THE REOPENING OF
THE AMERICAN MIND

VIBS

Volume 69

Robert Ginsberg
Executive Editor

Associate Editors

THE REOPENING OF THE AMERICAN MIND

On Skepticism and Constitutionalism

James W. Vice

Amsterdam - Atlanta, GA 1998

ISBN: 90-420-0521-1 (bound)
ISBN: 90-420-0511-4 (paper)
©Editions Rodopi B.V., Amsterdam - Atlanta, GA 1998
Printed in The Netherlands

To my family and to friends beyond numbering who have contributed to this book.

CONTENTS

EDITORIAL FOREWORD

James W. Vice offers a well-conceived and well-written study of social philosophy, including political theory and jurisprudence, as well as of American values and systems. He makes unusual use of Cicero, Tocqueville, and Felix Frankfurter, who are juxtaposed here in striking ways as major thinkers. By pointedly making his theoretical explorations bear on the United States, Vice reopens debate in American thought.

This is a cultured book, graced by writing reminiscent of Hume, Burke, Jefferson, and Madison. The articulation of Vice's delicately balanced position is well-served by his delicate choice of words. What he is saying is embodied in how he says it. This mind-opener is a pleasure to read and ponder.

James W. Vice became my mentor when I was sixteen years old and we were both students at the University of Chicago. By his example, he encouraged in me the love of great books and ideas. These were the Fundamentals. What made them fundamental was that they were always worthy of being discussed. Great discussions were the living substance of higher education and of useful scholarship. And what discussions we had! Jim and Gins uncovered the world in our frequent discourse. Vice had a feel for the textuality of ideas and a commitment to the opening and reopening of thought. These qualities are amply evident in the present book which is based on a lifetime of reflection on ideas, books, values, and culture.

The Value Inquiry Book Series is honored to make available this fundamental contribution by James W. Vice to the great discussion across the ages.

Robert Ginsberg
Executive Editor
Value Inquiry Book Series

GUEST FOREWORD

The Reopening of the American Mind: On Skepticism and Constitutionalism with its allusion to Allan Bloom suggests that James W. Vice wishes to do for the American Mind what Bloom wanted to do for the Student Mind. But especially for certain American minds: those influential and politically rigid minds of the day, whether conservative or liberal.

Vice is disturbed by assumed contemporary rigidities of thinking about public life, public institutions, and public policy, since he values thought itself, not only for itself but as beneficial for, essential to the goodness of, political action and living. But not just any thought. His aim is to blend, or rather to base, political thought on academic thought. But not just pure academic thought since that kind of thought is too centered on its own certainty, even when it is dealing with probability, to sell in a market in which true uncertainty is the principal product but which yet requires a degree of certainty in order to exist, even, or, better still, to succeed. Vice is like a university professional fund-raiser, trying to get the faculty member in want of money for faculty work or prestige to accommodate academic thought to the interests and desires of the donor, on the one hand, and to get the donor to be aware of the donor's own true interest and desires, as determined by academic thought, without corrupting either party.

To this end, Vice develops a theory of "academic skepticism." As an embodiment of that praising term of yesterday, the Renaissance Man or in its more bureaucratic form, the Generalist, Vice's reach for the idea of academic skepticism goes all the way back to Cicero, and through and around him to many of the principal Old Greek and Roman political reasoners. Then he tracks his trail like a jumping hare to the eighteenth century and digs deeply there into Hume, Burke, and Madison. Then with another jump, though the intermediate terrain is again seen flashing by, he ends up with Felix Frankfurter.

Each of these figures is treated fully, though not thickly, in a mix of biographical and intellectual texts, always accompanied by Vice's self text, which, combined with pellucidity of word arrangement and off-beat sudden interpretations, yields a drama a cut above the usual academic soap opera, though given the intellectual commonness of the subject matter itself, he cannot avoid some of its problems.

Academic skepticism as presented by Vice is worthy of center stage in public action and sometimes it even is shoved out there from the wings. For Vice, academic skepticism is a plea on behalf of sober, tolerant political judgment. It is not destructive skepticism, or a skepticism based upon a cynical view of human beings and of the possibilities of knowing anything about them. But it is not a plea for academic dogmatism either. The key issue involved in the concept seems to involve the question of the advocacy of political principle in a context of political probability. Vice is willing to recognize principle and even that it is derivable from that main academic mode of thought, reason. But he also recognizes that to fit political reality to principle is not only difficult but can be dangerous to freedom. As I read him, however, Vice is not advocating ancient or modern Pragmatism as the best political theory, whose principle is to accept as true anything that works. As already indicated, he believes in the academic. But he believes also in the variability and desirability of community thought, of the aggregation and synthesis of individual thought. So the problem is how to combine effectively the principle and the probable. His catalytic tool is judgment.

In my own governmental experience, his is the right way: reasoned principles, such data as you can get, a sense of the indeterminacy of the ever new context in which the issue presents itself, and then the judgment which takes all these things into account yet which is none of them. That is the only way to do the business of political life, and even it does not work most of the time.

Yet those of us who think well of this balanced, reasoned, probable approach to politics and life might do well to remember:

> Judgment and IQ, level of education, etc., are not related.
> Melville's concept of the certainty of reality: "Yet the sea is the sea and these drowning men do drown."
> If there is no certainty there is no probability: no bag, no balls, no output.
> Like Cicero himself they may end up being executed by the State.

William B. Cannon
Professor Emeritus
The University of Chicago

"A sermon should have a text, and I have found a suitable one in ...[Bishop Tallyrand]: The only good principle is to have no principles....It is, no doubt, usually enjoyed and dismissed as a witty cynicism; but I propose to treat it quite seriously, as a starting point. Not literally, I admit. It is an epigram; and an epigram has been defined as a half-truth so stated as to be especially annoying to those who believe the other half. I wish to stress both halves, the value of principles as well as their limitations. Accordingly I must reword the text into one of rather the opposite literal import. The right principle is to respect all principles, take them fully into account, and then use good judgment as to how far to follow one or another in the case at hand. All principles are false, because all are true— in a sense and to a degree; hence, none is true in a sense and to a degree which would deny to others a similarly qualified truth. There is always a principle, plausible and even sound within limits, to justify any possible course of action and, of course, the opposite one. The truly right course is a matter of the best compromise or the best or 'least worse' combination of good and evil. As in cookery, and in economic theory, it calls for enough and not too much, far enough and not too far, in any direction. Moreover, the ingredients of policy are always imponderable, hence there can be no principle, no formula, for the best compromise."

Frank H. Knight
Presidential Address
American Economic Association
28 December 1950[1]

PREFACE:
Standpoint

This is a book addressed to politicians and lawyers as well as to students of political philosophy and law. It is intended to serve practical as well as scholarly ends. I hope the reader will recognize the tentative character of what may appear didactic. One objective is to stimulate reconsideration of views now taken for granted and recovery of understandings now ignored or forgotten. Everyone in a democracy is widely presumed to know something about politics, but misunderstanding of some basic principles of American politics is widespread at present. I hope this book may stimulate without agitating. It restates familiar topics in different ways and introduces facts or juxtapositions not previously noticed. I am attempting what jurist Oliver Wendell Holmes had in mind when he said, in language often repeated by Felix Frankfurter, "at this time we need education in the obvious more than investigation of the obscure."[1] In private conversation, philosopher Richard P. McKeon put it as "the need to articulate the obvious."

I should like what I have written to be approached in what *The Federalist* refers to as a "spirit of moderation."[2] This may be expecting too much. Both scholarly and popular discourse often tend otherwise. Participants in public discourse find it more titillating or more newsworthy to point with glee to weaknesses in an argument rather than to explore ways to strengthen the argument and to improve its chances of creating a consensus. In scholarly matters, journals often publish constructive refinement in an on-going dialogue of critical and friendly commentary until a new "paradigm" or central issue is presented—a new fox to follow.

The skeptical tradition, more exactly called "academic skepticism," which is investigated in this book admits to points of choice, of decision. Nothing proves itself. In politics, one or more responsible persons must make a decision if action is to follow. In philosophy, the writer and the reader must each make choices about assumptions to make or accept and paths to follow or refuse. As many as possible of these choices should be made explicit, though not all will or can be. It is therefore incumbent on the writer to describe the ground from which the sequences of choices begin. Descartes started from something which he knew with certainty ("cogito ergo sum") and proceeded on a path of deduction which he thought clear and persuasive. The academic skeptic begins from where he or she stands and from the shaping experiences and influences of which he or she is conscious and proceeds by a method which will be described in detail below.

I start from where and who I am: a middle-aged, middlewestern, white male with a fairly broad education begun in a small town, continued at the University of Chicago, and furthered during university administration and teaching. My formative years in rural and small-town Indiana were spent in one of the safest and most plentiful of human habitations; my father, mother, and younger sister remained there to participate in local politics and to contribute to civic well-being. That should tell enough of the biographical where and who, except to add a few formative teachers and books. We are all captives of time. Our general ideas and our interests and approaches have been influenced by our particular lists (or "canons") of "great books"; and these lists have been constructed partly by chance.

Whatever plan we may have pursued in our education, some of the thinkers who have deeply impressed us came onto our paths by accident. I have often thought, as I read something, "Oh, how unfortunate that this writer never came across so-and-so." It is important that the reader know my so-and-sos.

My understanding of "political philosophy" has been dominated by many readings of various translations of Plato's *Republic* and *Symposium* and Aristotle's *Nicomachean Ethics* and *Politics*. Of more modern works, other than those discussed in the essays which follow, Tocqueville's *Democracy in America* has been the most influential classic work. While at the University of Chicago, I was much influenced by a disparate group of professors, all prolific writers in political or social thought. Daniel J. Boorstin's *The Genius of American Politics* introduced me to the idea that ambiguity can be "productive" and "compromise" can be constructive. My indebtedness to the essays of Frank H. Knight are beyond cataloging but are noted from time to time below. F. A. Hayek, too, is cited below. I became familiar with the work of another, and much younger, member of the Committee on Social Thought only later, Edward Shils whose three volumes of *Collected Essays* and *Tradition* have influenced me in the final preparation of this book. Another person whose writings and courses had a great deal of impact is often cited herein: Richard P. McKeon. These writers would consider themselves quite different. Justifying this eclecticism or syncretism will be one of the objects pursued in what follows.

While I have read a good deal of fiction, I have reread some books many times and, when available, in various translations over many years; and they have influenced my view of humanity. Tolstoy's *War and Peace*, Stendahl's *The Charterhouse of Parma*, Henry James's *Portrait of a Lady*, Cao Xuequin's *The Story of the Stone* (also called *The Dream of the Red Chamber*), and Lady Murasaki's *The Tale of Genji* each continue to remain suggestive.[3]

Finally, I have read widely in history. The political history of ancient Greece and Rome, Britain, and the United States have played a central role in my thought.

But to say I "start from where and who" is relevant in another way. Though these chapters extend across more than two thousand years, my concern is in the United States in the late twentieth century—with the problems of how to state the issues before us and most especially how to make use of (and improve) the social and political institutions we have inherited. In the words of Edmund Burke: "A disposition to preserve and ability to improve, taken together, would be my standard of a statesman."[4]

I start in the middle of things. In my view, we cannot see where we are going: we try to understand where we have been and see where we are; we make choices; we see what happens; and we make further choices. I have no overarching view or theory of things, such as has a committed and well-versed follower of St. Augustine or of Karl Marx. Neither do I expect to rely on any "least parts" on which I can build my argument with certainty—the sort of things which people may employ to understand all human action by reducing it to physics, chemistry, biology, psychology, statistics, linguistics, or various interdisciplinary combinations thereof. What we observe cannot be analyzed definitively into determinate units which permit certain predictions. As human beings, we do not have a definite nature: we have histories. But our biology and social settings limit our options. We are not infinitely pliable, and we cannot "make" ourselves according to a plan.

I am therefore here with my limited understanding, examining some commentators I think relevant to current politics, in part in an orderly fashion but always recognizing that fashion governs what is seen as orderly inquiry as well as it governs other things. This is not a critical study. It attempts to make evident (display; demonstrate) an intellectual pattern by juxtaposing the thoughts of the writers considered. While I have sought to make my own position explicit, my contribution is slight.

The problem, to restate, is how we should understand and make use of the institutions we call the American government and legal system, the constitutional system. I am especially concerned with the low estate into which American political and legal institutions and the occupants of their offices have fallen. Some of their low repute is deserved—well-earned by stupid or dishonest behavior. Part of the problem, though, is the spread in the United States of a virus which has been around a long time. Alexis de Tocqueville described the period immediately preceding the French Revolution in memorable terms:

> The general idea of the greatness of man, of the omnipotence of his reason, of the limitless powers of his intelligence had penetrated and pervaded the spirit of the century; yet this lofty conception of mankind in general was coupled with a particular contempt for the contemporary age and for contemporary society. The pride of humanity was madly inflated; the esteem of one's own times and one's own country was singularly low. All over the Continent that instinctive attachment and involuntary respect which men feel for their own institutions, for their traditional customs, and for the wisdom of their forefathers had almost ceased to exist among the educated classes.[5]

You may think we now have no such exalted view of humankind. Much of our literature, visual art, and television and cinema have a harsh or horrible view of the human situation. Views of reason lay at the heart of the matter for Tocqueville, however; and those views dominate public discourse today.

Three other preliminary points are needed. (1) I am interested in cooperation rather than domination. I recognize that domination exists. It is deeply rooted in the biological character of human beings. It is necessary to all human society, even the most democratic and constitutional. We may usefully think of ourselves as tribal creatures with primal tribal loyalties which often dispose us to "follow the (hunter-gatherer) leader."

John Adams and Thomas Jefferson, some years after retiring from active politics, resumed the friendly correspondence interrupted by the partisanship of the 1790s. One of their most interesting exchanges concerned leaders, the "natural aristocracy." Jefferson wished to establish a national educational system culminating in a national university to identify, educate, and promote the "natural aristocracy of virtue and talent." Adams reiterated the necessity of limiting the power of government, since the "aristocracy of wealth, beauty, and family name" will always prevail, in popular elections, over virtue and talent. The political potency of the Kennedys provides a nice illustration.

The success of tall men in business as well as government is another reminder of how primitive our view of a good leader is.[6] We only gradually and with great effort and to a limited degree transcend our tribal characteristics and become "civilized." We do this as societies through law, and as individuals through habituation and education. Thus we become potential citizens of a world community. But this potentiality depends on our efforts to achieve and understand cooperation. We will not achieve it if we only study and bemoan the facts of domination.

(2) Politics is about both disagreement and agreement, what is held in common as well as what is in contention. This was well illustrated by a dialogue shortly after the November 1994 elections. A political columnist on a prestigious television news program remarked, with intended profundity, that "politics is about differences." A counterpart, presumably from the other side of the political fence, shortly thereafter agreed with him and demonstrated their shared ground. Troubles come from these apparently small distortions. Much of contemporary political discourse focuses on differences—whether of opinion, interest, or background.

Politics is not possible without some common grounds, and we should explore and discuss them too. Even the lion and the lion-trainer share some communication and habit. Where there is no common ground, there will probably be violence. What is shared may be seen as the ground upon which the exploration of differences permits growth and progress. Or, differences may be seen as the ground upon which agreements must be constructed if human beings are to progress. Both approaches may be productive. The writers discussed here contribute to our understanding of the interplay of agreement and disagreement. Plato wrote in the *Symposium* about love as the search for that which completes or fulfills us. One aspect of our fulfillment is understanding how we can cooperate better with others. That is what I am seeking to understand.[7]

(3) The third point should be evident from the first and second points. I am interested mainly in what should be rather than simply what is, but I do not think of myself as a utopian. We cannot remake our society or even ourselves overnight. We are short-sighted creatures who must do the best we can. The three figures treated at greatest length here—Cicero, Burke, and Frankfurter—have detractors who believe they did not live up to their lofty pretensions. So be it. That does not detract from the worth of their ideas. "Do as I say and not as I do" is good advice, for injunction may confer more benefits than description. We are none of us as good as we should be, but that does not mean we should not try to do better.

In philosophy, the word "skepticism" is usually understood to refer to what in this volume I refer to as "Pyrrhonic skepticism." In law, politics, and general discourse, the word "skepticism" is used casually, without definition, and often without index citation in discussions not only of Felix Frankfurter but also of Holmes, Learned Hand, and others. Most writers of the past one hundred years have no relevant knowledge of Cicero, but all writers on subjects related to the American Constitution are familiar with *The Federalist*. Thus they have absorbed some of the teachings of academic skepticism which trace back to Cicero without noticing it. Most who use the word do not intend to imply the more extreme Pyrrhonic skepticism which is of greater interest to the epistemologist. This volume may encourage the historians of philosophy and the students of politics and law as well as the general public to be more exact in their usages.

On several occasions in the argument which follows, I have pursued peripheral points. Peripheral points often play an key role in our understanding and choices—whether we listen to or ignore an argument: "Hasn't this fellow even considered x, y, and z?" I am sure I have missed many xs and ys and zs. I hope I have some as and bs and cs right. I shall use quotation marks even though I am not quoting a particular source whenever I am referring to a word as a word or when words and phrases have taken on a fashionable life of their own. In these instances, I may not want to be associated with the connotations evoked; I at least consider the word to present some problem of interpretation. The quotation marks serve as the most convenient warning sign. Finally, I have spent so much time reading Cicero and Frankfurter and the several eighteenth-century authors that their shared style of long, complex sentences comes naturally to me. I believe the style accurately reflects the manner of thinking of the academic skeptic—a style of qualification and balance and diplomatic circumlocutions tending to discourage the reader from too-readily committing to a side. I trust the reader will find these at least correctly-constructed even if sometimes wearisome.

My special thanks for the formatting of this volume to Kathryn Hills and Ron Tabeta.

One

INTRODUCTION TO THE INQUIRY

More than forty years ago, while studying history, I began to search for what can be known certainly and stated unequivocally. I assumed that such knowledge could provide a basis for political agreement and action. At that time, logical positivism was still popular as a basis for social science, and social science seemed a basis for social engineering. "Sense data" or "atomic facts" based in experience and observable to everyone and which could be combined by a logical calculus seemed a perfect solution to the problem of certainty. Such might, indeed, be a perfect solution, but I found no end of sense data and atomic facts. At every moment, I am surrounded by an almost limitless number of facts plus additional sense data which I may not process as facts. A study of the major texts of logical positivism led me to Ludwig Wittgenstein. The early Wittgenstein led to the then recently published *Philosophical Investigations* and thence to his *Remarks on the Foundations of Mathematics*.[1] The "linguistic turn" in philosophy made clear to me that words are not simple, unambiguous tools for manipulating the world or communicating with one another. I also came to doubt the assumption that we can "apply" the work of contemporary philosophers to social knowledge in any way that would be final and certain—as an engineer is said to apply chemistry or physics. Put another way, the practical cannot be grounded in the theoretical as a way of achieving certainty. This was already clear to Aristotle. Any discussion of knowledge in the social sciences should begin with *Nicomachean Ethics*, Book 1, chapter 3:

> Our discussion will be adequate if it has as much clearness as the subject matter admits of, for precision is not to be sought for alike in all discussion....Now fine and just actions, which political scienc e investigates, admit of much variety and fluctuation of opinion....We must be content, then, in speaking of such subjects and with such premises to indicate the truth roughly and in outline....for it is the mark of an educated man to look for precision in each class of things just so far as the nature of the subject admits; for it is equally foolish to accept probable reasoning from a mathematician and to demand from a rhetorician scientific proofs.[2]

While we may now qualify, or reject, Aristotle's classes of things, we are more inclined to accept probable reasoning from a mathematician than we are to accept Aristotle's version of scientific proofs.

As was illustrated in the case of logical positivism and social scientists, by the time a philosophy is applied it is usually already falling out of favor with professional philosophers. The transfer of ideas from a field of scholarship to one of practice may be quite productive, but we will not achieve a final certainty that way. For example, the use of insights and information from psychology, sociology, and economics may be productive in the legal profession. That does not mean that law can be reduced to any of these disciplines or to all of them together. The productive insights may have been abandoned or left behind in their original home by the time they reveal their riches to the students of law.

Even before beginning the study which has culminated in this book, I had come to the conclusion that syllogistic reasoning is not as good a model for practical reasoning as the old saw about listing the pros and cons. At first, I focused my study on Felix Frankfurter and his view of judicial reasoning. Frankfurter, who was still at that time on the Supreme Court of the United States, provided an exemplar of self-conscious reasoning. Frankfurter followed, and even exceeded, his mentor Holmes in warning about the inadequacy of the syllogistic pattern in the law. Though highly self-conscious, Frankfurter did not readily show an alternative pattern. (In the chapter on him, I shall use "F.F." from time to time as shorthand for Felix Frankfurter to provide relief from repetition while preventing confusion. He himself often used his initials.)

When Holmes first wrote, powerful voices in legal circles were still arguing that judicial decisions are simply an exercise in deductive logic. That voice received revived expression in the Supreme Court opinions of the "conservatives" among the "nine old men" of the 1920s and 1930s, so response was of concern to Frankfurter.

Despite abandoning the syllogistic model, I still hoped that I could display some exact pattern in a form similar to that of symbolic logic to guarantee clarity and to insure consensus. It was not obvious to me at the time that the pros and cons combined with choice itself provide the general pattern of legal and practical reasoning. This view may be traced back to the sophistic contemporaries of Socrates, but the account here extends in detail only from Cicero to Frankfurter.

As I studied Frankfurter, I ceased following the dialogue of the mainstream of contemporary philosophy through its linguistic and post-linguistic phases. Coincidentally, I became interested in the work of Richard McKeon and—what is now trying to claim a place in the mainstream—"systematic pluralism."[3] Put simply, this is the position that many reasonable starting points, facts, and methods exist. No one position or philosophy exhausts the opportunities to say something true and fruitful. Therefore, these systematic pluralists create schemes for systematically comparing philosophers, presumably giving each her or his due and presumably preparatory to the resolution of some problem. Recently dipping back into the work of philosophy professors who write about what is "current" in professional philosophical discourse, I came across Richard Rorty and a discussion of "an ancient hope: the hope for a language which can receive no gloss, requires no interpretation, cannot be distanced, cannot be sneered at by later generations. It is the hope for a vocabulary which is intrinsically and self-evidently final...."[4]

This hope is now, in Rorty's view, properly abandoned. I take encompassing both Saul Kripke and Martin Heiddeger as Rorty does in his discussions to be a sufficient sign of awareness of "the mainstream." While Rorty and the systematic pluralists are not one in mind, I find the two positions convergent in this practical sense: the expectation of finding a final and definitive formulation of "truth" which will be accepted among educated persons as true universally and finally is unrealistic. The expectation was examined and dismissed as unrealistic by John Dewey in *The Quest for Certainty* in 1929.

As a matter of practical politics, we should acknowledge that within intellectually isolated "tribes" (whether in the anthropological or fundamentalist sense), much consensus may occur on the most profound matters. In such communities much is determined by habit and tradition or by conversion experiences. My views on such matters were much influenced by my maternal grandfather who claimed to believe literally every word of the Bible which he knew almost by memory. He read only the King James version, as befitted a good Protestant, and considered the Catholic edition with its differing text the devil's own work. I regret that he did not live to be shown the Anchor Translation of *Genesis* with its rich use of archeological materials and the comparison of ancient Hebrew with other, related ancient languages.[5]

If total and final agreement is not to be expected in philosophy, is it to be expected in practical affairs—even among the well-educated? On particular matters at particular times and places substantial agreement exists. In traditional societies, the extent of consensus may be broad and disagreement expressed in only limited ways. In modern societies, we must take disagreement to be a regular part of affairs. Disagreements and misunderstandings are common enough within families and sometimes result in violence. In this close context, love and hate have often been paired, in literature as in real life. In the public realm, political institutions have been said to exist to moderate the conflicts of interest groups. Legal institutions exist to resolve the disputes of individuals. In the American political consensus for two hundred years, no sophisticated person doubted that the rich or the famous had a leg up in the processes, but these short-comings were not thought to give grounds to dismiss the whole system. Now people are more inclined to see these institutions as devices of oppression of the various types of have-nots. This is, I assume, an application or popularization of the insights of Karl Marx. But I am not an expert on Marx and not trying to write an intellectual history of our age. A disinterested history sounds to me difficult but informative. It is, I gather, impossible from many points of view. As the decades of the second half of the twentieth century have passed, people have an increasing consciousness of, interest in, awareness of, and promotion of the lack of "consensus" about many matters in which it was previously assumed or positively thought that consensus existed. An earlier generation spoke of America as a "melting pot" in which traditional cultural or tribal distinctions were blurred so that homogenized "Americans" were produced from persons of many countries and religions. (Race was always cited as the troubling exception.) In recent years, the melting pot has been disputed both for its descriptive value and as an ideal. "Multiculturalism" is in vogue. Differences are emphasized as matters of fact and praised as matters of valuation. Most relevant to this discussion is the decline of consensus about the political and legal institutions. That the seats of both have been occupied at times by corrupt officeholders is common enough and is, indeed, a part of the traditional consensus about our institutions. But the view that the "white, Anglo-Saxon males" who occupy the seats of power cannot be fair to women or "minorities" has been slower to reach widespread public attention and constitutes a much more serious allegation of corruption. People once thought that government and the courts should try to be fair—to operate on the basis of some consensus about what fairness is. Some people apparently have never thought that any such consensus of fairness has existed, and more people apparently doubt it today.

These views present a major problem to the views I shall present. The difficulty is put concisely by reference to the epigraph to this book by Frank Knight. The multiplicity of "principles" is not so hard (though hard enough in practice). The real crunch comes in the phrase "good judgment." How much consensus exists about who has this "good judgment"? Cicero and Burke each undertook the defence of an oppressed national group, and Frankfurter took especial interest in legal developments throughout the multicultural British Commonwealth. All three thus tried to bridge the cultural gulfs of good judgment.

Rather than pretend that my views should be obvious or my lines of reasoning self-validating to every reader, I make stipulations on several points of what is presupposed by me for what follows. The justifications for these stipulations lie outside this text, though I provide references to direct the reader to justifying arguments. I suspect that one who disagrees with me in the main lines of my thought can be convinced only by a quasi-religious conversion or "paradigm shift." My own "canonical" writers on this have been Michael Polanyi and Stephen Toulmin rather than the more widely cited Thomas Kuhn. Polanyi traces the unarticulated and often unarticulatable elements in knowing. He also gives an explanation of the distinction between "knowing by attending to" and "knowing by relying on" which is a useful complement to Gilbert Ryle's distinction between "knowing how" and "knowing that" in *The Concept of Mind*. Toulmin in *Human Understanding* explicitly examines the problems addressed by Kuhn in *The Structure of Scientific Revolutions*.[6]

These remarks on the difficulties of "judgment" bring us back to Felix Frankfurter. Frankfurter's understanding of legal reasoning is better understood as a way of setting up the situation of judgment rather than as a pattern of logic. I am using "logic" and "epistemology" in the way the words are used in university bulletins—to indicate two separate areas within philosophy. Some philosophers have not separated epistemology from logic, considering the theory of knowledge a part of the more general field of logic or vice versa. In another view, the two words mark the difference, greater or less, between knowing and presenting what is known. By juxtaposing logic with judgment, I wish to contrast focus on a pattern of words or symbols with focus on an activity of choosing. I have not cited the vast literature familiar to any interested student of philosophy.[7]

In what follows, the key organizing topics are skepticism and constitutionalism. A brief starting point for these two will be provided here, but their explication and connections are developed throughout this book. The spelling "skepticism" will be used throughout the text, but some authors have spelled the word "scepticism." Frankfurter spelled it both ways. In quoting, the original spelling will be followed without benefit of "sic" or a note in each case.

Skepticism is an attitude concerning the difficulty or impossibility of knowing certainly and a strategy for dealing with uncertainty. The term does not appear often in Frankfurter's Supreme Court opinions. This is not surprising since the word is sometimes conflated with "cynicism" and has connotations which might distract from the argument. "Skepticism" appears often, and always as a word of praise, in Frankfurter's extrajudicial writings. Skepticism, properly understood, is a guiding principle throughout his Court opinions.

Pursuing "skepticism" in Frankfurter led me to those for whom it was a well-developed philosophy, first and foremost Cicero. Cicero combined his skeptical philosophy with an attachment to the so-called "mixed" form of constitution/government and a career in law and government. "Constitutionalism" is an expansion of the mechanism of the "mixed form" which has been alleged to produce a moderate or middle-of-the-road government or represent the interests or wishes of a "middle class." In Cicero, as in Frankfurter, I found a concern to display the characters of those who acted on republican virtues. The lessons of these exemplars will be discussed in what follows.

Reading Cicero gave me a new perspective on the preeminent commentary on the American Constitution, *The Federalist*. The text is so well-known that extended discussion here would be presumptuous and unnecessary, but the connection of the argument to skepticism has gone largely unnoticed. Since most readers have some familiarity with *The Federalist* and since James Madison gives such a concise summary of skepticism and links it so closely with his view of the Constitution, I have chosen to begin with a short chapter on Madison's papers. It seems the most relevant entry-point for the American reader.

The connection of the most famous *Federalist* Ten to the essays of David Hume is well-known among scholars; and Hume's reputation as a skeptic gave added ground for some consideration of him. I am no expert on Hume, so I shall not say anything original about him. Instead, I quote extensively from one essay and one book about Hume, both of which shed light on the relation of academic skepticism to constitutionalism. Edmund Burke shares some biographical parallels as well as ideas with both Cicero and Frankfurter and helps prepare the reader for Frankfurter, who is the original of this effort as well as the most directly relevant to contemporary thought and action.

I have not written an intellectual history: I have not attempted to trace the influences of one writer on another in a self-conscious tradition. The consensus existing among these five men owes more to similar experiences with government, law, and legal thought than to any conscious development of a line of philosophy.

Following are the most general of my stipulations. Others more specialized to the legal system will be necessary before my discussion of Frankfurter and will be made at that point in the text.

1. Stipulations about Social Knowledge

1. Social knowledge is a structuring of facts. Facts, as the parentage of the word (the Latin "facta") implies, are made. They are constituted or separated out of experience. As I write, I sit in a room surrounded by books, papers, my cats, and pictures and pieces of furniture. The window is open, with sounds coming in from outside. I have stated a few facts. But, depending on what I wish to take up, I can identify—or bring someone else to help me identify—more facts, almost without limit, of biology, chemistry, acoustics, interior design, and so forth, even without opening the books for all the facts asserted therein. There are non-facts: I have no tiger in my room, about to eat me—except perhaps in metaphorical fact associated with what I am trying to argue. So, major issues of "selection" or "point of view" or "nature of the inquiry" arise which might be called "relativism" except for the suggestion of arbitrariness which that suggests. When another person comes into the room, we might or might not get into disagreement about the facts in a particular line of inquiry. Almost certainly, two visitors, who after spending only one minute in the room were asked to describe it from memory, would not only make different selections of facts but would probably also disagree about what was factual.

This multiplicity of facts leads easily to controversy. We might say that "most people" or "the average person" would give a roughly similar description of the room: "book-filled, stacks of papers, heavy furniture, dusty." "Experts" might well, however, give different descriptions: "cats that aren't brushed enough"; "furniture of such-and-such style"; "lead-based paint"; "Eurocentric, white male books." Someone transported suddenly from a pre-literate society might note something like "edible small cats" or "bad spirits." (How should I distinguish this view from the metaphoric tiger?) A person from a different religious background might, from my books, identify me as an "heretic" or a "benighted creature needing to be saved." One of these might begin trashing my books and papers from the best of motives—a concern for my salvation or the desire to improve the world. Or, someone whose motives I could not grasp at all—whom I might, quite probably, consider insane—might begin doing the same thing. Thus, I am careful about whom I invite in. The definition of "most people" or the "average person" is crucial. Consensus cannot be taken for granted; it becomes problematic. Richard Rorty has discussed this "ethnocentrism."[8] To appeal to an older tradition and borrow from Cicero, my society depends upon some consensus of "justice and a partnership for the common good."

In the spring, I walk in the woods, hunting for the hard-to-see morel mushrooms. As any experienced hunter knows, it is easy to look right at a morel and not see it. That is why a person walks back and forth across a likely spot, looking from different angles, and why another hunter may spot a mushroom at the person's very feet. In this case, the "sense data"—the impressions falling on my eyes—are not formed into the "facts" relevant to my search.

The determination and selection of facts depends upon a context, whether one or more than one person is involved. We have developed disciplines and institutions to provide contexts for the determination and selection of facts. Within disciplines, principles and methods (which may be debased into prejudices or a narrowing of view) differentiate schools and traditions of thought. The conclusions of these schools may actually or only appear to conflict. In either case, they explore and use or abuse the richness of facts. Within institutions, organizations and procedures determine ends, allocate means, assign tasks, and resolve conflicts—all determining and selecting facts. Institutions themselves conflict. In all these processes of thought and action, facts are selected or ignored, agreed upon or disputed, as greater or lesser consensus is reached or fails.[9]

2. Frank H. Knight wrote extensively on the nature of social knowledge and the social nature of knowledge. He distinguished six levels of investigation of human beings. They can be considered as physical-chemical mechanisms, as biological organisms, as traditional beings who have to a great degree substituted habits for instincts (anthropology), as rational beings who allocate limited means among given ends (economics), as rational beings who choose ends (ethics), and as societies of persons who jointly determine their common ends and allocate common means. These "sciences of man" cannot be "reduced"—the latter subsumed under or derived from the earlier. The focus in this book is on the sixth of these levels—a society of (free) persons cooperatively (democratically) deciding on ends and through free markets and governments allocating resources to achieve those ends.[10]

3. Each of these sciences employs "ideal types" ("models") which involve selections of both "facts" and "laws" or "generalizations." They employ "hypotheses" which may only in part be directly "confirmed" by "empirical observation." In the case of the sixth level above, the previous statement bridges both the "is" and the "ought." The "ought" or "ideal" is so both in the sense of being "abstracted" and in the sense of implying "goals." This stipulation briefly covers a long and subtle series of disputes and a vast literature.[11]

4. "Political" agreement (as contrasted with coerced agreement) cannot depend on incorrigible truths. Ambiguity and differing perspectives are facts of political, as well as the rest of, communication. In political discourse, we proceed by the recognition of problematic situations, by the presentation of "relevant" information and arguments (not always sharply distinguished) to identify alternatives, and then by judgments made by the "responsible" person(s). Thus, instead of the difficulties of identifying atomic facts and selecting a logical calculus, we are faced with the difficulties of understanding judgment and responsibility and of recognizing/selecting responsible persons. "Responsibility" is a relatively new word, created about the time of the drafting of the American Constitution. Its origins and meaning are discussed by McKeon in *Freedom and History*.[12]

The aspect of responsibility on which my remarks focus is its relation to a division of labor. If we all take responsibility for everything, we can be confident that everything will be poorly handled. Only by distinguishing and allocating areas of responsibility can we hope to cope, and even then only in a partial way, with all that we must do together. Such a division of responsibility requires mutual confidence and a great deal of faith and charity. We shall return to this in the chapter on Frankfurter.

It is worth adding here, however, that John Stuart Mill, in *The Principles of Economics*, Book 5, justifies the oft-maligned principle of "laissez faire" on this basis. Like Adam Smith before him, Mill recognized many functions which government should perform *vis-à-vis* the economy, so long as it does not interfere with price movements. The principle is a warning to avoid placing too many optional responsibilities on government, lest it be unable to perform its most important functions properly. Unfortunately, the phrase has been torn asunder by those who would, on the one hand, use it to shelter mischief which should properly be illegal and, on the other, those who wish to scorn a price system which they think has been discredited.

2. Stipulations about the United States Constitution

5. Richard McKeon viewed the American Constitution as having been drafted by a group of men who held different philosophies but used a common vocabulary to reach practical agreement on the language of a constitutional framework which permits persons of differing philosophies to reach practical agreement on problems without first reaching philosophical agreement. This presents an ideal formulation of democracy as government by discussion rather than by the imposition of a philosophy or "democratic dogma." Thus we did not ground our polity in what can be known certainly and stated unequivocally.

McKeon developed this view in a course at the University of Chicago in late 1960s. The course proceeded from a careful examination of the position of various participants in the Constitutional convention (as presented in Madison's Notes) to show that they did not hold the same philosophy. Although they used a common vocabulary, they did not have the same meanings in mind for the terms they employed and employed different principles and methods. McKeon next examined the writings of two influential members of the founding generation, John Adams and Thomas Jefferson who were both in Europe at the time of the Convention, to reveal that they too did not share a common philosophy. The course concluded with an examination of two philosophers thought to have influenced the Founders, John Locke and David Hume, to reveal once again different philosophies. The Constitution is not simply an "application" of Locke's philosophy.

Through the course of many essays, McKeon distinguished the different methods philosophers have used, the different principles they have subscribed to, the different selections of material they have examined, and the different meanings they have given to the terms they have employed. His sort of analysis helps us to recognize the ambiguities and different perspectives referred to in the first and fourth stipulations. For example, one of the richest sources of ambiguity in political discourse lies in the undefined use of the words "freedom" and "liberty" and their cognates or presumed cognates in other languages. Depending on the writer, "freedom" may mean "the absence of restraint" (Hobbes), "doing as one wills" (Sartre), "ruling and being ruled in turn" (Aristotle), "doing what contributes to self-development" (Dewey), or "doing as one ought" (Plato).[13]

There have been many stimulating studies of the Constitution of the United States and constitutional government in general which start from different approaches and focus on different facts. The fact that I make no mention of them does not mean I denigrate their importance or dispute their truth.

3. This Text

The chapters, with the Madisonian exception, are arranged in historical order. Cicero is regaining a position in political philosophy but is typically treated as a Stoic. I believe this interpretation is wrong. Much that he wrote, if properly understood, is relevant for contemporary political philosophy, law, and government. At least since Edward Gibbon, Westerners have been interested in "the decline and fall of the Roman empire," especially as a tale of vice and corruption; but the decline and fall of the Roman republic, as a tale of failure to understand and improve the traditional institutions, are of more importance to us.[14]

In all of these chapters, I have made frequent use of quotation. I want the reader to recognize the writers I am considering, and not just my analysis and assertions. In the chapter on Cicero I have made extensive summaries of the texts because the originals are so remote from us. This is, however, my line of thought and the juxtaposition of quotes and summaries are within my argument. I have not hesitated to intrude my comments into this context, even though the reader may from time to time think I am continuing with a mere summary. In those chapters in which I have quoted extensively from the subject's writings, I have identified quotations from each writer by citations placed in parentheses in the text, rather than by endnotes. Abbreviations are explained in the first endnote for each chapter. In the chapters about authors who wrote in English, my citations are mainly to readily available editions.

Two

MADISON

Following after the godlike Washington, the leonine Adams, and the inspirational Jefferson, James Madison is almost a blank in our consciousness of American history.[1] His two predecessors advanced to the Presidency from the Vice Presidency. Like his two successors, Monroe and the second Adams, Madison was promoted from the position of Secretary of State. A small man physically as well as in our presidential consciousness, Madison was born in 1751 and died in 1836, the last of the signers of the Constitution. His presidential administration is generally modestly rated. His real claim to fame is as "the Father of the Constitution." His claims to this title are multiple. The Constitutional Convention in Philadelphia was presented at its opening with a set of "Virginia Resolutions" which laid down the main lines of subsequent discussion: this document was drafted by Madison. Along with Alexander Hamilton and John Jay, Madison wrote *The Federalist*: two of the three most famous papers were composed by Madison. Finally, among Madison's papers were found his detailed notes on the Constitutional Convention giving a day by day account of the course of debate and thus providing our most intimate insight into how the Constitution was put together. Although it goes beyond our concern here, it is worth adding that Madison also led the First Congress in creating the "Bill of Rights." He had thought an enumeration might be interpreted as restricting basic rights to those enumerated but yielded to political pressures in order to obtain ratification of the Constitution.

As mentioned in the Introduction, I am not attempting to prove direct lines of influence from Cicero to each of the later writers. Only a few and unilluminating explicit references to Cicero occur in *The Papers of James Madison*.[2] Madison learned Latin as a boy. His biographer Ralph Ketcham tells us "he must have known Cicero and Virgil by heart," but he was more likely to have concentrated on the speeches than on the dialogues. Ketcham also suggests that Madison may have absorbed many of the lessons of academic skepticism (though he does not use that term) from *The Spectator*, which often quoted Cicero for references to "moderation, the need to encourage good manners, hostility to any form of fanaticism, the necessity of high standards of public ethics, and the usefulness of good humor in a cultivated society." Ketcham, in his brief summary of *Federalist* No. 37, completely ignores the outline of skepticism. Neal Riemer claims a direct connection with Cicero's political thought, observes that Madison "may have read in Cicero a definition of the Commonwealth," and quotes directly from the *On the Republic*. Riemer does not explain how the passage may have come to Madison's attention: the Vatican Library palimpsest, the primary source for the text in modern times, was not discovered until 1820.[3]

The Federalist is unquestionably the most popular commentary on the government of the United States and has been so since shortly after the Founding. *The Federalist* is a group of eighty-five essays, usually following a line of argument over several sequential papers. They were written by Alexander Hamilton, James Madison, and John Jay for publication from autumn 1787 to spring 1788 in the New York press. They were intended to support the ratification of the new Constitution by that State's legislature, though their actual impact is a matter of debate. They were only one series in the newspaper wars of the era, and "antifederalist" writers were active too. The modern reader must be impressed with the level of discourse, which is far above that of popular newspapers in the late twentieth century.

While today we would scarcely think of *The Federalist* as popular reading to compare with paperback romance or murder mysteries, it is a common reference for high school and college courses and so has touched, though lightly, the lives of many Americans. If any book on American government might appear on a television quiz show, it would be *The Federalist*. The same work would be put by academics at the top of lists of the "must read" books for American studies. To give only one example, Clinton Rossiter says, in his Introduction to the Mentor edition: "*The Federalist* is the most important work in political science that has ever been written, or is likely ever to be written, in the United States. It is, indeed, the one product of the American mind that is rightly counted among the classics of political theory."[4]

The three most famous papers are Ten and Fifty-one, both written by Madison, and Seventy-eight, by Hamilton. Ten explains and defends the "federal system" of States and a central government; Fifty-one explains and defends the operating principle of "checks and balances" within the central government. Seventy-eight justifies the Supreme Court.

While a substantial literature of excellent and stimulating commentary on *The Federalist* exists, I find it all lacking in adequate appreciation of the role of skepticism in the explanation and justification of constitutionalism. I shall sample only a little of that literature here to illustrate my point. A most illuminating essay because of the position taken toward political theory is Martin Diamond's essay "The Federalist" in the Strauss and Cropsey *History of Political Theory*.[5] Diamond notes that Hamilton and Madison "could agree as to what the convention had done and what kind of country would be the result." This agreement seemingly prevented the authors from accomplishing what Rossiter claimed for them: that is, producing a "classic of political theory." Diamond comments on the agreement and consistency of the two principal authors, Hamilton and Madison, which permitted them to use the common name "Publius" even though we know from other writings that the two had many disagreements. According to Diamond's assessment: "...the literary character of *The Federalist* did not oblige them to push so far in the discussion as to lay bare their ultimate differences. Unfortunately, what helps explain Publius' consistency explains also why The Federalist falls short of those great works in which theoretical matters are pressed to their proper, that is, farthest limits." What is of most interest to the "theoretician" (the true political philosopher?) is "ultimate differences" and "farthest limits" rather than what we might call "a working agreement" such as a constitution.

The tendency to ultimate differences and farthest limits seems to promote a particular interpretation of "republic" in *The Federalist*. In Diamond's view, the authors articulated "Publius' exclusively democratic idea of republicanism." This is restated as: "...republican regimes...belong overwhelmingly to the democratic kind of rule" and later, "...republics are, so to speak, 'impure' democracies." This contrasts with the view that the Founders in establishing a "republic" were explicitly not creating a democracy—the characteristics of which they denigrated, as in Numbers 10, 49, and 51—but a "mixed form." According to Diamond, The Federalist concerns itself with the "second best" in two senses: it is a second-best type of political thought about what is a second-best ("impure") type of democracy. The book and its subject are presumably to be judged by comparison with pure or ideal forms of thoughts and institutions. In terms of the argument which is to follow, it is important to note that Diamond makes no use of or reference to Number 37.

A commentator who pays thanks to and remarks on his "reliance on" Diamond is David Epstein. In his 1984 book *The Political Theory of the Federalist*, Epstein examines the relation of "republican" and "liberal principles." For Epstein, "republican" is clearly identified with "popular" though he does not suggest it is second-best. He gives special status to Number 37 as the first paper in what he calls "Volume 2" of the collected papers. His treatment of 37 focuses on the tension between "stability and energy" on the one hand and "republican liberty" on the other. (Madison's explicit contrast in Number 37 is first stated as between "stability and energy" and "liberty and the republican form." He thus appears to distinguish liberty from the form of government.) The rest of Number 37 is referred to as "...a skeptical digression in the middle of a rather confident book." The discussion which follows focuses on the problem of giving a suitable definition to "republican." The full discussion extends over pages 114 to 125. There is, however, no entry for "skepticism" in the Index, nor any for Cicero. We are told at the end of the Introduction that "...The Federalist was the first book to recommend a 'wholly elective'... form of government...." While the authors of *The Federalist* might be excused for making such a claim since Cicero's *On the Republic* had not yet been recovered at the time they wrote, Epstein might have been expected to know of the existence of this justification of the "wholly elective" Roman republican government. Skepticism, for Epstein, presents a problem for republican government; but it is not integral to it.[6]

Still another excellent book is *The Federalist: Design for a Constitutional Republic* by George W. Carey. Carey's argument is structured by the exploration of four "principles"—republicanism, separation of powers, federalism, and limited government. These principles are explained without reference to the skeptical argument of Number 37 or any consideration of epistemological issues. Carey notes that "...Publius simply could not embrace the likes of Platonic 'Guardians'...," but his reason for making this assertion is not that no one possesses the necessary certain knowledge. It is rather that "[s]uch a solution would clearly verge on employing 'a power independent of the majority'."[7]

In his 1960 book *The Federalist: A Classic on Federalism and Freedom*, Gottfried Dietze treats Madison, Hamilton, and Jay separately; but in a twenty-nine page chapter on "Madison on Free Government," he makes no mention or use of the skepticism passages of Number 37. While Number 37 is often quoted throughout the volume, none of the quotations concerns the grounds or relevance of skepticism. Cicero is referred to only as one of the classics of political thought with which the Founders were familiar.[8]

It is thus a plausible generalization to assert that James Madison, "Father of the Constitution" and co-author of *The Federalist*, has not usually been treated as a skeptic. Scholars have found it easy to ignore the central passages of Number 37 and to miss their relevance to the more famous Numbers 10 and 51 and the papers on the branches of Congress. In Number 37, Madison begins a series of twenty-four papers ending with those on the Senate. (These are only interrupted by three on elections written by Hamilton—59, 60, and 61.) These papers lay out the principles of "checks and balances" within the central government. By its position, Number 37 might seem to play an introductory and important role in Madison's presentation. It does just that. It lays out the grounds for uncertainty in the understanding and statement of political truths. Tentativeness and compromise lie at the heart of the federal republic, and they follow reasonably from the theory of knowledge put forward by Madison.

In Number 37, Madison gives a concise summary of the principles of what was in his day called the "academical" philosophy and which I am calling academic skepticism. Though Madison does not use these words to characterize his position, he was certainly familiar with his older contemporary David Hume who refers, for example, to a "mitigated scepticism or academical philosophy" in his *An Enquiry Concerning Human Understanding*. (Hume is discussed in a subsequent chapter.)

The philosophy comes from the world of the Greeks and Romans but is nowhere more concisely summarized than by Madison himself. "Here, then, are three sources of vague and incorrect definitions: indistinctness in the object, imperfections in the organ of conception, inadequateness of the vehicle of ideas" (270). In the previous argument, he discusses "objects extensive and complicated in their nature" (268) and especially "the institutions of man, in which the obscurity arises...from the object itself....Questions daily occur in the course of practice, which prove the obscurity which reigns in these subjects, and which puzzle the greatest adepts in political science" (269). Madison particularly mentions the problems of discriminating and defining the three branches of government and their powers and the parts of law and justice. Moreover, "[the] faculties of the mind itself have never yet been distinguished and defined, with satisfactory precision, by all the efforts of the most acute and metaphysical philosophers. Sense, perception, judgment, desire, volition, memory, imagination, are found to be separated by such delicate shades and minute gradations that their boundaries have eluded the most subtle investigations, and remain a pregnant source of ingenious disquisition and controversy" (268). Finally, language is inadequate to express what it is we do understand of the complexity. "...the medium through which the conceptions of man are conveyed to each other adds a fresh embarrassment....no language is so copious as to supply words and phrases for every complex idea, or so correct as not to include many equivocally denoting different ideas" (269-270).

Earlier in Number 37, Madison mentions "that spirit of moderation which is essential to a just estimate of [the] real tendency to advance or obstruct the public good..." (266). He also notes that "a faultless plan [for the Constitution] was not to be expected" (266) for men are fallible. Here then are five aspects of Madison's skepticism. Things, particularly political things, are complex. The mind is limited in grasping that complexity. Language is inexact in expressing what is grasped. Thus, no verbal formulation is likely to be definitive and final. It is fallible and may require modification. (Even the Constitution provides for its amendment.) And thus, one ought to approach these matters in a spirit of moderation or, in a Ciceronian phrase, without contentiousness. I must add that Madison's list of the faculties of the mind, starting with sense perception, sounds very much like the skeptical writings of Cicero. We can easily trace the implications of Madison's moderate skepticism through major steps in the papers which follow.

Number 49 addresses a problem which is only answered, insofar as it is answered, by reading Hamilton's famous Number 78 on the Supreme Court. The problem first posed by Madison in Number 48 is how the (presumed) weaker departments, the executive and judicial, are to protect themselves from the "encroaching nature" of the power possessed by the legislative branch. Jefferson had suggested that a popular convention be called whenever two of the branches felt they were being imposed upon. Madison disagreed with his fellow Virginian: "...frequent appeals [to the people] would, in great measure, deprive the government of that veneration which time bestows on every thing, and without which perhaps the wisest and freest governments would not possess the requisite stability" (349). Madison then draws out the implications of his skepticism.

> If it be true that all governments rest on opinion, it is no less true that the strength of opinion in each individual, and its practical influence on his conduct, depend much on the number which he supposes to have entertained the same opinion. The reason of man, like man himself, is timid and cautious

when left alone, and acquires firmness and confidence in proportion to the
number with which it is associated. When the examples which fortify opinion
are ancient as well as numerous, they are known to have a double effect. In a
nation of philosophers, this consideration ought to be disregarded. A reverence
for the laws would be sufficiently inculcated by the voice of an enlightened
reason. But a nation of philosophers is as little to be expected as the
philosophical race of kings wished for by Plato. And in every other nation,
the most rational government will not find it a superfluous to have the
prejudices of the community on its side. (349; italics in the original)

This passage strongly suggests the influence of Hume, since it reads much
like one of the latter's essays:

...the bulk of mankind [is] governed by authority, not reason, and never
attribut[es] authority to any thing that has not the recommendation of antiquity.
To tamper, therefore, in this affair, or try experiments merely upon the credit
of supposed argument or philosophy, can never be the part of a wise magistrate,
who will bear a reverence to what carries the marks of age; and though he
may attempt some improvements for the public good, yet will he adjust his
innovations, as much as possible, to the ancient fabric, and preserve entire
the chief pillars and supports of the constitution.[9]

In Number 51, Madison sets forth the principal mechanism in the construction of the central government which we summarize as "checks and balances."
Having observed in Number 48 that the mere "parchment barriers" of the written
constitution will not prevent the concentration of power and dismissed Jefferson's
as well as other solutions, Madison explains that the Constitutional Convention
has "so contrived the interior structure of the government as that its several con-
stituent parts may, by their mutual relations, be the means of keeping each other
in their proper places" (355). The "great security against a gradual concentration
of the several powers in the same department, consists in giving to those who
administer each department the necessary constitutional means and personal motives to resist encroachments of the others....Ambition must be made to counter-
act ambition. The interests of the man must be connected with the constitutional
rights of the place" (356).

This contrivance depends upon an assumption about human nature sometimes ignored in more "realistic" views. The "personal motives" and the "interests of the man" center on the love of reputation or fame and glory rather than
love of wealth or greed. When moved by the latter motives, the occupants of
office simply combine to fleece the public (a situation which pertains all too often). The proper working of the Constitution depends upon the existence of of-
fice-holders who have an eye to their places in history. If a person is to be remembered as a great senator, he or she must do what is appropriate to the office, not
simply do the bidding of the President.

For Madison, the product of Christian culture, the love of fame is not looked upon as an especially ennobling motive. Like Edmund Burke, he looked upon it as powerful and therefore useful. In Burke's words, the "sense of fame and estimation" is "one of the greatest controlling powers on earth."[10] Such an approach may be deemed a "reflection on human nature....but what is government but the greatest of all reflections on human nature? If men were angels, no government would be necessary. If angels were to govern men, neither internal nor external controls on government would be necessary" (356). Angels or, one might add, philosopher kings. If rulers were available who both knew the truth and knew they knew it-that is, not only felt certain about their views but had certain validation of them-then these persons might best be the rulers. An argument might be constructed that a democratic rule guided only by opinion is better for personal development than an aristocratic or royal rule guided by truth; but that is unnecessary here. Madison clearly did not believe in the existence of such philosopher kings for the reasons set forth in 37. They are not available, as noted in Number 49. Without such all-knowing rulers, the system, Madison believed, is best which prevents or at least makes very difficult the concentration of all power in the hands of one person or class. As he noted in Number 47, "The accumulation of all powers, legislative, executive, and judiciary, in the same hands, whether of one, a few, or many, and whether hereditary, self-appointed, or elective, may justly be pronounced the very definition of tyranny" (336). This is simply an expansion of the same point made by Jefferson in the *Notes on Virginia* and quoted in Number 48 (345).

The structure of checks and balances set forth in Number 51 and the federal division of power maintained by the proliferation of interests set forth in Number 10 are the twin operating principles which minimize the likelihood of the concentration of power. A somewhat closer look at Number 10, the most famous paper, is in order to take note of the operation of the same skeptical principles.

The concentration of power of concern in Number 10 is the concentration in a "faction...amounting to a majority...who are united and actuated by some common impulse of passion, or of interest, adverse to the rights of other citizens, or to the permanent and aggregate interests of the community" (130). The argument made explicit in 37 is prefigured: "As long as the reason of man continues fallible, and he is at liberty to exercise it, different opinions will be formed. As long as the connection subsists between his reason and his self-love, his opinions and his passions will have a reciprocal influence on each other; and the former will be the objects to which the latter will attach themselves....the latent causes of faction are thus sown in the nature of man..." (130-131). The extensive federal republic makes less likely "the existence of the same passion or interest in a majority at the same time" or "concert[ing] and carry[ing] into effect schemes of oppression" (133). It does so by the "delegation...of the government...to a small number of citizens elected by the rest" (133) (rather than by direct democracy) and by extending the number of citizens and the extent of territory to "take in a greater variety of parties and interests" (135).

The benefit of representation rather than direct popular rule is made clearer in Number 63. The members of the House of Representatives stand for election every two years to promote their "fidelity to their constituents" (384) by their "dependence on the people" (385). The senators, on the other hand, have staggered six-year terms precisely to make them less immediately responsive to the people, as a defense against their own temporary errors and delusions." As a cool and deliberate sense of the community ought, in all governments, and actually will, in all free governments, ultimately prevail over the views of its rulers; so there are particular moments in public affairs when the people, stimulated by some irregular passion, or some illicit advantage, or misled by the artful misrepresentation of interested men, may call for measures which they themselves will afterwards be the most ready to lament and condemn" (415).

At these moments, the ability of the Senate to delay action, to postpone judgment, gives a corrected opinion time to develop. It does not guarantee that absolutely certain truth will emerge, but it provides the opportunity for more leisurely reflection upon the implications of the projected action.

One further passage from Hamilton is worth quoting at length since it expresses a view of political institutions articulated in different ways by Cicero and Burke and understood by Madison and Hume. In Number 9, Hamilton says:

> The science of politics.., like most other sciences, has received great improvement. The efficacy of various principles is now well understood which were either not known at all, or imperfectly known to the ancients. The regular distribution of power into distinct departments; the introduction of legislative balances and checks; the institution of courts composed of judges holding their offices during good behavior; the representation of the people in the legislature by deputies of their own election: these are wholly new discoveries, or have made their principal progress towards perfection in modern times. (125)

The resemblance of this view to Cicero's catalog of the contributions of each of the kings to the growth of Roman institutions will be evident to anyone familiar with it. We shall see Burke explain what he means by "liberty" with a parallel catalog of historically developed institutions.

We can see the distance of these views from those expressed by Martin Diamond in his essay on *The Federalist*. The "principles" listed by Hamilton are a far cry from the ultimate differences and farthest limits sought by Diamond. The procedural principles listed by Hamilton and those discussed by Burke under the heading of "liberty" are based on the experiments of many persons. They are working hypotheses which lie, when and where they are operative, in the realm of commonly-held opinions. Fifty years later, Alexis De Tocqueville could still refer to a "new science of politics" and mean the same thing as Hamilton.

Three

CICERO AND THE ORIGINS OF SKEPTICISM

1. Prologue: The Skeptical Tradition

The skepticism which has been of greatest interest to teachers of philosophy especially in recent years is more exactly "Pyrrhonic skepticism," tracing back to Pyrrho of Ellis (circa 360-275 B.C.). The type of skeptic which describes Cicero and the others discussed here is "academic skepticism."[1] Pyrrhonic skepticism comes down to us mostly through the works of Sextus Empiricus (circa 200 A.D.), unknown except for his works. It was of substantial importance in the history of philosophy especially from the sixteenth century to the time of David Hume and has a revived vitality from recent interest in Hume and from work in the history of philosophy especially by Richard H. Popkin.[2] According to Popkin, both forms of skepticism were found in the sixteenth century to be compatible with Christian belief based on faith rather than reason. (This "fideism" provides a kind of parallel to reliance on the commonly accepted opinions of the community which will be discussed in greater detail, especially in the chapters on Cicero, Hume, and Frankfurter.) Hume believed he had pursued pyrrhonic skepticism to its self-defeating end in *A Treatise of Human Nature*, but many of the issues have surfaced in various epistemological discussions in this century.[3]

The philosophies of skepticism developed in Athens and elsewhere in the Greek-speaking world during Aristotle's lifetime and continued thereafter in the Hellenistic period at about the same time as the better known philosophies of Stoicism and Epicureanism. Pyrrho was a younger contemporary of Aristotle. His followers stood aside from the larger schools which dominated the Hellenistic scene. Diogenes Laertius, in his *Lives of the Eminent Philosophers*, says they "were constantly engaged in overthrowing the dogmas of all schools, but enunciated none themselves; and though they would go so far as to bring forward and expound the dogmas of others, they themselves laid down nothing definitely, not even the laying down of nothing."[4]

Academic skepticism comes down to us mainly through the works of Cicero, the statesman and lawyer of the first century B.C. The school is usually traced to the Hellenistic philosophers Arcesilas and later Carneades. The name comes from those who claimed most direct descent from Plato's "Academy" by actually occupying the site of the school. A younger contemporary of Pyrrho, Arcesilas, founded the "Middle Academy" with what we would call skeptical doctrines. He proceeded by arguing on both sides of a question. He thus seemed to follow the Socrates of the "early" Platonic dialogues which are dramatic and "inconclusive."

Carneades, an acquaintance of Polybius and the founder of the "New Academy," lived in the middle of the second century B.C. and was sent by the Athenians on a diplomatic mission to Rome in 155 B.C. Still further developments in the tradition occurred; and Cicero learned his skepticism from Philo of Larissa, who subscribed to the teaching of Carneades. The purpose of this little history is to point out that differences existed even within the academic tradition, let alone differences from Pyrrhonian skepticism. Since Pyrrho and Arcesilas were said to have left no writings and we do not have the works of Carneades, we are dependent upon Cicero himself and writers of the second century A.D. and later for information about their methods and doctrines. Distinguishing the views of the founders is unnecessary for our purposes, except to note that Cicero had a good deal of material to choose from in developing and employing a "skeptical method."

Cicero asserted that Socrates, Plato, and Aristotle had only verbal differences (a suggestion so strange that Cicero's dismissal by most modern philosophers is not surprising). The common starting point for all the skeptics was disbelief that certainty in knowing is possible. Cicero's version of academic skepticism has the added dimension of connecting epistemological views with an attachment to the constitutional government expounded in Polybius' history of Rome.

A large body of Cicero's works survived and were read during the "Dark Ages" in Western Europe, but it is not always easy to identify which works were available in their entirety or trace his influence exactly. He was influential in the Renaissance, allegedly as a counter to Aristotle. The place of Cicero among the "classics" read in the eighteenth century was well-established, especially among those influenced by the Common Law and the English constitution. Of persons writing in English, David Hume, Edmund Burke, and James Madison were among eighteenth-century advocates of constitutional government who were familiar with Cicero; and we have documentation that the former two were aware specifically of his attachment to academic skepticism.[5]

2. Cicero's Life

Marcus Tullius Cicero was a prolific writer and a master of the Latin language.[6] His writings include speeches, works on rhetoric, philosophical works, and letters. This body of work has had repeated and enduring impact on Western literature and thought; but at different periods attention has focused on different aspects of his writings. Cicero thought of himself first and foremost as a statesman. He reached public notice and thence high office through his success as a legal advocate. His early cases concerned private law. Later he turned to public law, for in Rome the prosecution of former office holders was a major instrument of politics. One of his most famous cases, against the former governor of Sicily, Verres, was in prosecution; but for the most part he was a "defense lawyer." He reached the highest executive office in the Roman state, the consulship, in 63 B.C. and remained a public figure for the rest of his life.

At times in the two millennia since his death, Cicero's statesmanship has been the focus of attention. At other times, his role in law or his oratorical accomplishments or writing style have been of most interest. For some, he has mainly been a mine from which information about philosophers of the Hellenistic period has been drawn. Each of these aspects is of interest here, even though the treatment must at points be cursory.

Cicero was born in the small town of Arpinum, about sixty miles from Rome, probably in 106 B.C. His was a well-to-do but not politically distinguished family. It is reported by Plutarch, writing around the end of the first century A.D., that Cicero was a prodigy. In any case, he received a fine education and was early introduced into the company of some of the leading lawyers and public figures of Rome. He took to the study of Greek philosophy with such relish and showed such mastery of it that he was dismissed by some Romans as a "Greek and scholar," but his education was aimed throughout toward a career of public life. Cicero retained a life-long attachment to Arpinum and set some of his writings there. For a bright and ambitious person, however, Rome was the place to be, rhetoric the skill to master, and law and politics the fields in which to excel.

While still in his twenties, Cicero, the young lawyer, successfully defended a client against a charge brought by friends of the then-dictator Sulla. After winning the case and a good deal of public attention, Cicero, perhaps for reasons of health, went to advanced study in Greece for a couple of years. He studied under some of the leading philosophers of the day and developed a life-long attachment to the philosophic school called the New Academy. This was the first of several periods in which Cicero found himself at leisure from public life and gave himself to study and, from this early age, writing.

After his return from this first and voluntary exile, Cicero resumed his legal career and quickly earned distinction as the outstanding trial lawyer of his day. He also began the campaign for public office which saw him elected—in each case at the earliest year permissible by the law—to the positions of quaestor, aedile, praetor, and at age forty-two, consul. Whether by personal distinction or private arrangement, he managed to eclipse his colleague in the consulate and was preeminent during his year in office. His term saw the attempted revolution of Cataline which Cicero was instrumental in aborting. His service in the task caused him to be hailed by the Senate as "pater patriae," father of the country. He was never again to taste such success. The remainder of his life was lived in the lengthening shadow of Julius Caesar and then, in its last year and a half, under the storm clouds culminating in the Second Triumvirate and his own execution.

Cicero's political problems began not long after he left office. He refused to join the First Triumvirate of Caesar, Pompey, and Crassus. When he attempted to oppose some of their policies, he fell afoul of one of their allies Clodius and was obliged to leave Rome once again, this time involuntarily, for some months in 58-

57 B.C. The official charges were that he had misused his executive power while consul, but his problems with Clodius may in part have arisen from his great but sometimes ill-advised wit.[7] He returned to Rome amid such popular enthusiasm that he mistakenly thought his political preeminence again assured. Not long after his return, though, he was again excluded from public life when the First Triumvirate was renewed in 55 B.C. Late in the decade, he served reluctantly as proconsular governor in Cilicia, in what is now southeastern Turkey.

When the First Triumvirate came apart, Cicero attempted to mediate between Caesar, an old acquaintance for whom he seems always to have retained a certain personal fondness, and Pompey, whom he looked upon as the greater figure. After the rupture and a good deal of personal hesitation, Cicero followed Pompey out of Italy and spent some unhappy months in Pompey's camp. Caesar, victorious, welcomed Cicero back to Rome and seems to have enjoyed his company but did not seek his political advice. Some of Caesar's lieutenants, on the other hand, seem to have put themselves in Cicero's hands for an adult education course in rhetoric and Greek philosophy. This was Cicero's final period of enforced leisure, from 47 to 44 B.C., while Caesar dominated public life. Especially during this last period, he made use of his studies to write most of his philosophical works, mainly in dialogue form. With Caesar's assassination, Cicero returned briefly to active politics, helping to raise up Caesar's young heir Octavian and winning the enmity of Marc Antony. This led in turn to the deaths of both Marcus and his brother Quintus Cicero.

3. Cicero's Academic Philosophy

Many of Cicero's philosophical works and his speeches and court arguments (some perhaps extensively rewritten), works on oratory, and letters survived to insure his literary immortality. He undertook, especially during his last period of leisure, the task "of expounding in Latin literary form the famous old system of philosophy that took its rise from Socrates" (A: 413). His dialogues and other philosophical writings are a principal source for our knowledge of philosophy during the period from the death of Aristotle to Cicero's own time. In the construction of the philosophical works, especially the dialogues, Cicero typically juxtaposed materials which he borrowed—mostly from unknown or conjectured sources— to present views from the Stoic, Peripatetic, and Academic traditions on questions such as friendship, old age, and the nature of the gods. He admitted that the dialogues he wrote from 47 to 44 B.C. were written quickly and drew on various texts available to him (but now mostly lost). Most commentators consider Cicero's contribution to philosophy, other than as a transmitter, to be negligible. Often he is looked upon simply as a mouthpiece for Stoicism. This is curious since he explicitly and repeatedly acknowledged adherence to the New Academy (academic skepticism), and his dialogues follow that method.

George H. Sabine's long-popular college text *A History of Political Theory* is typical of the stoical interpretation of Cicero. Neal Wood's *Cicero's Social and Political Thought* (published after this chapter was first drafted) is a full and stimulating discussion but suffers from the typical errors of failing to recognize that Cicero actually used his method of academic skepticism, that the characters in the dialogues cannot be treated simply as mouthpieces for Cicero's positions, and therefore that Cicero cannot be treated simply as a Stoic.[8] The interpretation is conveniently available in the essay "Marcus Tullius Cicero" by James E. Holton appearing in the widely used *History of Political Philosophy*, and I shall use this version to criticize the view that Cicero was a Stoic.[9] Holton, like Wood, recognizes that Cicero professed to be an academic skeptic. Unlike Wood, Holton attaches significance to the fact that Cicero wrote dialogues but employs a distinction in the audiences addressed which I find ill-advised. Let me set down the major points of disagreement since they are fundamental to an understanding of Cicero's political philosophy.

Holton distinguishes two audiences for the dialogues, the "mass of men" and "serious students" (133). He thus traces two lines of thought which we may call exoteric (for the mass) and esoteric (for the serious students). This distinction accounts for the overt following of Stoic doctrines at various points but conceals another message. "While skepticism and the suspension of final judgment may be philosophically tenable, if such extreme views are taken seriously and developed to their logical extremity by the mass of men, the outcome may well be politically disastrous" (131). This seems to me to be misguided. Cicero was writing for the general reading public who took an active part in politics. While he asks the Academics to hold their fire at one point in *On the Laws*, all of his readers knew he adhered to the school of academic skeptics—the point is stated repeatedly in his works. He hoped to influence the political public and not just a select group of philosophy students. When he took on the tutelage of two of Caesar's lieutenants Hirtius and Dolabella, he surely viewed neither of them as "serious students." His writing is meant to constitute a public philosophy.

Closely related to this in Holton's argument is the view that there can be "little doubt" that Scipio, in the dialogue *On the Republic*, preferred "the philosophic rather than the active life" and that Cicero sought to show "the ultimate supremacy of the philosophic life" (135). In "Scipio's Dream," which Holton makes use of, the "rulers and preservers" of the "assemblies and gatherings of men" are the ones who will especially receive heavenly reward, not philosophical adepts (see R: 269). Cicero explains the attraction of the heavens which are described in Scipio's dream in the *Academica*: "for the study and observation of nature affords a sort of natural pasturage for the spirit and the intellect; we are uplifted, we seem to become more exalted.... There is delight in the mere investigation of matters at once of supreme magnitude and also of extreme obscurity.... [An Academic skeptic who can be called a wise man will be] afraid of forming rash opinions and to deem that all goes well with him if in matters of this kind he has discovered that which bears a likeness to the truth" (A: 633).

Cicero thought highly of the study of philosophy; but his position is one that Holton dismisses, a "union of experience in the management of great affairs with the study and mastery of those other arts," quoting Cicero (135). According to Holton, the "philosopher must be prepared at certain times to abandon his concern with 'eternal and divine' subjects and to place his particular talents at the service of the commonwealth" (136). But this is a position which Cicero, in his own voice, ridicules. One must lead a life of public voice from boyhood. "It has always seemed to me the most amazing of the teachings of learned men ['hominum doctorum'], who deny that they can steer ['gubernare'] when the sea is calm—having never learned nor cared to know—and at the same time proclaim they will take over steering when the waves are the most excited" (R: 25-27; my modification of the translation). Cicero blames Socrates for having separated philosophy from rhetoric. He repeatedly attacks the Epicureans for their views that withdraw them from public life. Cicero was not driven into politics. He framed his career to advance in politics even while he studied philosophy and rhetoric. During the time of Caesar's dominance, Cicero refers to himself as "deprived...of everything to which I had been accustomed by nature, inclination, and habit..." (quoted by Bailey at page 189 of his biography). Even at the end of his life, after he had completed the last group of dialogues, Cicero returned to politics, with fatal consequences.

In Holton's argument, it follows from the above that Cicero actually thought the "unqualified best regime" to be "that in which wisdom has an absolute right to rule: the absolute rule of the wise (the true aristocracy) and ultimately the absolute rule of the one man pre-eminent in wisdom and virtue (the true kingship) is the most desirable form of government" (142). Holton's subtle argument is defeated by recalling Cicero's commitment to academic skepticism. In the *Academica*, the academic argument is that there is no wise man equipped to rule on the basis of his wisdom. The wisdom of the wise man is knowing that he does not know. He never "assents" to anything; and "this being so, he holds the one plan in theory, so that he never assents, but the other in practice, so that he is guided by probability" (A: 601). And again, "the wise man will make use of whatever probable presentation [sense perception] he encounters" in action, but he does not fool himself into believing he is acting on the basis of anything other than probability (A: 595). In his defense of the academic position, Cicero says "the entire system and principle of the whole life is at issue"; and yet he refers to himself as an opinion-holder ["opinator"] rather than wise (A: 591).

Holton notes the similarity of Cicero to Edmund Burke in the treatment of the growth of the Roman state over a long time, but he dismisses this as more appearance than reality. Cicero is "closer to the classics [that is, Plato and Aristotle] than to Burke." For Holton the principle is "the superiority of planning to accident," and the Roman state was thus produced by a series of "fairly able men" (140-141). Yet, as Holton admits, the "history" which Scipio recounts in *On the Republic* of the development of the various institutions "is not meant to be simple history." From Holton's point of view, it is "in its essence a deliberate example of the Platonic 'noble lie'" to show "the citizens the wisdom and justice of the Roman origins" (141). While we are dealing with a foundation myth, this is also an assertion that the state developed its institutions over time through the admixture of experience—not by chance but by good counsel, by discipline, and by good fortune (R: 139). This view is not that of Burke, but it is more suggestive of Burke than of Plato.

Cicero is often dismissed as simply "eclectic," and this is understandable. Scholars are in general agreement that most of the works produced in Cicero's final period are translations and adaptations of Greek philosophical works. Rackham's evaluation is typical:

> His method was unambitious: he took some recent handbook of one or another of the leading schools of philosophy and reproduced it in Latin; but he set passages of continuous exposition in the frame of dialogue, and he added illustrations from Roman history and poetry. His object was to popularize among his fellow-countrymen the work of the great masters of thought; and he had made the masters' thought his own, having read widely and having heard the chief teachers of the day. But to learning and enthusiasm he did not add depth of insight or scientific precision. Nevertheless he performed a notable service to philosophy. With the Greek schools it had now fallen into crabbed technicality: Cicero raised it to literature, so commending it to all men of culture; and he created a Latin philosophical terminology which has passed into the language of modern Europe.[10]

We can agree with substantially all of this and yet believe it misses the point. Cicero addressed the literate public, not just professional philosophers. His method aims to articulate a common ground, not elucidate fine distinctions.

Cicero describes his approach as one that "by arguing on both sides" draws out and gives "shape to some result that either may be true or the nearest possible approximation to the truth. Nor is there any difference between ourselves and those who think that they have positive knowledge except that they have no doubts that their tenets are true, whereas we hold many doctrines as probable, which we can easily act upon but can scarcely advance as certain; yet we are more free and untrammelled, and are bound by no compulsion to support all the dogmas laid down for us almost as edicts by certain masters" (A: 475). This is quite different from the extreme skepticism of Pyrrhonism which acknowledges holding no doctrines because there are no grounds to do so.

Dismissing Cicero as eclectic is to give the word away to its pejorative connotations. It is a mistake to assume that Cicero's borrowing from earlier philosophers is merely casual or idiosyncratic. As an academic skeptic, he employed their method to make use of the valuable work done by others. His position may be summarized as follows. Many able persons have considered philosophical problems, and the problems themselves are multifaceted. Not all able persons find the same approach equally satisfying. Some problems may be more amenable to resolution by one approach than another. These two assertions are not obvious nonsense. Cicero selected his material carefully.

At the beginning of *De Officiis*, Cicero remarks that, "I shall, therefore, at this time and in this investigation follow chiefly the Stoics, not as a translator ["interpretes"], but, as is my custom, I shall at my own option and discretion draw from those sources in such measure and in such manner as shall suit my purposes" (Of: 9). He found Epicurean philosophy generally unacceptable because it promoted withdrawal from public life; but he tended to look for common ground among the other schools. So, shortly before the passage just quoted, he says, "...the teaching of ethics is particularly the right of the Stoics, the Academicians, and the Peripatetics: for the theories of Aristo, Pyrrho, and Erillus have long been rejected; and yet they would have the right to discuss duty if they had left us any power of choosing between things [that is, if their skepticism were not so extreme]..."(Of: 9). Indeed, "my philosophy is not very different from that of the Peripatetics for both they and I claim to be followers of Socrates and Plato" (Of: 3). Dismissing so readily the differences among philosophical schools is a substantial feat. How this is justified requires a more detailed look, especially at Cicero's book on epistemology.

The *Academica* addresses issues of epistemology directly and demonstrates Cicero's method most clearly. It along with the dialogue *On the Republic* which treats of the best state are of especial interest in this examination of skepticism and constitutionalism. In the *Academica*, men representative of different philosophical schools address a common concern, each from his own philosophical tradition. While the approach of academic skepticism moderates the entire discussion, no one view prevails completely. The reader, originally presumably a busy but concerned and serious Roman citizen, should be able to get some sense of the truth as a kind of middle ground among the positions articulated in the dialogue. To assist the busy reader even more, the several books or chapters of both of these dialogues are given an introduction in Cicero's own voice which explains the argument in a general way. The reader can thus either follow the discussion in considerable philosophical detail or can lay the work aside after getting a quick idea of its drift. The Roman reader could get a general idea of the best philosophical thought on important matters which was previously available only to those who could read Greek.

Cicero believed in education. He thought that philosophy could have practical importance if it could be made widely available within the upper classes. His emphasis is on citizenship. Cicero does not display the Stoic-Christian disposition to carry his message to all people, slaves as well as free. The Stoics, like the Christians after them, extended their doctrine of the community of gods and men to slaves. While Cicero expressed personal fondness for particular slaves, he often makes clear that he has little confidence in the mass of men as they were in his day.[11] His "republic" was no "democracy." The many, even among the well-to-do class, could not be expected to study another language, nor could they be expected to study the diverse doctrines of the many philosophers. Yet some such study was of importance if the republic were to survive. Cicero believed that there is some common truth underlying the many doctrines and that, by study, one can get a grasp of that truth sufficiently probable for common action.

I suggest that Cicero hoped to substitute popularized philosophy for the traditional customs of Rome (the "mos mores" or ways of those who have gone before) as a guide for political action. The traditional ways had decayed and were inadequate for the governance of Rome's empire. Cicero's educational task was thus central to his statesmanship: to make a properly conceived popular philosophy both of interest to the citizens and accessible to them. The Epicurean position, as indicated above, is not included in his dialectic because the Epicureans advocated withdrawal from public life. We now identify Epicureanism with a sybaritic love of bodily pleasure. This is untrue to the teachings of Epicurus, but the withdrawal from the public—what we might now call privatism—is true of the philosopher and his followers. (Cicero's closest friend Titus Pomponius Atticus was an Epicurean and avoided engagement in politics. So "neutral" was he in politics that he remained friends with both Cicero and, even after the latter's execution by them, with Mark Antony and Octavian.[12])

The *Academica*, as the title suggests, juxtaposes differing views on epistemology by the New Academy and the Old Academy. The Academy was considered to have been founded by Plato, while the other major philosophical schools, both more popular in Cicero's time, the Stoic and Epicurean schools, were founded later. The Peripatetics, derived from Aristotle, were minor. It is even alleged that Cicero was one of the first persons to take an active interest in Aristotle, after a long period in which his works were ignored or lost. As recounted by Richard McKeon, a set of Aristotle's works, "badly damaged by worms and damp" after a long sojourn in a cellar in Asia Minor, was brought to Rome by Sulla "after he took Athens in 86 B.C."[13]

It may at first glance seem strange that Cicero did not employ a character representing the Stoic tradition in his dialogue on epistemology, since the Stoics were especially interested in logic and methodology. The two Academies sufficed for Cicero's purposes, though. His argument is against certainty and for probability. The Old Academy held that some things, at least, can be known certainly while the New Academy held that, at best, one can only know with a degree of probability.

The *Academica* comes to us in fragments of two drafts, set at different times and with different casts of characters, although Cicero himself appears as a major participant in both drafts. In the earlier draft, set between 63 and 60 B.C., the interlocutors are leading statesmen (and the draft is usually called after the most famous of them the "Lucullus"). In the later draft, set approximately at the time of composition in 45 B.C., the principal sharing the dialogue with Cicero is a scholar-antiquarian. By chance, the second half of the first draft has come down to us and the first quarter or so of the second draft. The selections of characters in both drafts are suggestive. For the connections by blood and marriage of these persons and others of the Roman elite, see Erich S. Gruen.[14] The scholar gives a detailed history of philosophy, carefully distinguishing the different schools and doctrines. Cicero, as a character in the dialogue, presumably minimizes the differences among the schools, although his argument has not survived. This tendency to find common ground among philosophical schools is presented to us in the surviving second half of the first version where it is compared to the practice of the "popular" party in politics. The popular party claimed distinguished men from the past as a part of their tradition (most questionably, from the viewpoint of the speaker) just as the Academics claimed that Socrates, Plato, and Aristotle were all a part of their tradition and that Zeno the Stoic really differed only in terminology. What is to be made of such a philosophical conflation? We must turn to a more detailed examination of the *Academica*.

The first draft of the dialogue is set shortly after Cicero's year as consul in 63 B.C. In the missing first book, the aristocratic political leader Catulus, known for his upright character, puts forward the skeptical views of his father, also a distinguished political leader. The view that there is some certain knowledge is then advanced by Hortensius, a close associate of Catulus and the most distinguished lawyer in Rome until supplanted by Cicero. Cicero himself then puts forward a moderate skeptical position. In the second book, which will be considered in some detail, the dogmatic position that certain knowledge is available is defended by Lucullus, another associate of Catulus and an able general, distinguished governor, and a man of such wealth and taste that his name has passed into the vernacular. Cicero then again defends skepticism, this time particularly in the form developed by Carneades.

In the second draft, the position of the Old Academy, particularly that of the philosopher Antiochus, is expounded by the prolific Marcus Terentius Varro, an extremely learned man whose book *De Lingua Latina* was dedicated to Cicero. Cicero himself responds for the skeptical position, although only a short section of his response is extant. Atticus, attached to the Epicurean philosophy, is a minor participant in the dialogue. This second draft is set in Varro's villa, near Cicero's own country home, and is dedicated to Varro.

With this in the way of introduction, we can turn our attention to an examination of the first part of the second draft for a beginning to the argument.

The dialogue begins with a short first-person narrative which locates the participants at the country home of Marcus Varro, "a person united to us by identity of studies as well as old friendship." The three begin to talk about Roman politics. Both Cicero and Varro had sided with Pompey in the recent Civil War. Unlike many of Pompey's partisans, however, they had not sought death in defeat and had been pardoned by Caesar. They were politicians in retirement, curious about political doings but impotent to affect them. Atticus interrupts them, pointing out that they can indeed do nothing and that the conversation is only distressing. He opens a new line of discussion by inquiring about Varro's failure to publish anything recently. Varro responds that his work in progress, *De Lingua Latina*, is a large and complicated work, with which he is taking great pains. Cicero remarks that he himself has "embarked on the task of placing upon record the doctrines that [he has] learned in common with [Varro] and [is] expounding in Latin literary form the famous old system of philosophy that took its rise from Socrates" (A: 413). Cicero asks Varro why he has passed over this task when the subject of philosophy is of importance to all.

Varro's rejoinder is that anyone interested in philosophy will take the trouble to read the great philosophical works in their Greek original. He is thus unwilling to put in Latin "what the unlearned would not be able to understand and what the learned would not trouble to read...." For the Academics, unlike the Epicureans, do not "discuss matters that lie open to the view of ordinary language" but write with considerable technicality and employ a special vocabulary (415). Thus while he takes philosophy as a "guiding principle of life and as an intellectual pleasure," he sends his friends who are interested "to the Greeks, so that they may draw from the fountain-head..."(417). He writes instead on the history, institutions, language, and literature of Rome.

Cicero agrees that this is an important study, for it enables Romans to understand themselves better. But as for Varro's views of philosophy, his view has only some probability; for those who can read Greek may still enjoy reading even derivative philosophy in their own language and those who cannot read Greek may find some value in reading philosophy.

Varro's position is one familiar to the modern academic world. True philosophy is for the few, a scholar's business. The problems of philosophy are of such complexity that they can be treated only with the greatest care and precision by the highly trained. Varro could not see the point in trying to make philosophy accessible to the many. He chose instead the task of making Roman antiquities of interest to the most sophisticated Romans. This was an important task in Cicero's view (for he, after all, put the words in Varro's mouth). The well-being of the republic, which emerges as Cicero's overwhelming preoccupation, depends upon loyalty. Loyalty may serve rational understanding, but it also depends on a kind of affection for the mores of the community.[15]

Cicero himself thought that philosophy could have practical importance if it could be made widely available. The many could not be expected to study many languages, nor could they be expected to study the many doctrines of the philosophers. Yet such study is of importance for, as we have said, Cicero believed that there is some common truth underlying the many doctrines and that the reader can get a grasp of that truth sufficiently probable for action.

Cicero next notes that while he was preoccupied with politics, he kept "these studies within close bounds and relied merely on reading" (421). But now he is proceeding with his project of making philosophy accessible to the many. He is both out of office and suffering grievously from the recent death of his daughter. He seeks in philosophy both a cure for his grief and the most honorable way of spending his time. "For this occupation is the one most suited to my age; or it is the one more in harmony than any other with such praiseworthy achievements as I can claim; or else it is the most useful means of educating our fellow-citizens; or if these things are not the case, I see no other occupation that is within our power" (423).

Cicero has given us—not the one true reason for studying and writing philosophy—but four very good reasons, each of which has some probability. Philosophy may be the highest study; it may provide guidance in practical matters; it may be useful in education; and it may be the last pleasure when all else is taken away from us in adversity. Cicero makes clear, as he does in a number of dialogues, that practical affairs take some kind of priority over study; but philosophy is well worth study. The practical man needs to learn that philosophy is valuable; and the philosopher needs to learn that his philosophy should not withdraw him from the public life (see A: 421, 469-471; R: 17, 23, 27).

It has sometimes been argued that Cicero really believed the life of the scholar, withdrawn from the turmoil of public life and public affairs, is preferable. During the nineteenth century, Cicero was commonly valued for his literary qualities and was undervalued as a philosopher or statesman. The essay by Holton discussed above similarly attempts to show that Cicero sought to demonstrate "the ultimate supremacy of the philosophic life" to those sharp enough to bite through the outer husk of his argument. While it is clear that Cicero sought consolation in philosophy, both from the disappointments of his political life and from the death of his daughter, he seems always to have retained the hope of providing guidance in practical matters, for the mature as well as the young. Throughout the Fifties, while writing *De Oratore* and *On the Republic*, he hoped to influence Pompey to pursue a statesmanlike policy. Even in the Forties, during Caesar's dictatorship, Cicero may have retained some hope of influencing Caesar through his principal lieutenants. Thus it seems clear that even in the writing of the *Academica*, in the depths of his despair over Tullia's death, he retained hope for the practical potency of the right kind of philosophy. Biographically, too, it is hard to sustain the priority of philosophy. Cicero's letters, especially those to Atticus, are full of anguish during his exiles of 58-57 and 47-46 and impatience during his governorship in Cilicia—in each case because of his absence from Rome. It is difficult to explain the extremity of these feelings if literature and the philosophic life were supreme or first in his heart. The closing act of his life, too, is hard to explain. He abandoned his writing to return to politics following Caesar's death when the consuls proved inadequate to the situation. His vitriolic attacks on Antony led directly to his own death.

Immediate action in the political realm is the most direct way of benefitting the community. Cicero not only makes explicit that he has not let his philosophic work intrude on his public duties, but he is also careful to set this and other dialogues on a holiday or vacation. The dialogues typically take place in the country, not near the seat of government. Some are set on a religious holiday while governmental business is adjourned. In the *Academica* itself a special point is made that immediate political participation by Cicero and Varro is precluded by Caesar's dictatorship. We are told just before the beginning of the dialogue in the "Lucullus" that the persons involved had been in the country for some time and were planning to adjourn elsewhere outside Rome later. We can thus reasonably conjecture that a holiday justified the absence of Catulus, Hortensius, Lucullus, and Cicero from Rome.

We can make one further conjecture about the relation of philosophy, and especially the specialist's philosophy, to action. In this dialogue, Cicero emphasizes the pleasure to the sophisticated Roman reader of seeing the success with which Greek philosophy can be translated into Latin. There is no mention of intrinsic philosophic significance to the translation. In other works, however, Cicero discusses the "community of mankind," clearly arguing for a common humanity to be cultivated despite all the variation in peoples and customs. While the Greeks made a sharp distinction between themselves and "the barbarians" and directed their philosophy—their political philosophy at least—to themselves alone, Cicero's works display a catholic intention throughout. He promotes ideas and institutions to be available to all cultivated people. This view was developed in the Hellenistic world by the Stoics, but it has particular significance in the Roman cosmopolis. Is not the translation of Greek into Latin itself proof that there may be various ways of summing up what we know? The search for the truth, or at least a better approximation of it, is the common activity of humankind, not the preserve of an elect people.

After Cicero explains his efforts to write his dialogues, Varro asks Cicero the significance of the latter's shift from the Old Academy to the New Academy as a source of materials. Cicero lightly responds that people ought to be free to change their views but then adds that there are not really two Academies anyway. Varro retorts that view has been properly combatted, so Cicero asks that Varro outline the history of philosophy to clarify the point.

In what follows, Varro strives to distinguish philosophers and schools. Cicero, as a participant in the dialogue, strives to minimize differences and to find a fundamental unity in the whole course of philosophical investigation. Thus to the historian is given the task of differentiating and particularizing while to the philosopher and lawyer is given the task of finding unity amidst apparent diversity. Even the Epicureans, whose views are seldom canvased by Cicero, are represented by the friendly auditor to the conversation, Atticus, who expresses pleasure at hearing once again views with which he is familiar.

Varro begins his history with Socrates "who was the first to call philosophy away from preoccupation with things hidden in the intricacies of nature and to have focused it on the common life and on questions of the virtues and the vices and things good and bad" (A: 424-425; my translation). He did so because the earlier philosophic concerns with physics and astronomy were preoccupations with things hard to know and of no real significance in deciding how to live well. Socrates also introduced the method of affirming nothing himself and proceeded by the questioning of other people's opinions.

Plato and Aristotle abandoned this Socratic method and founded a philosophy containing positive doctrines. They divided philosophy (this Hellenistic distinction is anachronistic) into ethics, physics, and logic.[16] Their ethical views agreed in relating action to the natural development of man's mind and body and to the extension of his control over nature through possessions usefully employed in action. (The focus is on action and circumstance.) Their physics depended on the interplay of force and matter, and they did not recognize the existence of any fundamental particles from which the world is built up. During the course of the discussion, the word "qualitas" (from which we get "quality") is coined; and Cicero defends the creation of new words as almost as valuable as the discovery of new facts. In the third division of philosophy, epistemology and the philosophy of discourse, Plato and Aristotle agreed in believing that truth arises from the senses but is not solely a matter of sensation, distinguished opinion from knowledge, and distinguished dialectic from rhetoric.

Varro continues his history of philosophy on down through Zeno, the founder of the Stoic school. Despite the differences in doctrine articulated, each of the philosophers cited takes his beginnings in nature. While there are disagreements about what is the case, truth is not simply a convention.

The New Academy began in disagreement with Zeno, and Varro insists that Cicero himself explain this disagreement. Cicero responds by minimizing the departure of the Stoics from earlier philosophy. He then asserts that the pre-Socratics agreed with Socrates in doubting the certainty of sense perceptions. Arcesilas, the founder of the New Academy, was not moved by any obstinacy or commitment to besting others but simply by recognition of the obscurity of things. He therefore argued against the opinions of all men so that no one would affirm any positive statements or act on the basis of thinking he knows what he does not in fact know. At this point, the text of the second draft of the *Academica* is broken off.

What is to be made of the discussion so far? The two principal participants profess to disagree and to adhere to different philosophical schools. They find a common interest in the subject of epistemology, however; and they are able to discuss it in a calm and friendly manner. Even the representative of the school which took no interest in epistemology, while he makes little positive contribution to the discussion, professes to find it of interest. Though Varro outlines the disagreements among philosophers, he finds a common starting point in nature. While Cicero defends the position that certainty in philosophy is impossible, he finds a common thread running through the history of philosophy. Common ground and disagreement are common to both speakers.

We turn now to the first draft of the *Academica*, that set a year or two after Cicero's term as consul. We have only Book 2, the second half of the work. The principal speakers are Lucullus and Cicero. The other participants, who apparently were featured in Book 1, Catulus and Hortensius, contribute only an occasional remark.

Lucius Licinius Lucullus served under the dictator Sulla and emerged as one of the leaders of the Roman aristocracy (the "Optimates") in the years after Sulla's death. Though without significant previous military experience, he commanded the eastern armies opposing King Mithridates in Anatolia and had, for all practical purposes, won the war before he was supplanted by Pompey, his principal political opponent. He returned to Rome where, for a decade, he was the outstanding Optimate and leader of those who opposed Pompey's preeminence in the state. Lucullus is best remembered, though, for his cultivated life—especially identified in later history with good eating and drinking. The story is told by Plutarch that Cicero and Pompey one day found Lucullus in the Forum and asked to dine with him on that day just to see what the menu would be when Lucullus had expected to dine alone. When he was refused a day's delay or any opportunity to instruct his servants on the menu, Lucullus simply told the servants that he would dine in the Apollo room. So well-organized was his household that his servants knew by the one instruction that a lavish meal was to be served. Cicero and Pompey were said to have been amazed not so much by the lavishness of the meal as by the rapidity with which such a meal could be served up.

Book 2 has an introduction written in Cicero's own voice. He employed this device fairly frequently in his dialogues to introduce the characters and to summarize the general position to be developed in the dialogue. It is as though Cicero, alert to the pressures facing the busy men to whom his works were addressed, chose to insure that they would get at least some idea of his argument even if they did not take the time to follow through the details of the dialogue proper. The introduction begins with a reminder to the reader of the career of Lucullus and the great admiration he won for his devotion to duty and his ability. His intellectual gifts are particularly singled out for praise, especially his memory for detail. "So great," writes Cicero, "was his wisdom in practical affairs in the constituting and compounding properly of states and so great his sense of justice that twenty-five years later Asia [a section of Asia Minor] continues to observe the institutions of Lucullus and to follow the path he laid out" (A: 468-469; my translation). Cicero goes on to regret, however, that those talents were missed from the law-courts and Senate while Lucullus was absent in Asia. All of these things, Cicero asserts, were well known.

What is less well known, Cicero says, was that Lucullus was deeply dedicated to philosophy and literature. Even on his military campaigns, he kept philosophers near him. Given his remarkable memory, it is not surprising that he could recount in detail philosophical discussions he had heard. Cicero professes to have heard these things from Lucullus himself in private company. He then apologizes for letting out the secret, since it may diminish the stature of Lucullus in the eyes of those who do not like Greek literature and dislike philosophy even more. Cicero goes on to assert, nonetheless, that two outstanding statesmen of the preceding century had also been devotees of philosophy—Marcus Cato (a figure in Cicero's dialogue "On Old Age") and Scipio Africanus the Younger (the principal in the *On the Republic*). Marcus Cato took up Greek literature in his old age; Scipio had as a constant companion the Stoic philosopher Panaetius. Cato was the very embodiment of traditional Roman virtues, and Scipio was the outstanding general and statesman of his day. Succeeding generations looked back to the example of Scipio's statesmanship. Some critics may be reluctant, Cicero says, to see such important public figures as Lucullus, Cato, and Scipio employed in philosophical dialogues. Cicero dismisses such criticism: are these men to be thought of as simply congregating silently or to pass their time in ludicrous or light conversations? No; showing these men discussing philosophy is precisely worthy of their greatness and dignity so long as the precaution is taken that such private concerns are not shown as detracting from public business. Cicero asserts that it magnifies the glory of these statesmen to show them as using their leisure for serious and erudite conversation. And, he adds, it is proper for himself, when he can not be on active duty for the state, to spend his time being of service through writing philosophical dialogues.

Cicero later admitted in a letter to Atticus that he had rather miscast Lucullus, Catulus, and Hortensius in the first version of the *Academica*; for "the matter did not fit the persons, who could not have been supposed ever to have dreamed of such abstrusities."[17] This seems to have been one of the reasons for rewriting the dialogue to assign presentation of epistemological niceties to the scholarly Varro. It has been suggested that the build-up of Lucullus as a philosopher was simply patchwork, that the introduction was written as an after-thought in a lame effort to justify the cast of characters. In view of the facts that such preferences are common in the Ciceronian dialogues, however, and that Cicero typically assigned philosophical sophistication to leading Roman statesmen, such an interpretation of the introduction to the "Lucullus" is inadequate. Surely Cicero had in mind the building up and legitimizing of philosophy in the eyes of the Roman reader. While he is careful to combat the Epicurean position which would withdraw its adherents from public life, he sought to identify philosophy with statesmanship. The contribution which philosophy can make to public affairs recurs frequently in his work, as argued further below.

Cicero next gives a brief restatement of the position of the New Academy. Things in themselves are obscure and our powers of judgment infirm. In view of these limitations on the possibility of certainty, the Academics seek truth with the highest care and the most patient commitment of their energies and adopt positions "without contentiousness." They do this by "arguing on both sides of an issue to draw out and give shape to some result that may either be true or the nearest approximation to the truth" (A: 473-475). This produces probable doctrines which one can easily act upon but which cannot be asserted as absolutely certain. The academic method flourishes on the doctrines of other philosophies, for their statements and positions provide arguments pro and con to be employed by the Academics. While most people commit themselves early in life to a philosophy and then stubbornly adhere to it even though the original commitment was made when the person was young and impressionable, the Academics leave their judgment unfettered and are prepared to hear arguments pro and con, adhering, as a guide for action, to whatever seems probable.

To cast this in modern language, important problems have typically been canvased by serious students representing diverse points of view. Many of these points of view have something to contribute to understanding the issue at hand. No one of them is likely to be fully adequate for the richness, variety, and uncertainty of the situation. We can argue abstractly without end but are drawn up short when there is a need to act. When a person has heard or read the best formulations, he or she is in the best position to chose what seems most probable to guide decisions and action. The Ciceronian dialogues are designed to make available to the Roman man of affairs the major arguments examining the basic questions of life: how confident is he to be of what he thinks he knows? what are the proper ends of action? how should he judge his actions in relation to other people? what is the best political organization? The questions listed here are not only basic but big; but the discussions suggest options for more particular problems as well.

After this introduction, the dialogue itself resumes. Apparently on the proceeding day, Catulus outlined the views of his father which corresponded to those of the philosopher Carneades. Hortensius apparently responded by outlining the views of Antiochus of the Old Academy. Cicero apparently then responded to shake the position of Hortensius (A: "Introduction," 401). Lucullus begins his discourse by making clear that the doctrines which he is going to present are not necessarily his own. He puts them forward to be examined and then rejected if they should be found wanting. He is going to expound in some detail the views of Antiochus, which he heard from the master's mouth. He recounts a visit to Alexandria in the company of Antiochus and another philosopher of the "New" persuasion. As the two talked and Antiochus pressed his position without persuading the other, Antiochus began to lose his temper, something he did not usually do. It may be by this little story that Cicero means to give us a clew that those philosophies which believe some truths can be grasped with certainty are likely subtly to encourage anger and contentiousness, while the method of the New Academy hears all positions calmly and chooses among them dispassionately. On the other hand, a little further along, Lucullus makes the point that many of the skeptics, despite their profession that nothing can be known, "seem to be only too confident in some of their assertions and to profess to know more than they really do." Thus the skeptical school may lead to its own brand of doctrinaire certainty, here warned against.

After telling the story, which serves also to explain the occasions on which Lucullus heard Antiochus outline his views, Lucullus next compares the New Academy with the "Populares," political figures who appealed to the common people for support. Both groups rewrite history to emphasize resemblances. The politicians emphasize the similarity of their own position to all of the great predecessors, all of whom they claim to have been committed to the well-being of the people. The philosophers assert that all of their famous predecessors basically held the same position as they do. Both in fact blur distinctions and create perturbations—the one upsetting the public and the other disturbing solidly-based philosophy. The character of both is suspect.

What are we to make of this? Cicero has placed in the mouth of a leading Optimate the charge that those who adhere to Cicero's own philosophy are similar in character to the Populares. Cicero has been said to have been an Optimate himself. I find most persuasive the view that Cicero saw himself as neither one of the Optimates nor one of the Populares: he found some good and some bad in both positions and tried to create a middle ground in Roman politics. Some modern thought is inclined to look at class division simply into the "haves and the have-nots," the rich and the poor. Doing so may lead us to lump Cicero with the wealthy, especially since he, as a "new man," clearly hungered for the social approval of these people. As early as Aristotle, however, the point was made that stability is most likely to be found in a city state dominated by a position between the rich and the poor, a middle class. This is the position which Cicero promotes as a "mixed constitution."[18]

The passage in question here seems compatible with such a view. In the passages in the dialogue assigned to the character Cicero, the speaker does indeed emphasize similarity and continuity among the philosophers. The method outlined in the author's own voice at the beginning of the "Lucullus" suggests that each philosophy should be heard carefully and treated seriously to see what contribution it can make to wise action. Yet skeptics are typically criticized, in Cicero's time and our own, for simply being critics and nay-sayers, believing nothing themselves and contributing nothing. They are suspected of undercutting the established order, morally and politically as well as intellectually. To the contrary, Cicero the skeptic believed many things and had both affection and respect for the established order. Similar charges of pandering to or of undercutting the established order were also laid against David Hume.

Cicero takes seriously the comparison of skeptical philosophy with popular politics. This skeptical philosophy is a philosophy of common sense. Even when written in great detail, it is designed to challenge the certainty and usefulness of sharp distinctions and esoteric concepts. It is ironic that the skeptical philosophy has never been popular: most people, it would seem, are "true believers." The philosophy, certainly in the hands of Cicero, is designed to be popular. The very structure of the dialogues, with their introductions giving a general indication of the thrust of the work, and their characters, popular public figures, suggest that the dialogues were intended for a broad audience (within the meaning of that phrase in the Roman context).

The political position of Cicero, as we shall see it emerge in what follows, is indeed popular in a significant sense of the word. While accepting and recognizing diversity, it attempts to find a common ground to moderate differences. It is not a philosophy of aristocracy, though it recognizes and accepts differences and inequalities among human beings. Statesmen of varying points of view and policies contribute to the republic, and the proper republic permits citizens to cultivate their differences while it provides devices to encourage their cooperation. The skeptical position of Cicero seeks to spread as wide a net as possible, including if it can and excluding only in the most extreme cases.

Lucullus sets out a proper history of philosophy, sharply distinguishing the views and methods of the philosophers and showing progress in philosophic thought. According to this history, Arcesilas, the refounder of the Academy, attempted to throw into the shadows things that were very clear. While some philosophers preferred simply to ignore Arcesilas for this, others—believing that worthy human beings deserved to have their views discussed—took up the debate with the skeptics. It is clear to Lucullus from that debate that if the skeptics proved anything with their doubt, they proved too much. In the skeptical effort to attack any certainty of knowledge based on sense perceptions, they had in fact made it impossible to distinguish even probabilities. The position from which Lucullus himself argues has some characteristics in common with the logical positivism of the late 1930s, founding knowledge in clear and certain sense perceptions and building up a "chain of larger percepts" (495) with the help of a logical calculus. Lucullus, however, unlike most of the positivists, draws his examples from ethics. He is concerned to ground action in nature and in certain knowledge derived from sense perception. Thus when one "assents" ["adsensione"] to a truth, he does so with full confidence that other people must concur.

Lucullus attacks the skeptical argument as implausibly subtle and denies the validity of standard skeptical examples of the uncertainty of sense perception: the apparent bending of a stick when it is stuck into water, the apparently changing color of a pigeon's neck, and the evidence of dreams. He admits, nonetheless, that a wise man may delay his assent in order to take time to distinguish the true from the false. Lucullus distinguishes even the principal philosophers of the later Academy, Arcesilas and Carneades, on the grounds that the former was at least consistent while the latter thought that the wise man would sometimes give his assent to things even if he did not believe in the certainty of their truth. But in another sense, Lucullus challenges the consistency of both of them, pointing out that both of them made great use of a large supply of facts.

Lucullus closes his argument by pointing out to Cicero that if he denies that people do in fact know things he will be calling into question his own testimony at the time of the Catalinarian conspiracy when Cicero had testified under oath that he knew about the existence of a plot.

After a brief interlude in which Catulus encourages Cicero not to be intimidated by the authority and fluency of Lucullus, Cicero begins his response. He professes to be very nervous in the face of such an important task. In several of his writings, Cicero revealed that he was nervous at the beginning of his speeches. This from one of the greatest orators of all time! Plutarch alleges that Cicero began his speeches with great timidity "and in many cases scarcely left off trembling and shaking" until well into the substance of the speech. Cicero justifies this nervousness not only by the distinction of his auditors but also by the importance of the subject, for they are dealing with the whole grounding of life and the basis for wisdom in living life properly. It is because of this importance that he is so committed to seeking the truth. How can a person not be excited by the investigation of a question so basic to human life (549)?

Cicero summarizes his own position. A truly wise man would never give his "assent" in the sense in which they have been using the word, for he would recognize that there is no certain truth. But Cicero himself is not a wise man; he does hold opinions; and he does at times give his assent. He compares himself with one who navigates by a bright group of stars rather than by one rather dim star which would give the most accurate course. He follows "these theories of wider aspect, not fined down and over subtilized" with the result that he must "roam and wander more widely" (551). He accepts many appearances without being certain they are true.

This passage and the general argument which follows it suggest that perhaps the truly wise man, in the fullest sense, does not exist. The approximation to wisdom is left to those such as Cicero himself who recognize both that certainty is impossible and yet that action based on the best available evidence must still be taken.

The controversy, in Cicero's view, turns on the question as to whether anything can be perceived with such certainty that there can be no disagreement about it. He begins by pointing out that Antiochus, from whom Lucullus had drawn his arguments, himself changed his opinion late in life, converting from skepticism to a doctrinaire position. How could he suddenly have seen with certainty what before had been uncertain? Cicero then examines in considerable detail the grounds for doubting certainty: the disagreements of philosophers, occasions in which the senses err, the uncertainty that the structure of logic reflects the structure of the world, and the existence of logical fallacies. All of these challenge the doctrine of certainty.

Cicero next outlines the position of Carneades who employed a distinction between two ways of classifying appearances: those which are grasped certainly and those which are not grasped at all; and those which are probable and those which are not probable (593). While the grounds for certainty can be impugned, it is contrary to all experience to assert that nothing is probable since things of some sort, whatever their exact character, happen around us all the time. "Thus the wise man [and here Cicero has dropped his distinction between the truly wise and one such as himself] will make use of whatever apparently probable [appearances] he encounters, if nothing presents itself that is contrary to that probability," and this will govern his whole organization of life (595). The wise man holds one plan in theory and believes knowledge is derived from sense perceptions and is never certain and thus never really holds it as knowledge. He holds another view in practice and is guided in action by such order as he can make from appearances (601). This very way of formulating the matter, however, is only probable; and we should note that some people seem so successful in gaging probabilities that they can properly be thought of as experts ["versatus"] (609).

Cicero then expands his horizon, not with a history of philosophy but with a comparison and evaluation of doctrines. He particularly praises the peripatetic formulation of epistemology but finds some good in each of the schools. There is some truth, some reality outside ourselves; but it is never perceived or grasped with such finality that it can be asserted in a certain and permanent form. There will always be disagreements among human beings. We should not adopt an epistemology which would lead us to demand complete certainty. We should introduce an element of doubt into our own judgment and not expect complete agreement from others. While some positions may be quite improbable, there are various ways of formulating what is probable; and our choice of formulations may change over time.

Cicero particularly anticipates disagreements in cosmology and religion, for such subjects are so far removed from us. He praises such study nonetheless, for it lifts up the mind and somehow has a humanizing effect. (We shall return to a closer examination of this point in the discussion of *On the Republic*.) Cicero then turns, in somewhat greater detail which we shall not follow, to agreements and disagreements over ethics and logic. It is worth quoting Cicero's closing remarks on ethics, however:

I am just as much affected as you are, Lucullus, pray don't think I am less a human being than yourself. The only difference is that whereas you, when you have been deeply affected, acquiesce, assent, approve, hold the fact as certain, comprehended, perceived, ratified, firm, fixed, and are unable to be driven or moved away from it by any reason, I on the contrary am of the opinion that there is nothing of such a kind that if I assented to it I shall not often be assenting to a falsehood, since truths are not separated from falsehoods by any distinction, especially as those logical criteria of yours are non-existent. (A: 651)

While this is scarcely the stuff of conversation, it is an apt summary of the Ciceronian position. We should note particularly Cicero's desire to encompass different verbal formulations of what he takes to be basically one "doctrinaire" position opposed to his own.

Cicero, the participant in the dialogue, closes his remarks by returning to the charge Lucullus has made about swearing the truth concerning the conspiracy of Cataline. Cicero points out that his theory is actually supported by Roman law since the oaths taken by jurors required following one's own judgments of what appeared to happen. Closing with a point derived from the legal system under-scores the closeness of Cicero's epistemology and the method following from it to the legal mode of argument. When an issue arises, parties with differing views are brought together to argue out the matter fully. The argument does not provide a final proof or a logical demonstration but requires a judgment or decision to be made by a disinterested weighing of the probabilities. This too we shall have occasion to explore further.

In the closing passage of the dialogue, the participants agree that at some future time they will discuss the differences in opinion existing among men of the greatest distinction, the obscurity of nature, and the errors of philosophers. Lucullus expresses no regrets about the debate; Catulus thinks he may concur with the skeptical position; and Hortensius, in a Latin double entendre, says they should set sail for home and implies that they must do away with the prospect of certainty. The dialogue thus ends with an agreement somewhat ambiguous save for the acceptance of continuing discussion.

Having summarized in a general way Cicero's dialogue concerning the character of knowledge, I should like to pause to reflect on some problems in the interpretation of the philosophical method and intent.

We have been considering a philosophical dialogue on epistemology in which the author himself appears both as a participant in the dialogue and as a commentator on it. The dialogue was written, moreover, at the end of the author's life. Coveys of questions fly up before us.

Does an individual character within the dialogue carry the full message of the author? How does the author as commentator relate to the full message of the dialogue? What significance, if any, is to be attached to the use of the dialogue form, and what role does the character of the participants play? In a more general form, is philosophy and particularly political philosophy something which can be conveyed in a simple, clear, and straightforward form?

What is the purpose of such a dialogue? Is it simply the amusement and retreat from active politics of a tired and discouraged old man? Has the politician simply turned philosopher, or is there some political significance or practical implication of epistemology? In a more general form, what is the relation between thought and action; what is the relation between a person's words and deeds?

Is the position which Cicero outlines in the *Academica* one to which he adhered throughout his life, or does it represent the skepticism of old age? Is the position of the New Academy consistent with the youthful *De Inventione*? More importantly, is the mode of interpretation suggested by the *Academica* appropriate to the dialogues begun in the previous decade: *De Oratore, On the Republic,* and *On the Laws*? In a more general form, what is the nature of consistency in the philosopher-statesman?

The exploration of these questions will run through much of what follows. At this point I shall give only an indication of the proper answers.

Cicero can be said to participate at three levels in the *Academica*: he is the character arguing from the position of the New Academy; he is a commentator introducing the action in the variants and, in the "Lucullus," discussing at some length the character of the participants and the position of the New Academy; and he is the artistic creator of the entire work. Three variants of the Academy are articulated in the work: the position of Arcesilas of arguing against all positions and assenting to nothing; the position of Carneades of differentiating theory and practice, assenting to nothing in theory but in practice following the probabilities of appearance; and a third position usually identified with Cicero's teacher, Philo of Larissa. Cicero defends, but without adopting, the position of Arcesilas. He employs the position of Carneades but seems more interested in the use of probabilities in action than the exact formulation of theoretical detail. Varro says the Academic philosophy must employ a technical vocabulary accessible only to the scholarly. Cicero responds that such a view is only probable and in fact in the introduction to the "Lucullus" gives a simple, popularized summary of the Academic position. There is, thus, no simple, straight-forward, uncontroverted version of the New Academy presented in the *Academica*.

The summary at the beginning of the "Lucullus" may seem most tempting in suggesting a method which proceeds "by arguing on both sides to draw out and give shape to some results that may either be true or as near as possible an approximation of the truth," a position apparently very like the adversary position in law; but if it is really that simple, what is the point of the whole elaborate dialogue? It seems more rewarding to take the view that the total dialogue, including the presentation of character, carries the full Ciceronian message. No one character in the dialogue conveys the full truth about the character of knowledge and the relation of knowledge to action and to character. Even the Ciceronian preface gives only a general direction as a beginning and is not meant as an adequate, full statement for a person who is to bring wisdom to the service of action. The scholarly histories of Varro, the debating skill of Cicero, the confidence of Lucullus that there is a truth of some sort based in nature, and both the simple explanation of the Academic position and the elaborate ones all play their part in conveying the message of the dialogue.

The truth, whatever it is, is complex. A person may need a simple sense of direction in trying to get out of the woods, but he or she also needs an acquaintance with the fine details of forest life such as which animals to avoid and what ground to walk upon. We may advocate policies, not men; but the varying characters of human beings are the stuff of politics. History and even myths and the children's tales of the community help to establish the fundamental agreements on which cooperative action rests. The sympathetic historian and the antiquarian have important political roles. The antiquarian is the guardian of the common lore. The sympathetic historian recounts the successes of the community. Varro represents all of this. He also presents the need of the community for detailed and encyclopedic knowledge. Cicero, as a character in the dialogue, represents the need for the "big picture," a general view which gives coherence to the details and direction to the action. These insights may call into question our contemporary efforts to purge elementary education of the mythic accounts of the Founders and stories of "pure virtue" in order to substitute more realistic and even "debunking" histories.

It does not seem to me that Ciceronian epistemology should be looked upon as a retreat from practical action. The political problems of Rome were to be solved, in Cicero's view, not by the adoption of one doctrinaire position, whether that of Optimates or of Caesar. A proper respect for the complexity of reality and the diversity of human insights is at the heart of true politics, whatever the odds against their establishment or maintenance. While the probabilities of political life and Cicero' mood seem to have fluctuated greatly, it was surely Cicero's hope to make people see that republican politics are grounded in the very nature of human beings as knowing beings.

Cicero is at pains in both the first version of the *Academica* and in *On the Republic* to portray leading Roman statesmen as interested in philosophy, but only as a supplement to their public commitments: they are not professional philosophers. Their philosophizing is ultimately a matter of finding public common ground, not of promoting divisive distinctions.

It is also to be expected, if this view of the dialogue is correct, that consistency throughout a long life does not require an exact identity of expression in different contexts. Nor does it require that action will always be the same in "similar circumstances" or will always follow in a clear and simple way from a prior expression of principle. Reality being complex, circumstances are never exactly the same; no verbal formulation is ever fully adequate to reality. Even though there may be probabilities which approach so closely to certainty that they can be thought of as basic truths, one cannot be certain that any verbal formulation will be adequate and final for all time.

Unfortunately, we must acknowledge that other characteristics of human beings which Cicero did not discuss but partially illustrated are also grounded in human nature and constantly challenge republican politics. The writings of Frank Knight are replete with elaborations of his assertion that: "...human nature as we know it—the nature of man sufficiently advanced or civilized enough to think and talk about his own nature—is a tissue of paradox. It would be difficult to make any general statement about 'man' which would not contain substantial truth; and this means that the antithesis, or, indeed, several antitheses, would also be partly true and, on the average, equally so."[19]

These last few pages have already begun to suggest implications of relevance to politics. The epistemology of the *Academica* calls out for a political theory. In Cicero's case, the political theory was written first. I shall examine his formulation in detail below, but I wish to make my own interpretation of these implications explicit here.

We should not look, in politics, for a neat, orderly, and definitive model. While it is appropriate to seek coherence, what typically emerges is a series of overlapping, interconnected insights. We should not expect complete certainty nor complete agreement. When they are found, we should rather be suspicious of them. The things of politics can be approached in many ways through history, philosophy, and law; and the insights will be at best complementary rather than identical. What seems incompatible may be somewhat different answers to somewhat different questions. The political community depends on a degree of consensus, including a reasonable degree of patience and tolerance; but disagreement is also central both to human experience and republican politics.

In the *Academica*, the dialogue is simply between the doctrinaire and the skeptical positions. In other dialogues, various doctrines are employed against one another; and it is brought home even more sharply that skeptical truths may depend upon the juxtaposition of various doctrines. Many philosophical positions can reasonably coexist, each contributing insights of value to the common life; and different disciplines may contribute to the common life so long as they treat each other with mutual respect and an element of good humor. Skepticism may be said to be the basic doctrine of republican government, but it itself depends upon the existence of doctrinaire positions. Skepticism is, moreover, not just a "negative doctrine." The wise skeptic recognizes that he or she holds many beliefs and may retain them even in the face of apparently unassailable logical argument.

The second part of the *Academica* in its first version gives a detailed argument about the grounding of certainty in sense perception. There follows a detailed skeptical counter-argument, involving optical illusions for example, that only probability is available: things in themselves are obscure and our powers of judgment are infirm. Reading accounts of the idealists and the new and critical realists of the early years of this century makes the non-adept wonder how much discussion has progressed in the past two thousand years.[20] These important problems have been examined by serious students following various points of view. They concur in beginning with perceptions. This is true even of the Platonic dialogues which then make every effort to transcend appearance. No one of them is likely to be fully adequate for the richness, variety, and uncertainty of the situation. We can argue without end but are drawn up short by the need to act. Cicero expounds a practical philosophy: the "issue at hand" is something which ultimately requires action. When we have heard the best formulations of the best minds about relevant generalities, we are in the best position to choose what seems most probable for guidance in decision and action—and we must choose.

Participants in the philosophical dialogue employ important but fine distinctions and may become quite contentious in propounding their points of view. The observer of the dialogue may find much that is common among the philosophers when they and their dialogue are contrasted with other persons and ways of interacting. As an extreme case, the barbarian who executes all the philosophers and burns their books sees little difference among philosophers and philosophies. The common ground from Cicero's point of view includes what might be thought of as "political" aspects such as recognition of the importance of the enterprise and some accommodation of divergence.

Perhaps the most prescient of Cicero's insights is the recognition that a popular government requires the acceptance and integration of different formulations of what is the truth. Seemingly incompatible language may possibly encompass similar or congruent or supplementary views, so there should be a strong disposition to inclusion rather than exclusion. Reality is rich enough and political necessity strong enough to make such syncretism desirable, though it flies in the face of the scholarly desire for careful discriminations. At the end of the *Academica*, the participants all agree that the dialogue has been fruitful and should be continued. Their differences of approach have not foreclosed their continued cooperation.

Let me reiterate. The stuff of politics is complex. Knowledge is founded in sense perception, but sense perception itself is complex. Conclusions cannot be drawn with complete certainty. Instead of expecting certainty on an issue, we should seek to have arguments made on each side, providing both the general drift of the argument and detailed examination of the subtleties. What is sought is an approximate formulation of the issues and answers adequate for the person or persons responsible for action to make a decision that is either a true one or the most probably correct one. A judgment and a decision will be made. The person(s) making it should be as free from dogmatic precommitment as possible.

This formulation of course simplifies. The complications begin usually when some of those eligible to participate see a problematic situation and others do not (or, if problematic, important or not). Among those who see the situation as problematic, there will be differences in how the problem is identified and stated. Differences and agreements about means and ends (or procedural principles and terminal principles) occur, involving both the choice and the status of the principles. That is, people see different principles as relevant or more important; and they also disagree about the status of the principles as primarily means or ends. For example, is "democracy" an end in itself or is it the best means for achieving freedom?

"As free from dogmatic precommitment as possible" is a matter of degree. Everyone has to stand somewhere. Where and how, with what redeeming willingness to reconsider, make a great deal of difference. The character of the judge or decision-maker plays an important role: the argument cannot be laid out with a geometric or logistic form which proves itself. It is not like doing a set of sums. Reasonable and informed persons may make different judgments. A person of proper character will seek what can be found to be common among diverse positions and will recognize that each position may have some merit, some insight into the truth. Truth, that is, in the sense of something out there which we may trip over if we are not careful. We can never be completely sure that we have identified it and characterized it correctly even after we have tripped over it. When we act under these conditions, history and the lives of individuals (exemplars) are valuable resources, a kind of storehouse of possibilities for our consideration as we examine problems. History and biography are the teachers of character.

The general pattern of presenting arguments to make the best possible case on each side of an issue with an intelligent person of good intent (an impartial judge) to determine the action to be taken is a plausible outgrowth of an adversarial legal systems such as those of the Roman Republic and the English Common Law. In these legal systems, issues are combined so that there are two and only two sides before the court at a time. In philosophic dialogues, the form is less fixed. In the Ciceronian dialogues, more than two sides are often presented, but they are typically taken up two at a time. Judgment ultimately lies outside the dialogue, with the reader. In the Platonic dialogues, there are typically two engaged in discussion at one time; but the participants themselves find their way to the truth without a distinct judge (although the truth is often a recognition of ignorance). The Platonic dialectic, as it is developed in the *Republic*, is a method for reaching first principles which have previously been used only as hypotheses; but the method can only be employed by one who has had extensive training in abstraction from appearance.[21] Aristotle's dialogues for the general public were praised by Cicero for their graceful style but have not survived. Dialectic in Aristotle's research works, the material we have available today, is a preliminary procedure for examining what has been previously said as a preparation for undertaking a proper methodical or scientific investigation; this is treated in *Topics*. The situation is less clear in deliberative situations as discussed in the *Ethics* and the *Rhetoric*.[22]

Throughout the previous discussion, note has been taken of the dramatic character of the dialogue and the connections of the characters to their opinions in the dialogue. The skeptical position, depending upon judgment among probabilities, readily lends itself to being supplemented by examples of judgments and of persons with good judgment. The status of examples and exemplars in serious discourse has varied through the centuries. The importance of an image to the furtherance of understanding is evident in the Platonic dialogues: a character often exemplifies the virtue under discussion in the early dialogues. Socrates continually exemplifies the "lover of wisdom." Plato makes the point explicitly in the "Seventh Letter" that understanding depends upon the word, the line of reasoning, and the image. "For everything that exists there are three classes of objects through which knowledge about it must come....first, a name, second, a description, third, an image, and fourth, a knowledge of the object."[23] Even the very model of deductive reasoning, Euclidean geometry, typically employs drawings, albeit with disclaimers that they are not really necessary. Those disclaimers suggest that discursive reasoning, in its purest form, does not need examples. While modern physicists often warn us that we should not expect to visualize what their mathematical formulae conceptualize about subatomic particles or cosmology, it would appear from very limited observation that chemists reason together quite extensively through the use of "molecular diagrams."

In the past thirty or so years, the physicalist model has been called into question. Other forms of "demonstration" have gained acceptance, and "exemplars" once again provide a legitimate form of argument. As we shall see below, Felix Frankfurter composed many exemplary encomia; but he did so before the fashion changed in his favor. Cicero, on the other hand, was praised in the decades immediately following his death for both his statesmanship and his literary value. Augustus claimed to continue all the institutions and good examples of the Republic.[24] Cicero's use of exemplars, though, had no lasting impact even on the greatest work in this genre, Plutarch's *Lives*.[25]

The complementarity of Varro and Cicero as characters and the effort to draw Lucullus as a philosophy-loving (a lover of lovers of wisdom) statesman have already been noted. The character of Scipio and the important role that character plays in *On the Republic* are discussed below. Other dialogues similarly take advantage of the form to display the relevance of character to the matter under discussion. The modern reader no doubt finds it odd and even in poor taste for an author to feature and to praise his own character (through the words of his characters) in the way Cicero does. Even the ancient reader must have been struck by the contrast with Plato, who does not appear in the Socratic dialogues even when he might most reasonably have been present. Perhaps Cicero had higher hopes for political effectiveness than did Plato, though Plato too had political ambitions.[26] In any case, Cicero believed that the presentation of his "characters" was an important part of his "argument." In introducing a volume of Isaiah Berliñ's essays, Noel Annan says:

> These tributes, then, are not sketches thrown on one side, the refuse of the artist's studio. They are as much part of Isaiah Berlin's ouvre as are his essays on liberty and on the intellectuals of the Enlightenment and the nineteenth century. No one can understand ideas unless he sees them as the expressions of the passions, desires, longings and frustrations of human beings; and the word 'life' itself has no meaning unless it calls to mind men and women— past, present and to come.[27]

Berlin falls within the skeptical tradition; one of his essays is about his friend Felix Frankfurter during the latter's stay at Oxford. This subject will be examined at greater length in commenting on Frankfurter's many biographical sketches.

4. The Legal and Political Dialogues

The importance of Ciceronian skepticism is even more evident when its political implications are examined in Cicero's two dialogues which are explicitly about the state. *De Re Publica* or *On the Republic* and *De Legibus* or *On the Laws* were written, or in the case of the latter at least started, in the period from 54 to 51 B.C. while Cicero was excluded from political life by the renewed First Triumvirate and before he left to serve as governor of the province of Cilicia in Asia Minor. (He seems to have been a very competent governor.) Reading only these two dialogues as they come to us might give us a somewhat skewed view of Cicero's position, for in the passages extant both draw heavily on Stoic ideas. It is easy to dismiss the role of academic skepticism, especially in *On the Laws* where Cicero implores "the Academy, the new one formed by Arcesilas and Carneades,—to be silent, since it contributes nothing but confusion to all these problems; for if it should attack what we think we have constructed and arranged so beautifully, it would play too much havoc with it..." (L: 339-341).

This passage takes us back to the argument of Holton that Cicero had two doctrines, one for general consumption and one for philosophers. This sharp distinction is unnecessary and does not require Cicero, at heart, to favor monarchy. No one doubts James Madison's commitment to republican government, yet he confirms Cicero's position in *The Federalist* 49, quoted at length in the chapter on Madison. Madison recognized, as Cicero had before him, that political discourse calls for great care. Neither man thought this insight precluded republican government.

We cannot doubt Cicero's life-long allegiance to skepticism evident already in his earliest work, the *De Inventione* on the invention of legal arguments.

Yet, as discussed above, it remains usual to treat Cicero as though he simply espoused a Stoic position in his political works. The Stoics contribute useful insights and so are used as the author thought appropriate; but it is a mistake to treat the Stoic participants simply as Cicero's mouthpieces. This is recognized by Leo Strauss after reviewing the positions taken by the characters in *De re publica*: "It is then misleading to call Cicero an adherent of the Stoic natural law teaching."[28]

Both political dialogues were written with conscious parallels to the two great works of Plato, though the doctrines are quite unlike Plato. *On the Republic* was long lost and known only from quotation until a partial text was discovered on a palimpsest in the Vatican Library in 1820. According to Sabine, "the text of the *Republic* was lost after the twelfth century"; but he gives no sources. He apparently believed it was available to John of Salisbury when writing his *Policratus*.[29] From a third to a half of each dialogue is available today.

It is convenient briefly to discuss the later work first, though it is intended as an explicit follow-up to the prior work—to provide the laws for the republic. The first book of *On the Laws* is set at Cicero's country estate and without embellishment introduces the participants, Cicero himself, his brother Quintus, and his closest friend Atticus. The discussion moves from poetry to tradition to history. Atticus and Quintus first suggest that Cicero should give his leisure to the writing of history. In what is constructed as a natural development out of the conversation, the law of Rome is chosen as a topic instead. This context provides a subtle corrective to the reliance on the Stoic basing of law in nature. Law too is an inspired creation of generations of men.

The bulk of Book 1 is given over to the "whole range of universal Justice and Law in such a way that our own civil law... will be confined to a small and narrow corner" (L: 315). Justice inheres in "Law, which is right reason applied to command and prohibition" (L: 333). Because justice and law are based in nature and are apprehended by a reason which is common to all men and to the gods, both justice and law are common for all humankind. The laws of any particular society must be judged by reason which knows and can compare them with the natural law. The "whole universe is one commonwealth of which both gods and men are members" (L: 323). Particular societies have their own laws, but these must be judged by comparison with the common laws which are rooted in "nature." All of this is straightforward Stoic doctrine, although Roman judicial procedures recognized a "ius gentium" or law applicable to all peoples.

The reader may take these expressions of Stoic doctrine at face value, but that is to ignore Cicero's skepticism and the clews given in the text that suggest a more complex view. The reason that the academic skeptics are to remain silent is not that their criticisms would be in error but that they would call into question those views which it is to the advantage of society to have accepted as common ground. Leo Strauss, for example, attributes Cicero's apparent adherence to the Stoic position in *On the Laws* to what Cicero thought was "politically salutary."[30]

These are views that are created not by reason but by the common history and myths of a society. Compare the role of Varro in the discussion above. In the *On the Laws* itself, Cicero says: "But since our whole discussion has to do with the reasoning of the populace, it will sometimes be necessary to speak in the popular manner, and give the name of law to that which in written form decrees whatever it wishes, whether by command or prohibition" (L: 319).

At one point, in order to win the acceptance of Atticus to the idea that justice is rooted in nature, Cicero gives a whole range of possibilities for the governance of nature: the sheer force of the gods, their nature, their reasoning, their power (in a legitimated sense), their mind, or their will (L: 319-321). That is, we should not be prevented by preoccupation with details from accepting that justice is somehow rooted in "nature," in something more fundamental than the passing power of a particular state or moment. It is not simply the will of the current holders of power. Nor is it only for one people. All humankind shares something in justice. In modern terms, a delicate balance must be maintained between dogmatism and relativism. It is only with the work of F. A. Hayek that we have a clear view of moral rules which are the product of human action but are not consciously designed by human reason—which lie, that is to say, in an intermediate ground between "nature" and consciously designed convention or "contract."[31]

While Book 1 finds the sources of law in a reason which is more or less accessible to all men and a nature which can be grasped by all men, Book 2 begins by emphasizing the limitations of human reason: "Law is not a product of human thought, nor is it the enactment of peoples" but traces to the "primal and ultimate mind of God" (L: 381). The purpose of this emphasis in Book 2 is to ground the law in firmly-held opinion as well as to mark the limits of reasoning. "So in the very beginning we must persuade our citizens that the gods are the lords and rulers of all things, and that what is done, is done by their will and authority....for surely minds which are imbued with such ideas will not fail to form true and useful opinions" (L: 389). Although there is not an exact parallel, this passage is reminiscent of the "noble lie" in Plato's *Republic*, a founding myth which gives a non-rational or pre-rational grounding for the political community.

What follows in Book 2 is Cicero's summary of and commentary on the laws regarding public worship and related matters. Such laws are foreign to the American system (though not to the British) because of long-standing opposition, expressed in the First Amendment, to the establishment of religion. It is unnecessary to compare the religion of the Romans with the religions of Americans, but it is worth noting that commentators have remarked on the American "civic religion" which makes of the Constitution a kind of "ark of the covenant." The important point is that the state rests on a foundation in beliefs more firmly held than those opinions generated by the individual reasoning powers of the citizens.

Since the last surviving section of *On the Laws* concerns regulations governing the actions of magistrates, we may turn to *On the Republic* which provides general principles more relevant to the discussion here. The most dramatically satisfactory of Cicero's dialogues, even despite its fragmentary form, *On the Republic* is set in 129 B.C. and features leading political figures of the time. Like the *Academica*, this work has prefaces in Cicero's own voice. The dialogue takes place over three days, and each day's discussion is begun with a preface.

The beginning of Book 1 is lost, and the prefatory fragment starts with the naming of persons who have served the state with great commitment and distinction. Why have they served? According to Cicero, human beings have by nature ["a natura"] a need for virtue ["necessitatem virtutis"] and a desire to defend the common safety ["amorem ad communem salutem defendendam"] (R: 14-15). Virtue exists solely in its exercise; and "its noblest use is in the government of the State..." (R: 14-15). Cicero makes a further and more important assertion: the things said by philosophers concerning justice and right behavior have been given birth to and confirmed by those who have set forth the laws (R: 14-15). The civic virtues arise first in practice, displayed in the example of those who have been disciplined by customs or statutes. Cicero quotes Xenocrates who claimed to teach his students, "To do of their own accord what they are compelled to by the law." The philosophers can persuade only a few to follow their rules. Cicero concludes: "I believe that those who rule such cites by wise counsel and authority are to be deemed far superior, even in wisdom, to those who take no part at all in the business of government" (R: 17). The remainder of the preface is dominated by Cicero's rebuttals of arguments by those such as the Epicureans who avoid public service altogether and those such as philosophers who save their energies for an emergency.

Some people have argued, for example, that public service should be avoided because it is hard and dangerous and because other people are ungrateful. Avoiding a task because it is hard can only be met with scorn; no one is taken seriously who avoids tasks simply because they are hard. As for danger and death, they are at least worthy of consideration. Yet avoiding actions which may produce great deeds because of fear of death is curious. All human beings must die. Is it really more appealing to be consumed by nature and by old age? For Cicero, it is preferable to live properly in the public eye and for the public good than to live a long but useless life and succumb to the deteriorating diseases of old age.

Cicero catalogs statesmen, both Greek and Roman, who found their public service rewarded by death or exile. With his usual modesty he manages to include himself but adds that he has received more honor than hardship, more glory than annoyance. Even if he had not, he would still owe a controlling debt to the community which nurtured him. Loyalty and gratitude have their roots at the very foundation of human experience. What a contrast he paints to Henry David Thoreau: "For my own part, I should not like to think I ever rely on the protection of the state....however, the government does not concern me much, and I shall bestow the fewest possible thoughts on it. It is not many moments that I live under a government, even in this world." "Civil Disobedience" is a world away from Cicero. The peace at Warden Pond permitting Thoreau's quiet reflection was created for him by the state. His thoughts and language depended on those who had gone before. Thoreau denigrates the government and withdraws from it; Cicero argues that it is the greatest arena for human action and urges participation. Cicero argues that it is through the common life that human beings become better; Thoreau praises progress "toward a true respect for the individual" which seems reclusive and egocentric.

Cicero's arguments in favor of public service can be summarized as follows. Those who give their lives to public service are perceived by others as admirable. A life of public service is consonant with and is implicit in human social qualities and potential for self-development. Public service is the best and wisest life because it provides the greatest scope for action and development. It is preferable to letting the powers of government fall into the hands of bad men. The arguments against public service are either unworthy ("It is too dangerous") or wrong ("The benefits do not compensate for the pains"). The presentation is hortatory. Even those who suffered from the ingratitude of the public are magnified and made worthy of emulation. In the dialogue proper, the figure of Scipio Africanus is employed to further this argument.

An argument is made, also, against those who have asserted that a wise man will take part in public affairs only when an emergency forces him to do take up the leadership. Cicero ridicules this. How could a person be in the position to assist the state in times of emergency or understand what needs to be done if he has not already engaged in public service and mastered the art of politics? A person is not plausibly elected to high office who has not proved himself in the performance of lesser offices. Nor does a person learn what needs to be done in an emergency and how to do it except by mastering administration in ordinary times. How strange it is that learned men deny they can steer while the sea is calm, Cicero observes, but offer assurances about steering when the waves are at their greatest.

Despite the effective rhetoric, the argument is by no means unassailable. In times of stress, a leader may emerge from outside the cast of governmental officials. Ingrained routines may unfit the current leaders for dealing with extraordinary circumstances. The outsider may be precisely the one who grasps the extraordinary solution required. But Cicero is not primarily concerned with enlisting leaders in time of crisis; he desires to involve people in the normal course of public business and to sustain the regular vitality of public institutions. The regular participation of citizens in free institutions cannot guarantee that the state will not be engulfed by catastrophe, but it can help to minimize the slow erosion of the institutions.

The preface closes with a regular theme in Cicero's writings: the need for a union of words and deeds. Here the matter is put simply. Some have been skilled in the verbal arts but have accomplished nothing. Others have been successful in action but have been unable to explain or teach what they have accomplished. A person who has never acted in the public arena cannot simply from "book learning" hope to understand politics sufficiently to teach the younger generation. On the other hand, accounts, whether spoken or written, of the deeds of public servants require care if they are to be conveyed adequately and with benefit to the beginner or the general public. What is to be conveyed is neither esoteric nor new. It is the common property of public life. The challenge is to see more clearly and articulate better what it is known and done when people cooperate together through public institutions. Cicero is often criticized for not being a philosophical innovator. I should like to respond for him: "Of course not! I am simply trying to help people get more clear on what it is they already know so that they can cooperate or work out their differences better. What I am saying is what good lawyers and public servants regularly do; but they don't explain what they do very well. And when scholars try to describe it, they do so as outsiders who do not really understand what is going on."

To promote the view that these ideas are not new with Cicero but are the common property of Roman statesmen, he asserts that the dialogue which he is recounting was originally reported to him and to the unknown person to whom the dialogue is dedicated by one of the participants, Publius Rutilius Rufus. Thus the dialogue is alleged to be not the creation of Cicero but a discussion carried on by the most distinguished and wise statesmen of an earlier time. Rutilius, consul in 105 B.C., was a competent military commander, an exemplary provincial governor, and a distinguished jurist. He went into exile in Smyrna in 92 B.C., and it is there that he is alleged to have reported the dialogue to Cicero. The dialogue itself is set in 129 B.C. While we do not have exact dates, Rutilius must have been in his late twenties or early thirties at the time of the dialog and in his late sixties or early seventies at the time of recounting it.

The use of Rutilius as an intermediary permits Cicero to set up a pattern: the experienced and articulate statesmen of 129 B.C. instruct the young man who is just at the beginning of his public life. He in turn becomes a distinguished statesman and conveys the lessons to the young Cicero. Finally, Cicero, having in his turn become a leading statesman, passes the lesson on to the potential leaders of the next generation. We shall have occasion later to examine the question of whether Cicero means to imply that political knowledge does not grow or change but is merely transmitted from one generation to the next.

In the dialogue, the participants are Publius Cornelius Scipio Africanus the Younger, Gaius Laelius, Lucius Furus Philus, Manius Manilius, Quintus Allius Tubero, Rutilius, Spurius Mummius, Gaius Fannius, and Quintus Mucius Scaevola. Scipio, the general who finally conquered Carthage, was the preeminent political figure of his time—twice consul, censor, and the center of an intellectual and literary circle which included the Stoic philosopher Panaetius and the historian Polybius, both Greeks. Laelius, a close friend, had also been consul by the time of the dialogue. He was interested in philosophy and was remembered as a wise man. Philus and Manilius had also served as consul before the dialogue, and the others except Mummius served in that position later. Manilius, Tubero, and Scaevola were known as learned in the law. Several were known for their interest in Stoicism, and Scaevola was a teacher of Cicero. The dialogue thus presents a particularly brilliant cast of characters. It is also set at one of the major turning points in Roman history.

For over a decade and a half, Rome was in turmoil over class conflict and reforms proposed by the brothers Tiberius and Gaius Gracchus, distant relatives of Scipio. The violent deaths of Tiberius and then of Gaius put an end to the immediate controversy but appeared to subsequent generations to introduce an era of deepening problems which culminated in the fall of the republic. Scipio died in 129 B.C., shortly after the supposed date of this dialogue. Cicero believed that had Scipio, with his combination of political influence and political wisdom, lived the subsequent history of Rome might have been much different. Cicero may well have believed that his own time provided an opportunity to correct the things that had gone wrong, perhaps by himself playing Laelius to Pompey's Scipio. We shall not tarry, however, to sort out the historical details. Our focus is on Cicero's effort to bring together practical experience and philosophical and legal wisdom in solving political and constitutional problems.

The dialogue takes place on a public holiday. Study and philosophic discourse must be the complement to public business and should not interrupt it. Scipio has left the city for his country home. Several of his closest friends have indicated their intention to visit him. His nephew Tubero is the first to arrive and finds Scipio still in his bed chamber, most probably reading. His mind is busy. Though he greets Tubero warmly, there is the slightest hint that the young man, coming earlier than the others, has shortened the time his uncle might have spent alone with his work. Somewhat later he has occasion to quote his grandfather "that he was never doing more than when he was doing nothing, and never less alone that when alone" (R: 49). This day, however, has been constituted by the friends as an occasion when they should remind themselves of their commitment to and familiarity with learned doctrines. The day will be one of freedom from business and will be relaxing, but it is not to be simply recreation. It is instead an intentional taking of time, by the agreement of the group, to remind themselves of what they have already studied and to explore further serious matters. This is not a application of "work hard, play hard." The state has established holy days, and these should be used to raise up one's thoughts through discourse.

As in Plato's *Republic*, the discussion begins with a subject apparently remote from the major material of the dialogue. In this case, the question which Tubero raises concerns a celestial phenomenon. A "second sun" has been seen (apparently a parhelion, an optical event somewhat analogous to a rainbow). Such an event would by no means have been irrelevant to Roman politics, since it would occasion interpretation by the state augurs and might affect public business. The question is pursued at this point, though, as a matter of astronomy. Scipio responds in what appears to be an ambivalent fashion. He first regrets the absence of their friend the Stoic philosopher Panaetius, who was a careful student of celestial matters. But Scipio goes on to admit that he does not entirely approve of Panaetius's familiarity with such subjects, for the latter affirms things about these subjects as though they were immediately at hand when in fact they are quite hard to grasp. Scipio expresses a preference for Socrates who disavowed any interest in such natural science either because it was too difficult to understand or because it had no effect on men's lives.

There follows a brief aside of interest to the history of philosophy. Tubero points out that in the Platonic dialogues Socrates often expresses an interest in mathematics and natural science. Scipio explains this by telling of Plato's travels to Egypt and Italy, his interest in the doctrines of Pythagoras, and his subsequent attribution of Pythagorean ideas to Socrates as a way of building up the latter's standing. To Socrates, Scipio attributes charm and subtlety in talking while to Pythagoras he attributes obscurity and gravity.

The discussion is interrupted by the arrivals, first of Philus and Rutilius and then of Laelius and the others. Scipio dresses and goes out to meet the later arrivals. After evidences of mutual respect, the gentlemen seat themselves in the sun and resume the conversation about astronomy. Philus and Rutilius are already identified as taking an interest in astronomy. Laelius takes up where Scipio left off, inquiring whether enough is known about the republic to justify concern with what is happening in the sky. Philus responds with a proper Stoic doctrine that the whole universe is the common home and fatherland of gods and men and that, moreover, learning about such things is extremely enjoyable. Laelius accedes for the moment but makes a joke that the lawyer Manilius may well issue an edict compromising ["componendum"] between the two suns. Manilius first defends the legal profession as necessary for each man to identify what belongs to himself and then turns the discussion back to Philus. Instead of attempting to explain the phenomenon in question, however, Philus speaks of celestial globes, beautiful and elegant devices for keeping track of the apparent movement of the heavenly bodies. Such globes permitted the prediction of eclipses.

There is a brief interruption of the text; but when it resumes, Scipio recounts an occasion when knowledge of astronomy was useful in reassuring Roman troops about an eclipse. Simply by drawing on his knowledge and without ostentatious oratory, he was able to explain matters in a dignified but simple way to relieve the mens' fears. This illustrates one of the most important functions of leadership in a popularly-based regime (and even in the army of a popularly-based regime): the need to explain matters to the lay person in a simple but correct way. Too much of what passes for political rhetoric is simply the stringing together of elevated sentiments and generalities which clarify nothing. Scipio goes on to recount that a similar thing happened during the Peloponnesian War when Pericles—preeminent in his authority, eloquence, and practical wisdom—explained a solar eclipse to the Athenians on the basis of what he had learned from the philosopher Anaxagoras. As a curious aside on solar eclipses, Scipio remarks, Romulus (the legendary founder of Rome) disappeared or was carried up to heaven during such an eclipse. Tubero points out that in all of this Scipio seems to be contradicting what he had said earlier about the importance of studying astronomy.

The text is interrupted at this point. When it resumes, the subject is still astronomy with Scipio talking. The tone of his remarks has changed substantially. The long fragment of speech which follows would appear to cast considerable doubt on Cicero's express political philosophy and his view of the relation of a life of contemplation to one of action. We shall only have an adequate view of the passage, however, after we have examined the dream which concludes the dialogue. This is quite possibly in imitation of Plato. In the latter's *Republic* too, a topic taken up early in the work—the role of poetry in the state—can only be completed at the end of the dialogue.

Scipio asks how anyone can be impressed with human affairs, their permanence, or glory who has reflected upon astronomy, thought about its eternity, and recognized how small the whole earth is. The Romans themselves occupy only a small portion of the earth and are unknown to many nations. A person motivated by a love of fame must nonetheless recognize that personal fame or glory is a small thing after all. Similarly, a person may strive for vast possessions and be proud of those holdings, but a person with proper perspective recognizes the limitations on enjoyment and utility and the uncertainty of possessions. Scipio notes that the worst of men sometimes have immense possessions. Possessions are of value only to those who know how to use them properly. A person may seek military command and the highest offices of state for glory or profit; but these should be seen as necessary rather than desirable and be undertaken as a burden of responsibility. A person may envy the power and prestige of a great tyrant such as Dionysus of Syracuse, but the tyrant's way of associating with others provides no real satisfaction. It is far better to be alone with one's thoughts, if they are good, or in the company of learned men through their writings. The saying of Scipio the Elder to this effect has already been quoted. Better to be Archimedes of Syracuse, the maker of the sky globe they had discussed, than Dionysus. "Who in truth would consider anyone richer than the man who lacks nothing that his nature requires, or more powerful than one who gains all he strives for, or happier than one who is set free from all perturbation, or more secure in his wealth than one who possesses only what, as the saying goes, he can carry away with him from out of a shipwreck? What power, moreover, what officer, what kingdom, can be preferable to the state of one who despises all human possessions, considers them inferior to wisdom, and never meditates on any subject that is not eternal and divine; who believes that, though others may be called men, only those are men who are perfected in the arts appropriate to humanity?" (51) These arts are then illustrated by a story concerning geometry.

Scipio appears to have made an absolute about-face. He starts with the assertion that they ought not concern themselves with the problems of astronomy but rather with the questions of human life. He then recognizes that a knowledge of astronomy may be useful in certain practical situations. He then suggests that glory and wealth should be seen in proper context. He then asserts that possessions should be despised and that one should never direct his mind to anything but that which is unchanging and divine. What are we to make of this?

Surely we are not meant to take this position as the final and "really true" one. Neither Scipio nor Cicero was a withdrawn or ascetic philosopher. Both of these men's lives were committed to public affairs and were lived amidst considerable comfort. Nor does the dialogue end here; it has only just begun. As I have already said, we shall have to return to the question of astronomy at the end of the dialogue. Some general indications are already evident, however. If we are concerned with human affairs, we must be concerned that natural science and esoteric subjects do not cause us to lose our way in their details. On the other hand, a knowledge of natural science can be useful. The natural science in question here is not biology nor psychology but astronomy. Astronomy has a peculiar interest for us in that it makes us feel small. Even though we strive to be important in human affairs, we can still recognize limits to our greatness. The details are not marked out at this point in the dialogue. We simply see glory and power reduced by comparison with more magnificent things and regulated by a sense of context and purpose. Further it is hard to go further at this point, for there are hiatuses at the beginning and shortly after the end of Scipio's speech.

Laelius responds to Scipio. Part of that response is missing. The part we have seems to return to the point Laelius made earlier, the earliest position taken by Scipio. Laelius refers to a man "most intelligent and prudent" who was so "not because he sought what he could never find" but because he responded to those who came to him for advice and helped to resolve human concerns and affairs (53). The words however have been shifted. Scipio spoke of a man who was "sapiens," while Laelius speaks of a man who is "catus" and "cordatus" (48-51). The words may have been chosen to shift the discussion from heaven back to earth. All the words, "sapiens," "cordatus," and "catus" can be translated "wise," but sapiens is cognate with "sophos" and thus closer to Greek usage. "Catus," moreover can have a bad meaning—sly, crafty—as well as a good one. All three words seem to have the possible meaning "judicious" implying judgment or choice between alternatives; "catus" originally relates to hearing and "sapiens" to tasting. The distinction perhaps prefigures that in the *Academica* between the truly wise and those such as Cicero himself who are wise only in a lesser sense.

Laelius suggests that the study of philosophy is all right in moderation and says the things Scipio has been discussing are useful to sharpen and stir up the minds of the young; but there are other subjects of a more liberal and broad nature which are more useful for life and the republic. When asked by Tubero what these subjects are, Laelius responds that those things are more worthy of investigation which are immediately before our eyes. He then asks why one should be worried about two suns when there are two Senates and almost two peoples in the Roman state (R: 55). Reflections on celestial phenomena are decidedly out of place in the face of public disorder. Either the double sun does not exist, or we are unable to learn anything about it, or what we learn can never make us better or happier. But unity within the state is possible, understandable, and will make our lives better and happier.

We may usefully contrast the positions of Laelius and Scipio somewhat more concisely. For Laelius, celestial phenomena have no effect on human affairs, and the knowledge of them contributes nothing to make one better or happier. For Scipio, celestial phenomena may have an effect on human affairs, as for example in frightening the ignorant. We can thus have some useful, even if limited, knowledge. Moreover, the contemplation of these things is uplifting and may have the effect of making a person better and happier. Both men suggest a priority of the things available to immediate sight and touch, which are the things associated with human affairs. Both mention things immediately before the eyes; Scipio mentions things accessible to touch. The distinctions are commonsensical rather than philosophically sophisticated. It is worth remembering, however, that the sense of sight and touch are of especial relevance in the Academic discussion of the possibilities of knowledge. The stars may be visible, but they are far away. We must employ conjectures and sophisticated trains of reasoning in thinking about them. Laelius apparently believes there is something immediately available, concrete, more certain, and requiring less troublesome chains of reasoning. Modern epistemology would tear these distinctions apart, but so for that matter would the participants of the *Academica*. What then is the ground for such distinctions? They lie in common sense, not in the esoteric distinctions of philosophers but in the exoteric, usual distinctions of our common life together.

What is this common knowledge, this knowledge more liberal and of broader application, which distinguishes itself from astronomy and is more important to understand? Scaevola asks the question of Laelius, who responds, "those arts which encompass our usefulness to the corporate community. I consider that usefulness to be the most distinguished responsibility of wisdom [sapientiae] and either the greatest proof of virtue or the most important activity of virtue in our relations with others" (56; my translation). What we need to explore is not a body of facts but a group of acquired skills which are properly employed in participating in community activity, for it is in that participation that the noblest wisdom lies. This suggests that "catus and cordatus" rather that "sapiens" may be the highest "wisdom." It is there, in community activity, that a person most clearly shows possession of human excellence. It is there too that a person develops in the greatest degree the qualities of behaving well toward others which are the concern of "officium" [usually translated "duty"].

Laelius, hoping to insure that their civic holiday will be employed to the best service of the republic, next seeks to pin down the investigation by asking that Scipio tell them which form of government he considers the best. From that beginning, they can proceed to the other important subjects. A few lines are lost. Laelius continues by explaining why he thinks this will be a particularly fruitful way to proceed. The discussion will thus be led by someone himself accomplished in public affairs, but someone who also has had experience in discussion of the subject with Panaetius (philosophy) and Polybius (history). Both men were sophisticated Greeks, and discussion with them forced Scipio to collect his thoughts on the special preferability of the Roman republic.

Scipio accepts the invitation, acknowledging that no other subject concerns him more in thought or attention. Every craftsman tends to the development of skill in his own craft, and Scipio has had the superintendence and the administration of the republic passed on to him as a family responsibility. He is familiar with the Greek experts on the subject but is not satisfied with them. He does not speak simply from his own views, however, but as a Roman raised with a "not illiberal" education and enthusiastic for study, yet trained more by usage and family precepts than by books. Philus confirms that Scipio is qualified by ability and practice in the highest business of the republic and is, moreover, possessed of the ability to explain what he knows. He is, that is, a master of both words and deeds. Thus introduced, Scipio begins the discussion which preoccupies the remainder of the first two books of the dialogue.

Scipio starts by naming and defining that which is to be discussed. He says that the "res publica" (both "public business" and "republic" in Latin) is what they shall be investigating. He does not intend, however, to trace the state back to its elements in the union of man and woman and the growth of families and tribes, as a learned man would. This apparently is meant as a reference to Aristotle's *Politics*, Book I, in which Aristotle examines almost exactly these subjects, adding household management, but never providing—in what we have available— the discussion of tribes. Cicero was quite familiar with Aristotle's works (though not as familiar as he thought, at least as evidenced by his attempt to produce a commentary on the *Topics* in his own work of the same name). He typically treated Aristotle in a favorable way. Nor, Scipio says, will he attempt to sort out all of the different definitions exactly. He is talking to men of practical wisdom ["prudentes"], themselves distinguished servants of the republic; and he will not try to treat the subject in an overly exact fashion or as a teacher taking to pupils. Here again, Cicero may be reflecting in his own way on Aristotle's famous passage in *Nicomachean Ethics*, Book 1, Chapter 3 (1094b12): "Our discussion will be adequate if it has as much clearness as the subject matter admits of...).” The audience in the dialogue is just the sort Aristotle thinks appropriate for his *Ethics* when he remarks (following 1094b29) on those who will be good judges of such matters.

Scipio thus assumes a common understanding shared by practical people who live in a republic—a common understanding about their own status and activity. This is not to be, in our terms, a scientific treatment by a learned, outside observer who describes dispassionately the organization of a community. It is instead a pulling together of observations and thought by one practitioner for other practitioners of what it is they do together. Their goal is improving the common effort.

We must not be misled by the introductory discussion of astronomy. *On the Republic* does not approach political science from the point of view of an astronomer or physical scientist. The possible confusion which Cicero faced is not that facing us. We shall return later to the relation of astronomical interests and information to political knowledge in Cicero. At this point, it is more important to pay attention to our own possible confusion. While fewer professional teachers of philosophy than formerly are disposed to find in the physical sciences a paradigm for all knowledge, much respect for those studies which can be cast in mathematical form remains among the well-educated. The situation is similar in respect to “scientific laws” of human behavior. While they have fallen out of favor in much contemporary philosophical discussion, some inclination to hope for the certainty which such laws could provide lingers on.

The problems of scientific objectivity, value-free studies, and observer/participant had not yet been identified in Cicero’s time. If he thought much about the differences which we make between the “hard sciences” and other types of knowledge (and I find little evidence that he did), Cicero probably relied on the Epicurean-Stoic division of subject matters into logic, physics, and ethics. The laws Cicero is concerned with are not descriptive but constitutive. They are what they are not as descriptive of how we behave but because we or the gods made them as they are. A human being follows such a law not because bound by nature to do so independently of choice. A person obeys the law from having agreed to follow it, although perhaps under the threat of punishment. We can predict human behavior with some accuracy because we expect that people will keep their promises. The system of laws may permit some accommodation among different points of view and preferences, but it is in no sense “value-free.” As Cicero says in *On the Republic*, speaking in the voice of Scipio, society presupposes some agreement on the meaning and terms of justice. The closest we get in Cicero to scientific objectivity is disinterestedness. While the exploration of the political system is profoundly difficult and important, it is nonetheless the exploration of the system which arises for the most part from the daily, conscious choices and action of average men and women.

The "res publica" is a "res populi." The republic or public thing is the thing or business of the people. A people, however, is not every collection of persons assembled in whatever manner but a collection of people associated or united by an agreement about right ["iuris consensu"] and a mutual participation in what is useful ["utilitatis communione"]. This union arises not out of individual weakness, as in the view of Thomas Hobbes, but by a kind of natural disposition to associate with others ["quasi congregatio"] (65).

The discussion to this point prefigures all that follows. Scipio was originally asked to discuss the best "status" of a "civitas" or state. He has begun, however, with the definition of a "res publica." One might hope that Cicero would have kept the two terms strictly separated throughout the dialogue. He perhaps followed conversational usage in not doing so. Distinguishing the two terms, though, helps us to keep track of the argument. Scipio argues that the republic is the best form of government, and the characteristics of the best form of government are implied in the definition of the republic. The best form of government is one in which the government is the business of the people. It presupposes a society in which there is a consensus about the rules of justice, of what constitutes right and wrong, fairness and unfairness. It is a society too in which there will be general participation in what is useful or beneficial. The people participate in the government; they agree in a general way about what is fair; and they agree in a general way about how their benefits relate to the well-being of others. The individual's view of the good life recognizes the connections of her or his own well-being to that of others. Such a political society reflects not the weakness or deficiency of human nature but natural social inclinations.

Some lines are missing. The text resumes with Scipio still discussing how people come together to form a community. The opening fragment associates virtue with the republic. The principal line of argument, however, concerns the connection between the institutions of government and the character of the community. "Every people which is a union of the multitude, every state which is a constitution of people, and every republic which is a business of the people, must be ruled by a source of practical wisdom about affairs ["consilio"] if it is to last" (64-66; my translation). That is, the continued existence of a state is dependent on intelligence. The word employed, "consilium," means deliberation, consultation, a considering together. It relates to wisdom about practical affairs and is an interpersonal kind of knowledge. It may be given or received or taken together, but it is not the sort of thing Robinson Crusoe would employ alone on his desert island except perhaps in talking to himself. This "consilium," we are told by Scipio, must be referred back to the same cause as that which produced the state. The ongoing, operative device for introducing intelligence into the running of the community is determined by the kind of consensus which brought the community together and continues to hold it together.

The demands for intelligence which a community faces arise in part from the relation of the community to that which is outside itself, whether that be foreign communities or the non-human world. In part, the problems arise from the interaction of the people within the community. Social intelligence must deal with a complicated mixture of intransigent nature and more or less variable social arrangements. (While all intelligence arises "socially" and the phrase "social intelligence" is fundamentally redundant, it is nonetheless useful to distinguish Crusoe-type problems from others which directly imply the presence of other persons participating in one degree or another in the problem.) What human beings think of as appropriate or fair varies from community to community. What would be an intelligent judgment in one community may not be so in another. A leisurely speech outlining the pros and cons of a particular policy might be a consummate expression of parliamentary intelligence yet would neither look like nor be intelligent in a community oriented toward decisive and definitive decisions by one leader.

The relations of intelligence to the state thus lead Scipio into a discussion of the standard classical distinction of rule by the one, the few, and the many. Any of these forms of government, he says, may prove tolerable; but each has its shortcomings. In monarchies, the people have minimal experience in the rules of fairness and in the giving of practical advice. This implies that most are precluded from developing their truly human qualities: they are or are like slaves. In aristocracies also the many do not have a full portion of liberty since here too they are excluded from the common councils and from power. In a simple democracy, even one run justly and moderately, the very equality is unjust since it takes no note of distinctions in worth (R: 67-69). Aristotle had already made the point that it is unjust to treat equals unequally, but it is also unjust to treat unequals equally.

The very shortcomings of the simple forms give us a better view of the proper kind of government. People must be treated justly in the proper state. They must, in addition, participate in public deliberation if they are to develop their capacity for reflection and, we would add, self-respect. But a proper government also recognizes inequalities among persons. The word "worth" above is a translation of "dignitas." The inequalities in question here are not of race, skin color, nationality, nor even necessarily wealth. They are inequalities of reputation and position justified by character and performance. To fail to recognize such inequalities is to dismiss the idea of individual worth. If the community makes no distinction between those who have cultivated virtue and talent and those who have not, it cannot be the best sort of state.

Cicero's choice of "consilium" as a way of introducing the role of intelligence into political affairs predisposes the choice of the best form of government, though without dictating it entirely. If the word chosen had been "sapientia," the reader might have expected the choice of the best state to be that ruled by the philosopher-king, the person possessed of certain truth. If, on the other hand, the preferences of the people and not intelligence had been sought, democracy would seem preferable. "Consilium" leads in the direction of a group of persons consulting together in the search for practical wisdom. Moreover, Cicero connects "consilium" with "diaturnus"—of long duration (64-65). The right kind of intelligence is connected with stability, and thus Scipio shortly criticizes the simple forms of government because "before every one of them lies a slippery and precipitous path leading to a certain depraved form which is a close neighbor to it" (69).

This introduces the cycle of change, so interesting to the Greek and Roman writers. The discussion is brief from our point of view, since the text is fragmentary. Enough is available, however, to reveal that the cycle of change is, in the first instance, from the good form to its bad variant (monarchy to tyranny, aristocracy to oligarchy, and democracy to mob rule) and not, as in Plato, a downward slope from the rule of the philosopher-king through the intermediate forms to an ultimate tyranny. After a break in the text, Scipio speaks of the "periodical revolutions and circular courses followed by the constant changes in sequences in governmental forms" (71). It seems likely that the spirit or purpose may go out of a governmental form first, leaving the bad variant; but after that the form itself may well be overthrown. The text is too fragmentary to be confident of what produces the change, but it appears to be a loss of restraint. Whether among the many, the few, or in the individual ruler, some sort of restraint must hold in check the license ["licentia"] to which men are prone

Though Cicero makes no reference to Thucydides, he must have been familiar with the latter's account of the loss of restraint and sense of decency as the Peloponnesian War progressed. The modern reader is also reminded of eighteenth century concern about the importance of such restraint and the role of "fictions." In Gibbon's account of the decline of the Roman Empire, the action of Septimius Severus in exposing the fiction of Senatorial election led to the instability of the following century. Burke attacked the French Revolution for dissolving all "the pleasing illusions which made power gentle and obedience liberal, which harmonized the different shades of life, and...incorporated into politics the sentiments which beautify and soften private society" and for "rudely" tearing off all "the decent drapery of life."[32]

A truly wise person, says Scipio, would forestall the dangers; but it is quite unusual, indeed almost divine, to have those holding the reins of government able to keep track of tendencies and make the necessary adjustment in a simple form to keep it beneficial and stable. A fourth form of government is therefore introduced as the most to be approved, and this is a well regulated mixture of the three simple elements. Aristotle, especially in Books 3 and 4 of the *Politics*, had discussed three good forms—monarchy, aristocracy, and polity—and three bad forms—tyranny, oligarchy, and democracy—in much more detail than we have in Cicero. Aristotle even mentions a "mixed form" of sorts, the "polity"; but it is achieved by mixing elements of only two forms, democracy and oligarchy.

Laelius is unwilling to let Scipio proceed with the discussion of this fourth form, however. He presses him to reveal which of the simple forms is preferable. Most of the remainder of the dialogue in Book 1 is given over to this subject. In what follows, there are a number of lacunae. It is apparent that Scipio, in good skeptical fashion, presents arguments which have been put forward discussing the advantages and shortcomings of each of the simple forms. There is also a detailed discussion of the changes in constitutions. Enough of the text is missing, however, to make us cautious about the exact course of the argument and the conclusions to be drawn from it.

Scipio first sketches the argument for democracy, emphasizing the connection of democracy with liberty.[33] His understanding of liberty seems at this point to be participation in government: freedom consists in equal access to office, to participation in public deliberation, and to service on the law courts. Freedom is in legal contrast to slavery and involves the possession of legally defined rights. Thus democracy simply equals democracy. Scipio asserts that democracy can be stable where there is general agreement on interests and a willingness on the part of the people to test public measures by reference to their own safety and liberty. The last argument which we have on behalf of democracy is that a state can only truly be a partnership in justice if all the citizens have equal rights before the law. "For if we cannot agree to equalize men's wealth, and equality of innate ability is impossible, the legal rights of at least those who are citizens of the same commonwealth ought to be equal" (75-77).

Aristotle had made a different argument for democracy: that when the many meet together, they may become a better judge collectively than a few good men. Since the many do this in judging music and poetry, it may also be true of them in some democracies. This is an argument from prudence, a collective practical intelligence similar to Cicero's "consilium."[34] Freedom in Aristotle is given two definitions, ruling and being ruled in turn (participation) and doing as one wishes. The love of freedom is a characteristic of democracy but is neither univocally equated with it nor treated as an argument for it.[35]

In Cicero, the argument from intelligence is against democracy and for aristocracy. The dialogue shifts to consideration of that form. "It has been the difficulty of formulating policies ["consilii"] that has transferred the power from a king to a larger number; and the perversity and rashness ["error et temeritas"] of popular assemblies that have transferred it from the many to the few" (81). Infirmity in "consilium" in one person and temerity in "consilium" in the many require a group which will be dominated by moderation. "Infirmity," "temerity," and "moderation" are all transliterations. Only with "consilium" can the "equality of legal rights of which free peoples are so fond" be maintained (R: 81). It is these legal rights which insure the people's tranquility and freedom from cares. The analogy of the ship's pilot is employed to suggest that leaders ought not to be chosen by democratic procedures. If the people choose the best persons to lead them, all would be well. But the many often misjudge who possesses virtue, selecting on the basis of wealth and family name rather than good counsel and knowledge of how to live and rule over others. The reader may be reminded of the exchange between Adams and Jefferson, cited in the "Preface." The people, moreover, often give honors and create distinctions which are contrary to justice or to accurate perception of who is most deserving. The people do not long protect equality before the law for they are insensitive to or reject outright true differences among persons.

At this point, Laelius interrupts Scipio to ask once again which of the three forms is best; and Scipio, while not rejecting the question, once again asserts that the mixed form is best. If pressed to chose, he says, a monarchy is appealing in that the title of king is reminiscent of fatherhood and the protection of the citizens is like that of children. But then, an aristocracy can lay claim to be more reasonable and can better combine effectiveness with care. And finally, a popular government has freedom to offer; and nothing is sweeter than liberty, even to a wild beast. Thus, monarchy is appealing for its "caritas," or principle of affection, aristocracy for its "consilium," or practical wisdom, and democracy for its "libertas," liberty (R: 83).

Laelius impatiently remarks that they cannot really proceed if Scipio is unwilling to settle this matter. We witness a wise man ("sapiens") demanding a simple answer, even after being told there is no simple answer.

Scipio, in a lovely piece of Ciceronian self-promotion, remarks that they will have to imitate Aratus in beginning the discussion with Jupiter. (Cicero had translated Aratus' long poem on natural philosophy from the Greek.) Laelius, bemused, asks what relevance Aratus has to their current discussion. Scipio proceeds to develop an argument in favor of monarchy through a series of analogies: the rule of Jupiter over the other gods, the apparent government of the universe by its own coherent principles, the rule of reason over the body, the rule of the master over the household, and the rule of the navigator over the ship and the doctor over his patient. This richness of analogy is itself a rebuke to the demand for simplicity, since it marshals "proofs" from many traditions of argument. Scipio also draws on two aspects of Roman history and institutions: the fact that the Roman state began as a monarchy and the continued use of a constitutional dictator in time of emergency. The analogical and historical arguments are put forward largely in question and answer form, with Laelius simply the foil for Scipio. The argument concludes, after a short hiatus, with another poetic reference, this time to a long poem by Ennius about the early history of Rome. Though the poem refers to the fatherly and godlike qualities of kings, it recalls the instability of monarchy, since the Roman monarchy was overthrown by the injustice of one man, the seventh king Tarquinius Superbus.

Scipio provides grounds for doubting that monarchy is the best of the simple forms even while seeming to argue for it. These grounds are as follows. The analogy of the rule of Jupiter over the other gods is attenuated by the suggestion that the whole story is simply a useful, human fabrication. The analogy of the governance of the universe by a single mind is attributed to learned investigators of the physical universe whose teachings are elsewhere called into question. The first argument from Roman history is intertwined with a discussion of whether or not the Romans were "barbarians" at the time they had a king; and though the conclusion is that they were not inhuman and beastly at the time, the juxtaposition raises doubts rather than laying them to rest. The argument from the role of reason over the passions culminates in the assertion that "imperium" or command must be unitary. When Laelius questions whether that inevitably means one man, Scipio ignores him and moves to another line of argument. The next analogy is that of the master over the household. This is put in a slightly peculiar form by asking whether one man or many are left in charge when the master is away. The "proof" concerns an agent rather than a principal, and Laelius is only "almost" prepared to concur. The analogies of the pilot and the physician are stock arguments. The passage closes with a rather ambiguous passage about the excesses to which people went after the exile of Tarquin. While the quote from Ennius says the death of a just king is mourned almost as much as the passing of a father or a god-like figure, it is followed by the reminder that the injustice of only one man caused the collapse of the monarchy.

Laelius asks Scipio "quod optimum iudices" (which do you judge the best?), and again, "quod maxime probas" (which do you approve most greatly?) of the simple forms. Scipio responds that it is a legitimate question to ask "quod maxime probo" (which I think the greatest?). When Scipio finally sums up, however, he uses different language: "longe praestat regium" (monarchy stands first by a long way). The word "optimus" is reserved, in the same sentence, for the mixed form.

The primacy of monarchy is thus quite unlike the rule of the philosopher-king portrayed in Plato's *Republic*. Monarchy is not the most perfect introduction of reason into the state. It is rather the earliest form of government and one which in the simplest way fulfills a common human need for coherence in leadership. Human beings are drawn to the idea of unity and command, whether they employ the idea to explain the gods, the universe, their own mental operations, or the governance of the state. They readily develop a kind of affection for the one ruling principle which is the center of their attention.

In choosing "caritas" as the attraction of a monarchy, Cicero calls attention to a deep-seated human characteristic. The strong inclination of Britons and Americans to look for a leader in times of adversity rather than depending on their representative, deliberative assemblies is a case in point, as is the lingering and apparently wide-spread reluctance to believe evil of Joseph Stalin within the former Soviet Union.

Despite these warning signs, Laelius seems satisfied, and Scipio has once again made his central point about the best form. The dialogue can turn to the question of changes in basic constitutional structure. Before we proceed with this, however, some general observations on the discussion of the simple forms is in order.

It is apparent, first, that most of the discussion of the simple forms is elicited from a reluctant Scipio by Laelius. From Scipio's point of view, he needs only to show the principal deficiencies of the simple forms as a preface to showing the strengths of the mixed form which is his main objective. Monarchies are deficient in justice and prudential counsels; aristocracies in popular liberties; and democracies in adequate distinctions of individual worth. All of the simple forms are unstable. This is all Scipio really needs to introduce the mixed form which corrects the short-comings. The repeated requests from Laelius that Scipio indicate the best of simple forms serves to elicit detail about the simple forms. Though such detail is not intrinsically necessary to Scipio's argument, it is necessary to satisfy the cultivated reader. One familiar with early writings on political philosophy would not be prepared to see the simple forms dismissed so abruptly. It is therefore necessary, if Cicero is to carry along those familiar with Greek philosophy, that he show in some detail the disadvantages of the simple forms. Although Laelius eventually appears satisfied that Scipio has answered his question, Scipio never actually gives an unambiguous answer. Even monarchy, which appears to be preferred, is so only as a beginning and does not survive the argument as a satisfactory, permanent form of government.

Cicero's dialogue is directed to men of practical affairs; but his readers were more or less familiar with the classics of Greek political thought. Some in fact found philosophy an excuse to avoid public service: they had cultivated their intelligence yet chose to withdraw it from public uses. Each of the simple forms excuses such a withdrawal, for each turns the business of government over to the hands of one part of the community. Only the mixed form requires the participation of every member of the political community, though each need not participate in the same way.

Another characteristic of the discussion is the quality of the interaction between Scipio and Laelius: Laelius appears to be treated by Cicero rather badly. First, Laelius seems rather querulous in insisting that Scipio answer his question despite the fact that Scipio repeatedly puts him off. Second, when Scipio begins to develop the analogies which suggest that monarchy is the best of the simple forms, he leads Laelius through a sequence of questions which makes the older man look like a schoolboy. What are we to make of this? It seems in strange contrast both with Cicero's assessments elsewhere of Laelius and with his usual method of lending distinction to his argument by placing it in the mouths of notable characters and of altering somewhat the standard view of these men by displaying their interest in philosophy. This apparent mistreatment of Laelius is surely a false lead. It is hard to avoid the appearance, but perhaps the situation would be clearer is we had the entire text.

Most of the extant discussion is given over to democracy, and little of it concerns aristocracy. This is rather curious at first glance, since the discussion of the forms of government began with "consilium" and consilium is precisely what is said to attract us to aristocratic government. There is a hiatus in the text, but it appears comparatively brief (77). We are given a detailed treatment of the dependence of liberty on democracy and a variety of analogies to show how basic in human nature is the dependence on one recognized leader. Both the failure of democracy to make wise choices of leaders and the closeness of monarchy to tyranny are emphasized. By comparison, neither the strengths nor the weaknesses of aristocracy are well developed. It is clear that aristocracy occupies a middle ground between the one and the many. In this it seems to provide an analogue for the mixed form, though the latter combines elements of all three simple forms. Aristocracy is the rule of the few and the rule of the best. It provides wise counsel and is moderate, but it requires a way of designating the few who are wise. Are the few to choose themselves by cooptation? This may be unfair and surely deprives the many of the chance for self-development which comes from participating in the political process. The difficulty of connecting wise counsel with a political form remains unresolved at the level of the simple forms. Cicero apparently chose to avoid the difficulties in clearly distinguishing the rule of the few who are wise in an aristocracy from the rule of those chosen to serve in a constitutional or mixed form.

When apparently at last satisfied, Laelius indicates that he is prepared to turn to the cycle of changes of constitutions. If this subject were taken up next, the Ciceronian *Republic* would follow the format of that of Plato. Scipio responds that they will be in a position to take up the problems of change better after they have examined the best form of the republic. At this point, the treatment must be rather simple. When a king becomes unjust, the form has become a tyranny. A tyranny may be overthrown by either the aristocrats or the people. The people may, however, overthrow a just king; or, as may happen more frequently, they overthrow an aristocracy. There is then a long citation from Book 8 of Plato's *Republic*, describing the decline of popular rule into mob rule. The passage is parallel to the earlier argument in favor of democracy: where that passage shows the connection of liberty to popular elements in the government, this shows what happens where liberty becomes license and the people can stand no authority whatsoever over them.

The cycle of change is summarized as: everything going to excess engenders its opposite (101-103). The principle produces not one simple cycle, however, but permits a number of variations. Monarchy, gone to excess, produces tyranny. An excess of liberty in the people is likely to result in servitude, also through a tyranny. The patterns which emerge here are the possibilities to be kept in mind by statesmen, as we shall see later, and not inevitable laws of change. Central to these problems is the instability of the simple forms. Thus even a just monarchy cannot be preferred to a just and temperate balance of the three forms. The best government combines that which is outstanding and royal, to focus the affections of the community, with authority which is associated with the principal people of the state, and with that which takes into account the judgments and choices of the multitude. This constitution can combine justice with stability and is the central concern of *On the Republic*.

Book 1 closes with a transition to the subject of the mixed form of government as it is embodied in the Roman constitution. The philosophical cycle of change is converted to the historical development of Rome. Scipio reiterates that the subject already familiar to everyone must be discussed as among equals rather than being treated as a teacher would his pupils. Yet, and it bears repeating, even statesmen must remind themselves of the general character of their constitution, its division of things, and the discipline which it confers. They must also periodically remind themselves of how these topics relate to what can be said about the best form of government. It is thus an appropriate task, even for those learned in government, to remind themselves of first principles—both the organizing, operational principles of their own government and the relation of these to the principles of good government. The group assembled about Scipio will look to an earlier form of their government for their model, however. They will be discussing the state which their fathers received from their own ancestors. (Though there is no detailed explanation at this point of the weaknesses of the government of their own time, their clear reference is to the decline in the state they associate with Tiberius Gracchus.) Laelius praises the projected discussion, noting that Scipio is uniquely qualified for the task through his ancestral connection with government, his contemporary standing in the community, and his proven disposition to provide for the future.

Book 2 continues the discussion without interruption. Instead of recounting his own views, however, Scipio attributes what he is going to say to Cato, known to later generations as the "Censor" to contrast him with the Cato who was Cicero's contemporary. Scipio assures his auditors that he had the greatest affection and admiration for the old man who was the contemporary of his adoptive grandfather, the first Scipio Africanus. Scipio says, further, that he spent a lot of time with the old man both by his own choice and the advice of both his father by blood and his adoptive father. Scipio says he could never "get enough of his conversation, so remarkable was his experience of public affairs, with which he had dealt in both peace and war with the greatest success and for a very long period, his observance of due measure in speaking, his union of charm with dignity, his zeal for either learning or teaching, and the complete harmony between his life and his words" (111). Another of Cicero's dialogues *De Senectute* portrays a much younger Scipio and Laelius discussing old age with Cato. The dialogue reflects the very close and respectful relationship which is reported here. The great praise of Cato and the attribution of all the ideas that follow to him require some comment.

It is clear that Cato and Scipio Africanus the Elder were political antagonists.[36] It would appear that Cato was instrumental in Scipio's withdrawal from
public life. Cato outlived Scipio by many years. Cato played a role in having the
younger Scipio, the participant in the dialogue, promoted to command in the Third
Punic War, in which the latter too earned the name "Africanus." At what point
this change in relations between Cato and the Scipios took place, we cannot say.
I should be surprised to think it took place as early as suggested here, almost from
the childhood of the Scipio in the dialogue. Whatever the historical reality, however, this attribution of opinions to Cato serves a number of purposes. The disagreements of Cato and the elder Scipio were a matter of public record, under-
scored by a series of court trials. Instead of carrying on this opposition and perhaps promoting it into a family feud, Scipio's son encouraged his own son to
admire Cato and to study public affairs under him. This was certainly no turning
of the Scipios away from the first Africanus, for he was rightly seen as the most
remarkable of their line—the man who saved Rome from Hannibal. It is rather a
case in which political differences have been narrowed. Whatever the issues originally in dispute, the younger Scipio chose to focus on the character and political
wisdom of the erstwhile family antagonist rather than the bygone issues that had
separated them. Whatever the historical accuracy, the story in Cicero's hands is
one of men of deeply republican sentiments reaching across the gulf of divisive
issues to recognize good character. We have here something of the same general
sort as is depicted in the *Academica*: disagreement kept in bounds by civility. The
same device is employed in *De Oratore* and may play a critical role in republican
government. Observers of the behavior of members of Parliament and of the
American Congress have often commented on seeing those from opposing parties attack each other viciously in floor debate, only to appear later in close and
amiable discussion: the enemy on the floor may not be so off the floor.

Cato was known to subsequent generations as an opponent of philosophy.
He introduced legislation which forbade philosophers from practicing in Rome.
The story is told in detail in Plutarch.[37] The Athenians sent Carneades the Academic philosopher and Diogenes the Stoic philosopher to Rome to plead their
city's case in a dispute. While there, the two philosophers won a great deal of
interest and admiration from the young. Cato responded by introducing a resolution banning all philosophers from Rome "because he wholly despised philosophy, and out of a kind of pride scoffed at the Greek study of literature...." Moreover, " he pronounced, as it were, with the voice of an oracle, that the Romans
would certainly be destroyed when they began to be infected with Greek literature...." Cato would be remembered to Cicero's contemporaries as the champion
of the traditional Roman way, suspicious of philosophizing and anxious to reform
the state in the direction of reestablishing the earlier ways of doing things. During
his term as censor, for example, he was anxious to root out innovations in form or

personnel and reestablish earlier morality.

The Scipio of the dialogue, on the other hand, who has learned so much from Cato, was a friend and patron to Greek philosophy and literature. It is true that in his own remarks in the dialogue he suggests the need to recapture some genius of the Roman state already lost by his time. His own identification with philosophy and history, however, precludes the idea of reestablishing an earlier simplicity. It is quite likely that if Scipio held ideas at all like those placed in his mouth he derived them from acquaintance with Polybius, not Cato. Polybius seems the most likely source for Cicero's own ideas on the mixed form. By attributing these ideas to Cato, Cicero manages to blend the restoration of the Roman constitution with a method derived from philosophy and with a culture and sophistication foreign to the earlier community in which that constitution operated.

In the portrayal of Cato's character, we have an indication of the character of a proper republican. His long participation in public affairs is obvious enough. "Moderation in speaking" points up both the necessity of participating in the public debate and the necessity of restraining the inclination to speak too much. "Charm mixed with gravity" indicates a similar combination of seriousness about public affairs and about one's own role combined with a certain good-humored openness to others. The "zeal for learning and teaching" connects a person with both contemporaries and with predecessors and successors. The final characteristic, "the congruence between one's life and one's words," may seem obvious enough, yet is often absent. (Incongruence between words and deeds is alleged not only of Cicero but of Edmund Burke and Felix Frankfurter.) We have here a brief but suggestive lead in the exploration of the type of character appropriate to a republic.

We come now to the first and central idea attributed to Cato. According to Scipio, Cato asserted that the form of the Roman state was better than that of other states because the others had each been established by one man, the founding law-giver. The Roman republic, on the other hand, was based not on the genius of one but of many; it was constituted not in one generation but over many generations. "For, said he, there never has lived a man possessed of so great a genius that nothing could escape him, nor could the combined powers of all the men living at one time possibly make all necessary provisions for the future without the aid of actual experience in the test of time" (111-113). The idea may well be derived from Polybius:

> The Romans while they have arrived at the final same place as regards their form of government, have not reached it by any process of reasoning, but by the discipline of many struggles and troubles, and always choosing the best by light of   experience gained in disaster have thus reached the same result of Lycurgus [at Sparta], that is to say, the best of allexisting constitutions.[38]

In *On the Republic*, though, it is made clear that the Roman constitution is preferable even to that designed by Lycurgus for Sparta.

Having Scipio put this idea in the mouth of Cato helps to make the whole discussion exemplify the very process which is being described. Instead of simply announcing the views in *On the Republic* as his own, instead even of simply attributing them in a simple sense to Scipio, Cicero has attempted to show, both through the dialogue form and through the Catonian prior formulation, the way many minds work together over time in developing the best form of government. As is maintained by the skeptical position, no one person's mind can fully grasp the truth. Nor is any one articulation of the truth fully adequate and final. Political truth is built up by the experiments of people over a long time, and its fundamental formulation is in the functioning of institutions by which human beings cooperate. Discourse is by no means irrelevant to the process, neither the discourse which takes place in the resolution of particular problems nor that which takes place when those experienced in the resolution of practical problems take time out from those problems to reflect on the general operation of their institutions. The fullest political truth lies not in ideas laid up in heaven, to use the Platonic view, nor in philosophical or scientific treatises but in political institutions, in the "system of actions" of free human beings which includes both their words and deeds.

Cato was often portrayed as hostile to philosophy, very practical, and concerned solely with the restoration of the ancient ways. In Cicero's hands, he is a part of the ongoing process of establishing the best form of government. The dialogue extends not merely through Scipio to Laelius and the other participants immediately portrayed but on a time dimension from Cato through Scipio to Cicero. It does not even stopped there. The full dialectic exploration of the political community extends through the whole Ciceronian corpus from discussion of the basic nature of the constitution to the modes or argument by which people communicate to the judgments made as individual persons interact.

Scipio proposes to follow Cato, who wrote an historical work on the origins of the Roman people, in tracing for his auditors the birth of the Roman state, its growth, and its adulthood. He specifically contrasts his project with that of Socrates in Plato's *Republic* who made up his ideal state. The history that follows, the portrayal of the best kind of state, is a brief sketch of the monarchical period and the early years of the republic. The kings are treated in their traditional chronological order; and we are shown what each king contributed to the improving state. The principal source is revealed by Scipio when he says, in referring to the second king: "...to follow as our chief authority our friend Polybius, who is unsurpassed in chronological accuracy" (137).

The story begins with Romulus. It is reasonable to assume that the tale of the kings was a commonplace to educated Romans, though Cicero may have embellished the record for his own purposes. In any case, the information which he has chosen to include must have a purpose. He is not, in short, simply recounting a history to inform his audience; he has selected certain aspects of history to suggest critical elements of the best constitution. I shall therefore examine the history not to retell the story of the early years of Rome but to point to those critical elements and expand upon their significance.

Cicero's history of the early days of Rome, with its catalogue of institutions gradually added to the constitution, is rich and suggestive despite its brevity. The details of history and the list of institutions both include many that seem, at first glance, of little interest to the modern reader. There is of course a danger in associating too rich an interpretation with Cicero's words. Yet Cicero was "versatus" in constitutional government, and his feel for what is necessary to it may well have been much greater than his ability to articulate the relevance in ways that would satisfy us.[39] What follows is an effort to understand the implications and significance of Cicero's history.

Scipio's account begins with the story of the founding of Rome by Romulus. Romulus was, Scipio tells us, the son of Mars, the god of war. This should be conceded, Scipio says, not just because it is an ancient view but because it is actually wise that "those who have deserved well of the commonwealth should be deemed actual descendants of the gods, as well as endowed with godlike qualities..." (113). Two aspects of this are of interest. In the first place, the state is descended from war. Even the best republic springs out of force and violence. It may well be that the best form transforms force. We shall see this idea developed in the discussion of the second and third kings and again, and in a different way, in the discussion of *De Inventione*. Force is the primordial way; and constitutional government remains, even in its most developed state, as a way of controlling and regulating force. It is a device for cooperation, but it retains even in its developed state a proper reminder that, in James Madison's words:

> ...what is government itself but the greatest of all reflections on human nature? If men were angels, no government would be necessary. If angels were to govern men, neither external nor internal controls on government would be necessary. In framing a government which is to be administered by men over men, the greatest difficulty lies in this; you must first enable the government to control the governed; and in the next place oblige it to control itself.[40]

Other traditions may see human beings as peaceful creatures "corrupted" by institutions or may view them as creatures susceptible to a revolutionary reformation if "saved" by the proper religious or scientific insight or by the proper institutional adjustments. In constitutional views, the disposition to force is almost an original sin, but not one to be purged by any expected reformation in human nature. The disposition is rather controlled by the development of institutions which serve that purpose.

The commentary on the allegation of divine birth is equally interesting. Those who have deserved well of the commonwealth have a divine gene in them. They do not simply possess godlike qualities, the virtues in a high degree. The founders of states are recognized to have performed an extraordinary deed. The ancients typically ascribed the founding of a state to a god or demigod; but even modern commentators have recognized that there is something special about the person or persons who successfully found states. In Rousseau's *The Social Contract*, the "legislator," the one who assists the people in giving birth to the true republic, is godlike.[41] The American "Founding Fathers" are recognized to be at least an extraordinary group, and Washington in particular has been subjected to a good deal of myth-making. The cult of Lenin provides a conspicuous example of the deification of a founder in a state which was avowedly anti-religious. In all these cases, there is a recognition that a people requires something to hold it together more than simply a rational understanding of the benefits of organized society. The birth in war and the founding by an extraordinary person or persons are both ways of achieving group solidarity in societies which may later take on any form of government. Something extra is required if a constitutional republic is to flourish, however: some continuing spark of almost divine creativity. Other states have their divine founders once. The constitutional republic is continually refounded "by those who deserve well of he commonwealth." The constitution is not set once for all time by the divine founder. It is refounded with each progressive institution created by the care and genius of those who tend the republic. This point is embellished by the story of the founding of Rome which Scipio recalls for his listeners.

Romulus and his brother Remus were exposed on the banks of the Tiber by order of Amulius, the Alban king, who had been warned to fear for the overthrow of his own powers by these babes. The infants were suckled by a wild beast and rescued and raised by shepherds, until they carried out the very prediction which Amulius had feared. The story is a common one in the ancient world: Pharaoh and Moses, Laius and Oedipus, Herod and Jesus. In each case, the child is a threat to the man. The infant represents the supplanter of what the man has established and represents. Rome too was founded by one who grew up to supplant an older order by something new. But the Roman government, whether intended that way by Romulus or not (presumably not), created a new order in a new sense. No longer was the constitution established by one generation held as firmly restricting subsequent generations. The constitution of Romulus was not overthrown by his successors but repeatedly amended, improved, and expanded.

The American Constitution, as has often been remarked, has institutionalized this very process in "Article V" with the explicit introduction of the amending process. The constitutional order may have a kind of divine quality about its origin, but it does not pretend to perfection. Its improvement is a cooperative enterprise of generations working together—the older recognizing that its handiwork will be altered as new insights are attained, the younger recognizing the wisdom of what has been achieved and changing not simply for the sake of change but only as such changes emerge through experience. In reality the constitutional temper is hard to come by. People are usually disposed either to blind worship of what has been or equally blind enthusiasm to "try something new." Neither temper is satisfied with the patient adjustment of institutional arrangements since we may not live to judge their success or failure.

Scipio next comments on the wisdom and foresight of Romulus in his selection of a site for his new city. It was not built on the sea and yet had access to the sea. Scipio outlines two dangers arising for cities located on the seacoast. In the first place, foes can approach the city rapidly and with little advance warning by sea while an army must move much more slowly over land and gives more occasions for early discovery. Secondly, Scipio says, maritime cities are subject to a kind of corruption and degeneration of traditional customs. New ways of speaking and acting and foreign customs are imported with the merchant trade, and the ancestral institutions cannot maintain their integrity. The populace of the city becomes unstable, either through actual physical mobility or through preoccupation with foreign customs. Scipio also mentions the dangers of abandoning agriculture and the cultivation of arms for trade and preoccupation with luxury items. Scipio attributes the political instability of Greece to these causes. He adds that some access to the sea is, however, advantageous since "all the products of the world could be brought by water to the city in which you live, and your people in turn can convey or send whatever their own fields produce to any country they like" (119). He adds one further significant remark concerning the siting of the city: it should be so situated as to be naturally defensible, healthful, and possessed of an adequate water supply.

Two themes raised in the discussion of the site of Rome are of particular interest: a successful political community requires a kind of geographic coherence; and there is an interplay among geography, economy, and institutions of particular significance in maintaining a constitutional republic. The advantage of natural barriers for the growth of a state are obvious, but the advantage to a constitutional or mixed form may be particularly important. The relative isolation of Britain from the Continent surely assisted in the growth of the English constitutional form. The remoteness of the United States from other major powers has had comparable significance. Debilitating incursions are rare in English history and unique in that of the United States. The English community was able to develop the complex balances of the English constitution relatively free both from the meddling of external powers and the pressures of a large, standing military establishment. Rome, unlike England or the United States, was a republic in arms;, but it sustained until fairly late in its history an army of citizens who continued to perform their apportioned constitutional responsibilities.

Cicero's remarks about agriculture, water supply, and a healthful environment are also suggestive. The association of agriculture with republican virtues and a citizen army was a commonplace both to the Romans and to our own Founding Fathers. Another dimension exists in the question of whether a constitutional government may not require a degree of economic and material independence. Cicero's perception of the problem is quite simple. A city besieged must have enough water to hold out. A populace dependent on large grain imports was not a reliable element in a mixed constitution.

The connection of seaports with the corruption of morals must be nearly as old as the existence of seaports. The Latin "mos" from which we derive "morals" means customs; and it is not surprising that seaports should provide the point of entry into a society for foreign ways of doing things. What Cicero focuses on, however, is not the corruption of morals in our sense of the expression but on the strain put on the "instituti patrorum" by the foreign ways of speaking and acting. Institutions are established ways of interacting. They may be consciously amended, or they may be gradually changed as individuals introduce new behavior. The established institutions may or may not be able to accommodate new behavior patterns. Some behavior may be subtly incompatible with the existing institutions. There is, moreover, an interdependence of institutions and individual roles. High mobility such as Scipio attributes to maritime cities may diminish the likelihood that people will adequately fill the roles necessary for the continuance of the institutions. The love of change for change's sake and the admiration for the "foreign" both threaten coherent institutional development.

Thus, in modern dress, Scipio's comments on the selection of the site of Rome make some sense. It is also worthy of note that the whole discussion does not imply a hatred of all things foreign. It is not an expression of xenophobia. It simply recognizes the importance of balancing the advantages of trade and international contact against the dangers of institutional disruption.

In discussing physical setting, Cicero examines a topic which has concerned political scientist since Aristotle. The relevance of physical setting has been overvalued, for example, by those geographic determinists who have thought climate controls temperament which in turn limits political alternatives. It has been undervalued by some would-be founders of states. The choice of Roanoke Island by the first Virginia Company proved quite unsatisfactory. The states established in Africa especially in the 1960s provide a somewhat different example. Most of their boundaries were laid out by diplomats in Europe late in the nineteenth century, quite independently of natural boundaries or traditional tribal loyalties. The states thus formed lack "natural" coherence, and circumstances have frustrated the republican governments which were established upon independence. Aristotle, Cicero, and more recently Rousseau remind us that it may not be possible to convert just any group of people under any environing circumstances into a free republic.[42]

Rome is typically identified with conquest and the creation of empire. One element in the creation of this empire is often missed, and it is one touched upon next in the account of the contributions of Romulus. The "rape of the Sabine women" is a familiar story: the Sabine women who came to Rome for a religious holiday were seized and married off to young Romans. The war that followed, according to Cicero, ended in a truce with the Sabines joining the Romans in citizenship and the Sabine king joining Romulus in the kingship. The solution may have been out of necessity rather than choice (see R: 131); but it marked a pattern in Roman history, a pattern of the gradual extension of citizenship to the people incorporated in the state. Though some of those conquered admittedly became slaves, others sired distinguished lines of Roman public figures. While the greatest and most rapid expansion of the citizenship came during the Principate when most of the spirit had gone out of republican forms, citizenship still had significance in legal proceedings and in local government. Many cities of the empire seem to have maintained more than just the forms of the republic. The purpose here is not to trace the actual history of the expansion of empire and of citizenship but rather to point out that the republic Cicero is discussing is not exclusive. It was in a position to reach out to all who had the virtues necessary to participate. The republic of the Romans was in this respect quite unlike the democracy of Athens. In its prime, Athens excluded from citizenship anyone not born of two Athenian parents. This non-exclusiveness of the Roman republic is further illustrated by Cicero's report that the second king Numa Pompilius was selected by the people for his virtue and wisdom even though he was a foreigner.

In summary to this point, we may say that a republic cannot be formed simply as an act of reasoned decision and without regard to circumstances. Once formed its genius is open rather than closed. Participation is not restricted to those of a certain ancestry. Newcomers to the state, though, must have or pursue certain kinds of virtues—developed qualities—necessary for participation. This further suggests that the degree of incorporation into the political community is important. Rome itself never managed this; its institutions did not possess the flexibility and were not amended to accommodate the flood of people to the metropolis. Public business was focused in popular assemblies at the seat of government. Too many who congregated at the seat of government did not possess the requisite virtues to participate knowledgeably in the common business of the state.

The importance of war and circumstance in the founding of a republic was recognized by the American Founders and addressed by Alexander Hamilton in the first paragraph of *The Federalist* 1:

> It has been frequently remarked that it seems to have been left to the people of this country, by their conduct and example, to decide the important question, whether societies of men are really capable or not of establishing good government from reflection and choice, or whether they are forever destined to depend for their political constitutions on accident and force. If there be

any truth in the remark, the crisis at which we are arrived may with propriety be regarded as the era in which that decision is to be made; and a wrong election of the part we shall act may, in this view, deserve to be considered as the general misfortune of mankind.

A casual reading may place the sole emphasis on the first sentence, with its proud hopes for human reasoning; but circumstance in the form of the Revolutionary War and its aftermath played a crucial role in structuring the opportunity.

The final two contributions attributed to Romulus in the remarks of Scipio are said, in the summary of the reign, to be the "two surpassing foundations of the republic"—the establishment of the Senate and the taking of the auspices (125). The first of these is fairly obvious. The stability of the state is increased if the authority of the "best men," the most influential, is joined to the raw force or domination of the king. Sheer force becomes, as it were, domesticated, regulated, and legitimized. At this point in the presentation, focus is not on wisdom or virtue as the contribution of the few.

The taking of auspices is a Roman practice which seems particularly remote from us today. That the carrying forward of public business should depend on the interpretation put on the flight of birds seems flighty indeed. Roman history is filled with stories in which military choices depend on the interpretation of such signs and portents. The functioning of the assemblies in the first century B.C. was often frustrated by magistrates who blocked legislation by finding the occasion inauspicious. One need not justify all these eccentricities in suggesting that the taking of auspices has a certain suggestive or propaedeutic value. It served the Romans as a reminder that events did not turn solely on their own determination. It provided an antidote to the danger of hubris.

The point is perhaps best illustrated by contrast with the Athenian assembly, in its pride and self-confidence, in committing the cream of its young manhood to an unnecessary expedition to remote Syracuse during the Peloponnesian War. The assembly did not consider the possibility that their great expeditionary force could be overthrown and completely destroyed. The event proved the turning point in the war. The American people too find it hard to believe that there is anything which they cannot do ("no problem is too hard to solve"). We can use institutionalized reminders that intractable circumstance, whether of nature or chance, may influence possibilities and outcomes and that not everything is simply a matter of our will and choice.

Scipio reports that, upon the death of Romulus, the Senate tried to rule without a king ["rex"]; but "the people would not tolerate it, but, in their affectionate longing for Romulus, continually demanded a king" (131). We see exemplified here the point made in Book 1 that "kings attract us by our affection for them" (83). The king is a focus of loyalty to the state. To satisfy the people and provide continuity, the Senate created an interregnum and an interrex to lead the state until a foreigner Numa Pompilius was chosen to succeed. Numa was known for his "kingly virtue and wisdom, not royal ancestry" (133). The people were involved in his elevation which was confirmed by the popular assembly.

Numa's contributions to Rome's growth were in matters of peace. He established religious ceremonies and officials, encouraged agriculture, and instituted markets and games. He set an example of benevolence and kindliness. His long reign was marked by "the two elements which most conspicuously contribute to the stability of a State—religion and the spirit of tranquility" (137). At this point in his account, Scipio is interrupted by a question: was Numa a pupil or follower of Pythagoras? Scipio readily proves this chronologically impossible. When his interrogator expresses pleasure that advances have come "from the native excellence of our own people," Scipio does not demur yet goes on to remark that "even of those institutions that have been borrowed from abroad, many have been improved by us until they are much better than they were in the countries from which we obtained them and where they had their origin" (139). The institutions of Rome include the borrowed as well as the old.

The next king (Scipio's accounts become briefer with the remaining kings), again chosen in the assembly, was Tullus Hostilius. Tullus was of contrasting character from his predecessor and a man of war, but he introduced "rules for the declaration of war." In classic style, he used the proceeds of war to build meeting places for the Senate and the assemblies. He was succeeded by Ancus Martius, Numa's grandson, who incorporated the surrounding Latin peoples into the state and built a harbor at the mouth of the Tiber. Even war and conquest result in the development of Roman institutions.

The next king, Lucius Tarquinius, was of Greek origin and came to Rome via Etruria. (No mention is made of Etruscan conquest though this is now considered a possibility.) Lucius is given credit for beginning the class organization which played so important a part in Roman politics and government. It was a reflection of both economic and familial positions and served, through the "client" system, to bind the classes and perhaps soften the impact of class divisions. Lucius too was a conqueror and builder. Laelius sums up at this point that "every king contributed many good and useful institutions" (145).

The last good king Servius Tullius is described in somewhat more detail, though the picture leaves as many questions as answers. Servius was reported to have been of slave birth, raised by Lucius, and ascended the throne by subterfuge in concealing Lucius' death until he had consolidated power. In the course of his reign, he carried much further the class organization. Many aspects familiar to the Roman of Scipio's time are ascribed to Servius. While the text is patchy, Servius—whom Laelius claims had the best understanding of government—apparently is given credit for the balance among classes and powers which distinguished the excellence of the Roman constitution from the point of view of Scipio (and Cicero).

Even the last king Tarquinius Superbus ("the haughty") used the proceeds of his conquests to build the Capitol. Tarquin's most important "contribution" was his misuse of power leading to his overthrow and the end of the use of the title king. Commenting on the end of the monarchy, Scipio introduces the cycle of change, the "regular curving path through which governments travel," only to drop it. While he refers to knowledge of it as "the foundation of that political wisdom ["civilis prudentiae"] which is the aim of our whole discourse," he in fact attributes the fall of the monarchy to the bad character and behavior of one man (155-163). Even this explanation is not entirely satisfactory. Several of the earlier kings died under suspicious circumstances and may not have been exemplary or popular characters.

Progress in institutional development did not cease with the beginning of the republic. Early in his discussion of this continuing process, Scipio explains the mixture of elements in a well-constituted republic: "...unless there is in the State an even balance of rights, duties, and functions ["iuris et officii et muneris"], so that the magistrates have enough power, the counsels of the eminent citizens enough influence, and the people enough liberty, this kind of government cannot be safe from revolution" (169). In presenting this, Scipio makes a curious but correct remark: "...the essential nature of the commonwealth often defeats reason" (169). The comments concern an early controversy in which "the people...claimed a somewhat greater measure of rights" (169). Were they claiming "too much"? Reason cannot, in advance, give a clear answer. If the balance is overthrown, the republic falls; but there is no a priori rule which dictates how much of each element is "enough." The task of balancing rights, duties, and functions will come to the fore in the chapter on Felix Frankfurter.

Our text for Book 2 becomes fragmentary toward the end, but we can see some of the institutional changes which are discussed. Appeal from the magistrates was made possible. The offices of consulate and dictatorship were created. Reforms were introduced to smooth class conflicts, including ending enslavement for debt and creating the plebeian tribunate. The question then raised is apparently whether such a state can survive. Scipio reaffirms that the republic is the most stable form, but even this would appear to require statesmanship since, by a transition which is lost, talk now shifts to the ideal statesman (179-183). We are told that such a person must be "a mirror to his fellow-citizens by reason of the supreme excellence of his life and character" (181). He must be an example and must reveal to others what they should seek to make of themselves in respect to service to the state. His challenge is to assist in "a fair and reasonable blending together of the upper, middle, and lower classes" to produce harmony or concord in the state (183). This requires justice.

Plato's *Republic* is at many points clearly the model for Cicero, with many inclusions made on Plato's example. It is important to note, however, that justice is the central topic of Plato's masterwork; and other matters, such as the forms of state and the best state and the cycle of change, are stretched on a framework provided by an investigation of justice. In *On the Republic* justice becomes central only in Book 3. The best state, while it clearly requires justice, is discussed first in the context of change, the growth of institutions into the best state. Stability is treated rather more frequently than justice in the first two books.

Book 3, which comes to us in fragmented form, is a discussion of justice. After an introduction in Cicero's own voice, the dialogue proceeds with a presentation by Philus of an argument from the point of view of the New Academy. He is then answered by Laelius who presents the Stoic position.

The preface seems to begin with a consideration of the development of humankind. On the authority of St. Augustine, "the book begins with some reflections on man's weakness at birth, and how it is overcome by the divine spirit within him" (185). What we have refers to the improvement of mobility and the growth of language and then mathematics. The latter encouraged individuals to look up to the stars and to lift up their thoughts—to aspire. (We shall return to this at the end of *On the Republic*.) Cicero then recurs to topics from his introduction to Book 1. "...two paths to wisdom" ["via prudentiae"] are distinguished: a "quiet life devoted to the study of the noblest arts" and "the life of a statesman" (189). We do not see here the Aristotelian distinction between philosophical and practical wisdom based on the distinction of things invariable and things variable by nature.[43] The distinction seems to be based on an active versus a retired life and on the mode of "teaching": between those who are "teachers of truth and virtue" by "admonition and instruction" ["verbis et artibus"] and those who are knowledgeable in the "art of government and the training of peoples" ["ratio civilis et disciplina populorum"] and teach by "institutions and laws" ["institutis et legibus"] (187-189). This distinction between teaching through the laws and through discourse was made by Aristotle, and it is reasonable to think Cicero was familiar with it.[44] Those who teach through laws, Cicero says, should be praised more highly. They combine experience in leading the state with book-learning and familiarity with the traditional ways of their own country with "acquired learning" and "foreign learning" (187-189).

One brief, parenthetical remark reminds us of the *Academica*. Scipio refers to "men, who, if they have not been 'wise,' ["sapientis"] since that name is so carefully restricted..." (189). Keyes, the translator, notes: "i.e., by and to the philosophers" without further specification; but this surely coincides with the Academic position expounded by Cicero in *Academica*.

Philus expresses regret that he should be cast in the role of defending "wickedness" ["inprobitatis"], though Laelius responds by praising Philus's old-fashioned probity ["antiquae probitatis"] and noting that he is in the "habit of arguing on the other side, because [he thinks] it is the easiest means of reaching the truth" (190-191). Both from what is available and from references elsewhere, Philus's approach is apparently drawn from writings of Carneades. Some of the arguments put forward are rather like some of those of Glaucon and Adeimantus at the beginning of Book 2 of Plato's *Republic*. Laws are obeyed out of fear of punishment rather than an innate sense of justice (199). They are thus, in Plato's presentation, a kind of compromise between doing and suffering injustice (201-203). Plato's suggestion by Glaucon and reinforced by Adeimantus that it is better to be wicked but appear just than to be just but appear wicked is even echoed by Philus.

Philus calls attention to the differences among laws in different places and at different times and so denies that there are any universal laws of justice. His central conclusion reinforces the argument for a mixed constitution: "But when there is mutual fear, man fearing man and class fearing class, then, because no one is confident of his own strength, a sort of bargain is made between the common people and the powerful; this results in that mixed form of government which Scipio has been recommending; and thus, not nature or desire, but weakness, is the mother of justice" (203). This compromise of the many and the powerful recalls the polity of Aristotle which arises from a mixture of democracy and oligarchy.

Laelius's response has many lacunae. In what we have, he first makes the Aristotelian point similar to that already noted in discussing *On the Laws*, that young men, who are impressionable, ought not to hear this skeptical argument. He then gives the Stoic manifesto: "True law is right reason in agreement with nature; it is of universal application, unchanging and everlasting....It is a sin to try to alter this law....We cannot be freed from its obligations by senate or people, and we need not look outside ourselves for an expounder or interpreter of it" (211). He draws the conclusions that there should not be different laws for Rome and Athens, that violators of the law will ultimately be punished even if that punishment is not readily apparent, and that a state founded on such law will be eternal ("death is not natural for a State as for a human being...") (212-213).

Later fragments of Book 3 contain an exchange between Laelius and Scipio which makes the point that the absolute rule of the people is as much a tyranny as is the vicious rule of one man. A republic can exist only where there is a "partnership in justice" ["consensu iuris"] (222-223). It is a point reaffirmed by Madison and then by Tocqueville. Madison says: "The accumulation of all powers, legislative, executive, and judiciary, in the same hands, whether of one, a few, or many, and whether hereditary, self-appointed, or elective, may justly be pronounced the very definition of tyranny." And Tocqueville: "I regard it as an impious and detestable maxim that in matters of government the majority has the right to do everything, and nonetheless I place the origin of all powers in the will of a majority." Tocqueville's appeal is to the "majority of all mankind" over time.[45]

Of Book 4 almost nothing remains. It apparently dealt, at least in part, with "wise provisions for that association of citizens in a happy and honorable life; for that is the original purpose for men's coming together, and it should be accomplished for them in their commonwealth partly by established customs and partly by laws" (233).

The few fragments of Book 5 remaining make interesting points. Some may have been made in Cicero's own voice. Even the order is uncertain. One point notes the interplay of customs, individuals of excellence, and institutions: "...the customs of our ancestors produced excellent men, and eminent men preserved our ancient customs and the institutions of their forefathers" (245). Individual responsibility extends to the preservation of custom, a point not popular with those who would reduce all politics to reason and will. Keyes believes Book 5 dealt principally with "the qualifications and functions of the ideal statesman" (245), and this seems plausible in terms of the topics offered by Plato and Aristotle and Cicero's own ambitions. We are told that "nothing is so regal" as the "explanationem aequitatis," which Keyes translates as "the administration of justice" (247). The Latin is suggestive, though, in conveying the sense that officials must not only do justice, but explain it. The passage goes on to make explicit that the doing of justice is more important than the waging of war. A further fragment contrasts the corrupting of the people by money with the more dangerous corrupting of them by words: even the virtuous can be corrupted by words.

The only section of the *On the Republic* which is likely to have been read by persons such as Hume, Burke, and Madison occurs in Book 6, the long fragment known as "Scipio's Dream." This section, standing at the end and in obvious parallel with the "Myth of Er" which concludes Plato's *Republic*, merited an independent commentary which put it among the works of the Church Fathers and helped to preserve it. The "Dream" returns to the question discussed by Cicero in his own voice at the beginning of Book 1: the value of a life of public service. Just as the story of Er affirms in mythic language the advantage of the just life, so the story told by Scipio reaffirms in cosmic language the value of the public life.

Scipio tells his auditors that, on his first visit to Africa, he met King Masinissa whom his grandfather had befriended and confirmed on his throne. The young man and the king stayed long into the night recalling the greatness of the elder Scipio Africanus. The young man retired exhausted and fell into a dream. In the dream, his grandfather, the conqueror of Hannibal, talks with him and then guides him on tour which displays to him the vast scope of the heavens and the small space assigned to the earth. The account of earth is notable for recognizing its sphericity, the existence of two cold polar regions, and the "small portion" (275) occupied by the Roman empire. But though the earth is small, it is central to the whole structure of the heavens—a point to be kept in mind in assessing the importance of earthly experiences.

Scipio the Elder makes certain predictions about his grandson, including the prospect that he may survive the turmoil created by the Gracchi to be the refounder of the state. (He did not, and the refounding remained to face Cicero's own time.) The life facing Scipio is the best preparation for an "eternal life of happiness," for "nothing of all that is done on earth is more pleasing to that supreme god who rules the whole universe than the assemblies and gatherings of men associated in justice, which are called States" (265-267). The life is a burdensome one, but it is the human way ["munus humanum"] which is "the road to the skies..." (266-269). The cosmic spectacle portrayed by Scipio and thus by Cicero might tempt one to think that its contemplation ("pure" philosophy) is the highest life; but the centrality of the earth to the scheme and the path established to the heavens remind the reader that the active, not the passive, life is prior.

Without attempting an analysis of the cosmology and geography of the Dream, we can nonetheless be clear that political service is noble. Good states are committed to justice and sustained by attachment to tested ways of operating. The preservation and improvement of such states are the highest form of human action, but one ought not to count on earthly rewards for such service. Performing such service is in harmony with the universe and is thus its own reward.

The significance of Cicero's "best republic" is more clearly grasped by contrast with that of Plato. In Plato's *Republic*, it is suggested that the best state or the nearest approximation to it can come into being if a philosopher-king can be identified. This is a person (or persons, and may be male or female) who knows the truth and knows that he or she knows the truth. The possession of knowledge is certain. In such a case, the governance of the state can be given over to this philosopher-king who rules with complete discretion based on a grasp of the truth. (There will be little business for the law courts, we are told.[46]) In Cicero's republic, on the other hand, a mixed government combining institutions of rule by one, rule by the few, and rule by the many functions in ways we have come to call "checks and balances" because no one person or group can be expected to have the full and complete truth. The best government comes from the interaction of these institutional elements. The Roman government which is the concrete embodiment of this mixed form was a "popular" government in the sense that all of the offices were filled by elections in which all of the citizens played a role. This government arose not from the insight or wisdom of one man or group of men at a particular time, but from the experimentation of many men over a long time. (Unlike the republic of Plato, this one requires law courts to resolve the many issues which arise when there is no one center of or source for truth.)

5. Other Works

Many of Cicero's other works contribute to his social/political philosophy. Several of the works, most notably *De Oratore*, relate to public discourse. *De Officiis*, usually translated as *On Duties*, treats mutual obligations. *De Finibus Bonorum et Malorum* or *On the Ends of Good and Bad* and a number of other works treat ethics or particular subjects within the broad questions of living well. And *De Natura Deorum* or *On the Nature of the Gods* lays some basis for human society in the "order of things": human society is not simply a matter of unconstrained individual choice. Detailed consideration of these works is beyond the scope of this study but would add to a fuller picture of skepticism and constitutionalism.

A few comments on *De Oratore*, however, give a useful supplement to our understanding of the kind of "political science" implied by Scipio's presentation. Scipio indicated that he would not go back to the elements of which a state is constructed but would instead speak as one informed participant in the state to other informed participants. He would speak in the common language of public life. The *De Oratore* is Cicero's most comprehensive treatment of the art of discourse, so what he has to say can be expected to shed some light on the common language of public life.

De Oratore was written in 55 B.C. in the year before *On the Republic* and contains references to the "science of community building ["sapientiam constituedae civitatis"] and to Scipio, Laelius, and Furius (Or: 309). It makes use of the works of Carneades and other Academics. The work is Cicero's longest, three books of some 330 pages in English translation, and is a dialogue. The dialogue form enables Cicero to present two views of oratory and orators, each of which has some claim on our support. In one view, oratory is closely allied with liberal education (Or: 17, 201) and a free man's life (Or: 23) and is broadly applicable to that life. It is "the trained skill of highly educated men." In the other view, it is more of a knack to be used mainly in the law courts, dependent on "a sort of natural talent and on practice" (Or: 7). Between them, the positions provide a framework for presenting a comprehensive discussion of all aspects of rhetoric.

The status of rhetoric as an "art" in a technical sense is a subject of dispute in the dialogue. Rhetoric is unlike other arts. While "the subjects of the other arts are derived as a rule from hidden and remote sources,.. the whole art of oratory lies open to the view, and is concerned in some measure with the common practice, customs, and speech of mankind, so that, whereas in all other arts that is most excellent which is furthest removed from the understanding and mental capacity of the untrained, in oratory the very cardinal sin is to depart from the language of ordinary life, and the usage approved by the sense of the community ["communis sensus"]" (Or: 11).

That we human beings talk among ourselves ["colloquimur inter nos"] distinguishes us from other animals. Speaking was the power ["vis"] which gathered people into a common place, promoted the cultivation of the human in us, established communites, and gave shape to "laws, tribunals, and civic rights" (Or: 25). For modern Americans, "the law" is a "mysterious science" which is both complex and available only to the professionally trained; so it is difficult to grasp Cicero's view of law as the common possession and common sense of a people. While the phrase the "mysterious science of the law" traces to Blackstone late in the eighteenth century, the most important formulation of the esoteric character of English law was made by Edward Coke at the beginning of the seventeenth century. Coke argued that King James I (unlike the kings of the Middle Ages) could not sit in the hearing of legal cases because the law had become too specialized and could only be applied by those versed in its details. Since Coke's time, the law has grown even more esoteric. It is thus hard for us to think of the law as materials lying "open to view, having their setting in everyday custom, in the intercourse of men, and in public scenes..." (Or: 133). Our language of the law is so esoteric that it is hard to think of a sense in which it could properly be commonly understood. Cicero's writings on rhetoric are concerned mostly with the presentation of arguments in the courts of law, though he always gives at least passing reference to the other fora for oratory. Such treatises on legal reasoning are remote from us. Further and more detailed examination here is unnecessary, but the relation of the "common" language to "political science" will remain for consideration in the chapters which follow. The explanation of the workings of the Supreme Court were of especial importance to Felix Frankfurter.

De Inventione, On Invention, is by general agreement the earliest of Cicero's works, perhaps written as early as age nineteen.[47] The substance is taken from some no-longer-available Greek handbook and may well have been written by Cicero as a kind of exercise book to further his legal studies. It concerns the "invention" of legal arguments. Each of the two books into which it is organized has an introduction which seems original to Cicero and is consistent with his academic skepticism and method. These introductions may have been written later, since we do not know when the work actually became public property. The consistency with other works is particularly evident in the introduction to Book 2. Cicero tells of a famous Greek artist Zeuxis of Heraclea who asked the city of Croton to provide him with five of its most beautiful young women to serve as models for a picture he was to paint of Helen of Troy, "because in no single case has Nature made anything perfect and finished in every part" (I: 169). Similarly, Cicero claims that he collected "all the works on the subject... [and] excerpted what seemed most suitable precepts from each...." He goes on to observe: "And it is also true of other pursuits that if men would choose the most appropriate contributions from many sources rather than devote themselves unreservedly to one leader only, they would offend less by arrogance, they would not be so obstinate in wrong courses, and would suffer somewhat less from ignorance" (169-171).

Cicero concludes his introduction with another observation: "For disgrace lies not imperfect knowledge but in foolish and obstinate continuance in a state of imperfect knowledge; for ignorance is attributed to the infirmity common to the human race, but obstinacy to a man's own fault. Therefore without affirming anything positively, I shall proceed with an inquiring mind and make each statement with a degree of hesitation..." (175). This may be the original version of a quotation often used by economist-philosopher Frank Knight and attributed to nineteenth century American humorist Josh Billings: "It ain't ignorance that does the most harm; it's knowing so durned much that ain't so." Anthologies of quotations attribute to Billings the following variants: "It is better to know nothing than to know what ain't so" and "The trouble with people is not that they don't know but that they know so much that ain't so."

Book 1 begins with a discussion common in Cicero: the importance of combining wisdom ["sapientia"] with eloquence ["eloquentia"]. This is congruent with his concern to unite words and deeds and also philosophy and rhetoric. Cicero traces these diremptions to Socrates, whom in other respects he much praised. One may guess that he saw himself as putting back together what the master had mistakenly divided. He gives a little hypothetical anthropology about the role of speech—perhaps from the mouth of a man great and wise ["magnus and sapiens"]—in converting human beings from "wild savages into a kind and gentle folk," by substituting speech for force (5-7). But speech can be put to bad uses as well as good; and thus facility in using words must be balanced by reasoned understanding of the ends which may be sought. Once eloquence and rightful reasoning ["eloquentia" and "ratio rectissimus"] had been separated, classes of professors of rhetoric and professors of philosophy grew, implying speech and action without reason and reason without speech and action. Cicero wishes to bring reason and action into teamwork and harmony in the service of civil association.

The work on invention which follows is worthy of reading by those interested in lawyer's arguments, brainstorming, or creativity. It lays out in great detail a structure of "places" you may look or possibilities you may consider in trying to figure out the best way to argue a legal case. It requires choices among the possibilities in selecting arguments which may probably be persuasive to the audience of jurors. With our inclination to emphasize imagination and originality and to depend on intelligence or even genius, we moderns may underestimate the potential value of devices or schemas which prompt us to consider possibilities methodically. We are also inclined to look for "proofs" which provide answers which in effect choose themselves. The Roman legal system was much less developed than our own in niceties of evidence and court procedures and thus permitted kinds of argument which cannot be used in an American court. Even so, *De Inventione* is surprisingly rich in offerings for a contemporary lawyer.

The last of Cicero's philosophical writings is also the last we shall comment on here. It too lays out an elaborate schema. *De Officiis* is usually translated "on duties," but the English word "duties" may be somewhat misleading. "Officium" comes from "opus facio," which means to do work. Robin Seager has translated the word as "reciprocal personal relationships."[48] We might think of the title of this work as "on the principled way of thinking through our interactions with others." The book is in Cicero's own voice and is addressed to his son. It urges young Marcus to concern himself with both oratory and philosophy so that he will become adept at both speaking and judging (Of: 3). In every aspect of life,

we must be able to think through and decide how we should behave in interacting
with others. This subject is the "common property of all philosophers" (7). Cicero
says his views are not very different from those of the Peripatetics with whom his
son was studying. He indicates that he will draw principally on the Stoic Panaetius
(whose work is now lost) of whom Cicero says he "has given us what is unquestionably the most thorough discussion of moral duties that we have..." (277). But
Cicero says, in a passage I have quoted earlier, he will follow his own method: "I
shall, therefore, at this time and in this investigation follow chiefly the Stoics, not
as a translator, but, as is my custom, I shall at my own option and discretion draw
from those sources in such measure and in such manner as shall suit my purpose"
(9). He reasserts his commitment to academic skepticism again at the beginning
of Book 2 (173-175).

Cicero asserts that all treatments of this subject have two divisions: one
pertains to the supreme good or hierarchy of goods ["finem bonorum"]; the other
to the practical rules ["praeceptis"] by which all the aspects of life can be lived in
conformity together (7-8). The former subject he has already treated in *De Finibus*.
This book focuses on the latter set of issues. This division parallels another between what is right absolutely and what is done with an adequate reason ["ratio
probabilis"]. On these bases Panaetius divided the problems into three sorts: the
relation of the morally right to the morally wrong, the relation of the more and the
less expedient, and cases in which what is morally right seems in conflict with
what seems expedient. Cicero corrects this organization by focusing on the problem of choice rather than simply classifying right and wrong, useful and useless.
He adds two kinds of problems: choosing when two right actions are in conflict
and choosing when two expedient options are in conflict. After warning against
the two dangers of treating the unknown as known (thinking one knows what is
not in fact the case) and working too hard at the obscure (which is likely to be
useless), Cicero begins his detailed outline of possibilities (19-21).

In the creation of legal arguments and in the resolution of practical problems, we deal with probabilities, not certainties. We must exercise choice. We can
approach these matters in a very methodical way, but that does not imply anything like a mathematical calculus which will free us from uncertainty and choice.
Having no claim to certainty, we can have no claim to unrestrained authority.

6. Cicero's Influence

The ancient school of Academic Skepticism did not produce surviving works
after Cicero. Nor did the ancient world produce further books connecting skepticism with limited government; discussing limited government fell out of style.
While the trappings of restraint on authority lasted for a while, real restraints on
political authority were abandoned. Pyrrhonic skepticism which had no concern
with politics and the practical life may well have continued as an active tradition

in the following centuries of the Roman Empire; at least, important summaries of arguments were produced by Sextus Empiricus. Cicero continued to be read and retained some popularity for his style and perhaps especially with Christian writers as a conduit of Stoicism. St. Augustine, to mention only the most famous, was influenced by Cicero's introduction to philosophy, the now-missing *Hortensius*. The problems treated by Ciceronian skepticism, the need for practical resolution of conflicting dogmas, only occasionally emerged in the next fifteen hundred years. *On the Republic* disappeared, though there appear to be traces of Ciceronian political thought in such medieval writers as John of Salisbury. Cicero was popular in the Renaissance and at various times since, especially in the eighteenth century. In recent years, he has been a major source for investigation of the Roman legal system. His contribution to philosophy has been more elusive.[49] This book is based on the belief that Cicero's career and philosophy shed light on the greatest political achievement of the West—limited, popular government.

Four

HUME

1. Hume and His Interpreters

The preeminent philosopher of skepticism for the modern world is David Hume. Hume, born in 1711, was an older contemporary of Edmund Burke and James Madison.[1] When Hume died in August 1776, Burke had just begun the speeches and writings for which he became famous and Madison was just beginning his long career of public service. Hume was acquainted with Burke and was a close friend of another famous contemporary Adam Smith. Hume's influence on James Madison has been partially traced in Douglas Adair's examination of the connections of his work with Madison's argument in the Tenth *Federalist* paper.[2] Hume himself was never actively involved in government or politics and held only minor public office. His reputation is based solely on his writings. He was best known in his own time for his essays and then for *The History of England*; but his first book *A Treatise of Human Nature*, published while he was still in his twenties, has received the most attention in this century. Hume is usually identified with the Pyrrhonic skepticism which occupies the first book of *A Treatise of Human Nature*. For at least the first half of this century, Hume the epistemologist was of primary interest to professional philosophers. He has been called by J.H. Randall, Jr., "beyond all doubt the ablest British philosopher." Philosophy students have tended to distinguish Hume's essays and his history from his philosophy. Two volumes edited by V.C. Chappell illustrate the point in several ways. The *Philosophy of David Hume* includes only "Of the Standard of Taste" from the *Essays Moral, Political, and Literary*. Roughly twice as much space is given to excerpts from Book 1 of the *Treatise* as to the other two books. Chappell also edited *Hume: A Collection of Critical Essays* for the "Modern Studies in Philosophy" series. The volume is primarily given over to discussions of epistemological issues. It does, as an exception, contain F.A. Hayek's essay, discussed below, but for the most part distinguishes Hume's "philosophical writings" from his essays as T.E. Jessop does explicitly in his friendly essay. The assessment of Hume by Randall is quoted in the essay by E.C. Mossner in the same volume. This focus and assessment have changed only in part.

Hayek and Donald Livingston dispute the approach. As Hayek says, "It is no accident that Hume develops his political and legal ideas in his philosophical work. They are most intimately connected with his general philosophical conceptions, especially with his sceptical views on the 'narrow bounds of human understanding'."[3]

The *Treatise*, in Hume's own words and emphasis, "fell *dead-born from the press*, without reaching such distinction, as even to excite a murmur among the zealots" (E: xxxiv; italics in the original). He restated his argument a decade later in two long essays *An Enquiry Concerning Human Understanding* and *An Enquiry Concerning the Principles of Morals*. In the former of these, after pursuing Pyrrhonism to a dead end, Hume says: "There is, indeed, a more *mitigated* scepticism or *academical* philosophy which may be both durable and useful, and which may, in part, be the result of the Pyrrhonism or *excessive* scepticism when its undistinguished doubts are, in some measure, corrected by common sense and reflection" (HU: 111, emphasis in the original). The status of this mitigated skepticism is a matter of some scholarly dispute: which brand, Pyrrhonic or mitigated, is the real Humean skepticism? and where does the mitigated skepticism come from—Hume's immediate predecessors or directly from Cicero? In Richard Popkin's view, such "mitigated skepticism" developed out of Pyrrhonism in the early seventeenth century with Mersenne, Gassendi, and others. Quoting Mersenne, Popkin says that though our knowledge is severely restricted, "it still has some value of a pragmatic variety, since 'this little knowledge suffices to serve as a guide in our actions'." Peter Jones argues that Hume's mitigated skepticism comes directly from Cicero. The details of this scholarly dispute will not be considered here. I take the view that Hume is a mitigated or academic skeptic and that in holding this position he was in part directly influenced by Cicero.[4]

Hume stands at a critical juncture in transmitting academic skepticism to the modern world, but a full treatment is both beyond my capacity and unnecessary to my line of argument. Only two of Hume's contributions will be considered here and each in only summary form: his insights into institutional growth and his recognition of our dependence upon the "common sense" of a community. The approach to these two points will be primarily by way of recent commentators rather than Hume's own texts: F.A. Hayek mainly for the former point and Donald W. Livingston mainly for the latter. These recent interpretations of Hume are readily available and make detailed comment here unnecessary. Hayek and Livingston broke with most earlier twentieth-century treatments in English by setting Hume's epistemological contributions into the broader context of his social and political thought. His Pyrrhonism is properly treated as a way-station in his argument. In Hayek's words, "Hume is of course known mainly for his theory of knowledge, and in Germany largely as the author who stated the problems which Immanuel Kant endeavored to solve. But to Hume the chief task was from the beginning a general science of human nature, for which morals and politics were as important as the sources of knowledge" (H: 103). Neither Hayek nor Livingston explicitly refers to him as an academic skeptic nor traces his skepticism to Cicero; but their interpretations assume this position and expand these two aspects of Ciceronian constitutional-skeptical views. The argument here will rely mainly on quotation from them.

2. Hayek

Hayek treated Hume and Cicero as a part of the same intellectual tradition but never seems to have made use of Cicero's *Academica*, discussed at length above. Hayek, initially an economist, became popularly known for his attacks on socialism and on governmental interference in free markets, especially as presented in *The Road to Serfdom*.[5] Many persons were so prejudiced by the line of argument in *Serfdom* that they ignored his further and more profound works. When he published *The Constitution of Liberty*, it was widely assumed by his readers to be the culmination of his life's study and his masterpiece.[6] During the course of his discussion in *The Constitution*, he referred to what he "called the 'British tradition' [which] was made explicit mainly by a group of Scottish moral philosophers led by David Hume, Adam Smith, and Adam Ferguson, seconded by their English contemporaries Josiah Tucker, Edmund Burke, and William Paley, and drawing largely on a tradition rooted in the jurisprudence of the common law" (p. 54). In the footnote citation for his reference to the Scots, he says: "An adequate account of this philosophy of growth which provided the intellectual foundations for a policy of freedom has yet to be written and cannot be attempted here" (431). This account he went on to provide in the three volumes of *Law, Legislation, and Liberty*.[7] Running through all of these works is an attack on what Hayek called "constructive rationality"—a misplaced understanding of and confidence in reasoning. Central economic planning, the problem addressed in *The Road to Serfdom*, is simply one manifestation of the hubris of reason. Hume is quoted frequently in *The Constitution of Liberty*, but it is my personal impression that Tocqueville may have played a greater role in inspiring the book than did Hume. *Law, Legislation, and Liberty* is another matter. *The Constitution of Liberty* grew out of a lecture on "The Political Ideal of the Rule of Law" delivered in Egypt but perhaps stimulated by a year-long University of Chicago seminar Hayek gave on Tocqueville in 1953-1954. *Law, Legislation, and Liberty* seems to have grown out of the essay on Hume originally given as a lecture at the University of Freiburg in 1963.[8]

In tracing the gradual construction of the Roman constitution through the contributions of each of the Roman kings, Cicero provided a conscious contrast with the republic constructed by Plato and by most subsequent architects of ideal states. Plato's republic sprang like Athena full-grown from the head of its creator. Its realization depended upon the existence of wise men and women who know and know that they know: possessors of certain knowledge. Cicero did not fully depart from the master's example. The contributions of the Roman kings, in Cicero's account, are intentional even if the kings did not foresee how their individual contributions would culminate in the form of the Roman constitution of Cicero's day. Hume made significant advances over this. He understood that the most important institutional developments can not, for the most part, be traced to

98 HUME

known persons who intended what resulted. The experimental and gradual method operates much more subtly than the addition of great stones to a grand edifice. In understanding the growth of institutions, moreover, Hume emphasized the moral and legal underpinnings of the explicitly political institutions. He expands upon Cicero's point that political society presupposes a consensus on justice.[9]

In Hayek's interpretation of Hume and here quoting from him, three related rules emerged early in human association through trial and error: "*the stability of possession, of its transfer by consent,and of the performance of promises*'" (H: 109, emphasis in the original). Not all individuals in any society follow these rules, and not all societies have equally attempted to promote them. Following them and developing and elaborating them is the path of progress. The substitution of general laws expressing these principles for the discretionary acts of government—the "rule of law, not men"—has permitted the development of more free and prosperous societies. Hayek even offers evidence that Darwin's idea of biological evolution was derived from Hume's idea of social evolution by way of Darwin's grandfather, Erasmus Darwin (H: 114-116).

In Hayek's words, "What [Hume] produced was above all a theory of the growth of human institutions....His work also provided the foundation on which the authors of the American constitution built and in some measure for the political philosophy of Edmund Burke which is much closer to, and more directly indebted to, Hume than is generally recognized" (H: 106-107). Hayek expands the point by quoting Christian Bay, *The Structure of Freedom* (Palo Alto: Stanford University Press, p. 33):

> Standards of morality and justice are what Hume calls "artifacts"; they are neither divinely ordained, nor an integral part of original human nature, nor revealed by pure reason. They are an outcome of the practical experience of mankind, and the sole consideration in the slow test of time is the utility each moral rule can demonstrate towards promoting human welfare. Hume may be called a precursor of Darwin in the field of ethics. In effect, he proclaimed a doctrine of the survival of the fittest among human conventions—fittest not in terms of good teeth but in terms of maximum social utility. (H: 107)

Note that what Bay and Hayek are talking about is not the much-despised "social Darwinism." The survival in question is of "moral rules" not individual human beings nor classes thereof.

Unlike the kingly contributions to political institutions sketched by Cicero,

> What [Hume] undertakes is to show that certain characteristics of modern society which we prize are dependent on conditions which were not created in order to bring about these results, yet are their indispensable presuppositions....Hume shows...that an orderly society can develop only if men learn to obey certain rules of conduct....These rules were not, however,

deliberately intended by men to solve a problem which they saw (though it has become a task of legislation to improve them). (H: 108-109)

"Law and morals, like language and money, are, as we would say, not deliberate inventions but grown institutions or 'formations'" (H: 109). The moral rules which concern Hume and Hayek are not, however, those which most likely now come to mind from the phrase. They concern justice, property and contract, and honesty rather than sexual practices and such. Political society presupposes a consensus on justice; and justice requires above all the stability of property. What Hume examines in detail is precisely what Cicero took for granted: the critical elements of the consensus on justice. Hayek traces the genesis of Hume's insights back to Cicero.[10]

Hume came at so important a juncture because he provided a philosophical antidote to another line of skeptical reasoning, Descartes' method of doubt. In *The Discourse on Method,* Descartes had proceeded by doubting everything of which he could not be completely certain. The certainty which he could not doubt was the famous "cogito, ergo sum"—I think; therefore I am. From this certain beginning, he constructed by a deductive and apparently certain procedure a whole system of thought on the model of Euclidian geometry. Descartes's achievement, bolstered by the intellectual successes of the physical scientists of the seventeenth century and following, seemed to establish this deductive method as the only method for arriving at truth. Most philosophers and scientists did not avail themselves of the Humean antidote. As recently as the middle of this century, the physical sciences and the syllogistic procedure treated as a "method" were seen as the paradigm for all knowledge worthy of the name

Aristotle claimed to have invented the syllogism, which he treats in detail in the *Prior Analytics.* The "analytics" do not provide a "method." For Aristotle, method varied by subject matter. Comments on methods occur in many of his studies. Some methodical instruments were of broad applicability such as examining a thing in its process of growth and dividing composite wholes into parts. The general discussion of methods presumably occurred in books listed in Diogenes Laertius's catalogue of Aristotle's works but now long missing.[11] Euclid cast his work on geometry in syllogistic form and created what was generally considered the paradigmatic form for "scientific" knowledge—a form considered exemplary by writers as diverse as Descartes, Spinoza, Hobbes, Newton, and later physical scientists. For two millennia, geometry was considered a perfect and basically completed science until the introduction of "non-Euclidean" geometries at the end of the last century.

In this century, Bertrand Russell and the Vienna Circle promoted the idea that truth is based on sense perceptions from which, properly handled by a "scientific" (read "geometric") method, all knowledge can be derived. "Sense" could thus be distinguished from "nonsense." Issues of "method" centered on examinations of "induction" and its relation to "deduction."[12]

Hayek, who knew members of the Vienna Circle and was related by marriage to Wittgenstein, spent the latter half of his life attacking this "method," which he called "constructive rationalism."[13] In his words: "Reason was for the [Cartesian] rationalist no longer a capacity to recognize truth when he found it expressed, but a capacity to arrive at truth by deductive reasoning from explicit premises" (H: 102). Hayek goes on to connect this manner of reasoning with reasoning about institutions and the importance of the Common Law tradition in English thought: "The older tradition, which had been represented by the earlier theorists of the law of nature, survived chiefly in England in the works of the great common lawyers, especially Sir Edward Coke and Matthew Hale, the opponents of Bacon and Hobbes [both constructive rationalists], who were able to hand on an understanding of the growth of institutions which was elsewhere displaced by the ruling desire deliberately to remake them" (H: 102-3).

Hayek returned to these subjects in *Law, Legislation, and Liberty* in which there are more citations to Hume than to any other person. He here—in substitution for the common distinction between the natural and the artificial—makes use of three Greek terms for which he provides his own translations: *physei* ("'by nature'"), *nomoi* ("best rendered as 'by convention'") and *thesei* ("which means roughly 'by deliberate decision'"). Of special interest is the *nomoi*: "... a distinct third class of phenomena [distinct from natural and artificial], later described by Adam Ferguson as 'the result of human action but not of human design.'" Recognizing the existence of and understanding this class of phenomena—neither natural nor consciously made—are crucial to understanding the truly "social" sciences. Two disciplines have typically, though not always self-consciously, done so: law and economics. It was to these processes that the founder of economics Adam Smith referred in the oft-maligned phrase "invisible hand." Far-seeing Reason has not constructed from its own wisdom the institutional arrangements which permit great societies to flourish, and it is not capable of massive reconstruction. (Thus, revolutionaries such as Danton and Robespierre and the Old Bolsheviks were destroyed by the revolutions they helped to bring about.) On the other hand, "...the so-called anti-rationalists [Bernard Mandeville and Hume] insist that to make reason as effective as possible requires an insight into the limitations of the powers of conscious reason and into the assistance we obtain from processes of which we are not aware..." (LLLi: 29). These two approaches to reasoning about institutions are illustrated: "We find one great tradition extending from the ancient Greeks and Cicero through the Middle ages to the classical liberals like John Locke, David Hume, Immanuel Kant and the Scottish moral philosophers, down to various American statesmen of the nineteenth and twentieth centuries, for whom law and liberty could not exist apart from each other; while to Thomas Hobbes, Jeremy Bentham and many French thinkers and the modern legal positivists law of necessity means an encroachment of freedom"

(LLLi: 52; footnotes omitted).

The obvious issue raised by this approach is the limited role played by reasoning in social and political change. Everything important at first seems assigned to the unforeseen consequences of self-interested acts. The role of reason in the "great tradition" referred to by Hayek is not the starring one assigned by rationalists and revolutionaries, but neither is reason driven from the stage entirely. In discussing his *History* in one of his letters, Hume said that his "views of *things* are more conformable to Whig principles; my representations of *persons* to Tory prejudices" (Quoted CL: 263, emphasis in the original). The complementarity of lines of reasoning with portraits of character has been discussed in the chapters on Cicero and Frankfurter. Hayek provides a kind of gloss on this in the postscript to *The Constitution of Liberty*, "Why I Am Not a Conservative." In brief, Hayek thinks most conservatives flow with the dominant current of history but simply backstroke enough to slow their movement. He, on the other hand, swims in a direction determined by his principles, toward liberty.

Hayek provides an example of the important but limited role of reason in a quotation which, in contemplation of the common law, sheds light on the task which faces a judge:

> The distinct character of the rules which the judge will have to apply, and must endeavor to articulate and improve, is best understood if we remember that he is called in to correct disturbances of an order that has not been made by anyone and does not rest on the individuals having been told what they must do. In most instances no authority will even have known at the time the disputed action took place what the individuals did or why they did it. The judge is in this sense an institution of a spontaneous order. He will always find such an order in existence as an attribute of an ongoing process in which the individuals are able successfully to pursue their plans because they can form expectations about the actions of their fellows which have a good chance of being met....It is only as a result of individuals observing certain common rules that a group of men can live together in those orderly relations that we call a society....No group is likely to agree on articulated rules unless its members already hold opinions that coincide in some degree....Persons differing in their general values may occasionally agree on, and effectively collaborate for, the achievement of particular concrete purposes, but such agreement on particular ends will never suffice for forming the lasting order which we call a society. (LLLi: 95)

In the third volume of *Law, Legislation, and Liberty*, Hayek says that sometimes the legal system, in its slow accrual, makes errors which take it on a wrong turn. In such a situation, substantial change may be necessary in the laws or the constitution. He proposes drastic separation of the institutions for making the general rules or laws which are guidelines for individual behavior from the institutions which make the "laws" for the administration of government. The conditions of society change, so we must constantly make changes in the personnel of government, the rules of private behavior, and even the constitution. The more extreme the changes we make, however, the more unpredictable the outcome. Whatever pride we take in our intellectual constructs, we are always building on—even as we depart from—what is currently the case. We carry with us all sorts of unrecognized habits, prejudices, and assumptions. We shall return to this after examining the commentary of David W. Livingston.

3. Livingston

Livingston, like Hayek, believes that Hume must be understood through consideration of all of his works: he must not be trifurcated into philosopher, essayist, and historian. While Hayek relies mostly on the *Treatise* and the two *Enquiries*, Livingston also makes great use of the *History* and the essays and provides a far more detailed analysis of Hume's position. In a simple comparison, we may say that Hayek expands upon Hume for the general, educated reader while Livingston corrects, clarifies, and explicates Hume for the professional philosopher. It should be noted that Livingston makes no reference whatsoever to Hayek's work, completed a decade before Livingston published. Their interpretations are congruent but independently arrived at. Livingston makes many interesting additions to our understanding of Hume's views on institutional growth, but central for this discussion is his examination of Hume's "philosophy of common life."

As was said above, we are always of necessity building on where we are. We cannot think our way onto some perfectly "objective" ground, and we cannot instantly reconstruct humanity to our wishes. As Livingston frequently remarks, we have no place outside our experience to provide a fulcrum for an Archimedean lever with which to move the world. Even the most objective or abstract philosopher is to a considerable degree a product and captive of her or his background and circumstances. To achieve as much objectivity as possible, Cicero (though he does not use the term "objectivity") reviews what the several philosophical schools have to say about important issues so that the prudent man of affairs can decide upon some probable course of action—some kind of "middle ground" from the point of practicality. Livingston finds, in Hume's idea of the "common life," a far more adequate statement of this "middle ground."

The Pied Piper who led Western philosophy astray, for Livingston as for Hume and Hayek, is Descartes (CL: pp. 275 ff.). His method of doubt is an instrument for the ultimate achievement of certainty—that is, for the pursuit of a false hope, a will-o'-the-wisp. Cartesianism, what Hayek calls "constructive rationalism," found its way into practical affairs where it has a result comparable to Platonism by making a distinction between the world of here and now and a much better, and supposedly realizable, ideal world.

Two brief asides may clarify this point. One of the most famous outcomes of the Cartesian view of knowledge is Rousseau's paradoxical opening of *The Social Contract:* "Man is born free, but he is everywhere in chains." This language has inspired many and is often said to have influenced the coming of the French Revolution, despite or perhaps because of its paradoxical quality. A person is "born free" only on an assertion of principle and scarcely describes the condition of a new-born nor the circumstances (including a lot of "investment") which result in an adult competent to act freely in society.

While many political reformers and revolutionaries were influenced by the Cartesian approach, it found fertile ground also in what might seem a quite implausible place—the common thought patterns of Americans. Not all western thinkers were led astray by Descartes; and one of the exceptions was the shrewdest observer of the United States, Alexis de Tocqueville. Tocqueville begins the second volume of *Democracy in America* with a chapter on the "Philosophical Method of the Americans." "America," he writes, "is therefore one of the countries where the precepts of Descartes are least studied and are best applied. Nor is this surprising. The Americans do not read the works of Descartes, because their social condition deters them from speculative studies; but they follow his maxims...." The principal result of this method is to demand clarity and simplicity in all things, whether or not the subject matter is amenable to such clarification and simplification. Tocqueville elaborates (in a passage which sheds light on contemporary media intrusion into private lives):

> ...each American appeals only to the individual effort of his own understanding [and] fixes [his] standard of judgment in [himself] alone....Thus they fall to denying what they cannot comprehend....As it is on their own testimony that they are accustomed to rely, they like to discern the object which engages their attention with extreme clearness; they therefore strip off as much as possible all that covers it; they rid themselves of whatever separates them from it, they remove whatever conceals it from sight, in order to view it more closely and in the broad light of day. This disposition of mind soon leads them to condemn forms, which they regard as useless and inconvenient veils placed between them and the truth.[14]

The result of this tendency of thought is that "the tie that unites one generation to another is relaxed or broken....Everyone...makes it his boast to form his opinions on all subjects. Men are no longer bound together by ideas, but by interests; and it would seem as if human opinions were reduced to a sort of intellectual dust, scattered on every side, unable to collect, unable to cohere."[15]

To return to Livingston and Hume, Livingston argues that the Pyrhhonism of Book 1 of *A Treatise of Human Nature* is an attack on Cartesianism and is designed to prove that "philosophy conceived as an autonomous and ultimate inquiry leads to absurdity" (CL: 23). So conceived, philosophy is false.

> False philosophy has many forms ranging from religious superstition to
> metaphysics, but they are all cases of seeking, by way of the autonomy
> principle, some Archimedean point outside the prejudices and customs of
> common life from which the order as a whole can be judged....false philosophy
> in politics leads to a frame of mind we may call metaphysical rebellion: the
> conceptual destruction of the authority of the prejudices and customs that
> constitute the order of common life. The order as a whole is viewed as
> illegitimate and the Archimedean principles which lead to this judgment are
> logically of a type that make it impossible to discern the goods and evils that
> exist within common life, and so make it impossible to reform that order.
> (CL: 6)

Hume's philosophy is not intended as a justification of the status quo but as a way
to successful, because realistic, reform. To comprehend this philosophy requires
a vision of Hume's entire body of work and the way he views history as giving
specificity and content to the general principles of "human nature."

Livingston argues that most commentators on Hume have completely misunderstood the central role of historical perspective. Livingston here explicates
the insight which was of such central interest to Hayek. "The concept of convention is, perhaps, the most important in Hume's philosophy. A Humean convention
is not the result of conscious agreement but is arrived at over time as the unin-
tended result of man's involvement with the world and with his fellows. The
concepts that it is the task of true philosophy to bring to light (language, justice,
religion, causality) are housed in the rules and principles that are implicit in a
historically developed convention" (CL: 4). These "conventions" constitute what
a community of persons share in common; they define the community. They are,
moreover, specific to a specific historic community except insofar as and until
they can be abstracted and refined by "true philosophy" which can then be related
to other historic communities. None of us is "simply a human being" who can
philosophize as such: we are all someone from somewhere. Our intellect, however one defines that, takes its origin in a particular cultural tradition and can
only, with effort, reach out from that beginning toward and into other traditions.
To be realistic, one must accept that "true philosophy...presupposes the authority
of common life as a whole. A reformed version of the autonomy principle [which
asserts that 'philosophy has an authority to command belief and judgment independent of the unreflectively received beliefs, customs, and prejudices of common life'] survives: philosophy may form abstract principles and ideals to criticize any judgment in common life; what it cannot do, on pain of total skepticism,
is throw into question the whole order" (CL: 3).

Tocqueville makes a derivative point. Not only is there no Archimedean
point from which to criticize the whole; but there is also not the time to critique
each part:

There is no philosopher in the world so great but that he believes a million things on the faith of other people and accepts a great many more truths than he demonstrates. This is not only necessary but desirable. A man who should undertake to inquire into everything for himself could devote to each thing but little time and attention....He must therefore make his choice from among the various objects of human belief and adopt many opinions without discussion in order to search the better into that smaller number which he sets apart for investigation.[16]

Livingston provides us with a detailed comparison of the relation of valid philosophical work to the common life as Hume understood this relation:

The moral world is a set of conventions which have developed unreflectively over time. The task of philosophy is to bring to explicit awareness the standards implicit in these conventions.... They were hammered out, unreflectively, over long periods of time as constituents of the process of common life, and cannot be known without an understanding of their history....The idea or rationale of the convention can be grasped only after it is established....Philosophers may criticize and reform these standards but only on condition that they recognize their independent authority; failure to do so yields total Pyrrhonism. (CL: 247-248; notes omitted)

Philosophy has a critical function, but philosophers must recognize that they cannot step outside the everyday universe in performing this function. As Livingston puts it:

In Hume's conception, philosophy must begin *within* the frame-work of common life, for in the end "we can give no reason for our most general and most refined principles, beside our experience of reality; which is the reason of the mere vulgar, and what it required no study at first to have discovered" [T,xviii]. What [philosophers] can do is become self-conscious of the practices of common life, codify these, discover their rationale, order them into systems, and correct them by reference to their coherence with other practices: "philosophical decisions are nothing but the reflections of common life, methodized and corrected" [EU, 162]. (CL: 24)

Livingston formulates and reformulates to convey his meaning. His interpretation of Hume is well summarized by a comparison:

The judgments of common life are concrete, particular, and provincial; those of philosophy are abstract, universal, and cosmopolitan. Yet philosophical judgments are parasitic upon the authority of those very provincial judgments of common life which it seeks to correct. (CL: 251)

The "common life" from which Hume operated was that of Britain and more broadly Western Europe. As Livingston uses the phrase, "common life" itself is an abstraction—a generalization from what was only partially shared between Englishmen and Scotsmen and to a diminishing degree with the French, Germans, and so on. Livingston does not address the distinctness and possible convergence of high cultures, only the relation of the civilized to the "barbarian" (CL: 235-246). The difficulty of studying the latter is that of understanding "the rationale behind their actions" (CL: 241) because the barbarians do not fully understand themselves. By definition, they are "virtually unreflective." The barbarian "lacks the cosmopolitan idea of himself as a human being" (CL: 240). The relation of high cultures will be addressed further below. The conventions of the "common life" of Hume's own experience, however, were given concreteness in his *History*. According to Livingston:

> That there are such conventions [of justice and political order] at all is due to tenselessly conceived structures: the nature of the world (scarce goods) and certain original human propensities (limited benevolence). But beyond this we cannot understand the principles of justice and politics without some grasp of the history of how men have become aware of these principles in their own experience and what they have thought about their significance. This would be the story of man's progressive self-awareness of the principles of civil society, and would be the story of civilization....[The story line] is concretely presented in the *History*, one main theme of which is the story of how the principles of civility became established in Britain. (CL: 249)

4. Toward Humanity

The word "civilization" apparently appeared first in France, perhaps used by Mirabeau who later played an important role in the coming of the French Revolution. Its first recorded use in English is in Boswell who failed to persuade Dr. Johnson to include the word in his dictionary.[17] The word was used to refer to a general level of civility envisioned to be most fully achieved at that time in Europe but potentially global, that is, applicable to all people. Writers using the term were, as we would now say, "Eurocentric"; but they recognized that a high level of civility had also been reached by the Chinese and Persians. Much of Edmund Burke's impeachment of Warren Hastings in the last quarter of the century was based on the argument that Hastings had behaved in an uncivilized fashion toward highly civilized people in India. In its original meaning, "civilization" referred to a level of conscious cultivation which could be reached by any people - not to different "civilizations."

Beginning perhaps late in the nineteenth century and now commonly in this century, the word "culture," typically in the plural "cultures," has been used to refer to distinct traditions defined by language group, nationality, ethnicity, or so forth. ("Or so forth" seems to be almost infinitely open-ended with a progression of new "cultures" defining themselves to become eligible for participation in "multiculturalism.") Starting even with the use of multiple "civilizations" and now typically with the use of "cultures," the issue arises about the incommensurability or, to the contrary, the hierarchical ordering of these traditions (relativist versus absolutist).

For Hume, the "common life" is shared among everyone who can understand one another, that is, to a considerable degree grasp one another's motives. According to Livingston, Hume originally dismissed the pre-Roman and Dark Age occupants of Britain as "barbarians" precisely because he thought one could not grasp their motives but only describe their movements. He later modified his view of the Anglo-Saxons in a review of another person's book on English history which gave him access to the "rational interior [of the Anglo-Saxons], however historically alien they [at first appeared]" CL: 246-247). The extent of the "common life" is an empirical matter: it is "common" just so far as it is in fact common. Nothing precludes the boundaries being gradually extended by the inclusion of newly-shared experiences. For that matter, nothing precludes the boundaries being constricted by the narrowing of the shared humanity.

Hume began writing his *History* with the Stuart regime because, in Livingston's interpretation, he could grasp the motives of the actors more fully than for earlier periods. This helps to explain his remark about preferring Whig principles but Tory personalities. As individuals, King Charles and his supporters behaved virtuously and conscientiously, while the Roundheads behaved like political and religious fanatics. But changes were occurring in the society and the economy which neither party understood. They actively misunderstood those changes, with violent results. At the time of the English Civil War, "deep social and economic changes, with political implications, were occurring that neither the Commons nor the Crown understood....these changes, which were felt but not understood, were given theological and metaphysical interpretations so that what should have been a question of common life, namely, reasonably adjusting a historical constitution to changing historical conditions, hardened into a metaphysical question, placing the contending parties in implacable opposition" (CL: 261).

Hume believed in the principles of liberty which were advanced by the experiences of the seventeenth century and were identified with the Whigs, but he thought the Whigs of his own day mistook the origins and nature of their own principles. The Whigs read "the present constitution into the remote past" of the Saxon forests and thought the Commons party of the previous century had simply been defending the "ancient liberties." The institutions of English liberty had in fact grown over time (CL: 252-253). The Whigs treated these liberties as timeless and identified them with "natural rights": "This theory [which Hume criticizes] is the application of what I call Cartesianism in politics and is exemplified in the natural-right, original-contract, and natural law theories common in Hume's time" (CL: 7). Assuming a-historical, timeless, and certainly-known political principles is a recipe for disaster: "...Hume's analysis of the Puritan Revolution in *The History of England* closely parallels Burke's analysis of the French Revolution in *Reflections on the Revolution* in France. Both events are seen as cases of the violent intrusion of misplace philosophy into politics..." (CL: 7). The growth of principles of liberty are examined further in the chapter on Burke, but Hume's approach to the "growth" of an historical consensus can be illustrated by examining another topic, aesthetics.

Here we part company with Hayek and Livingston to turn directly to Hume's essay "Of the Standard of Taste." In 1758, this essay was one of the last added to what we now call the *Essays Moral, Political, and Literary*. Hume began publishing his essays in collections beginning in 1741, and they established his reputation in his own lifetime. Over the succeeding years, he both added to the number of essays and rewrote what he had already published.

"Of the Standard of Taste" begins with "every one's observation" of the "great variety of Taste, as well as of opinion, which prevails in the world" (E: 226). In some matters, the variety of opinion is not as great as it first appears, since careful examination of meanings reveals that many disputes are merely about definitions. In other cases, though, disagreement is even greater than appears to be the case since persons using the same general words of approbation and disapproval ("virtuous, "vicious") have quite different specifics in mind. Hume illustrates from the *Iliad*: Achilles' heroism has a good deal more of "ferocity" in it than eighteenth-century civility would find appropriate. What is at issue is the existence of some "standard of taste"—a "rule whereby the various sentiments of men can be reconciled" (E: 229).

Hume addresses and dismisses an old saw, "there is no arguing about taste." (Frank Knight used to say there is no point in arguing about anything else.) Certainly to say, "I like it" is to assert what no one else at that time and place can dispute; only consistency with other more or less comparable occasions can be brought forth. But "another species of common sense" is relevant: we continuously compare and agree upon what is better and worse. Hume employs both a specific story and a general observation to defend the existence of "general principles of approbation or blame, whose influence a careful eye may trace in all operations of the mind" (E: 233). He recounts the story from *Don Quixote* in which two men, asked their judgment of a barrel of wine, both pronounce it quite good though one notes a slight leather-like taste while the other a slight flavor of iron. Their judgments are ridiculed until the barrel is emptied to reveal an iron key on a leather thong. Hume's general observation is that experience reveals some works which have pleased human beings over centuries of change.

Hume is led to believe that "there are certain qualities in objects, which are fitted by nature to produce those particular feelings" of beauty and ugliness (E: 235). That is, like Cicero, Hume believed that our judgments are not completely arbitrary or "relative" but instead depend in some part on the connections of the

characteristics of human beings with the environing world. But, "though the principles of taste be universal, and nearly, if not entirely the same for all men; yet
few are qualified to give judgment on any work of art, or establish their own
sentiment as the standard of beauty" (E: 241). He discusses a number of complications facing any attempt at definitive statement.

Like the winetasters and their critics in *Don Quixote*, we differ in the "perfection" of the relevant "sense or faculty" (E: 236); we are not all equally endowed by nature with the abilities of discrimination. Secondly, we must practice
contemplating beauty, analyzing the parts of a work and their connection to the
"purpose for which it is calculated," and, especially, practice in making compari-
sons (E: 237-240). Thirdly, we must avoid "prejudice"—the intrusion of extraneous considerations into the assessment of the fitness of the work to its desired
effects. Especially, this requires the ability to place oneself "in the same situation
as the audience" for whom the work was created and "make allowance for their
peculiar views and prejudices" (E: 239). We cannot judge the "Venus de Milo"
from the same point of view as we do a Raphael "Madonna," nor even *Huckle-
berry Finn* from the same point of view as a Toni Morrison novel.

Thus, the "standard of taste" has been converted into the qualifications of
the "critic" or, in other words, a person who is capable of judging.

> But where are such critics to be found? by what marks are they to be known?
> How distinguish them from pretenders?...if we consider the matter aright,
> these are questions of fact, not of sentiment. Whether any particular person
> be endowed with good sense and delicate imagination, free from prejudice,
> may often be the subject of dispute, and be liable to great discussion and
> enquiry....Where these doubts occur, men can do no more than in other
> disputable questions, which are submitted to the understanding: They must
> produce the best arguments, that their invention suggests to them; they must
> acknowledge a true and decisive standard to exist somewhere, to wit, real
> existence and matter of fact; and they must have indulgence to such as differ
> from them in their appeals to this standard. (E: 241-242)

Finally, both most troubling and most promising, we must recognize the
role of the "different humors of particular men" and "the particular manners and
opinions" of different countries and different times in judgments of taste. Even
the same, exquisitely prepared, critic may differ in her or his preferences at different times of life. But across the differences of personality and age as well as
the differences of geography and ages, the persons who are both careful and committed can conduct a productive dialogue and find considerable consensus on
great works of beauty. None of us, however, can wholly transcend the baggage of
her or his human upbringing.

Five

BURKE

Edmund Burke is, like Cicero, one of the most acclaimed public speakers in history and was, like Cicero, a "new man"—an outsider to a dominant, largely hereditary aristocracy.[1] Born in 1729 to a middle class Anglo-Irish family in Dublin, Burke inherited two religious traditions: his father was Protestant, his mother Roman Catholic. The likelihood of his being disposed toward religious toleration was perhaps increased by elementary education under a Quaker teacher. Though Burke was a life-long adherent of the Church of England, he had to cope throughout his public life with charges of Catholicism which was at that time still nearly equated with treasonable inclinations. His wife too, though she later followed her husband's faith, came from a mixed background with a Catholic father and a Presbyterian mother. Burke graduated from Trinity College, Dublin, and at his father's insistence went to London to study law. While he found law interesting and seems to have continued his studies informally over many years, he had no wish to practice it and followed his literary and political inclinations instead. He became a member of the famous circle of literature and wit which surrounded Samuel Johnson. By the time Burke entered Parliament in 1766, he had a creditable reputation for his writings.

Burke remained in Parliament, with occasional lapses, until almost the end of his life. He was seldom in the government and was consistently in opposition to the king's party in Parliament until the French Revolution. Though we know from his Parliamentary speeches and his correspondence that he was active in many political controversies, his career has always been closely identified with three great matters: the American Revolution, the impeachment of Warren Hastings for mal-administration in India, and the French Revolution.

1. Interpretations of Burke

Burke's reputation, like that of Cicero earlier and Felix Frankfurter later, has been influenced by an alleged switch from an early "liberalism" to a later "conservatism." In Burke's case, this is allegedly confirmed by his support of the American Colonies in their revolution and his vitriolic opposition to the French revolution. The charge was first leveled against Burke by his erstwhile Parliamentary allies, most notably Charles James Fox, and responded to directly by Burke, especially in his *An Appeal from the New to the Old Whigs*.

We have been warned by the essayist Hazlett that the only way to understand Burke is to read all he wrote. Francis Canavan, S.J., expands upon the point in his essay on Burke:

> The student must pick Burke's philosophy out of the large number of pamphlets, speeches, letters, and polemical tracts which poured from the prolific pen of this unusually gifted practicing politician. Almost everything Burke wrote on politics refers to an immediate issue of his day....To summarize Burke's political thought in series of abstract propositions, therefore, is inevitably to distort the perspective in which he originally expressed it. Brevity, however, requires the distortion.[2]

Reading all of Burke is more than is to be expected of any but the specialist—especially now that his extensive correspondence is also available—but has more merit than the reader may credit.

The same point may be made of each of the persons studied here. Academic skepticism permits much leeway in argumentation: outcomes are unpredictable because the paths of argument are not predetermined and judgment (choice) is required. Thus one needs to see how each problem is addressed and resolved. This is especially true in politics, but it does not preclude generalizations. Each of these authors, for example, is both conservative (slow to make changes) and liberal (committed to freedom) and as a result certain "options" are precluded. "Options" is in quotes because the apparent option is often not really possible, that is, if chosen, it will not have the desired outcome. This is a point Burke makes concisely in a quotation given below.

Burke's writings are full of wise remarks and captivating images, but many today find it difficult to be patient with either his style or substance. His style is complex and florid. (He is considered one of the precursors of the Romantic Movement.) Burke's preoccupation with complexity may seem simply an apology for conservativism or for the rich. His opposition to the French Revolution is not generally compatible with modern assessments even though several of his most dramatic predictions came true. Burke accepted social and economic inequality and the political consequences which flowed from them. Burke's view traces back to the *Old Testament*. He did not foresee the possibility that the world might produce enough to provide a comfortable life for all.[3] The opening up of the "new world" and the development by Adam Smith of ideas about the increase of the wealth of nations raised to the level of possibility what had earlier seemed impossible: that all persons might have enough material wealth to have the leisure necessary for political participation. This idea did not mature until after Burke's time.

The difficulty of Burke is not only the quantity of his writings but also their focus on particular controversies. It is often difficult to assess his comments without a detailed acquaintance with the personalities and issues of the day and, in some cases, without information about what occurred later. His own emphasis was repeatedly and insistently on the circumstances in which action must be taken.

The first challenge in discussing Burke is thus to determine where to focus. So much is colorful, insightful, and highly quotable. How is the analyst to select? The principles a reader finds in Burke may be all too dependent on the principles the reader carries to Burke. It is my own thesis that the consistency of Burke arises from his understanding of the role and limitations of reason in human affairs—the position I identify as the combination of academic skepticism with constitutionalism. His philosophy does not depend simply, as has been argued, on his personal or conservative attachment to the interests of the Whig aristocracy or, on the other hand, to a conservative "natural law" philosophy. In my view, he is as much "liberal" as "conservative"—a lover of liberty who expresses a prudent caution rather than a deep-seated hostility toward change.

Two terms—"experience" and "precedent"—are used repeatedly by Burke and seem intimately connected with his principles. The question immediately raised by these terms is how to know what experiences are crucial and what precedents to follow. How do we discover order or meaning in our experience or in history? The late Richard Weaver, himself considered a leading conservative, denied that Burke was truly a conservative. In Weaver's view, a true conservative must have principles while Burke, Weaver thought, was guided merely by circumstance. Weaver's statement deserves quoting:

> It is essential to see that government either moves with something in view or it does not, and to say that people may be governed merely by following precedent begs the question. What line do the precedents mark out for us? How do we know that this particular act is in conformity with the body of precedents unless we can extract the essence of the precedents? And if one extracts the essence of a body of precedents, does not one have a "speculative idea"? However one turns, one cannot evade the truth that there is no practice without theory, and no government without some science of government.[4]

In Weaver's view, Burke's position thus "turns out to be...a position which is defined by other positions because it will not conceive ultimate goals...." Its politics is "a politics without vision....It could almost be said that he raised 'muddling through' to the height of a science...." The indictment is a severe challenge to anyone claiming more for Burke—and indeed for Cicero and Felix Frankfurter— than simply a reputation as a man of affairs.

Biographer and editor Peter J. Stanlis, another conservative praised by no less a founder of modern academic conservativism than Russell Kirk, found in Burke conservative principles of Natural Law and proclaimed Burke "essentially a Thomist."[5] "Burke regarded the Natural Law as a divinely ordained imperative ethical norm which, without consulting man, fixed forever his moral duties in civil society" (73). In pursuing his interpretation of Burke, Stanlis makes many interesting observations about Burke; but his central thesis is most dubious partly because his history and understanding of "natural law" is so loose. Burke's "world of right reason and Nature was the Stoical world of Aristotle and Cicero and the Christian world of St. Thomas and Hooker" (84). Stanlis attributes to Burke the view that the "British constitution [was] merely the practical means of guaranteeing the 'rights' of Natural Law..." (48). Anachronistically placing Aristotle in the Stoical world requires more argumentation than Stanlis offers. Of greater importance, Stanlis does not address the crucial question for Cicero of how we know this natural law and what degree of certainty we can have: the skeptical issue. Stanlis seems not to have followed up seriously on his own assertion: "There is universal agreement among scholars about the early and sustained importance of Cicero's influence on Burke, in matters of style, temperament, and beliefs. Burke read practically everything that Cicero has left us" (36). It is difficult to believe that Stanlis has done likewise.

Stanlis has made the mistake of reading Cicero's *On the Republic* as though Laelius' advocacy of the Stoical position spoke for Cicero. Leo Strauss on the other hand, after reviewing the roles taken by the various characters in the dialogue, recognizes that: "It is misleading to call Cicero an adherent of the Stoic natural law teaching." In terms of relating Burke to his contemporaries, Strauss also offers better insight. Stanlis asserts that "Bentham [was] the logical heir of [Adam] Smith's theory" (56). Strauss says:

> Accordingly, the sound political order for him [Burke], in the last analysis, is the unintended outcome of accidental causation (or "accidental causation modified by the prudential handling of situations as they arose"). He applied to the production of the sound political order what modern political economy had taught about the production of public prosperity: the common good is the product of activities which are not themselves ordered toward the common good.[6]

Although it is not crucial to our argument, we should also note that Stanlis wrongly claims Cicero's *On the Republic* to have been among the list of books in Burke's library "published before the death of Burke in 1797" (265). The volume may well have been among the books when the library was sold in 1833, but the text was not rediscovered in the Vatican Library until 1820.

Stanlis makes a point of disputing the "liberal" interpretation that "Burke was a utilitarian" which Stanlis attributes to John Morley (31). Morley (1838-1923) was a prolific writer on topics political and literary and was representative of the great age of nineteenth-century "classical" liberalism. He published two books about Burke as well as books developing what he considered to be the vital principles of Burke's position. It will be helpful to expand briefly on Morley's understanding here, though one of his books *On Compromise* must be examined in a later chapter since it influenced Felix Frankfurter. Morley had a high opinion of Burke but thought the latter had missed the long-term beneficial effects of the

French Revolution, especially "the greatest of all the positive and constructive forces of the Revolution—the generous and sublime sentiment of the brotherhood of men."[7] Burke had, it is alleged, helped to push the Revolution into its destructive course by the harshness of his attack and its effect on the British ruling class and policy.

To assert that Morley thought Burke a utilitarian is to mislead regarding both Burke and Morley, insofar as the term calls up the shades of Jeremy Bentham and James Mill. Stanlis probably makes this error in part because both Burke and Morley refuse to consider "rights" as absolutes.[8]. Both Burke and Morley appeal to "general advantage" (*cf*. R: 33), but the challenge is to appreciate how they understood this to be arrived at. They certainly did not believe it could be reduced to calculation by a formula such as "the greatest good of the greatest number." Neither did they agree with Stanlis that it established itself by a simple parsing of the natural law. General well-being must be interpreted more loosely. Morley shows us a Burke "whose whole soul was bound up in order, peace, and gently enlarged precedent" and who understood "the elements of social stability, of its priceless value, of its power over the happiness of men."[9]

In pursuing Burke's understanding of experience and precedent, we shall look at three questions: What is Burke's view of language and what does that imply about principles? More specifically, how does Burke understand liberty, his lifelong concern and a matter about which, if anywhere, he must have held principles permitting him to separate true from false, beneficial from harmful precedents? Finally, what can we learn from Burke about human nature and social change? We shall, that is, be asking the questions of skepticism and constitutionalism.

2. Language and Meaning

Burke was quite familiar with academic skepticism. He knew Hume personally and was, as Stanlis attests, well-read in the writings of Cicero. His own contributions to the tradition are especially his insights into the problems of language and the relation of "metaphysical" to operational definitions, into the slow experimental growth of institutions and of human nature itself, and into the process by which we reach toward our common humanity.

As an example of his acquaintance with the tradition, in the preface to the second edition of his first book, *A Philosophical Enquiry into the Origin of our Ideas of the Sublime and Beautiful,* Burke refers to "Cicero, true as he was to the Academic philosophy" and quotes—or rather misquotes—from the *Academica* (S: 5-6; emphasis in the original). Modes of thought derived from this skeptical approach are scattered through Burke's writings.

Elaborating on Burke's views of the role and limits of reason plausibly starts with his view of language—that in which principles, once they are discovered, are expressed. In the *Enquiry*, Burke first makes a distinction between what he calls "aggregate words" and "simple abstract words." "Aggregate words" refer to "ideas united by nature," exemplified by "man," "horse," and "tree." They are the primary unities of which our experience consists. "Simple abstract words" consist of "one simple idea" such as "red" and "round." These were, for Burke, more simple than aggregate words and yet more abstract.

We shall especially concern ourselves with a third type of words, "compounded abstract words." "The common notion of the power of...words...is that they effect the mind by raising in it the ideas of those things for which custom has appointed them to stand." But of compounded abstract words this is not true. "No body, I believe, immediately upon hearing the sounds, virtue, liberty, or honor, conceives any precise notion of the particular modes of action and thinking" which these words somehow suggest (E: 163-165).

Compounded abstract words, "whatever power they may have on the passions" do not create "any representation raised in the mind of the things for which they stand. As compositions, they are not real essences, and hardly cause...any real ideas." "Such words are in reality but mere sounds; but they are sounds...wherein we receive some good, or suffer some evil, or see others affected with good or evil; or which we here apply to other interesting events or things; and being applied in such a variety of cases that we know readily by habit to what things they belong, they produce in the mind, whenever they are afterwards mentioned, effects similar to those of their occasions" (E: 163-165).

Our understanding of these words and the effect of these words on our minds are quite different. For Burke, we apply these words "in such a variety of cases" which, while somehow hanging together and suggesting to us good or evil effects, still raise no one particular image or idea before our mind. In fact, we employ such a term in a number of different, though vaguely related, contexts. Burke did not suggest that we might not properly try to find some commonness which inheres in all of those instances where we might, for example, use the word "liberty"; but he was inclined to be extremely cautious about such attempts. For example, he wrote, "metaphysics cannot live without definition, but Prudence is cautious how she defines" (A: 20). He had a certain willingness for the mind to explore such matters, play as it were with them, but he felt a great caution about acting on such investigations. Playful thought and even playful action must always keep in mind that ideas and acts have effects. Much of the *Reflections* concerns consequences, existent and anticipated, of the ideas of Rousseau and other "metaphysical" thinkers.

Burke also addresses the academic connection of character and argument. For example, referring to the "right of taxation" and the "general principle of legislation," Burke says: "These are deep questions, where great names militate against each other, where reason is perplexed, and an appeal to authorities only thickens the confusion; for high and reverend authorities lift up their heads on both sides, and there is no sure footing in the middle" (C: 78-79). This is a generalization of Cicero's dialogues of notable people and sounds very like the conclusion of the *Academica*. Commenting on the "Revolution Society" which had sent its complements to the French Assembly, Burke says: "Their signatures ought, in my opinion, to have been annexed to their instrument. The world would then have the means of knowing how many they are; who they are; and of what value their opinions may be, from their personal abilities, from their knowledge, their experience, or their lead and authority in this state" since the document could not be judged from the strength of the argument itself (R: 5-6; on "authority" and "men of consequence," see 48).

The general discussion of words can be illuminated by turning to the particulars of Burke's leading principle. Liberty is listed as one of the compounded abstract words in the *Enquiry*. Burke repeats his view of such words in a letter of 1789 to Monsieur Dupont in France, the man to whom the *Reflections on the Revolution in France* was addressed: "You have kindly said that you began to love freedom from your intercourse with me. Permit me then to continue our conversation, and to tell you what the freedom is that I love, and that to which I think all men entitled. This is the more necessary because, of all the loose terms in the world, liberty is the most indefinite" (W: 420).

At various points in his writings, Burke attempts to get at what is common to all of the different uses of the word. Perhaps the best of these is very close to nineteenth-century formulations of liberty: "whatever each man can separately do, without trespassing on others, he has a right to do for himself" (R: 67). This is put another way in the letter to Dupont in distinguishing "solitary, unconnected, individual, selfish liberty" from "social freedom" which is "that state of things in which liberty is secured by equality of restraint." "To give freedom...only requires to let go the rein" (R: 288-289). But proper freedom is "but another name for justice; ascertained by wise laws, and secured by well construed institutions." Proper freedom in all of its forms is required for progress in virtue. It is thus a prerequisite to all of those things in which human beings perfect themselves (W: 420).

In his "Letter to the Sheriffs of Bristol" Burke asked rhetorically what a free government is and, in answering, addresses the effect of the words: "for any practical purpose it [free government] is what the people think so—and that they, and not I, are the natural, lawful, and competent judges in the matter" (W: 202). One of the central complications in making a useful "metaphysical" definition is that people do not typically want to do all things or think it fair that all things be done at any given place or time. Thus those things that are the concern of freedom cannot be definitively catalogued.[10] Freedom can be identified by a feeling which accompanies the use of the word: when "I have that inward and dignified consciousness of my own security and independence, which constitutes, and is the only thing which does constitute, the proud and comfortable sentiment of freedom in the human breast" (W: 334).

We may summarize to make a metaphysical definition of liberty in the following terms: liberty is a state of political and social arrangements which permits to each person the opportunity to cultivate an inner dignity and which can arise only when consciousness of security is balanced with absence of restraint. Such a definition is interesting but tells us little, for it leaves us without specifics for cultivating these particular feelings.

In his letter to Dupont, Burke offers another way of telling what that freedom is which he loves and to which he thinks all men entitled. He proceeds to enumerate the variety of laws, rights, and political institutions and procedures necessary if a "solid and rational scheme of liberty" is to be in effect among a people. All of these laws, rights, and institutions were formulated by many people over centuries of experimentation. They include legal security for the life and property of the individual, freedom of movement, speech, and self-development, and fair compensation for property taken by the state. They include an authoritative, independent, freely-chosen legislature which: controls the military; is made up of legislators working responsibly and not simply concerned with their own election; produces legislation directed to the long-run economic well-being of the nation; respects the rights of individuals; and protects the nation from foreign dangers. They include a properly constituted, independent judiciary with regular, fair modes of proceeding and rules of decision, free from external interference, and following clear, equitable, promulgated laws. Such would be a society we call free and such the context in which we would use the word liberty (W: 421-423).

Long experience has proved that these laws and institutions are necessary for a free society. They do not exhaust the possibilities for operating principles. Presumably other principles can be created and articulated. Conceivably conditions might change so that one or another of the existing principles could loose much of its significance without diminishing freedom. These principles are founded in the nature of man but yet developed over many generations by the trials, experience, and wisdom of many people. They establish the conditions in which people have in fact felt free.

The liberal institutions of a society cohere, but only imperfectly. Such institutions, with an adequate degree of coherence, permit some feeling of freedom. But this feeling of freedom is not the "existential freedom" to make oneself through action but general attachments—to the words "freedom" and "liberty," to a set of institutions, and to a set of feelings and images evoked by the words and institutions. Burke illustrates this in his speech *On Conciliation*: "[The American colonists, having come from England] are therefore not only devoted to liberty, but to liberty according to English ideas, and on English principles. Abstract liberty, like other mere abstractions, is not to be found. Liberty inheres in some sensible object; and every nation has formed to itself some favorite point, which by way of eminence becomes the criterion of their happiness" (C: 59). Burke asserts that English history had located that point in taxation (and thus, the central popularity of "no taxation without representation").[11]

Understanding liberty, for Burke, means turning to one's own traditions.

> The [English] Revolution [of 1688] was made to preserve our *ancient*, indisputable laws and liberties and that *ancient* constitution of government which is our only security for law and liberty. If you are desirous of knowing the spirit of our constitution and the policy which predominated in that great period which has secured it to this hour, pray look for both in our histories, in our records, in our acts of parliament, and journals of parliament, and not in [the speeches of philosophizers]. (R: 35; emphasis in the original)

Burke's effort to find a prudential definition of liberty may seem frustratingly vague and prolix. It shows similarities to the efforts which dominated British philosophy in the middle of this century and are associated with Ludwig Wittgenstein. In his preface to the *Philosophical Investigations*, Wittgenstein wrote of exploring meaning as one would wander back and forth over a field—noting first one and then another aspect of the field, eventually coming to know it very well, but never able to put that "knowing" down on paper in a completely organized and definitive way. After examining the meaning and use of such words as "Werkzeuge" ["tools"] and "Spiele" ["games"], Wittgenstein concluded that we must not over-simplify our understanding of the meaning of a word and suggests that instead "we see a complicated network of similarities overlapping and crisscrossing: sometimes overall similarities, sometimes similarities of detail." He went on to suggest that he could "think of no better expression to characterize the similarities than 'family resemblance'."[12]

Wittgenstein, like Burke, turns us from preoccupation with finding one definition of a term which will serve us in all circumstances and at all times and instead directs us to examine the context in which the word is used. A proper understanding retains a sense of the diverse and complex. Wittgenstein employed no such simple distinction of types of words as Burke employed in the *Philosophical Enquiry*, and his understanding of meaning as use is more comprehensive than Burke's examination of compounded abstract words. In each case though, we are turned from efforts to find one comprehensive, completely adequate definition.

Wittgenstein sees "the speaking of language" as "part of an activity, or of a form of life."[13] The meanings of words must thus be examined in the contexts of life and of ways of behaving which may vary from culture to culture and period to period, although the words which Wittgenstein examined appear to pertain to experiences and behavior common to many or all traditions. Even words which we associate with what we consider "obviously common" aspects of human experience may raise difficulties, though. The many Innuit words for what in English is simply "snow" is an oft-cited example. I have not followed the later history of "linguistic analysis" sufficient to know whether any of Wittgenstein's successors have pursued cross-language studies or even explored possible subtle differences between Wittgenstein's German and his translators' English.

Wittgenstein's thoughts and his writings, at once particular and elusive, were addressed to professional philosophers; Burke's, particular and illuminating, were addressed to the political public, both politicians and voters. Wittgenstein was interested in logic, epistemology, and psychology. Burke's exploration of meaning came only in part from philosophical study and was primarily influenced by his observations and efforts in politics. Each nonetheless abandoned the effort to find one thing in common to all the uses of a particular word, opposed the picture theory of meaning, and turned instead to the examination of the diverse aspects of the contexts in which terms are used.

This meant, for Wittgenstein, that meaning must be examined as a part of human activity and ways of behaving. After exploring the interpretation of meaning as the "obeying of a rule," Wittgenstein remarked that "'obeying a rule' is a practice. And to *think* one is obeying a rule is not to obey a rule. Hence it is not possible to 'obey a rule privately'; otherwise thinking one was obeying a rule would be the same as obeying it." He goes on to say: "The common behavior of mankind is the system of reference by means of which we interpret an unknown language."[14] The meanings of words must thus be considered in the contexts of life and of ways of behaving which—although Wittgenstein did not discuss this in the *Philosophical Investigations*—may vary from culture to culture and period to period. This sentence must be qualified by the fact that I have read none of Wittgenstein's works translated and published after *Remarks on the Foundations of Mathematics*.

For Burke the meaning of a word such as liberty has to be examined in terms of the history and institutions of particular peoples. We can only imagine a period in the future when liberty and all of its cognates in the many languages will be truly universal.

For both Burke and Wittgenstein, reason both leads and misleads. One of its ways of misleading is to produce simple definitions in those moments we are thinking about meaning. Such definitions then hide from us the many ways we normally use the words in question and the many conditions which must be present for their employment. The result is a kind of "philosopher's problem." Burke repeatedly warns of the dangers of "metaphysics"—of geometric reasoning and abstraction and says that "no rational man ever did govern himself by abstractions and universals." He did not "put abstract ideas wholly out of any question; because under that name I should dismiss principles, and without the light of sound, well-understood principles, all reasoning in politics, as in everything else, would be only a confused jumble of particular facts and details....A statesman differs from a professor in an university: the latter has only the general view of society; the former, the statesman, has a number of circumstances to combine with those general ideas...." He calls one who ignores circumstances "metaphysically mad" (W: 313). For Wittgenstein, "Philosophy [done properly] is a battle against the bewitchment of our intelligence by means of language....What we [Wittgenstein himself] do is to bring words back from their metaphysical to their everyday usage."[15]

The linguistic concerns of Burke and Wittgenstein are not the same. Wittgenstein makes his famous explanation of purpose in question-answer form: "What is your aim in philosophy?—To show the fly the way out of the fly-bottle."[16] Burke's concerns were political and practical. Too simple a view of the meaning of words can have markedly bad effects in politics. What is at issue is not simply a bedroom ailment of philosophers. Treatment for the political ailment is a careful examination of the traditions and institutions of particular nations, formulations of problems and possible solutions that are adequate to the complexities of people and circumstances, and avoidance of blind adherence to the past as well as of extravagant optimism or careless relativism.

3. The Grounding and Growth of Principles

Before we turn to the content and origin of Burke's principles of government, some of the impressions conveyed by such phrases as "mere metaphysics" and "abstract theorizing" which appear so frequently in Burke require further explanation. In a speech of 1782, he said "I do not vilify theory and speculation: no, because that would be to vilify reason itself.... No—whenever I speak against theory, I mean always a weak, erroneous, fallacious, unfounded, or imperfect theory..." (W: 332). Where then are we to get strong, sound theories; and how are we to distinguish the sound from the weak?

Principles, for Burke, arise from the nature of things and of human beings. To examine this connection in detail would take us into the sort of controversy concerning natural law which arises in discussion of Cicero. That controversy can be avoided with Burke as with Cicero by reminding ourselves of the skeptical approach—whatever we "know" of things and of humankind, we know only imperfectly and can express only inexactly. Both the world and human beings have their own kinds of orders. We can perceive these orders only imperfectly, but even so the perceptions reveal principles. Principles are both summaries of previous experiences and guides to further action: both conclusions and starting points. They are part of on-going response to circumstance. These principles are not only hard to arrive at but also can only be articulated tentatively. They typically take years of experimentation and reflection on the part of many people before they come to find some generally acceptable, common expression. The discovery of truth for Burke as for Cicero centers in the practical person rather than in the scholar. For Burke, true political principles are defined prudentially by many people acting together through history and not metaphysically by the lonely philosopher in the study.

How do we go about finding these principles? First, a kind of preparatory bath seems necessary to divest ourselves of pride and great expectations. True humility, "is the low, but deep and firm foundation of all real virtue" (W: 512). The first of all virtues, as I have noted, is said to be prudence. That is, before we can begin to comprehend whatever it is that prudence does comprehend, we must be extremely aware of the difficulties we face and the limitations of our particular intellects. We must do this while not forgetting that there is something to understand. The whole world is not reduced to a dream by the weakness of reason. The consequence for the realm of action is that we should make extreme moves only when driven by necessity. We should not casually make drastic moves except when compelled by circumstance. Thus, for example, Burke found the French revolutionaries to have proceeded in a misguided pride, eschewing proper humility.

"I must see with my own eyes; I must in a manner touch with my own hands...before I could venture to suggest any political project whatsoever" (W: 507). There is a kind of acquaintance with reality, a kind of knowledge, which is more extensive than that which we can reduce to words. We would certainly say, for example, that we know a friend—indeed we would say we know her or him very well. We can predict how the friend is going to act. We can tell when she is being cruel, as we can tell when he is being kind. And yet I suspect the more thoughtful of us would be slow in attempting a definitive statement about that friend—a statement from which we should be prepared to derive all of our subsequent actions. For Burke, something of the same happens in all one's perceptions. As long as we do not gloss over all that we know, we can begin to have an apprehension even of something as abstract as "the rights of man." Burke says of them "the Rights of Man are in a sort of middle, incapable of definition, but not impossible to be discerned" (R: 71).

We must then start with that which is known to us immediately out of our lives' experiences. We should be extremely cautious with any theory which seems false to those beginnings in our own concrete relationships with other people and to those things we "know" even though we find the reasons for them difficult to enunciate. This does not mean that we may not rise by stages above immediate, face-to-face experience. It does, however, suggest we should build our theories— at least insofar as we expect them to influence our actions—slowly and experimentally, testing them out gradually to insure that they are not false to that which we know immediately.

In Burke's view, human nature is made what it is over time and is best perceived through the study of history and experience. Cicero knew the Roman antiquarians and the great Greek historians and drew especially from Polybius. He saw that the state had grown over time but did not consider the change of humankind over time. Burke drew a somewhat fuller lesson from the ancients. Of the "legislators who framed ancient republics," he says: "They had to do with men, and they were obliged to study human nature. They had to do with citizens, and they were obliged to study the effects of those habits which are communicated by the circumstances of civil life. They were sensible that the operation of this second nature on the first produced a new combination" (R: 215). Burke recognized that the European countries had produced different kinds of communities. More significantly, he recognized that in India there was a distinctively different but highly civilized people deserving of respect and fair treatment. Some parts of human relations trace to our first nature as human beings: the "law of humanity, justice, equity" (W: 406). But he also recognized, for example, that Indians were a "people for ages civilized and cultivated—cultivated by all the arts of polished life, whilst we were yet in the woods" (W: 374) and asserted that their "morality is equal to ours" (W: 399).

This still leaves problems. If a group of Americans try to define the "rights of man," they will probably lapse quickly into divisive controversy. If, on the other hand, the police were to bring a suspect before them and begin torturing the person to extract evidence, most observers would be pretty sure that a violation of human rights was occurring. That is, there is a kind of felt agreement in some cases which we all know when we are not being argumentative. But that felt agreement is within a community. We have heard of societies in which people had or even still have no such reluctance to torture to discover judicial evidence. Thus this dependence on our felt reaction requires a prior dependence on our felt reaction to or connection with a community of other people. The community and its understandings, perceptions, and feelings precede the language of specific philosophic discourse. This is a considerable disadvantage. For Burke, it is a given: we cannot escape the communities into which we are born, although, as I shall explore a bit more in a moment, we can somehow grow with them beyond what they have been.

Unlike most of the American Founding Fathers, Burke was a strong believer in party allegiance. On a number of occasions, from his earliest service in Parliament, he defended the association of parties and of friends on the grounds that this is one of the few ways we can develop the trust and agreement necessary to act. Action beyond the realm of friends and associates is action substantially in the dark, for it is to act by reason unaided by all of the other kinds of knowledge people do, to a degree, possess. And it is to be dependent upon assertions and actions made by those whose competence and honesty we do not know.

Burke's violent objection to the men he thought behind the French Revolution arose from his belief that their theories led them to "temper and harden the breast in order to prepare it for the desperate strokes which are sometimes used on extreme occasions" and to do so before they had tried and found inadequate more moderate solutions. They had "perverted in themselves...all the well-placed sympathies of the human breast" (R: 74). Their theories had hardened their hearts—made possible for them acts they would not in their normal, daily lives have committed. Their theories led most drastically to the execution of men and women for acts not defined as crimes at the time they were done or indeed for no specific act at all but merely for being a member of a particular class or possessing a particular family name.

Humankind is not necessarily permanently confined by the limits of separate communities. We can hope for a progression from all of the many separate communities into which we have been collected toward some ultimate common community of humankind, just as human beings have developed ways of transcending their immediate associations of family and friends in national communities. "To be attached to the subdivision, to love the little platoon we belong to in society, is the first principle (the germ as it were) of public affections. It is the first link in the series by which we proceed toward a love to our country and to mankind" (R: 53; and compare 231). Burke could find, for example, in the moral code and religion of India some common ground that would permit him to feel for and defend the Indians and demand, in his long prosecution of Warren Hastings before Parliament, that the conquering race must abide by a moral code toward the conquered.

We can hope to bring into being a community of humankind in time. This can not be done by flying immediately to some imaginary community that does not exist. It can not be done by being untrue to the good of the communities into which we have been born and in which we exist. Burke, in this respect, was a child of his age—one who believed that the whole world might move toward a standard of conduct acceptable and natural to all which would still not destroy the diversities of individuals and peoples. Peculiarly enough, therefore, for Burke the nature of man "as he ought to be made" remained yet in the future. For Burke, common principles remain to be derived from the common experience of humankind rather than being derived now from definition based on human nature as seen in partial communities. The whole process requires a slow, cautious building up—a search toward what we share in common, an effort to associate that precedes our attempts to define. Burke was no blind conservative. He anticipated progress but feared opportunities would be wasted.

I mentioned above that Burke is commonly considered a precursor of romanticism. I think he was also a precursor of a richer view of humankind than his "philosophe" contemporaries. During Burke's lifetime, the novel as a western literary form was just taking shape. The noun "novel" had been in use in English for some time but had not yet come to be attached solely to such works as *Pamela* and *Tom Jones*. Burke certainly could not have foreseen the novel's potentiality for broadening our sense of a common humanity.

The great European novelists of the nineteenth century reached across lines of Western nationality, time, and social class as they expanded their readers' vi-

,sion of the human condition. The novel in the twentieth century has made an even wider range of experiences available to the literate. Some explore aspects of human activity which many may feel best left in the dark. Books as old as Petronius's *Satyricon* or the eighteenth-century works of the Marquis de Sade are now easily available in cheap translations, and the reading-list has been much expanded in this century. More to the point than this expansion of vision into the marginalia of human experience, however, is the increase both of translations of old works and new works from non-Western sources and the addressing in Western languages of inter-cultural contact. Translations of such works as the eleventh-century Japanese novel by Lady Murasaki, *The Tale of Genji* and the eighteenth-century Chinese *The Story of the Stone* by Cao Xuequin portray societies of delight in beauty and love as well as great inequality. Our insight has been supplemented by authors too numerous to mention except as expressions of personal preference: Kawabata and Mishima from Japan and Mahfouz from Egypt. Vikram Seth's delightful family portrait *A Suitable Boy* is written in English but is aimed at Indian readers as well as Americans or British. E.M. Forster's *A Passage to India* and Paul Scott's *The Raj Quartet* sympathetically detail the ambivalences of inter-cultural relations.

4. Human Nature and Government

As suggested above, the complexities of language—what Madison calls the "inadequateness of the vehicle of ideas"—does not force the statesman to forgo principles or generalities. Certain generalizations can be made which are consistent with the common experiences of political life, though as simplisms they may easily mislead. The significance of the generalizations is subject to reinterpretation as we examine their employment in a variety of issues. With these caveats, Burke's central views can be summarized very briefly. Human nature is complex and human wants and purposes are many. Social and political structures must reflect that complexity and protect those diversities. Reason is very limited, and human ability to deal with the complexities arising from our own nature is very narrow. Progress is achieved by cautious trial and on-going evaluation of success and failure.

The complexity of human nature may tempt us to emphasize either differences or commonnesses. Burke's *Enquiry* starts from the "probability" that the standard of taste and reason is the same in all men and argues that common objects of perception have common effects in men. Burke thus presupposes some common ground founded in biological nature. In the argument of the *Enquiry*, the focus is on the agreement which is present among men rather than on the difference among their tastes. Concern with what is common to humankind produces many references to "natural rights," "natural reasonableness," and even to the "natural equality" of men scattered throughout Burke's writing. Weaver dismisses these references as rhetorical flourishes. Stanlis, on the other hand, has assumed too much from them. They are properly taken as evidence for some "common nature" which springs from basic human construction (whether that be thought of as physiologically or as divinely given). But they do not imply detailed definition of that "nature." Much more significant for political discussion is the fact that we only know human beings as they are the products of history. Even "primitive" people have their stories of the past and attribute their characteristics to the ways of their forebears.

The crucial point is that we do not have access to the individual "natural man," only the historical human being formed in part by the society in which he or she was reared. Any generalizations we make about "human nature," therefore, are conjectures and hypotheses which remain open to reformulation as time passes and we have more "history" to draw upon. We rightly have great confidence in some of our "truths" and "rights"; we cannot be absolutely certain, though, that we shall not have to reformulate them in the future based on new information or analysis.

John Locke, usually considered the founder of the Whig tradition, had derived the essential elements of his argument for limiting the power of government from his view of human character in the "state of nature." These "natural" characteristics included both certain rights and the "reason" in which the rights were founded. (In Thomas Jefferson's popularization, men "are endowed by their creator with certain inalienable rights...."[17]) The problem for Locke was the insecurity of rights, not their existence. For Burke, despite all of his profession of the Whig tradition, reflection does not properly start with the characteristics of human beings in any such "state of nature." Indeed, in his late essay, *An Appeal from the New to the Old Whigs*, he completely redefines the "state of nature" and says that "man is never so perfectly in his natural state but when he is placed where reason may be best cultivated and most predominates. Art is man's nature" (A: 105). To investigate the proper relation between human nature and government, we must consult the histories of particular nations. One of Burke's early literary attempts was an history of England. (He got only as far as King John and did not publish most of what he wrote.) In dealing with the origin of English society, he pictured no Lockean state of nature. Instead, "the Romans conquered Britain and made the Britons exchange a savage liberty for a polite and easy subjection." Culture, civilization, and advanced social organization came to Britain by the force of Roman legions. Early life was primitive, perhaps comparable to that portrayed by Hobbes in his version of the "state of nature" as "brutish, nasty, and short." Burke recognized that all earlier societies began with force—conquest, revolution, or coup—and not with any sort of "contract." Only the passage of time has given legitimacy to these regimes—the "long usage [which] mellows into legality governments that were violent in their commencement" (R: 192).

One of Burke's few resemblances to his contemporary Rousseau is in the following respect: both asserted that the most significant human characteristics from a political point of view arise within society rather than prior to it. This assertion may readily be questioned, especially since Rousseau was not long on consistency. I have in mind Rousseau's treatment of the "social contract" as transforming human beings from "a circumscribed and stupid animal to an intelligent being and a man."[18] Burke and Rousseau have radically different views of the transition from the primitive, however. For Rousseau, a dramatic transition comes through the intervention of some great innovator; and it may be implied that other such sudden innovations may take place in a society which falls short. At least, the French of 1789-1793 drew such implications. For Burke, human beings have made ourselves what we are but only through history, not by a sudden revolution or revelation. We are a product of our communal history. A simile helps to explain Burke's view. Human life together is like a giant flower garden. Each generation tends the parts which were planted earlier as well as planting new sections, sometimes with new types of flowers and sometimes only in new patterns. Now and again one section dies out and must be replanted, but we should not casually or constantly redo all of the older sections; for there are many plants, century plants and such, that grow only slowly and flower infrequently. The growth of civilization is the expansion of the garden as well as the tending of the older sections. Weeding is a necessary part of proper care. (An example of "weeding" is provided by the impeachment of Warren Hastings. The attack on Hastings was sustained for so long, more than a decade, because of Burke's concern with the corrupting influence on British politics as well as his concern for the Indians.[19]) But Burke would never envision, as Rousseau could have done, the tearing up of the entire garden with some vision of starting all over again. Wittgenstein, interestingly enough, compares language to a city: "Our language can be seen as an ancient city: a maze of little streets and squares, of old and new houses, and of houses with additions from various periods; and this surrounded by a multitude of new boroughs with straight regular streets and uniform houses."[20]

This complexity and diversity of human nature for Burke are both facts and facts to be approved.[21] The growth of human nature in appealing and satisfying ways takes place under conditions in which human interests and passions are guided by reason. But reason is not a solitary virtue. This guiding by reason takes place in society and under government; and the society and government must both recognize that diversity and tolerate it. Society, we are told, "is a partnership in all science; a partnership in all art; a partnership in every virtue and in all perfection" (R: 111). Government exists as our device to control our own diversity; "government is a contrivance of human wisdom to provide for human wants....Among these wants is to be reckoned the want...of the sufficient restraint upon their passions" (R: 68). To cultivate and to control human diversity and complexity simultaneously, the structure of government must be complex. Burke, like Madison in *Federalist* 10, believed that the proper government juxtaposes

128   BURKE

the diverse interests in the expectation that the common good will be found as a
kind of middle ground among the conflicting interests. According to Burke, the
ancient French constitution was close to being a proper government and

> possessed that variety of parts corresponding with the various descriptions of
> which your community was happily composed; you had all that combination
> and all that opposition of interests; you had that action and counteraction
> which, in the natural and in the political world, from the discordant powers,
> draws out the harmony of the universe. These opposed and conflicting interests
> which you considered as so great a blemish in your old and in our present
> constitution imposed a salutary check to all precipitate resolutions. They render
> deliberation a matter, not of choice, but of necessity; they make all change a
> subject of *compromise*, which naturally begets moderation; they produce
> *temperaments* preventing the sore evil of harsh, crude, unqualified reformations
> and rendering all the headlong exertions of arbitrary power, in the few or in
> the many, forever impracticable" (R: 40; emphasis in the original).

Here again, the similarity to Madison (in this case *Federalist* 51) is striking. Despite favorable treatment of some of the general principles of the French government, Burke asserted that the government was "full of abuses" (R: 145) and the
aristocracy "not without considerable faults and errors," including "habitual dis-
soluteness of manners, continued beyond the pardonable period of life" (R: 158-
9). What the French needed was reform based on traditional principles, not revolution.

Such a complex form of government is not produced by the genius of the
philosopher. Institutions are the result of discussion, reasoning, and—most of
all—experimenting over much time. Unfortunately, most of those who have been
committed to experimentation ignore or forget one of Burke's most powerful passages.

> The science of constructing a commonwealth, or renovating it, or reforming
> it, is, like every other experimental science, not to be taught *a priori*. Nor is it
> a short experience that can instruct us in that practical science, because the
> real effects of moral causes are not always immediate; but that which in the
> first instance is prejudicial may be excellent in its remoter operation, and its
> excellence may arise even from the ill effects it produces in the beginning.
> The reverse also happens: and very plausible schemes, with very pleasing
> commencements, have often shameful and lamentable conclusions. In states
> there are often some obscure and almost latent causes, things which appear at
> first view of very little moment, on which a very great part of its prosperity or
> adversity may most essentially depend. (R:69)

Rereading this pregnant passage always brings to my mind a modern illustration of well-intentioned but misguided efforts to improve the situation of the

very poor. In the ultimate statement of classical free-market economics, the *Principles of Political Economy*, John Stuart Mill argues on behalf of governmental charity to the poor but with this qualification: "If the condition of a person receiving relief is made as eligible as that of the labourer who supports himself by his own exertion, the system strikes at the root of all individual industry and self-government."[22]

Late in the nineteenth century and during the course of the twentieth, the view became common that because poverty is not the fault of the poor but is the fault of "the economic system," no stigma should be attached to receiving public aid. Since all human beings deserve "respect," nothing should be done in the distribution of public aid to make the recipient "feel inferior"—as for example, by leaving the person without television, telephone, and so forth. Most recently, of course, such aid has become an "entitlement." With all the admirable motives involved, this "plausible scheme" has nonetheless had "lamentable conclusions."

Many of the difficulties of government start with the tendency to approach a problem by assigning guilt or fault either to individuals or to what is now called "the system" when fault actually lies in expecting too much of reason. Guilt or fault seem to lend themselves to quick solutions. In the illustration just mentioned, the standard of living has risen remarkably in the free-market world over the past two hundred years despite the great increase of population. But free markets, like free individuals and free governments, do not work perfectly—only better than the alternatives—in satisfying the unlimited desires of a growing population. Deliberate experiment takes time and the awaiting of results. The institutions of government must insure that adequate time and an experimental approach be taken. This is done by the juxtaposition of the differences among individuals. While complexity in government is not good in itself, "every free constitution is complicated" because it must establish elaborate mechanisms for making decisions and controlling the passions. The end of government is happiness, the happiness of all of the people to be determined by the people themselves, "estimated by their feelings and sentiments, and not by any theories of their rights..." (W: 316).

Those who run the government must include persons of prudence. (In the texts examined here, prudence is restricted to its political applications. The practical reasoning of the courts is not considered until the chapter on Frankfurter. Comments made below about the wealthy being "slow to make changes" seem less applicable to the late twentieth century captains of the corporate world, and I have some doubts about the applicability of the word "prudence" in many cases.) For Burke and all of his predecessors it was a given of the economic world that most people had to spend their time working to get the minimal necessities of life; few people had the leisure to study the complicated subjects of politics in order to cultivate the prudence useful in government. Burke considered prudence to guide a person's action by apprehending the complex world in which he or she operates. Its most notable aspect in reflecting on government is this apprehension of complexity: "The excellence of mathematics and metaphysics is, to have but one thing before you: but he forms the best judgment in all moral disquisitions who has the greatest number and variety of considerations in one view before him, and can take them in with the best possible consideration of the middle results of all..." (W: 321). While even the most poor and illiterate can judge when they are being oppressed, they cannot judge of the "real cause" or the "appropriate remedy" of that which oppresses them.

Burke denied that he was a special friend to aristocracy; but he thought that only among the people of leisure could one hope to find many who have studied politics enough to have cultivated this prudence. Not all aristocrats will have done so, and some who are not aristocrats (Burke himself, for instance) may through good fortune and dedication cultivate prudence. Such persons should be expected to prove themselves; there should be no predisposition in favor of "new men." Burke did not romanticize the poor—the "natural man." Neither did he romanticize the aristocrats: he refers to the "creeping sycophants and the blind, abject admirers of power" who idolize "hereditary wealth" (R: 58-59). He recognized that the wealthy have much to lose by drastic change. Thus, even the stupid among them are likely to be slow to make changes and thus to give more time for reason and discussion to arrive at rational judgement. The true aristocracy of prudence is judged ultimately by the people on its total performance in maintaining and improving a happy society (R: 56-59).

Most people are attached to a government and controlled in their passions and interests by "prejudices" of various kinds and not by reason, even prudential reason. In American public discourse, the word "prejudice" has been so tainted by the bigotry of race that it is scarcely usable. Yet it is hard to find a suitable substitute. Burke means by the word pre-judgment: an intellectual movement from "a" to "m" without consciously rehearsing all the intermediate judgments. While this permits just the sort of "stereotyping" associated with bigotry, it is nonetheless necessary for our intellectual operations. We cannot review all the intermediate steps each time we make a decision and thus cannot function without "prejudices." Our prejudices are sometimes accepted unthinkingly from others and are sometimes the vestiges of our own lines of reasoning. While modern sociobiology may suggest that some prejudices may be "instinctual" in some sense, Burke emphasized that man is "in a great degree a creature of his own making" (R: 105).

Burke thought it a great mistake to imagine that people can associate simply on the basis of their reasoned perception of self-interest. On such a basis, the "commonwealth itself would, in a few generations, crumble away, be disconnected into the dust and powder of individuality, and at length dispersed to all the winds of heaven" (R: 109). People need something more than a "sense of present convenience" (R: 100). "People will not look forward to posterity, who never look backward to their ancestors" (R: 38). By "prejudice" Burke means "ancient opinions and rules of life"(R: 89). These substitute for reason for most people most of the time. A proper system of government is hard to come by, for it can exist only when there is a consensus of many such "prejudices." As an example, Burke points out that when the Romans withdrew from Britain, there were left to lead them "none of those titles to government, confirmed by opinion and long use"; "personal merit" was the "only pretense to power" (W: 70). Good governors must have personal merit, but it is often quite difficult to identify personal merit—to separate the wheat of merit from the chaff of appearance. The post-Roman society failed in the face of the Anglo-Saxon invasions.

This focus on complexity explains Burke's "conservatism." We have become so accustomed to using the "liberal-conservative" contrast that we have ceased to make distinctions in the meaning of "conservative." The following are not exhaustive of earlier meanings: appreciative of the past; cautious about change; and identified with the interests of the wealthy class. Burke's conservatism is often, and mistakenly, identified with the third of these. He was no toady to the rich and did not seek riches for himself. His conservatism is fundamentally of the second sort, but there are some tinges of the first. Two famous early American conservatives were John Adams and Alexander Hamilton; but Adams's focus was on caution in making changes, while Hamilton was an advocate of changes which would promote a rising mercantile-industrial wealthy class.

The options are now compounded by the reversal of meaning in "liberal" referred to elsewhere in this book. Now "conservative" may also mean preferring liberty to equality when the two are in conflict or desiring to limit the role and power of government. "Conservative" is also used to include those enthusiastically attached to religious or moralistic views which have never been central to American religious and moral practice. (It is not uncommon for some "fundamentalists" to attribute religious beliefs to the Founding Fathers which they did not hold.)

As Burke justified his conservatism: "it is with infinite caution that a man ought to venture upon pulling down an edifice which has answered in any tolerable degree for ages the common purposes of society" (R: 70). This is especially apt when some considerable degree of freedom has been enjoyed: "...to form a *free government*, that is, to temper together these opposite elements of liberty and restraint in one consistent work, requires much thought, deep reflection, a sagacious, powerful, and combining mind" (R: 289, emphasis in the original). As we shall see in the next chapter, Felix Frankfurter repeatedly emphasized that a free democracy is the most demanding form of government.[23] Burke appealed repeatedly to the past, to precedent, and to experience. He denigrated the "restless and unstable minds" who explored "mischievous theory" and "mere metaphysics" which he contrasted with "profitable experience."

We thus have before us an idealized picture of a complex political society. The complexity is a response to the diversity of human nature and the variety of human interests, seen both as material and as final causes. The good society is governed by an aristocracy of prudent people who understand complexity and are slow but steady in making improvement in human institutions and conditions. The circumstances of an affluent society mean that governance need not be limited by an hereditary aristocracy, as in Burke's time. Circumstance does not, however, free democratic governors from the need for prudence. Affluence does not mean that ends and means are unlimited nor that the connections of causes and effects become obvious.

5. Reason, in Sickness and in Health

Edmund Burke was the first great critic of the sickness of reason which affects the modern age. Aristotle pointed out that it is a mistake to expect the same degree of exactness out of every subject. Subject matters differ in variability. Oversimplifying, replacing prudence with imagination and hypothetical reasoning, and taking the exceptional for the rule are the great sins which the philosophic disposition may bring upon civil society. Aristotle somewhere says there is truth and beauty but no goodness in mathematics. This should provide a caution to our age of "sophisters, economists, and calculators" (R: 86). Conjectures and speculations not grounded on some basis in common experience and elaborate chains of hypothetical reasoning not tested by cautious experimentation are, as Burke quoted Milton, the "Serbonian bog...where armies whole have sunk" (C: 79).

Focusing on extreme cases rather than on the normal case or on exceptions rather than the rule is equally dangerous. Dr. Richard Price and others in Britain and France interpreted the English Revolution of 1688 as expressing the rule that the people might cashier their kings at will. To the contrary, the consistent pattern of British conduct both before and after was that the king succeeded to the throne without any explicit permission on the part of the people. The conclusion drawn by the French, that it is easy to establish a free government felt by those to be governed to be "legitimate," was wrong; but the lesson remains unlearned today. Burke knew better.

> Political arrangement, as it is a work for social ends, is to be only wrought by social means. There mind must conspire with mind. Time is required to produce that union of minds which alone can produce all the good we aim at....I have known and...cooperated with great men; and I have never yet seen any plan which has not been mended by the observations of those who were much inferior in understanding to the person who took the lead in the business. By a slow but well-sustained progress the effect of each step is watched; the good or ill- success of the first gives light to us in the second; and so, from light to light, we are conducted with safety through the whole series....We are enabled to unite into a consistent whole the various anomalies and contending principles of men. From hence arises, not an excellence in simplicity, but one

far superior, an excellence in composition. (R: 197-198)

Or, put more concisely: "All government, indeed every human benefit and enjoyment, every virtue, every prudent act, is founded on compromise and barter (C:
107).

In addressing reason itself, we must not confuse the exception, the sickness,
for the rule. Despite all of his animadversions against "metaphysics," Burke was
a friend to reasoning properly conceived as a collective enterprise.

> We are afraid to put men to live and trade each on his own private stock of
> reason, because we suspect that this stock in each man is small, and that the
> individuals would do better to avail themselves of the general bank and
> capital of nations and of ages. Many of our men of speculation [and here he
> was no doubt thinking of David Hume and Adam Smith], instead of exploding
> general prejudices, employ their sagacity to discover latent wisdom which
> prevails in them. If they find what they seek, and they seldom fail, they think
> it more wise to continue the prejudice, with the reason involved, than to cast
> away the coat of prejudice and to leave nothing but the naked reason; because
> prejudice, with its reason, has a motive to give action to that reason, and an
> affection which will give it permanence....Prejudice renders a man's virtue
> his habit, and not a series of unconnected acts. Through just prejudice, his
> duty becomes a part of his nature. (R: 99)

This passage is reminiscent of Madison's objection to frequent appeals to the
people in *Federalist* 49 and of the passage from *Democracy in America*, Volume
2, Book 1, Chapter 2, in which Tocqueville points out that it is impossible for
anyone to reason everything out for her or himself. These passages from Burke,
Madison, and Tocqueville have a common message. Our "rational" actions spring
mostly from habits. These, in turn, are dependent upon many "pre-judgments"—
made in part by ourselves but largely by unknown forebears. This is a "given" of
the human condition and a pre-condition of reasoning.

The point was first made and explored in detail by Aristotle in the
Nichomachean Ethics, a rebuttal of the pride of reason expounded by Plato. The
point is precisely that "human nature" is a nature in which instinct has largely
been replaced by habit—not reason. It must be added that Aristotle and the three
writers mentioned in the text also recognize the role of law and enforcement in
the creation of civil habits.

Burke expands upon his view:

> The legislators who framed ancient republics knew that their business was
> too arduous to be accomplished with no better apparatus than the metaphysics
> of an undergraduate, and the mathematics of an exciseman. They had to do
> with men, and they were obliged to study human nature. They had to do with
> citizens, and they were obliged to study the effects of those habits which are

communicated by the circumstances of civil life. They were sensible that the
operation of this second nature on the first produced a new combination; and
thence arose many diversities amongst men, according to their birth, their
education, their professions, the periods of their lives, their residence in towns
or in the country, their several ways of acquiring and of fixing property, and
according to the quality of the property itself—all which rendered them as it
were so many different species of animals. (R: 215)

Reason restrained is not reason dismissed. Caution is not the same as standing
pat. In words well remembered, the committed friend of liberty (the liberal) is a
conservative and the true conservative in the United States and the rest of the
"free world" is a liberal.

We shall let Burke have the closing words: "...where the great interests of
mankind are concerned through a long succession of generations, that succession
ought to be admitted into some share in the councils which are so deeply to affect
them. If justice requires this, the work itself requires the aid of more minds than
one age can furnish" (R: 198).

Six

FELIX FRANKFURTER

1. Stipulations about Law

Chapters One through Five do not require detailed statements about the Anglo-American legal system. This chapter, however, will assume certain views of law and of this system; so the following stipulations are added. The first five stipulations summarize views which Felix Frankfurter shared more or less with most of his American legal contemporaries. They conditioned his thinking and appear in many of his writings, including his Supreme Court opinions. They will not be argued here even though some are now controversial in some circles. They will, instead, be illustrated and exemplified in Frankfurter's thought and action.[1]

1. A distinction is made in what follows between "judicial reasoning" and "legal reasoning." Legal reasoning is broader and includes what a lawyer does in preparing a presentation before the legal system. It must include her or his whole strategy of representing the client, whether a private party or the state, in the formulation and prosecution/defense of a case. This may include many tactics, as for example in the selection and influencing of a jury, which are more plausibly called dramatic or emotive rather than reasonable. Those presenting cases to a tribunal may employ verbal and non-verbal, persuasive devices from profound arguments to cheap tricks to win a decision from a jury or even a judge. One aspect of the lawyer's strategy is the matter of conjecturing what a judge or judges will find persuasive as grounds for deciding the case—what, that is, a judge would find acceptable to present to the public as the judge's own justification for decision.

The latter is the subject of judicial reasoning. A judge must decide between the parties presenting arguments before the court. The judge must ask: what is the applicable law? what makes most sense in understanding the applicable law? what seems fairest in applying the applicable law? and related questions. The understanding of the law put forth by Oliver Wendell Holmes, a prediction of what the judge will decide, is of no help to the decider: "The prophecies of what the courts will do in fact, and nothing more pretentious, are what I mean by the law."[2] This recognizes the role of judicial choice but does nothing to justify particular choices.

2. Focus is on the legal system. The system is not simply a group of laws, though laws are at the heart of the system. The system has grown up over more than eight centuries, first in England and more recently in the countries colonized or controlled by the British. The system encompasses complex processes of recognizing (especially in the early days when judges articulated "the common law")

and creating (through judicial decision or legislative enactment) laws. The system also includes executive and judicial structures of offices to enforce and apply the laws to particular cases. The sheriff and the police officer, the prosecutor, the bailiff, and others, as well as the judge and jury are all a part of the system. So too are all of the lawyers who "practice" in the system. These institutions—powers, offices, and laws—interact in complex ways, perform many functions, and serve many purposes. To use one of Frankfurter's images, we must be careful not to pull threads from the cloth when attempting to understand the system.[3]

3. We may plausibly view such a complex system from any of a number of points—does it, for example, result in some specified sort of "justice"? The focus here is on the resolution of disputes between parties. The parties are typically two, or grouped into two sides. One party may be a governmental body. The parties may be individual human beings or groups or corporations. At issue must be a real "case or controversy," that is, an issue between parties which have a substantial interest in the outcome. The issue cannot be of purely speculative or theoretical concern. The two sides must have reasons to put forward the strongest possible arguments on their behalf. (This presumption is now weakened in two ways. Strategies are often developed to pursue an issue along what is anticipated to be the most favorable course. When a large corporation or a public interest group has an option of cases to appeal, it can choose the one which has the most appealing facts or the most friendly appeal courts. In addition, the definition of "substantial interest" has now been broadened.)

Many conflicts are resolved or forgotten by the parties without benefit of the legal processes, and others are rejected by the legal system as not suitable (for example, philosophical debates). The problematic situation, once in the hands of lawyers or other officials of the system, is subjected to a process of invention ("brainstorming") and selection and discovery of facts and arguments. Documents or evidence is produced, and conjectures may lead to the discovery of further documents or new evidence. Lawyers lay out lines of reasoning and select among potentially relevant laws and procedures and facts (make choices) for presentation to a court as the "legal issues" and their relevant facts and laws. Courts, sequentially in hierarchy, then make choices among the offerings presented to them and such other options as they may properly notice. The American process may culminate before the Supreme Court of the United States which makes a decision between the parties to the dispute and issues an "opinion" justifying the decision with lines of reasoning available to it under complex selection procedures. This opinion, ideally, not only persuades the parties that they have been fairly heard but also guides various audiences such as lower courts, lawyers, legislatures, and perhaps the general public as to probabilities of future decisions. Concurring and dissenting opinions explore competing lines of selection and argumentation which may prove helpful in the analysis and presentation of subsequent cases.

4. The courts in this system function within an elaborate division of labor. Not all courts do all things indiscriminately to achieve justice. There are both State and Federal courts and courts of first instance and appellate courts. "Jurisdiction" is a primary issue in determining which court properly hears a particular case. This is not simply legal legerdemain. Such division of labor is crucial to the operation of such an elaborate system, and the elaborate system is crucial to the resolution of disputes in such an extensive society.[4]

5. A court is not only a forum for hearing arguments but also provides a mechanism for deciding controversies. After hearing arguments pro and con, the court must make a choice. If it cannot do so, because a jury cannot make up its mind for example, a new trial must be held (unless one of the parties gives up). The court's decision is a choice based on a "weighing" of some sort. While the pros and cons may be "added up," they do not "total" in any sense comparable to an arithmetic calculation. The decision mechanism may be an individual judge, a panel of judges, or a jury. In more important matters, a panel of persons—whether jury or judges—strengthens "objectivity" by its numbers. Jury trials in criminal cases recognize the importance of what is at issue by demanding unanimity and a standard "beyond all reasonable doubt." At the level of the Supreme Court, to refuse to decide is to leave standing a lower court decision and is thus itself a decision. Unanimity in the Supreme Court is not required. Objectivity is served by the written opinions which outline the course of reasoning for public scrutiny. The opinion may be cast in the form of a syllogism; but the decision is unlikely to have been reached that way. The problems of choice and responsibility for choice run through much of what follows. Felix Frankfurter was a prolific commentator on the process and believed the Justices of the Supreme Court have a special obligation to expose the complexities of the process. He believed discussion of disagreements helps to educate the public.

This is a view of reasoning similar to that advocated by John Dewey, someone both Oliver Wendell Holmes and Frankfurter read approvingly. For Dewey, logic involves "controlled inquiry," and "judgment" is the "settled outcome of inquiry." Dewey defines logic as "an account of the procedures followed in reaching decisions ...." While some action occurs with a "minimum of foresight," in other cases "action follows upon a decision, and the decision is the outcome of inquiry, comparison of alternatives, weighing of facts; deliberation or thinking has intervened." This inquiry, comparison, weighing does not necessarily or even typically follow the syllogistic form, which is seen as a special case. Logic "is ultimately an empirical and concrete discipline" which explores the fact that "some methods which are used work better than others." Dewey may have been influenced by Holmes and praises Holmes's assertion that the "life of the law has not been logic," for in Dewey's view Holmes recognized the dangers of a "logic of rigid demonstration" or of "fixed forms" which is not "search and discovery" or "methods of reaching intelligent decision in concrete situations, or methods employed in adjusting disputed issues...." The "logic of judicial decisions must be a "logic of prediction of probabilities." "For the purposes of a logic of inquiry into probable consequences, general principles can only be tools justified by the work they do. They are means of intellectual survey, analysis, and insight into the factors of the situation to be dealt with. Like other tools they must be modified when they are applied to new conditions and new results have to be achieved."

This logic lacks the formal certainty of the syllogism, but it permits a considerable degree of confidence: "Enormous confusion has resulted...from confusion of *theoretical* certainty and practical certainty." Judicial decisions should enable persons to "foresee the legal import of their acts," but it is "absurd because impossible that every decision should flow with formal logical necessity from antecedently known premises." It is worth adding that Dewey agreed with C.S. Peirce's "fallibilism." "By 'fallibilism' Peirce means the scientist's recognition that he or she might be wrong, since those propositions recognized as 'established truths' are 'established' merely in the sense that for the time being it would not be useful to inquire further into them. They are not 'true' in the sense of being incorrigible; included within the idea of them as 'scientific truth' is the fact that they are in some measure erroneous."[5]

In my view, Stephen Toulmin most helpfully lays out the pattern of legal arguments in the course of establishing that jurisprudence rather than formal logic provides the best model of practical reasoning. The changing concepts employed in legal reasoning are best addressed by the "moving classification system" with "competing analogies" described in Edward H. Levi's *An Introduction to Legal Reasoning*. Both books deny that syllogistic reasoning is archetypal, and both repudiate the "quest for certainty."[6]

6. Currently, two popular approaches to legal studies involve the application of insights derived from economics, or related studies, to the law. One, using the tools of modern economic analysis, examines the cost-benefits of various legal alternatives. The other, expressing concerns derived from Marx, looks upon the legal system as the oppressive tool of the ruling class. Each appears to shed light on interesting aspects of the legal system. While Frankfurter was very aware of the problems the economy presented to the legal and political systems and very hopeful about the usefulness of the "social sciences" to legal study, he believed in approaching the law through its own system of thought and its own institutions. Neither of the current views would have appealed to him; neither will be employed here; and neither will be denounced here.

These "stipulations" by no means exhaust the common ground which must be shared if writer and reader are to communicate fruitfully. They are meant only to highlight some possibly controversial general positions which will not be argued in this chapter.

2. The Status of Frankfurter

Felix Frankfurter, Associate Justice of the Supreme Court of the United States from 1939 until 1962, was a controversial figure in his lifetime and remains so today.[7] When he was appointed to the Court by his good friend Franklin Roosevelt, it was widely assumed that he would have a substantial impact on Constitutional law. While he has been the subject of several books and numerous articles especially since his death in 1965, his views on Constitutional law have not influenced either Constitutional doctrine or public discourse as much as he would have hoped. Robert Bork's best-selling rejoinder after his nomination to the Court was rejected in the Senate was a vigorous attack on "judicial activism." While it attacked the approach of Frankfurter protege Alexander Bickel, it contained only insignificant references to Frankfurter himself.[8] Ruth Bader Ginsburg's nomination evoked no comparison with Frankfurter, though various commentators suggested she might be more "restrained" on the Court than her record as a reforming advocate might imply. Some change of awareness may be underway in academic circles. Richard A. Posner provides quantitative information on citations to "well-known judges" in law review articles from 1982 to 1989. Frankfurter is high on each of the four tables, higher than either Brandeis or Cardozo. In two of the three comparable tables, he also leads Hugo Black.[9]

Frankfurter was a well-known "liberal" on the Harvard Law School faculty and one of the most widely recognized of Roosevelt's advisers when he was appointed to the Supreme Court. After a few years of service, he came to be thought of as the principal "conservative" on the Court. The majority of the "Warren Court" developed many of its most notable doctrines under other influences and in ways quite contrary to those promoted by Frankfurter. Yet the "more conservative" Court under the stewardship of Chief Justice Burger did not refer back to the "conservative" doctrines of Justice Frankfurter; nor has that happened under Chief Justice Rehnquist. Several of F.F.'s biographers have been at pains to explain why his influence has been less substantial and less lasting than had been anticipated. All have had to consider his "shift from liberal to conservative." The shift in question was in fact one of role, not of principles. He behaved on the Court as Professor Frankfurter had, repeatedly and consistently, earlier argued a Justice of the Supreme Court should behave.

Several factors—changes in the "Zeitgeist," to use one of Frankfurter's favorite words—have reduced his stature from the perspective of our contemporary eyes. Frankfurter focused on the long-run and on process rather than specific results. American preference is for quick results. Arguments for "long-run" considerations have been viewed as evasions. This sense of evasion perhaps traces in part to generalization from reassurances given to Blacks that things are getting better if they will only be patient. This is not the sole source of modern impatience, however. It was John Maynard Keynes who dismissively pointed out that "in the long run, we are all dead." The two World Wars and the New Deal response to the Great Depression appeared to prove what can be done by a centrally organized, unified, and uniform approach to national problems. The "War on Poverty" of the Johnson administration, various "wars on drugs" and "wars on crime," the demands for a war on AIDS, and the Clinton administration's approach to the health care crisis all illustrate the mind-set as well as its short-comings.

Localism, another political principle defended by Frankfurter, was also discredited because it was used as an excuse to deny rights to Blacks. Frankfurter accepted variety and defended federalism as an experimental method for finding solutions to social problems. Frankfurter was no stranger to the appeal of centralized direction. He was in Washington during both World Wars and saw the need for coordinated effort. In advising FDR on New Deal issues, however, he was the spokesman for Louis Brandeis and what came to be called the "second New Deal" which abandoned the centralized planning of the National Recovery Act and the Agricultural Adjustment Act.

In recent decades, the tendency has been to treat the fight for Black rights as the leading or exemplary case for the promotion of other previously-acknowledged or newly-alleged rights. This proliferation of "rights" came mostly after Frankfurter's death. (A 1994 radio advertisement in the Chicago area asserted a universal right to comfortable eye glasses.) Frankfurter was a founder of the American Civil Liberties Union. He considered defense of the voting rights of the Negroes, the usual term during his lifetime, to be a special case because of the relevant Constitutional amendments. His understanding of "rights" will be examined in detail below.

For reasons connected with confidence in planning, dismissal of localism, and a particular view of rights, "compromise" has been in intellectual disfavor and has been seen as an abandonment of principle rather than as a method of accommodating multiple principles. Frankfurter believed in the existence and validity of multiple principles which are not entirely and inevitably consistent with one another and in the consequent necessity of "balancing" principles. Preoccupation with equality and democracy has made many people uncomfortable with any sort of elite and especially with an elite which lays claim to better judgment. Frankfurter believed that judging—especially in a highly differentiated society and governmental structure—is a skill cultivated and exercised only with considerable effort. Thus, Frankfurter has been out of step with the music to which society has marched for the past thirty years.

This problem is not new. Edmund Burke and Thomas Paine disagreed on virtually the same point about compromise. Burke thought that political matters are inherently complex and require time and commitment to be understood; he advocated a complex government to make it more likely that those charged with governing have the experience and leisure to grasp complexity. Paine believed that everyone is qualified to participate equally in government and held that government is basically a simple matter. Later, Tocqueville addressed this in his examination of the trend toward equality and the effects of this trend on our ways of thinking and our demand for simplicity.

Much of Frankfurter's sometimes bitter response to the influence of his colleague Justice Hugo Black probably traced to incredulity that Black's "simple" and "unschooled" use of principles and his unwillingness to see that principles must be "balanced" in competition with each other could be found competitive with and even preferable to Frankfurter's own self-conscious and artful compromising of principles. As Black's biographers make clear, he read extensively in history and philosophy after joining the Court and cannot be considered unschooled in these subjects. He was probably better read in the classics of philosophy than F.F. though less well read in law. Thus, his principles may be in a technical sense "simple principles" but they are not unschooled. From Frankfurter's point of view, Black was doctrinaire; but his doctrines, at least for a time, proved more persuasive than F.F.'s skepticism.

In the skeptical tradition, judgment and character are related. I shall treat Frankfurter as an "exemplar." What I mean by this will be treated below. It is only fair to note that his character has been subject to great criticism and the objectivity of his diaries and other accounts have been severely questioned. The diaries are dismissed by Black's most recent biographer, Roger K. Newman: "Very little he wrote about the Court [in the diaries] is, if true, verifiable; much of it is outright false" (298). No citations are given at the point of generalization. Newman as well as H.N. Hirsch, Mark Silverstein, and Melvin L. Urofsky, follow William O. Douglas's assessment that Frankfurter was "utterly dishonest intellectually, that he was very, very devious...[and] spent his time going up and down the halls putting poison in everybody's spring, trying to set one justice against another..." (quoted by Newman, p. 297). It is interesting that Newman does not appear to trace the notorious Black-Jackson difficulties of 1945-1946 to F.F. at least proximately (333-348) but perhaps to the fact that "Jackson was unstable, a walking time-bomb" (336) and "something of a bully" (342).

Of those fully in the know about the inner workings of the Supreme Court during Frankfurter's years on it, Douglas had the last word on personal relations within the Court by outliving the others. We shall probably get more data as the several clerks release more papers; and we shall probably get more interpretations from a generation of scholars not raised on the triumph of Black-Douglas doctrines. For decades, Black was intellectually devoted to Douglas. Black seems to have developed some doubts about his colleague's character as the latter progressed through his series of divorces and marriages. Whether this had any influence on doctrine remains to be explored, insofar as I know.

Frankfurter's influence lived on more in the students and clerks who studied under him and in their students than in the doctrines of the Supreme Court. Some whom he influenced followed him into the academy. They achieved prominent positions at influential law schools and have published much. Their indebtedness to F.F. is usually evident in their writings though they are not usually the persons who write about Felix Frankfurter. Max Friedman, the one whom Frankfurter chose to write his biography, did not live to do so. F.F.'s law clerks have undoubtedly contributed greatly to his reputation. One may wonder, though, what his influence and reputation would have been if he had never served on the Court and had remained at Harvard. His facility in explaining the business of the Supreme Court to the educated public has never been matched. The additional students sent into public service, the further scholarship, and popular education would have weighed heavily in scales of comparison. In rejecting a nomination to the Supreme Judicial court of Massachusetts in 1932, Frankfurter thanked the Governor for the honor but added: "But I have other obligations to the law which, after much anguish of mind, I feel I ought not to sever. As against the opportunities for immediate achievement on the bench, the long-term effects of legal education make their claim. The grave problems already upon us and those looming on the horizon require as never before a courageous and learned bar. And from such a bar alone can come an enlightened judiciary" (RF: 71). Though he may at the time have thought the "grave problems" and even those "looming on the horizon" would pass, they have only been succeeded by even more puzzling challenges.

Frankfurter was and remains a scholar's judge. His opinions and dissents were seldom popularly acclaimed at the time of their delivery. Even when they concurred with popular feeling, they did not please the "opinion makers."[10] Unfortunately, he did not have a popular expositor to match his own efforts on behalf of Holmes. Perhaps most scholars would concur that he is a major figure in the history of the Supreme Court. Fewer would consider his opinions of major influence today. The importance of his views greatly exceeds their current influence. But the wheel turns. Perhaps it is time again to listen to the advocate of combining local experimentation with democratic and liberal humanity.

Felix Frankfurter's career is no longer well-known even among lawyers, and his character has been subjected to the most divergent scholarly interpretations. A brief biographical sketch will connect that career with views which will be examined in subsequent sections.

3. Biographical Sketch

Felix Frankfurter was born in Vienna in 1883, accompanied his family to the United States in 1894, and became a citizen when his father was naturalized in 1898. While still a youth, he delivered a paper on the Dreyfus affair which, along with his enthusiasm for William Jennings Bryan, gives early evidence of his concern for the underdog. He became an avid user of the Cooper Union with its reading room and debates and attended City College of New York from which he was graduated in 1902. He entered the Harvard Law School in the fall of 1903 and led his class academically for all three years. One cannot doubt that his life at Harvard witnessed many signs of prejudice against a short, Jewish youth from New York; yet repeatedly throughout his later life, Frankfurter emphasized the democracy of the school and its concern with intellectual excellence, not family or wealth. Like Cicero and Burke, he was an outsider given a degree of access to the aristocracy of family and wealth. Like them, in later life he chose to emphasize the openness which permitted talent some access to the inner sanctum of the state.

Upon graduation, F.F. was placed, with some difficulty, in a New York law firm where it was suggested he change his name to something less Jewish. He refused. Though not religious, he had a strong sense of himself and did not wish to bend to the pressures of conformity. In a *Reader's Digest* article years later on "The Best Advice I Ever Had," he discussed the incident in connection with the admonition from his mother to "Hold yourself dear!" (LL: 38-39) He displayed resistance to such pressures throughout his life while, at the same time, he was careful to ingratiate himself with selected mentors, contemporaries, and protégés. After a short time, he joined the United States Attorney's office under Henry L. Stimson. Stimson, a friend and ally of Theodore Roosevelt, quickly became a model and mentor for Frankfurter. When Stimson went to Washington as Secretary of War, F.F. accompanied him, served as his general assistant, and had an insider's introduction to the Federal government and its politics.

Frankfurter took with him to Washington an introduction to Justice Oliver Wendell Holmes. He cultivated this acquaintance and one he established with soon-to-be Justice Louis D. Brandeis. One of Frankfurter's "three most influential books" was Boswell's life of Samuel Johnson.[11] Perhaps F.F. saw in Johnson's fierce conversation and pursuit of principle a kindred spirit if not an actual model. While F.F. is unlikely to have exposed either Holmes or Brandeis to his aggressive side, his conversation must often have verged on debate. Even on the bench, Frankfurter pursued his own dialogue with counsel before the Court in a combatitive fashion which irritated some of his colleagues.

The intellectual life of Washington in these years was dominated by the Progressive movement embodied in Theodore Roosevelt and articulated especially in Herbert Croly's book *The Promise of American Life*. These were the years in which the definition of "liberalism" in the United States was being transformed. "Liberalism" in nineteenth-century Britain had implied a reduction of governmental regulations and an increase of individual freedom ("negative freedom"). It now was coming to imply a government which would promote freedom through actions to increase economic and social equality ("positive freedom").[12] In the United States, this change occurred under the banner of progressivism. Though working for a Republican administration, Frankfurter supported the "Bull Moose" candidacy of "TR" in 1912. Stimson was a close associate of Roosevelt and resigned his office to support the campaign. At Stimson's urging, however,

Frankfurter stayed in his position to carry forward work in progress. He never declared party affiliation, but he remained most closely identified with progressive Republicanism until the New Deal was well underway. He was not a great admirer of Woodrow Wilson and saw him only as preferable to W.H. Taft.

Frankfurter's increasing attachment to Brandeis created a life-long tension in his intellectual position. Put in simple terms, Brandeis shared Wilson's traditional Democratic opposition to bigness. Frankfurter thus supported an energetic Federal government (both Roosevelts) and the States as laboratories of democracy (Brandeis). By the end of his life, Frankfurter was almost isolated as a defender of federalism when that word had come to be seen as a code-word for "States' rights," prejudice, and reaction.

F.F. stayed in Washington only briefly after the beginning of the Wilson administration. Complex negotiations by others produced the funds to create a suitable position on the Harvard Law faculty. Once back in Boston, F.F.'s friendship with Brandeis flourished, eventually in the 1920s into a very close relationship between the professor and the Justice. Since both men preached the necessity of abandoning concern with policy in going onto the Supreme Court, recent publication of the memoranda and correspondence which connected the two over a considerable period has called into question their intellectual honesty as well as their candor. Frankfurter was deeply involved in lining up support for the controversial nomination of Brandeis to the Court in 1916. Brandeis had supported unpopular popular causes and cases—he was called "the people's lawyer"—and both before the bar and in personal life had done little to ingratiate himself with many of the leaders of business and their legal counsels.

Frankfurter came to national attention after his return to Washington to help in the World War I effort; and he gained a reputation as a radical or friend of radicals. He served as counsel for the commission created to mediate labor problems. His work took him to Bisbee, Arizona, site of a major piece of injustice in the struggle of labor and management. Unfortunately for Frankfurter's reputation, one of the management perpetrators was a former "Rough Rider." Teddy Roosevelt remained fiercely loyal to his men, even when they were guilty of deplorable actions, and blasted Frankfurter when he and the commission sided with labor rather than management. The reputation for radicalism increased when, in San Francisco, F.F. became aware of and publicized procedural irregularities in the conviction for murder of labor activist Tom Mooney. These were two pieces of injustice in the long struggle between labor and management which, today, look clear enough: Frankfurter was on the side of procedural fairness. Contemporary opinion divided over the matter differently. F.F. was viewed either as a supporter of dangerous revolutionaries or as a true son of the Left. During these Washington years in which he lost the confidence of one Roosevelt, he developed a friendship with another—Franklin, the Assistant Secretary of the Navy and only a year his senior.

F.F. returned to the academic life at Harvard but by no means to an "ivory tower" of remoteness from public affairs. In a long letter of 1932 to Walter Lippmann, he said: "You know me well enough to know that temperamentally the ivory tower is not my congenial habitat" (RF: 66). Throughout the two decades remaining before his elevation to the Court, he was often involved in important and sometimes controversial issues. He addressed many of them in popular publications, especially *The New Republic*. Frankfurter was involved in both public controversies and behind-the-scenes issues of university politics: antisemitic quotas and faculty appointments. As a teacher, F.F. seems to have been for the few rather than the many. As the years passed, he tended more toward small, upper-level courses, taught in seminar style. He was impatient with the slow but both gave devotion to and received it from the quick and "jugular." His specialties were administrative law—the functioning of the administrative agencies which had begun to permeate American government—and the "business of the Supreme Court." The phrase is F.F.'s own, the title of a book he published in conjunction with one of his students James Landis. It is indicative of Frankfurter's concern with the whole institutional setting and process of judging rather than simply the doctrines evolved through that process.

While some people were not enchanted by him, those who were constituted a very able group.[13] In assembling proteges, Frankfurter had the advantage of regard accorded him by Holmes and Brandeis. He was permitted to select for each of the Justices the law clerks who worked for them, usually for one year. The young men so chosen thereby received their tickets to distinction. These men, and they were all men in those days, achieved a remarkable record of success in the law and in government. F.F. had an eye for talent, and he had a great willingness to promote those of whom he thought well. While he worked closely with many women in various "reform" activities, he seems never to have fought for women in the legal profession. In the Thirties, many of his protégés came to be known as the "happy hot dogs" of the New Deal.[14] It is worth noting that F.F. did not restrict his favorable views and recommendations to his own students. We are told that Frankfurter "used to recall with relish that he had chosen Magruder [Calvert Magruder, later chief judge of the Court of Appeals for the First Circuit] to be Brandeis' first law clerk even though Magruder had shunned all three courses offered by Frankfurter at the Harvard Law School" (RF: 491).

Like many professors today, Frankfurter had his own consulting business. In his case, the work did not earn him much money. In recent years it has been revealed that he was subsidized by the wealthy Justice Brandeis, sporadically after 1916 and regularly after 1925. This has been treated as scandalous.[15] The two men's concerns and views were similar. Brandeis believed that he must withdraw from public involvement in many of the issues which had preoccupied him; but he felt no wrong in making it possible for Frankfurter to pursue these problems. The question arises with regard to Brandeis as to whether he maintained a proper disinterestedness in matters when they came before him on the Court—a question which I shall leave to others. The question relating to Frankfurter is whether the disinterestedness which he so often praised was a mere sham. There seems little doubt but that in the journalistic atmosphere today, Brandeis would be driven from the Court by the revelation of such a relationship and Frankfurter would never be appointed. The gifts were made in an ethically simpler era, and I am unsure that the greater sophistication of the later time is greatly ethically superior. Did Brandeis tell Frankfurter more than any of his colleagues told their own close friends about the inner workings of the Court? Was Brandeis covertly active in matters inappropriate for the proper performance of his role? That Brandeis was a source of ideas for the Administration was no great secret in the 1930s .[16]

There is little evidence that Frankfurter's judgment was purchased by the support he received. The outside consulting which Brandeis made possible was *pro bono*. F.F. took over from his friend the preparation of a "Brandeis brief" for argument before the Court in *Bunting v. Oregon*, 243 U.S. 426 (1917). This was a detailed "factual" presentation of the implications of the law as it affected social welfare matters. He was involved in various civil liberties issues and became an early member of the national committee of the American Civil Liberties Union. In the early 1920s, F.F. was involved with Roscoe Pound, by then Dean of the Law School, in an empirical study of the criminal justice system in Cleveland. He wrote for the general public explanations of Supreme Court opinions and their implications. He had the benefit of Brandeis's insider views, and he may have even contributed to the formulation of those views.

The mystique of the Court was great in the 1920s, and Frankfurter strove to make the public understand that choices were being made and not always wisely nor in the general interest and certainly not simply dictated by the Constitution. Perhaps the most remarkable of these efforts appeared in *The New Republic* as an unsigned editorial 1 October 1924. "The Red Terror of Judicial Reform" concluded: "We have had fifty years of experiment with the Fourteenth Amendment, and the centralizing authority lodged with the Supreme Court over domestic affairs of forty-eight widely different states is an authority which it cannot discharge with safety either to itself or to the states. The due process clauses ought to go" (LP: 16). While he later gave up effort to remove the clause from the Fourteenth Amendment, he remained expansively cautious about it. Many of his most controversial opinions and dissents on the Court concerned the use and meaning of the phrase, and he was fond of pointing out that other free and democratic countries got along very well without such a "safeguard."

Frankfurter's most publicized involvement of the 1920s was with the Sacco and Vanzetti case in Massachusetts, discussed below. Frankfurter was both praised and attacked for his efforts, often on the basis of views of the opinions of Sacco and Vanzetti rather than on F.F.'s views of fair legal proceedings.

Frankfurter also took an interest in the national political scene and supported LaFollette's "third party" Presidential candidacy in 1924 for its progressivism. In 1928, he supported the Democratic candidate Al Smith. At this time, he began to cultivate his friendship with the Democratic candidate for Governor of New York, Franklin Delano Roosevelt, whose efforts, unlike those of Smith, were successful. In the following months and years, the FDR-F.F. friendship developed with Frankfurter paying visits to Roosevelt's home and advising him on personnel and legislation. As the 1932 Presidential campaign proceeded, F.F. became increasingly involved in giving advice and support. His published correspondence with Roosevelt shows the beginning of weekly and often daily communication.

After the election, Roosevelt tried to persuade Frankfurter to become the Solicitor General and mentioned appointment to the Supreme Court as the probable reward. F.F. refused, explaining that the position would require full-time commitment of his thought and energy. He felt he would be more useful if he did not "abandon what I am doing" to "take a job I don't want because it may lead to another, which also I'm not at all sure I'd want" (RF: 112-13). He also did not serve as a member of the "Brains Trust," the group of idea-men for the new administration led by Raymond Moley. F.F. provided his own supply of ideas and personnel for the new President and also served as a conduit for ideas from Justice Brandeis—ideas not in accord with those of the "Brains Trust." To put very simply what was in fact an extended and often piecemeal series of experiments, the "Brains Trust" was more inclined toward centralized direction of bigness and Brandeis more inclined to local control and smallness. Frankfurter not only accepted no position in the administration but shortly left for a year as visiting professor at Oxford, a year which reinforced his Anglophile and cosmopolitan tendencies.

The stay abroad permitted the renewal of earlier friendships and the making of many others. Frankfurter became an almost omni-present publicity-man for the New Deal and for close Anglo-American ties. He debated George Bernard Shaw on the viability of the American Constitution. He conducted a discrete but effective campaign with the brightest lights of the British publishing world. Not least, he sharpened and up-dated insights into international affaôrs. He was one of the first Americans to recognize the threat posed by the anti-semitism of Hitler and the Nazi regime in Germany. In October 1933, he wrote to the President "[t]here surely can be little doubt that Germany and Japan are moving on converging lines, full of ominous significance to the growing tensions between Russia and Japan..." (RF: 166). By September 1936, he was writing of the President's riding "the great storm of the next four years and guid[ing this] country's destiny in what may well be a world war" (RF: 358).

Beginning even before his attendance at the World War I Peace Conference, F.F. established a set of friendships reaching across all national boundaries. These friends both provided him with views and information and sought advice and assistance. His diaries and correspondence with FDR give a small taste of this. While the new administration was being formed, he gave FDR a suggestion for the Governor Generalship of the Philippines based on information he had received from "half a dozen of the advisers to the King of Siam" (Thailand) whom he knew (RF: 122). In 1943, Reinhold Niebuhr consulted him about whether to take a position at Harvard; and the same evening, Jean Monnet, the French statesman, sought his advice on the difficult wartime relations between French generals Giraud and DeGaulle (D: 184-185). The same year, Sir Girji Bajpai, the chief Indian diplomatic representative in Washington, visited F.F. to discuss Congress Party politics in the context of Gandhi's latest hunger strike and to request personal advice about what to do if Gandhi should die (D: 194-195). Edward R. Murrow asked advice about whether to accept a position with the BBC (D: 256-257). Those who were praised by Frankfurter and those who praised him (in both cases, from personal acquaintance) will be discussed at greater length later in this chapter. The biographical point here is that F.F. was the center of a network—old and young, female and male, from many nations and cultures.

Frankfurter contributed significantly to the New Deal in both personnel and substance. His frequent correspondence with the President frequently praised him in terms so lavish they seem sycophantic to the casual reader of the correspondence. We must not forget, however, how easy it would have been for little misunderstandings to arise and grow, especially during the years when one was in Cambridge and the other in Washington. The history of the New Deal (and of Washington since) is replete with political rifts of insubstantial origin. Roosevelt and Frankfurter not only avoided such rifts but kept very much "on the same wave length." In notes and letters both trivial and earth-shaking, F.F. continued to address the President as "Frank" unless the situation dictated greater formality. I shall examine in some detail later Frankfurter's trait of emphasizing the positive in people.

When Roosevelt finally named F.F. to the Supreme Court in January 1939, it was widely assumed that Frankfurter, with his brilliance and scholarship, would greatly influence and perhaps dominate the Court. His public record of scholarship on the Supreme Court was matched by behind-the-scenes familiarity with the workings of the Court which was unprecedented for someone not already on the Court. In his diaries, he noted: "I learnt a good deal, of course, about the Court's doings since the time Holmes came on in 1902, and after Brandeis came here in 1916 and Cardozo in 1932, I learnt with cumulative intimacy from them about the inner workings of the Institution and the behavior of the various personalities" (D: 175). He later told his colleague Frank Murphy that he had a "firsthand detailed knowledge of what has been going on inside the Court during the last thirty-five years" (D: 264).

Despite this preparation, the anticipated dominance was not to be. Various explanations have been offered. Perhaps the simplest are that the Court is not easily dominated and that Frankfurter remained too professorial toward his peers on the Court, too inclined to lecture them. Frankfurter was quite candid about his trait of lecturing his colleagues in his diaries. He refers to speaking in conference "rather at length" (D: 211), speaking "at some length" (227), speaking "at length" (241), and speaking "somewhat at length" (316).

To some extent, his behavior was encouraged even before he reached the Court. He was urged to meet with Roosevelt's first appointment Hugo Black to teach the latter something about the ways of the Supreme Court. Black, a leading Senatorial supporter of Roosevelt during the "Court packing" controversy, had no significant judicial experience and was selected in part as a way of getting back at those who had frustrated the scheme. That Professor Frankfurter should undertake to educate Senator Black is ironic. The two were eventually seen as the chief spokesmen for judicial restraint and judicial activism—to use only one pair of phrases which may distinguish their approaches. The relations of the two remained at least for the most part polite, unlike Black's relations with Justice Robert Jackson. William O. Douglas, another disciple of Brandeis, and later Chief Justice Earl Warren at times openly displayed their frustration with Frankfurter, however. He returned the sentiments. His diaries and correspondence reflect deep distrust of Douglas, both for the latter's political ambitions and for his opinions. It is interesting that F.F. objected vigorously to the Douglas interest in political office but showed no knowledge of Black's political interests in 1940 and 1944 as described in Roger Newman's biography of Black. Like F.F. but apparently more occasionally, Black did political chores for FDR.[17]

As is well documented, despite their strong disagreement about how to interpret and apply "due process," relations between Black and Frankfurter never reached the level of acrimony of those between Frankfurter and Douglas. They even seemed to warm up in F.F.'s final years. Newman quotes Black, presumably at the time of the *Rochin* "stomach-pump" case in 1952 and thus while controversy was still strong, as saying: "Felix is one of the nicest guys anywhere....If I had to find someone to tell me what's right or wrong for society, I'd pick him. There's no other man I would rather leave that choice to....[But y]ou can't put Felix into a bottle and see what comes out for due process....There have to be some fundamental rules." The comment was made to Black's law clerk David J. Vann. This does not appear to jibe with the assessment of F.F. by Douglas quoted above. Each man was apparently a severe trial to the other at times, despite or perhaps because of mutual intellectual respect. Unlike F.F., Black ordered his personal Court notes destroyed.[18] Rather amusingly in view of his own subsequent reputation, F.F. considered Douglas "the most systematic exploiter of flattery [he had] ever encountered" (D: 175) The "Roosevelt Court" split into two camps, especially after Harlan Fiske Stone succeeded Charles Evans Hughes as Chief Justice. The split continued throughout Frankfurter's years on the Court. The later years under Chief Justice Warren saw many of Frankfurter's views fall into the minority. Frankfurter, the fighting liberal, came to be viewed as the leader of the conservative block on the Court.

The two "Flag Salute" cases, with Frankfurter's majority opinion of 1940 reversed in 1943, marked the start of F.F.'s fall from liberal grace. Several of the Justice's colleagues and friends from earlier civil liberties causes argued on behalf of the Jehovah's Witnesses that their children ought not to be required to recite the "Pledge of Allegiance to the Flag" because it violated Constitutionally guaranteed rights. Frankfurter viewed the matter as properly left to the discretion of the States and of the legislatures. In both the opinion of 1940 and the dissent of 1943, which will be considered at some length below, he made every effort to teach his former allies that they were on a misguided path of judicial intervention and innovation.

In this brief biographical sketch, it is not possible to detail all of the major issues Frankfurter addressed, let alone provide a history of the Court during his tenure. It is possible, though, to summarize the main lines of controversy from his point of view. His primary concern was to maintain what he considered proper Constitutional balances: limitation of the role of the judiciary in the initiation of change, a balance between the Federal government and the States, and a balance between the government and the individual. He pursued these problematic areas during an era in which many on the Court and off saw a need to expand the meaning or deepen the understanding of individual rights and saw the Supreme Court as the primary forum for expanding, deepening, or defending these rights. From the viewpoint of his opponents, he was willing to sacrifice Constitutionally guaranteed rights of individuals and groups to the temporary majorities of legislative bodies. Frankfurter insisted that the legislatures, Federal and State, and the electoral process were the primary forums for such developments. Against those who asserted that the Supreme Court is the only protection a threatened minority has against an overweening majority, Frankfurter argued that ultimately reliance must be on the education provided by the democratic process: the Supreme Court cannot long stand against a misguided electorate. He did not even think the Court should attempt to correct inadequate representation, as in the failures of the State legislatures to effect appropriate redistricting. These issues will be examined in more detail below.

The several volumes of Frankfurter's articles and occasional pieces contain a number of eulogies of persons living and dead. Some were remarks made on memorial events, others letters or articles for newspapers. Some discussed close friends or former colleagues or students; others major figures such as John Dewey, Alfred North Whitehead, and Thomas Mann. Frankfurter always found much good to say of these people. His effusive praise of Franklin Roosevelt comes to mind. F.F. had his enemies, and he certainly thought poorly of or took no interest in many people who passed through his acquaintance. But the range of those he took an interest in and cultivated as friends was enormous, and his readiness and perspicacity in finding their good points gleams from every paragraph of these epideictic gems. Essays by F.F. discussed in Section V show some of the variety of his friends and acquaintances. The contributors to Wallace Mendelson's *A Tribute* illustrate it further. These essays will require further examination.

Felix Frankfurter retired from the Supreme Court on 28 August 1962 and died on 22 February 1965.

4. The Canonical Figures

How does a person come to hold the views he or she holds? Whence did they come? With what detail can these "influences" be traced in the person's works? The first and third of these questions will not be pursued here. Some exploration of the second permits elaborations of the skeptical approach which Frankfurter did not make explicitly, though he often commented on his personal divinities Thayer, Holmes, and Brandeis. Study of the Anglo-American legal system and the teaching and practice of law were no doubt the greatest influences on Felix Frankfurter; but these influences, like the Constitution itself, are ambiguous. Lawyers and legal scholars disagree on how to interpret the lessons of the law. The stipulations at the beginning of this chapter outline the interpretation followed here.

We are told that Frankfurter's "three favorite books," excluding legal works, were James Boswell's *The Life of Samuel Johnson, LL.D.*, *The Federalist*, and John Morley's *On Compromise* (RF: 721). While they are not included on this list, F.F. claimed to have read all of Abraham Lincoln's speeches and writings (RF: 361) and often referred to his admiration for Lincoln. It is a curious sidelight that Hugo Black, on the other hand, "was no Lincolnphile" but thought "Andrew Johnson was a great man."[19] The first two books on the list need receive little extra attention at this point. "Federalism" and "checks and balances" are the most obvious lessons of *The Federalist* and will be addressed throughout what follows. We have no evidence as to whether Frankfurter took any special note of Number 37 with its explicit summary of the skeptical position. Samuel Johnson was such a bundle of strong opinions that it is easy to miss the degree to which he combined his beliefs or "prejudices" with skepticism. His beliefs were based on faith, not the power of reason; and he often used his reasoning powers to cut down the pretensions of reasoners. Despite his doubts, he was a vigorous advocate of his views. This leaves us with Morley.

John Morley is little read today, but we are told by Alexander Bickel that Frankfurter's copy of *On Compromise* was well-annotated.[20] Morley was an editor of and published essays on politics and history regularly in the *Fortnightly Review*. Like much of the fiction of his time, his books appeared in installment in periodicals. He was a prolific writer and produced books on Machiavelli, Rousseau, Diderot and the encyclopedists, and "English men of letters" as well as on

Cromwell, Walpole, Cobden, Gladstone, and, most relevantly, Edmund Burke. As mentioned above, Morley was a great admirer of Burke's political wisdom even though he thought Burke had gone seriously wrong in his attacks on the French Revolution. Morley considered himself an heir of Burke and, as a good heir, tried to improve the inherited estate.

On Compromise, first published in book form in 1874, takes up where Burke left off. Burke was both a liberal and a conservative. His reflections on the French revolution appeared to emphasize only the conservative Burke, an opponent of progress. In Morley's correction of this appearance, "The world grows better, even in the moderate way is does grow better, because people wish that it should, and take the right steps to make it better." Burke had remarked that "it is a very great mistake to imagine that mankind follow up practically any speculative principle, either of government or of freedom, as far as it will go in argument and logical illation." Morley expanded approvingly: "What Burke means is that we ought never to press ideas up to their remotest logical issues, without reference to the conditions in which we are applying them." But Morley also corrected a potential short-coming of Burke: "The object of these chapters [Morley's own] is to reiterate the importance of self-assertion, tenacity, and positiveness of principle."[21] Skepticism about the power of reason and emphasis on finding a middle ground between competing positions may leave the skeptic restricted to the agenda presented by others. The skeptic is then a mere compromiser. Skepticism when making a judgment is not theoretically incompatible with initiative in introducing proposals. Incompatibility in practice arises from the enthusiasm a person typically develops for her or his own suggestions. Bias in favor of our own ideas can be controlled by a sufficiently developed skepticism.

Skepticism and a preference for the long view over the quick-fix need not mean passivity. Morley used an example that one can well imagine stuck with Frankfurter.

> You pass a law (if you can) putting down drunkenness; there is a neatness in such a method very attractive to fervid and impatient natures. Would you not have done better to leave the law unpassed, and apply yourselves instead to the improvement of the dwellings of the more drunken class, to the provision of amusements that might compete with the ale-house, to the extension and elevation of instruction and so on? You may say that this should be done, and yet the other not left undone; but, as a matter of fact and history, the doing of one has always gone with the neglect of the other, and ascetic law-making in the interests of virtue has never been accompanied either by law-making or any other kind of activity for making virtue easier or more attractive. It is the recognition how little punishment can do, that leaves men free to see how much social prevention can do.[22]

The skeptical position, with its emphasis on suspension of judgment and the balancing of two or more sides, easily lends itself to inaction. Practical decisions have a time limitation of some sort and must not be "sicklied o'er with the pale cast of thought." Cicero himself was guilty of great indecisiveness at various points in his career, including the delay in flight from the soldiers of Marc Antony which cost him his life. As a practical matter, the academic skeptic becomes one with the Pyrrhonic skeptic and the cynic if he or she takes so long to make a decision that events pass on by. Moreover, the skeptical position easily leaves itself dependent upon the initiatives of others. Here again, Cicero is easily treated as derivative because he juxtaposes the opinions formulated by prior philosophers. This is the main concern of Morley's book—that skepticism, with all that it implies about compromise and accommodation not discourage people from vigorous exploration of how far a line of endeavor should be pressed. This creates a tension within the individual if the same person is to develop and promote one side of an issue and then exercise dispassionate judgment comparing the position he or she has contributed with those contributed by others. It is not without reason that so many thinkers have remarked that one ought not to be a judge in one's own case. But the skeptical position is one of resolving disputes, and even this is not beyond some accommodation. It seems likely that Frankfurter wrestled with this difficulty throughout his life. He was a man with very strong opinions and commitments, including not least a commitment to disinterested judgment. To a degree, this tension is expressed in his efforts to encompass both Holmes and Brandeis within his skeptical position. Brandeis comes closer to Morley in his concern with the initiation of ideas; Holmes more closely exemplifies the judge who is disinterested and above the fray.

Before turning to Holmes and Brandeis, something must be said of James Bradley Thayer, a sometime law-partner of Holmes and his colleague on the Harvard faculty. Thayer retired from the Harvard Law School faculty shortly before Frankfurter arrived as a student.[23] Late in life, F.F. summed up Thayer's importance in his thought: "...undoubtedly both Holmes and Brandeis influenced me in my constitutional outlook, but both of them derived theirs from the same source from which I derived mine, namely, Professor James Bradley Thayer, with whom both had personal relations but whose views influenced me only through his writings..." (RF: 25). Thayer's views were expounded in his essay, "The Origin and Scope of the American Doctrine of Constitutional Law," published in 1893. The "doctrine" which Thayer discusses is the power given to or claimed by the judicial branch to declare legislative acts unconstitutional. The Constitution did not explicitly provide for this power, so the essay is in part an account of its "origin." In discussing the "scope," Thayer makes several points which F.F. often reiterated. They became, in fact, Frankfurter's operating principles in constitutional interpretation. First, other governments with written constitutions do not give such power to the judiciary; the power is not logically implied in the concept of a written constitution. Second, we must distinguish the acts of a "co-ordinate" department from those of a department which is "not co-ordinate." That is, the judicial review of Congressional action, asserted in *Marbury v. Madison*, 1 Cranch 137 (1803) is not the same as judicial review of State action, asserted in *M'Culloch v. Maryland*, 4 Wheat. 316 (1819). The latter is necessary for a federal system; the former is not. Third, the power in question is "purely judicial": that is, it is exercised solely for the purpose of deciding a specific litigated question. Fourth, we must not confuse wisdom with constitutionality; many acts are constitutional which are not wise. They may not even be just in the broadest meaning of the word. Fifth, "[u]nder no system can the power of courts go far to save a people from ruin; our chief protection lies elsewhere." It lies with a citizenry informed about the great power the legislature must have and the leeways it must have in exercising that power "so that responsibility may be sharply brought home where it belongs." The Supreme Court, that is, cannot play the role of philosopher king. Finally, legislation is the primary way of coping with the changing needs of society; and the views of Congress should be given considerable leeway in the assessment of what options are permitted by the Constitution. Justice Frankfurter's interpretations of this "conclusion" has invoked the greatest opposition to his position. It is all too common (and often all too appropriate) to think of legislators as posturing "politicians," to expect little of them, and to fail to hold them to high standards. Especially to the point, they are not expected to protect individual rights as they exercise governmental powers; this responsibility is left to the courts.

Frankfurter followed Thayer in believing that the courts cannot save a country if popular practice is not compatible with liberty: *"quid leges sine moribus?"*— what are laws without customs?[24] F.F. made use of the point in a speech draft for FDR:

> ...unless government can succeed in creating conditions under which the great mass of people do feel convinced of justice, economic security and ample scope for human dignity, that tolerance of differences and that general concern for fair play which are the real protection of the individual and minorities will disappear. As a practical matter that tolerance and that concern rest only in small part upon legal formulas. Far more importantly they are the natural reflection of magnanimity of spirit in the masses which in turn depends upon generally distributed well-being. (RF: 414)

The writer, jurist, and mentor with whom Frankfurter is most frequently identified is Oliver Wendell Holmes, Jr. This is not surprising since Frankfurter himself did much to associate himself with Holmes and was a major contributor to the mythic stature of Holmes.[25] The transformation of jurist into myth started with an issue of the *Harvard Law Review*, arranged by Frankfurter, celebrating Holmes' seventy-fifth birthday and proclaiming him a great Constitutional jurist. F.F. spoke and wrote so frequently about Holmes that he identified himself as the principal heir and interpreter of "the great man" (to quote Frankfurter quoting

Brandeis). Frankfurter's admiration was expressed in many ways, not least in some ten pieces published both during and after Holmes's lifetime. F.F. repeated himself quite a bit by borrowing passages from earlier essays, so there is a good deal of repetition both of favorite quotations and his own phrases.

Holmes was many things Frankfurter was not: a tall, reserved, New England aristocrat. Frankfurter often referred to Holmes's skepticism. Holmes's skepticism, unlike that of Frankfurter, was accompanied by an aloofness from the issues and sentiments of the day. Holmes prided himself on not reading the newspapers; F.F. read many every day (LL: 48; RF: 211). Holmes was inclined to accept classical economic theory and doubted the efficacy of "reform" movements; F.F. became a friend and admirer of Keynes and identified himself with almost every available reform movement. Frankfurter was an enthusiast; Holmes was not. Yet Holmes is the person Frankfurter idealized and idolized as the embodiment of American democratic jurisprudence.

One word is repeated again and again in Frankfurter's references to the older man: skepticism and its cognates. Holmes was indeed a skeptic. Frankfurter liked to call attention to Holmes' own reference to his skepticism: "He read omnivorously to 'multiply my scepticisms' (unpublished letter)" (MJH: 21). In Holmes' case, skepticism seems to have been ingrained in his personality and to have been associated at times with a kind of pessimism.

G. Edmund White's biography of Holmes has no index entry for "skepticism" and uses the word without explicit definition. Evidences of traditional academic skepticism occur, though. For example, in discussing the "two organizing methodological perspectives in *The Common Law*," White remarks that, unlike "the majority of his contemporary reviewers," Holmes "never treated them as uniformly self-reinforcing" and "was careful, in his language, to convey subtleties, note exceptions to his generalizations, give attention to anomalies, and emphasize his paradox of form and substance...." Holmes also acknowledged the existence of many situations in which, in White's words, "principles of comparable importance were in collision." Such situations require "balancing," "drawing lines," and—above all—"choice.".[26]

The skeptical views attributed in what follows to Holmes are as seen through the eyes of Frankfurter and are perhaps best summed up as follows: "His [Holmes] imagination and humility, rigorously cultivated, enables him to transcend the narrowness of his immediate experience. Probably no man who ever sat on the Court was by temperament and discipline freer from emotional commitments compelling him to translate his own economic views into constitutional commands" (MJH: 21). Frankfurter explained the basis of this skepticism:

> Since the whole of truth has not yet been, and is not likely to be, brought up from its bottomless well, the first duty of an educated man was to doubt his major premise even while he continues to act upon it. This was the sceptical

conviction with which he [Holmes] distrusted dogma, whether economic or intellectual. But his was never the paralyzing scepticism which easily becomes comfortable or corroding cynicism. He had a positive faith—faith in the gradual power to pierce nature's mysteries through man's indomitable endeavors. This was the road by which he reached an attitude of widest tolerance towards views which were strange and uncongenial to him, lest by a premature stifling even of crude or groping ideas society might be deprived of eventual wisdom for attaining a gracious civilization. (MJH: 85)

As in Madison, both the richness of the object of knowledge and the inadequacy of the instrument of knowing are remarked upon. As in Cicero, there is concern to distinguish the position from one which would withdraw the adherent from active, public life.

The skeptical position thus provided the underpinning for "judicial restraint":

It was not for him [Holmes] to prescribe for society or deny it the right of experimentation within very wide limits. This was to be left for political contest by the political forces in the state. The duty of the Court was to keep the ring free. He reached the democratic result by the philosophic route of scepticism— by his disbelief in ultimate answers to social questions. (MJH: 22)

In Holmes's case, however, "the democratic result" was more a fact to be acknowledged than a principle to be valued. Holmes believed that the most powerful interest groups in society would prevail and was very candid about this: "All that can be expected from modern improvements is that legislation should easily and quickly, yet not too quickly, modify itself in accordance with the will of the de facto supreme power in the community, and that the spread of an educated sympathy should reduce the sacrifice of minorities to a minimum...."[27]

In his biography, White considers Holmes inconsistent for his willingness to limit jury discretion in tort liability cases. White disparages his position as "countermajoritarian" because "[j]urors were representative of the community." The fact that "judges...were unelected, unaccountable officials" makes them no less representative of the "sovereign power" of the state than jurors (who are, for that matter, also unelected). White had already, at the passage cited earlier, permitted Holmes to make his point about who best "represented" the "community": "In many areas of negligence, Holmes believed, 'a state of facts' was 'often repeated in practice.' In such instances '[a] judge who has long sat at *nisi prius* ought gradually to acquire a fund of experience which enables him to represent the common sense of the community in ordinary instances far better than the average jury'." That our legal tradition places choice about "facts" in the hands of a lay group (a jury) does not imply that it needs to or should place in such hands the choice of conclusions to be drawn from these "facts."[28]

Democracy had quite different standing in the thought of Louis D. Brandeis.

Brandeis, Jewish and originally from Louisville, was doubly an outsider at Harvard and in Boston but nonetheless was very successful in legal practice in the Northeast. After insuring a comfortable fortune, he began to contribute his legal skill to the working poor and to what he saw as the public good. His career coincided with the growth of large business enterprises, efforts to organize industrial labor, and State legislation addressed to various economic and social problems. In the first decade of this century, he introduced into argument before the Supreme Court what came to be called the "Brandeis brief"—a massing of factual information to explain or justify State regulation. He was a progressive without being a "Progressive." Unlike those associated with Theodore Roosevelt, he did not accept the inevitability of Big Business, Big Labor, and Big (Federal) Government. He emphasized the potential benefits of using the States as laboratories for experimentation in social legislation. His views were quite compatible with those of Woodrow Wilson, who nominated him to be Associate Justice of the Supreme Court in 1916.

As with Holmes, we shall look at Brandeis with the eyes of Frankfurter. A few quotations from Frankfurter's 1931 essay, "Mr. Justice Brandeis and the Constitution" display F.F.'s understanding of Brandeis.

A philosophy of humility determines Mr. Justice Brandeis's conception of the Supreme Court's function: an instinct against the tyranny of dogma and a skepticism regarding the perdurance of any man's wisdom, though he be a judge. No one knows better than he how slender a reed is reason—how recent its emergence in man, how powerful the countervailing instincts and passions, how treacherous the whole rational process. But just because the efforts of reason are tenuous, a constant process of critical scrutiny of the tentative claims of reason is essential to the very progress of reason.   (FC: 264)

We should note that—as with Cicero, Holmes, and Frankfurter himself—a "philosophy of humility" and a personal style of humility are not the same thing.

Echoing the concern of Morley, F.F. expands upon the importance of rigorous advocacy:

Passionate convictions are too often in the service of the doctrinaire....But Mr. Justice Brandeis is the very negation of a dogmatist. He has remained scrupulously flexible, constantly subjecting experience to the test of wider experience....[H]is opinions reveal consciousness of a world for which no absolute is adequate. It is a world of more or less, of give and take, of live and let live. Interests clash, but no single one must yield. Self-willed power must be guarded against, but government must not be paralyzed. And even liberty must have its bounds....Problems, for him, are never solved. Civilization is a sequence of new tasks. Hence his insistence on the extreme difficulty of government and its dependence on sustained interest and effort, on the need for constant alertness to the fact that the introduction of new forces is

accompanied by new difficulties. This...makes him mindful of the limited
range of human foresight, and leads him to practice humility in attempting
to preclude the freedom of action of those who are to follow. (FC: 267-270)

Despite their oft-commented on frequent agreement on the Court, Brandeis
was Holmes's opposite when it came to producing opinions and dissents. In "Some
Reflections on the Reading of Statutes" (LM: 50-51), F.F. compared the two.
Holmes typically produced his work very quickly, delighted in his facility with
English style, and often leaves the reader rather in the dark as to how he reached
his conclusion and even exactly what he means. Brandeis laboriously marshaled
facts and arguments and often employed technical terms of law and other fields.
Once on the Court, Frankfurter himself was more inclined to follow Brandeis in
his manner of presentation and in a number of cases added detailed appendices to
justify or elaborate on his views.

Brandeis drew from his skepticism a preoccupation with localism and the
importance of the States as social laboratories. Frankfurter took this very seriously:

> The veto power of the Supreme Court over the social-economic legislation of
> the States, when exercised by a narrow conception of due process and equal
> protection of the law clauses, presents undue centralization in its most
> destructive and least reasonable form. The most destructive, because it stops
> experiment at its source, preventing an increase of social knowledge by the
> only scientific method available, namely, the test of trial and error. The least
> responsible, because it so often turns on the fortuitous circumstances which
> determine a majority decision, and shelters the fallible judgment of individual
> justices, in matters of fact and opinion not particularly within the special
> competence of judges.... (FC: 255-256)

Despite his involvement in the New Deal, F.F. was not committed to one of
the major effects of that period—the translation of almost all important issues to
the Federal arena. His commitment to the viability and importance of the States
marked many of his judicial statements and helped give him his "conservative"
reputation. As he says in the essay on Brandeis, so it can be said of him:

> [His] regard for the States is no mere lip service. He is greatly tolerant of their
> powers because he believes intensely in the opportunities which they afford
> for decentralization. And he believes in decentralization not because of any
> persistent habit of political allegiance or through an anachronistic theory of
> States' rights. His views are founded on deep convictions regarding the
> manageable size for the effective conduct of human affairs and the most
> favorable conditions for the exercise of wise judgment. (FC: 259)

Neither Brandeis nor Frankfurter participated in the revival of interest in

Alexis de Tocqueville, although these remarks about "manageable size" and "favorable conditions" could almost have been taken from *Democracy in America*, especially Volume 1, Chapter 16 and Volume 2, Book 2, chapter 4.[29]

Just as Frankfurter left the Court and then this life, others began to praise localism under the banner of "participatory democracy." The focal principle of Students for a Democratic Society (SDS), however, was individual development through participation rather than the skeptical connection of localism, experimentation, and the search for more adequate truths. In the 1990s, the principle of localism seems to be in dispute between those who adhere to the experimental approach and those who wish to deny any authority to government.

5. The Harvard Publications and Their Applications

During his years as a professor of law at Harvard, Frankfurter produced a substantial scholarly and popular written record which gives a clear preview of the skeptical, experimental, and process-oriented principles which would guide him on the Supreme Court. Comparison of these pre-Court writings with his opinions and dissents makes quite clear that there was no dramatic shift from "liberal" to "conservative." Most of his contemporaries did not have quite so full a picture as we have since a number of his commentaries and editorials appeared in the *New Republic* in unsigned form. In many cases and over a long period, F.F. borrowed his own language, sometimes again and again, in both his essays and his Court opinions. He loved to think of preserving things "in the amber of history." He often repeated quotes or misquotes of others, too: "think things, not words" from Holmes; "it is a constitution we are interpreting" from John Marshall; and, from Macaulay, "you must reform in order to preserve" (RF: 192-194).

It appears to me that he gradually changed his economic views. Though I do not intend to examine it here, I believe he modified these, but always around an experimental approach as contrasted with acceptance of a theory. He seems never to have engaged in sustained study of economic theory. He disagreed with Holmes, who was attached to free-market theory, but never found their differences enough to influence his view of the older man. To F.F., the important thing about Holmes's dissent in *Lochner v. New York*, 198 U.S. 45 (1905) was his willingness to let experimentation proceed even though he doubted its efficacy. Brandeis, like Holmes, was better read in economic theory than F.F.; but his major focus was on applications to institutional organization and finance. F.F. seems to have shared the interest in applications without any attendant interest in theory. He sympathized with the interventionalism of Harold Laski and the British socialists without ever subscribing to their theories. He seems to have been of a mind with FDR whose approach to the Great Depression was to try and try again—to "experiment" (RF: 63-72). When the time came, Frankfurter showed a readiness to accept the practical "solutions" of Keynes. By the late 1950s and 1960s, however,

F.F. showed a bit more respect for free-market views of business enterprise. This too was probably just his experimental approach rather than conversion to a different theory of economics.

Frankfurter's first major work was a case-book on the work of a regulative agency, *A Selection of Cases Under the Interstate Commerce Act* (1915). His organization of the text, though straight-forward enough, is also revealing: the scope of the commerce regulated by the Act, the "duties" of "carriers" under the Act, the functions of the Interstate Commerce Commission under the Act, and the functions of the courts under the Act. He emphasized the "quasi-judicial" role of the Commission and its primary jurisdiction. The Commission could properly create its own procedures and need not mimic the traditional forms of the court system. The judicial system should review the Commission's decisions only under restricted circumstances and should not attempt to substitute court procedures or judgments for those of the Commission. A new institution with new procedures should be seen as a reasonable and proper response to new developments in the national economy. The judiciary should recognize that primary responsibility lies elsewhere and should be appropriately modest in inserting its traditional procedures into the way chosen by Congress for dealing with these problems.

Once on the Court, Frankfurter applied and expanded upon these views but did not contradict them. He made clear that when an agency chose to follow the procedures of the court system, it was bound by its choice. *In Securities and Exchange Commission v. Chenery Corporation*, 318 U.S. 80 (1943), the Commission "purported to be acting only as it assumed a court of equity would have acted in a similar case. Since the decision of the Commission was explicitly based upon the applicability of principles of equity announced by courts, its validity must likewise be judged on that basis. The grounds upon which an administrative order must be judged are those upon which the record discloses that its action was based" (87). In accord with the case-book, F.F. makes clear that the Commission is "not bound by settled judicial precedents" if it, "acting upon its experience and peculiar competence, promulgated a general rule of which its order...was a particular application..." (92).

The authority of a regulatory commission to establish rules unlike those of the judicial system was affirmed over the objections of Justice Murphy the next term in *National Broadcasting Company, Inc. v. United States*, 319 U.S. 190 (1943). The Federal Communications Commission had promulgated regulations which were "assailed as 'arbitrary and capricious.' If this contention means that the Regulations are unwise, that they are unlikely to succeed in accomplishing what the Commission intended, we can only say that the appellants have selected the wrong forum for such a plea....Our duty is at an end when we find that the action of the Commission was based upon findings supported by evidence, and was made pursuant to authority granted by Congress. It is not for us to say that the 'public interest' will be furthered or retarded by the [regulations]" (224).

The relation of the courts to the other branches, moreover, varies with the legislation establishing the regulatory measures. As F.F. pointed out in dissent in *Stark v. Wickard, Secretary of Agriculture* 321 U.S. 288, 311 (1944), "there is the greatest contrariety in the extent to which, and the procedures by which, different measures of control afford judicial review of administrative action....Except in...rare instances.., whether judicial review is available at all, and, if so, who may invoke it, and under what circumstances, in what manner, and to what end, are questions that depend for their answer upon the particular enactment under which judicial review is claimed....There is no such thing as a common law of judicial review in the federal courts" (312).

F.F.'s interest, following Brandeis, in the place of "facts" in the operation of the legal system and the development of legal concepts and doctrines were evidenced both in the presentation of a "Brandeis brief" *The Case for a Shorter Work Day* before the Supreme Court in 1917 and in his participation with Roscoe Pound in the work which produced in 1922 a study of *Criminal Justice in Cleveland.* The former also sheds light on Frankfurter's understanding of "principles": "...the principle is the beginning and not the end of inquiry. The field of contention is in its application" (SWD: 981)

These early writings shed light on Frankfurter's understanding of a phrase by Holmes which he quoted often: "think things, not words." The "things" at issue are problems and institutions. By "words" he understands etymologies and "logical analysis"—word structures without explicit consideration of what the words refer to. The Interstate Commerce Commission, for example, was created by Congress to cope with problems in the nation's economy. As Congress recognized these problems and provided institutional response, it gave new meanings to old words. As business enterprises introduced new production techniques and experts in health sciences came to a new recognition of causal connections, the States passed new laws and established new procedures to deal with new (or newly understood) facts. The meaning of words and phrases such as "reason" and "public welfare" changes over time. Legislative bodies have primary responsibility for making or recognizing these changes. When we move beyond the reading of the texts of the published laws to the ways people in various organizations actually respond to the situations which face them, we see that the doing of justice is not as straight-forward as it seems. In the process of inquiry, a "principle"— which can be viewed as a summation of previous experience—is the starting point for further investigation. New facts may be recognized, so questions must be raised about the relation of these new facts to the old summation of experience.

In *The Public and Its Government,* discussed below, Frankfurter examined the regulatory agencies and their staffing in more general terms. Once on the Court, he saw cases involving the agencies as one of his specialties. He had competition from William O. Douglas who had chaired the Securities and Exchange Commission. In one of F.F.'s earliest opinions for the Court, *F.C.C. v Pottsville*

Broadcasting Co., 309 U.S. 134 (1940), he discussed the relation of court procedures to those of regulatory agencies.

> [The] history of Anglo-American courts and the more or less n a r r o w l y
> defined range of their staple business have determined the basic characteristics
> of trial procedure, the rules of evidence, and the general principles of appellate
> review. Modern administrative tribunals are the outgrowth of conditions far
> different from those [in which the courts arose]. To a large degree [the
> administrative agencies] have been a response to the felt need of governmental
> supervision over economic enterprise—a supervision which could effectively
> be exercised neither directly through self-executing legislation nor by the
> judicial process (142).

There is nothing wrong or inappropriate for Congress to create

> administrative agencies with powers...different from the conventional judicial
> modes for adjusting conflicting claims....These differences in origin and
> function preclude wholesale transplantation of the rules of procedure, trial,
> and review which have evolved from all the history and experience of
> courts....[Although t]o be sure the laws under which these agencies operate
> prescribe the fundamentals of fair play. (143)

Thus,

> technical rules derived from the interrelationship of judicial tribunals forming
> a hierarchical system are taken out of their environment when mechanically
> applied to determine the extent to which congressional power, exercised
> through a delegated   agency, can be controlled within the limited scope of
> "judicial power" conferred by Congress under the Constitution. (141)

That is to say, while such fundamentals as opportunity for a hearing and a reasoned conclusion are appropriate for a wide variety of institutions, we should not
assume that they can be achieved by only one set of familiar procedures nor that
institutional innovation must follow familiar patterns. We must resist the intellectual laziness which forgets that—to put it in rather infelicitous terms—there is
more than one way to skin a cat.

Frankfurter's preoccupation with the legal system rather than just the laws
came to focus on the Supreme Court. Especially with the assistance of his student
and later colleague James M. Landis, Frankfurter for many years published an
annual article in the *Harvard Law Review* on the "business of the Supreme Court."
A book of that title was published in 1928, dedicated to Justice Holmes. These
articles were not just reportage of doctrines promulgated by the Court. The "business" reviewed the kinds of public problems coming before the Court, the changing jurisdiction of the Court, and the importance of the Court's focusing its ener-

gies on issues which it is uniquely situated to resolve. In the book, F.F. noted the need for more empirical data—"judicial statistics"—on the judicial process. These include "...the types and volumes of issues, the duration of trials, the speed of disposition, the delay of appeals," and the creation of standard procedures for collecting the data (BSC: 220). These essays and the book probably contributed more than any other work F.F. did while at Harvard to build the reputation which made his appointment to the Supreme Court so acceptable. Those who read this work with care would have no reason to think he shifted to the right once on the Court.

Of particular concern is the problem of accountability. Since the Federal judiciary is not elected by the people and should not be controlled by the "political" branches, accountability raises especially delicate issues of information and scrutiny—first of all, self-scrutiny and then that of the "profession and the public" (BSC: 281). Accountability is necessary in popular government. In the judiciary, in Frankfurter's view, it is best not achieved through popular review in elections. He argues that it can be achieved through ongoing, publicized procedures for gathering and interpreting data along with judicial structure and procedures which are as clearly defined and well-publicized as possible. These methods will permit the judiciary itself, the legal profession, and the public to exercise adequate and proper control. (His popular essays, which will be discussed below, were a part of public "control.") As early as 1911, he attacked "this sacrosanct notion of our judiciary....[avoided] a natural tendency of self reverence by members of an institution...[and stressed the role of] the bar to keep alert eyes on our courts" (D: 113).

To function in an accountable manner, the judiciary requires conditions and procedures conducive to good judgments and the facts necessary for an informed judgment. Frankfurter enumerated "the methods and practices in the discharge of its business which are within the Court's own making." He lists six "conditions which are indispensable to a seasoned, collective judicial judgment": (1) oral argument stimulating and stimulated by vigorous questioning by the Justices; (2) "fixed, frequent and long conferences" for which each of the Justices has prepared with care; (3) recognition of individual "talents and energies" in the assignment of opinions; (4) circulation of draft opinions with ample time for critiquing, revision, and the preparation of alternative lines of argument; (5) discouragement of rehearings to encourage thoroughness.

Finally, (6) to "these specific procedural habits must be added the traditions of the Court, the public scrutiny which it enjoys, and the long tenure of the Justices. The inspiration which comes from a great past is reinforced by sensitiveness to healthy criticism. Continuity and experience in adjudication are secured through length of service, as distinguished from the method of selection" (BSC: vii). The last point implies that persons change as they are influenced by the role they assume on the Court, but only if they are aware or are made aware of the traditions of the Court and if they are subjected to healthy criticism. Both as professor and as Justice, Frankfurter considered himself both a teacher of the traditions and an exemplary critic.

Frankfurter also showed lasting concern, derived from Brandeis, with the ways the Court obtains access to factual information of relevance to decision. Traditionally, courts rely on contesting parties to bring forth the most relevant information and most powerful arguments on behalf of each side of a case. This is a powerful reason for restricting judicial business to "cases and controversies." When the outcome is of concern only to the contesting parties, we may think each gets only what is deserved by the care in preparation. In the types of cases coming before the Supreme Court, however, this may not be adequate because other substantial interests, including especially public interests, may be implicated in the outcome. How is the judiciary to insure it has all the facts it needs? In F.F.'s view, inadequate attention had been paid to this problem. The legal profession needs to "put its mind to devising the necessary method and machinery by which knowledge of the facts, which are the foundation of constitutional judgment, may be formally at the service of courts." This requires the "inventive powers" of lawyers and experimentation with different procedures. Frankfurter himself enumerates five modes for bringing before the Court relevant facts not limited by the vision of counsel. The first of these is one aspect of "judicial restraint": "deference to legislative judgment that circumstances exist warranting a change in the policy of the law." That is, even if justifying facts are not presented, a court should proceed on the assumption that the legislature had such facts. (This may of course be an error, as illustrated by the curious history of the Mann Act. The Act was adopted by Congress on the assumption that an extensive slave trade existed to ship young white maidens to the Orient to satisfy exotic sexual lusts. There was no factual basis for this concern, but the Act remained on the books and courts found other applications.[30]) Second, the legislature may include in the legislation a recital of the relevant facts. Third, the Justices may draw on "common knowledge" or information readily accessible, though it is important that they not accept as obvious what is actually controversial. Fourth, counsel arguing the case may bring forth more facts than a narrow view of the case would elicit. (This has especially justified amicus curiae briefs since Frankfurter wrote.) Finally, the Court itself may request opposing counsel to provide additional evidence (BSC: 312 ff.). (In Brown v Board of Education, 347 U.S. 483 [1954] the Court followed F.F.'s suggested use of his fifth procedure by addressing to opposing counsel a series of questions for their responses.) To improve upon these resources requires cooperation among active lawyers, those involved with legal education and research, and students of social change.

These prescriptions have been followed only sporadically, and the recommended cooperation has been infrequent. In The Public and Its Government, F.F. expressed concern about imbalance rather than cooperation—the imbalance of rewards available to those lawyers serving the public and those serving private interests. A new form of imbalance has developed since then between those serving State governments and those serving interests challenging the State. The latter are often graduates or faculty members of the most prestigious law schools or members of national law firms serving as *amicus curiae*.

Frankfurter's concerns that the Supreme Court focus on those issues it is uniquely situated to resolve and limit its business to insure adequate time for thorough consideration of such cases continued throughout his tenure on the Court and produced some of his most acrimonious conflicts with colleagues. His book traces the changing pattern by which cases come before the Court. Very few cases come before the Court because the Constitution specifies that they must do so as a matter of constitutional right. Most come on appeal as provided by various judiciary acts adopted by Congress. In earlier decades, these appeals were themselves matters of legal right; the Court had to accept them.

In the twentieth century, the Court finally gained substantial control over its business by making its review of each case a matter of choice determined by the Court itself. While the Court is still obliged by law to review some types of cases, for the most part it decides—with the positive vote of four members—whether it will grant certiorari (a writ calling up the case for its review). The Court thus has jurisdiction over many cases which it does not choose to review. F.F.'s opposites on the Court, most notably Black and Douglas, saw the Court's responsibility to be the doing of justice in individual cases where justice has not or seems not to have been done in the lower courts. F.F. considered this view irrational and irresponsible. All cases require choice on the part of the deciding judge. Reasonable, careful, and fair persons may arrive at different conclusions. To pretend to review all such cases is irrational because the number of cases where there remains some doubt is far beyond the time available to the Justices. Irresponsible because such second-guessing of the lower courts justifies carelessness below. He made the point explicit in *Adams, Warden v. United States ex rel McCann*, 317 U.S. 269 (1942) in attacking "legal formalisms" and "distrust of courts to accommodate judgment to the varying circumstances of individual cases. But this is to express want of faith in the very tribunals which are charged with enforcement of the Constitution. 'Universal distrust,' Mr. Justice Holmes admonishes us, 'creates universal incompetence'" (280). Irresponsible too because, as the process has operated, it has favored one class of parties.

The process was underway even as he wrote his initial article chronicling the business of the Court. Of cases arising under the Federal Employers' Liability Act, he notes: "Although the increased role played by certiorari has greatly enlarged the Court's power of preventing cases without real public interest from reaching it, in several instances during the last term the Court assumed jurisdiction in cases where a public or general interest is hardly discernible" (FC: 196). He was even more outspoken in the book:

...it is almost grotesque that the ultimate voice of the Constitution should be invoked to determine whether "the requisite employment in interstate commerce" exists where a car repairer is replacing a draw bar in a car then in use in such commerce as contrasted with a worker in a railroad machine shop who alters the location of a fixture communicating power to machinery used in repairing engines hauling both intrastate and interstate trains! (BSC: 209)

Once on the Court, with his own time at issue, he found the FELA cases an especial irritant. As Wallace Mendelson has pointed out in his comparison *Justices Black and Frankfurter*, Black found the votes to grant certiorari to workmen; but no one was similarly disposed to grant certiorari on behalf of employers.[31] F.F.'s diaries show that he thought perhaps he had succeeded in changing Court practice, but his success was short-lived. Frankfurter's comments in *Ferguson v. Moore-McCormack Lines, Inc.*, 352 U.S. 521, 524 (1957) typify his views. "...[Brandeis's] regard for the bearing on the judicial product of what business comes to the Court and how the Court deals with it, have been neglected in the name of 'doing justice' in individual cases" (525). "...a justice who believes that such cases raise insignificant and unimportant questions—insignificant and unimportant from the point of view of the Court's duties—and that an increasing amount of the Court's time is unduly drained by adjudication of these cases cannot forego the duty to voice his dissent to the Court's action" (529). There was no showing that the lower courts had been consistently biased; and the cases, moreover, often required inspection of extensive technical information for an adequate grasp of the issues.

The more general problems of responsibility in judging emerge in *National Labor Relations Board v. Mexia Textile Mills, Inc.*, 339 U.S. 563, 570 (1950), in which F.F. called attention to the growing difficulty of multiplying appeals. "One does not have to be an easy generalizer of national characteristics to believe that litigiousness is one of our besetting sins. A relaxed observance of the considerations that supposedly govern our certiorari jurisdiction is not calculated to discourage litigiousness" (573-574). Connected with this is the appearance that the Supreme Court regards the Circuit Courts of Appeal "merely as way-stations to this court" (574).

In establishing Courts of Appeals, Congress intended to create courts of great dignity and ability whose decisions were to be final except in very limited instances where the Supreme Bench should pronounce for the whole nation....The volume of business...was assumed to preclude the grant of certiorari, however decided below, in which the instance of error was too small compared with the drain their consideration would make on the thought and energy demanded of this Court in cases which invariably belong here. (572-573)

In F.F.'s view, Congress intended the Circuit Courts to have "final determination of this type of controversy" except "where the constitutional issues, or conflicts of circuits, or obvious considerations of public importance call for consideration" (572).

As a part of the proper management of the business coming before the Supreme Court for its decision, Frankfurter was also concerned that cases and the issues they raise not reach the Court prematurely. Unlike those who want to get a matter settled and done with, he was cautious in permitting the introduction of issues. In *Joint Anti-Fascist Refugee Committee v. McGrath, Attorney General, et al.*, 341 U.S. 123,149 (1951), he reviewed some of the issues to be faced in deciding jurisdiction. "...a court will not decide a question unless the nature of the action challenged, the kind of injury inflicted, and the relationship between the parties are such that judicial determination is consonant with what was, generally speaking, the business of the Colonial courts and the courts of Westminster when the Constitution was framed" (150). Only the "expert feel of lawyers" can recognize what constitutes a "cases or controversy," but some guidance can be given. There must be a "real controversy" so that issues are "presented in an adversary manner" based on "adverse personal interest" (150-151). In more detail, three questions follow in cases such as this seeking relief from governmental action. "Will the action challenged at any time substantially affect the 'legal' interest of any person? A litigant ordinarily has standing to challenge governmental action of a sort that, if taken by a private person, would create a right of action cognizable by the courts....Does the action challenged affect the petitioners with sufficient 'directness'?" And, "Is the action sufficiently final?" (152-155). All of this, to make sense, presupposes the tradition of the Anglo-American legal profession—manned (as it was in those days) by those who had undergone a severe and complete apprenticeship. The master lawyer, like the master physicist, has learned to read the record, verbal or photographic, and to distinguish the traces of the elementary particles of the craft among the photographic debris.

The point is made in an early case, *Dennis J. Driscoll v. Edison Light and Power Co.*, 307 U.S. 104, 122 (1939), a utility rate case. F.F. enlarged upon "questions of an essentially legal nature" by adding "in the sense that legal education and lawyer's learning afford peculiar competence" (122). By contrast, the setting of utility rates may call on the "knowledge of economics and finance" and the "practicalities of business enterprise." He continues, "The only relevant function of law in dealing with this intersection of government and enterprise is to secure observance of those procedural safeguards in the exercise of legislative powers which are the historic foundation of due process" (122). A system of such complexity as modern society can function only by recognition of our limitations as well as our expertise—what is and what is not our individual "business." That business is not simply a matter of book-learning but requires a "feel" for the material which may be developed over time. As in every art, not everyone suc-

ceeds in becoming a master; but every competent lawyer, in F.F.'s view, has developed a feel for the "procedural safeguards" of due process. This idea of feel
has been explored by Gilbert Ryle as the distinction between "knowing how" and
"knowing that" and by Michael Polanyi in his exploration of "learning how" as at
the foundation of each discipline.[32]

The situation has changed since Frankfurter wrote. The consensus about the
art or craft of law among practicing lawyers has diminished. Women and minorities have entered the profession in larger numbers and have done so partly as
"outsiders" unwilling to be wholly assimilated or compromised by the "white
western males" of the tradition. The intellectual milieu has also changed. The
legal tradition itself has been "compromised" by the introduction of "social sciences" and "philosophy." I use the quote marks to acknowledge that the changes
are seen by many as improvements and to note that the ideas and insights brought
to legal study are from disciplines explicitly external to the law.

Another of F.F.'s controversial dissents growing out of his understanding of
"the business of the Supreme Court" which further alienated liberals occurred in
Adler et al. v. Board of Education, 342 U.S. 485, 497 (1952). He wished to avoid
or postpone judicial decision on the grounds that the plaintiffs lacked standing.
What was at issue was an effort to enjoin the State board from promulgating rules
intended to eliminate "communist" teachers from New York schools. He com-
plains that the case has gone forward though the "intricate machinery has not yet
been set in motion" (500). He would defer on grounds that the several persons
who have brought the suit do not have standing: the taxpayers because this is not
a "pocketbook issue"; parents because the "hurt to [their] sensibilities is too tenuous or the inroad upon rightful claims to public education too argumentative to
serve as the earthy stuff required for legal right justicially enforceable" (501-
503). Even the teachers "merely allege that the Statutes and Rules permit" actions
depriving some teachers of rights under the First Amendment. Earlier laws have
been on the books for years without being enforced, so it remains to be seen
whether these regulations will actually be enforced.

> This case proves anew the wisdom of rigorous adherence to the prerequisites
> for pronouncement by the court on matters of constitutional law. The absence
> in the plaintiffs of the immediacy and solidity of interest necessary to support
> jurisdiction is reflected in the atmosphere of abstraction and ambiguity in
> which the constitutional issues are presented. The broad, generalized claims
> urged at the bar touch the deepest interests of a democratic society: its right to
> self-preservation and the ample scope for the individual's freedom, especially
> the teacher's freedom of thought, inquiry and expression. (504)

Too much of the scheme of enforcement was not yet clear. It is not the words of
the statute and regulations which should be found unconstitutional, if that is appropriate, but the actions taken allegedly in pursuance of the words. (506-507)

The value of the doctrine of "ripeness" took another and more general form in *Radio Corporation of America et al. v. United States et al.*, 341 U.S. 412, 421 (1951). At issue was the question of judicial review of the FCC. The Commission had settled on one technical solution for the transmission of color television. Black wrote the opinion of the Court approving the Commission's action. F.F. proclaimed himself *"dubitante."* While acknowledging that the Commission very broadly ought to be "allowed to exercise its powers unhampered by the restrictive procedures appropriate for litigation in the courts," Congress had given to the Court the power to review. "What may be an obvious matter of judgment for the Commission in one situation may so profoundly affect the public interest in another as not to be a mere exercise of conventional discretion" (423). Should the Court second-guess in such a situation? F.F., without making a final commitment, made a case for intervention. "What the Commission here decided is that it could not wait...a little while longer....[though] nothing was submitted to us on argument...which gives any hint as to the public interest that brooks no delay" (424). In a passage with the flavor of Burke, F.F. reflects:

> One of the more important sources of the retardation or regression of civilization is man's tendency to use new inventions indiscriminately or too hurriedly without adequate reflection of long-range consequences....The rational process of trial and error implies a wary use of novelty and a critical adoption of change....What evil would be encouraged, what good retarded by delay? By haste, would morality be enhanced, insight deepened, and judgment enlightened?.... prophecy of technological feasibility is hardly in the domain of expertness so long as scientific and technological barriers do not make the prospect fanciful....One need not have the insight of a great scientific investigator, nor the rashness of the untutored, to be confident that the prognostications now made in regard to the feasibility of a "compatible" color television system will be falsified in the very near future.   (425-427)

F.F.'s dubiety was shortly validated by events.

In another book, *The Labor Injunction*, written with Nathan Greene and published in 1930, Frankfurter sought to provide facts and analysis on a "technical" matter which had considerable public impact. The injunction had become a common tool in the hands of management, forcing organized (or organizing) labor to postpone or cease activities under the threat of court punishment. Frankfurter believed the courts were issuing injunctions both too frequently and in a biased way. This work too employed the genetic method: "Here, as elsewhere in the law, a full understanding of the history of a legal institution under scrutiny is necessary to wise reform" (LI: 1). Frankfurter had come to his own assessment some years before in an unsigned 1922 editorial for the *New Republic*, "Labor Injunctions Must Go" (FC: 104). (The essay was an occasion for one of F.F.'s sharpest public personal attacks and illustrates his bluntness: "There is probably agreement by informed professional opinion that in the history of this country there has never been a more unlearned and professionally less equipped Attorney General than Harry M. Daugherty. The spectacle of this man, unrestrained by the statesman's wisdom or the lawyer's tradition from attempting to write his economic prejudices into the law of the land, has a touch of humor which alone saves it from tragedy" (FC: 106).)

As a matter of biography, Frankfurter "sided with" labor. His argument against the labor injunction is not, however, a matter of special pleading for a favored interest group. In the case of the labor injunction, the legal profession had adapted a legal instrument to changing conditions; but it had done so in a way which undercut confidence in the fairness of the courts. The labor injunction had been used in such ways as to make the courts seem allies of management in advance of any full hearing instead of the neutral arbiters of such a hearing. The injunction was a "shortcut." What was prevented by injunction could be assessed and, as appropriate, penalized after the fact. The legal system, using the tools available to it, had created its own response to dynamic changes in the nation's economy. The response was neither comprehensive nor fair. The judicial system should abandoned its innovations and the field left to legislative response.

Book and editorial are reminders that, for Felix Frankfurter, learned and professional opinion must go hand in hand with popular opinion in a democracy. He produced a series of articles and editorials designed to explain to the general public just how important the "technicalities" of the legal system are. The most famous of his popular efforts was a long article published in the *Atlantic Monthly* in 1927 and shortly thereafter printed as a small book, *The Case of Sacco and Vanzetti*. The book was subtitled "A Critical Analysis for Lawyers and Laymen." The book does not argue the guilt or innocence of Sacco or Vanzetti, although F.F. eventually came to think them innocent.[33] It argues, rather, that the prosecution and the trial judge were patently unfair. The book is a withering indictment of prosecutor and judge. In the course of explaining how they sharpened and directed prejudice and bias against the accused, the book also painted a harsh picture of Boston, "one of the worst centers of [the] lawlessness and hysteria" (SV: 43) stirred by Attorney General Palmer's outburst of "native Americanism."

Frankfurter originally had paid little attention to the colorful and well-publicized trial of Nicola Sacco and Bartolomeo Vanzetti for robbery and murder. He made a point of not attempting to assess legal cases from accounts in the popular media (F.F.R: 208) It was only when the case reached appeal and was taken over by a highly respected figure of the Boston bar who was also a friend of Stimson that F.F. finally began to study the record. What he found was that the prosecutor had intentionally and conspiratorially framed a question so that the testimony of a ballistics expert seemed to say what the expert did not believe. "That outraged my sensibilities, outraged my whole conviction of what the administration of justice calls for, and my whole antecedents propelled me into action" (F.F.R: 213).

This case was even more extreme than the Mooney case as an example of those entrusted with doing justice choosing to do injustice.

Frankfurter was widely attacked and praised for the book, both for the wrong reasons. The book contributed much to his radical reputation and was to mislead many about what to expect from his appointment to the Court. Many readers of the time read the book as an argument for the innocence of the accused and others, even, as a statement in behalf of their anarchistic views. He tried to define his own middle position at the end of the book.

> I have sought to give in perspective...the facts of a particular case which has attracted world-wide attention, and not to call into question the Anglo-American system of criminal justice in general, or that of Massachusetts in particular. American criminal procedure has its defects. That we know on the authority of all who have made a special study of its working. But its essentials have behind them the vindication of centuries. Only ignorant and uncritical minds will find in an occasional striking illustration of its fallibilities an attack upon its foundations or lack of loyalty to its purposes. All systems of law, however wise, are administered through men, and therefore may occasionally disclose the frailties of men. Perfection may not be demanded of law, but the capacity to correct errors of inevitable frailty is the mark of a civilized legal mechanism. Grave injustices, as a matter of fact, do arise even under the most civilized systems of law and despite adherence to the forms of procedure intended to safeguard against them.
>
> [Efforts to correct such errors] reveal confidence in our institutions and their capacity to rectify errors. They also serve to warn us that, because ordinarily the criminal machinery affords ample safeguards against perversions of justice, a situation may not arise where extraordinary circumstances have deflected the operation of the normal procedure. (SV: 107-110)

This statement neatly reaffirms the traditional blending of skepticism with constitutional procedures. Unfortunately, all too many readers proved to have "ignorant and uncritical minds" and, whether taking it for good or ill, thought Frankfurter to be sharply critical of the foundations of the legal order. In fact, he had great "confidence in our institutions and their capacity to rectify errors."

On the Court, F.F. several times found occasion to reiterate the importance that those enforcing the law should do so in exemplary fashion. In dissent in a search and seizure case, *Harris v. United States*, 331 U.S. 145, 155 (1947), he pointed out that "[s]tooping to questionable methods neither enhances that respect for law which is the most potent element in law enforcement, nor, in the long-run, do such methods promote successful prosecution ....Respect for law by law officers promotes respect generally, just as lawlessness by law officers sets a contagious and competitive example to others" (172). And concurring in a case involving the allegation of entrapment, *Sherman v. United States*, 356 U.S. 369, 378 (1958), "[p]ublic confidence in the fair and honorable administration of justice, upon which ultimately depends the rule of law, is the transcending value at stake" (380).

One "error," however, which our institutions had not "rectified" was to trouble Frankfurter throughout his term on the Supreme Court. He thought interpretation of the Due Process Clause of the Fourteenth Amendment had taken a wrong turn which had in turn infected even the understanding of the phrase in the Fifth Amendment (which "had lain inactive or strictly confined" for a hundred years). In an unsigned *New Republic* editorial of 1924, "The Red Terror of Judicial Reform," mentioned earlier, he concluded that the "due process clauses ought to go" (FC: 167).

Both of the major party candidates for President in 1924 had given Labor Day speeches endorsing the responsibility of the Supreme Court to protect the "rights" guaranteed by the Constitution and Bill of Rights. Frankfurter understood their speeches to be attempts to question the Americanism of third-party candidate Senator Robert LaFollette and other critics of certain Court decisions which had limited legislative power over labor issues. In his response, F.F. distinguishes three "classes" of Constitutional cases which come before the Court: Commerce Clause cases which require the Court to "mediate between the States and the nation"; "specific prohibitions upon the legislative power" which offer narrowly limited scope for judicial review because of the "definiteness of the terms of these specific prohibitions, the definiteness of their history, [or] the definiteness of their aims"; and the "due process of law" and the "equal protection of the laws" clauses. These "broad 'guarantees' in favor of the individual are expressed in words so undefined, either by their intrinsic meaning, or by history, or by tradition, that they leave the individual Justice free, if indeed they do not actually compel him, to fill in the vacuum with his own controlling notions of economic, social, and industrial facts with reference to which they are invoked" (161-163). Frankfurter concludes that "no nine men are wise enough and good enough to be entrusted with the power which the unlimited provisions of the due process clauses confer" and points out that "not a single constitution framed for English-speaking countries since the Fourteenth Amendment has embodied its provisions" (166-167).

F.F.'s views of "due process" will be examined in more detail below. By the time he reached the Court, he had given up any hope of eliminating the due process clauses. He never ceased to call attention to the fact that other popular governments get along well enough without such a rubric, however. Much of his most acrimonious conflict with his colleagues, as well as a good deal of his reputation for conservativism, centered on efforts to find a way of circumscribing judicial discretion.

Two of Frankfurter's books published in the 1930s were the result of lectures: *The Public and its Government*, based on lectures at Yale, and *The Commerce Clause under Marshall, Taney, and Waite*, delivered at the University of

North Carolina.

The Public and Its Government begins by examining "The Demands of Modern Society" and finds that changes in the economic order "make the tasks of government today really different in kind" and require "wholly new interactions between citizen and government" than those which pertained in the early days of the Republic (27). F.F. then asks whether "law obstruct[s] government" and answers that "the difficulties that government encounters from law do not inhere in the Constitution" but "are due to the judges who interpret it" (79). In F.F.'s view, the Supreme Court in the 1880s and 1890s began to "stereotype ephemeral facts into legal absolutes" (45) and essentially tried to deny that "government means experimentation" (49). The "framers of the Constitution intentionally bounded it with outlines not sharp and contemporary, but flexible and prophetic" (75). John Marshall, who did so much to articulate the meaning of the Constitution, was supreme "in his recognition of the practical needs of government. Those of his successors whose labors history has vindicated were men who brought to their task insight into the problems of their generation. The great judges are those to whom the Constitution is not primarily a text for interpretation but the means of ordering the life of a progressive people" (75-76). They have recognized both their responsibility to make choices and the limits on the range of choices.

One of the specific areas in which government needed to display its competence in the 1920s and 1930s was the regulation of public utilities. F.F. reviews in some detail the need for regulatory agencies and the difficulties lawyers and courts face in adjusting their old legal ideas and attitudes to such "new political inventions" (88). Frankfurter had high hopes that economic problems might be resolved through governmental agencies. He thought they might generate "an esteem in the public such as the public now entertains for the judiciary" (122). Administrative agencies proliferated during the following decade under the New Deal.

The final chapter of the book laid out F.F.'s hopes for "Expert Administration and Democracy" (123-167). He contrasts an "early democratic faith" with a more sophisticated view. The early, and shallow, faith was based on a view of the "innate goodness of mankind" and required only the abolition of man's shackles: "It was indeed largely a negative faith." The newer view recognizes the "complexities of life" and the "forces inimical to the play of reason" (126-127). The earlier proponents of democracy "thought they were writing on a clean slate" and "forgot the obduracy of the past" so they lacked "patience" (128). (As he wrote, F.F. was aware of growing impatience with democracy in Europe and at home in the face of the Depression.) We must remember the "human origin of all government" and "recognize the essentially provisional nature of all political arrangements. Such an attitude will treat governments not only as a mechanism for day-to-day adjustments but also as an hypothesis in action, to be modified by the experience which it adduces" (129). Frankfurter, especially influenced by what

he knew of Great Britain, placed his hopes in bureaucracy, though he did not call
it that. What he called for was a "highly trained and disinterested permanent service, charged with the task of administering the broad policies formulated by [the
legislative branch] and of putting at the disposal of government that ascertainable
body of knowledge on which the choice of policies must be based" (145). F.F.
was in part influenced in his views by the example of Governor LaFollette and
the State of Wisconsin. As he had noted in 1911: "The Union between politics and
the university, energizing organized knowledge in the interests of the state as
LaFollette has done in Wisconsin is to me one of the most vital contributions he
has made" (D: 121).

　　These closing passages of *The Public and Its Government* show the skeptical optimist in fullest flower. "The ultimate justification for democracy still remains the lack, in the long run, of a decent and workable substitute" (124). To
refer to "science in politics" does not imply the existence of "an irrefrangible
fund of knowledge" but to "an intellectual procedure and a temper of mind" (151).
The cultivation of knowledgeable "disinterestedness" (a favorite word and concept for F.F., used often in this text and elsewhere) is in the special keeping of the
universities—the "reservoirs of disinterestedness" (164). In a sophisticated democracy, "*expertise* is indispensable [emphasis in the original]" (161). All
"[g]overnment...is the art of *making* men live together in peace and reasonable
happiness" [emphasis not in the original] (160). Though F.F. does not say it, much
coercion may be used in the "making"; and "reasonable happiness" may not be
very much by demanding standards. But in a democracy, "politics is a process of
popular education—the task of adjusting the conflicting interests of diverse groups
in the community, and bending the hostility and suspicion and ignorance engendered by group interests toward a comprehension of mutual understanding" (161).
Two kinds of experts are actually under consideration here: the politicians who
are expert in the "task of adjusting" and the disinterested experts who "sift out
issues, elucidate them, [and] bring the light of fact and experience to bear upon
them" (159-160). F.F. had high praise for the best politicians and here cites Walpole,
Pitt, Gladstone, Disraeli, Asquith, Lincoln, and the first Roosevelt. His epideictic
writings praised both kinds of experts, but more of his efforts are given to the
second sort. Statesmen are widely admired and receive their due biographical
attention. Most of us sing too little praise of those who give their lives to disinterested investigation; not so of Frankfurter.

　　Less need be said of the series of lectures on the Commerce Clause. Frankfurter finds a thread of continuity from Marshall through Taney to Waite where
others have focused on contrast. It is a thread of "tentative, experimental adjustments within the legal process" to accommodate local and national concerns (21-
22; 96). State-and-nation along with individual-and-society represent principles
which require balancing. The Court under these three Chief Justices managed to
resolve individual disputes without lapsing into rigid formulas which would have

unwisely limited future governing.

6. The Flag Salute Cases

One of Frankfurter's earliest opinions turned out to be one of his most unpopular with advancing liberal thought.[34] In *Minersville School District v. Gobitis*, 310 U.S. 586 (1939), Frankfurter gave a lecture on judicial restraint and sounded a call for the "unifying sentiment without which there can ultimately be no liberties" (597). The Gobitis family belonged to a religious group, the Jehovah's Witnesses, which believed (along with expecting an imminent end of the world) that pledging allegiance to the American flag violated the Biblical injunction against worshiping graven images. At the time and probably particularly in small cites and towns, the Witnesses were perceived as disruptive nuisances especially because they were traveling outsiders who were very persistent and scarcely civil in their attempts at proselytizing. Their doctrines were especially hostile to Roman Catholics and distressful in predominantly Catholic communities. Even small-town Protestants found this preaching distasteful perhaps because they still had a rather bad conscience about their own love-affair with the Catholic-bating Ku Klux Klan. I say this based on personal recollection as well as scholarly testimony.[35] The Witnesses inspired a good deal of local regulatory legislation. A growing group of urban, sophisticated friends of civil liberties (one of whom had long been Frankfurter himself) took up the cause of protecting the rights of this persecuted religious minority and thus of promoting civil freedoms in general. *Amici curiae* briefs were filed in the *Gobitis* case by the Committee on the Bill of Rights of the American Bar Association and by the American Civil Liberties Union. Participating lawyers included friends, Harvard colleagues, and former students of the new Justice Frankfurter. Instead of sticking to a citation of precedent, he delivered a civics lesson.

A number of points are made in a fairly brief opinion, and these are made without extensive argumentation. Frankfurter treats them as clear and straightforward, needing only to be marshaled to be persuasive. He begins with an assertion of principles in conflict which require balancing. The most general formulation of the principles is "liberty and authority," and the general argument is to point out that authority is a prerequisite to liberty. That is to say, for F.F. as for Edmund Burke, liberties are historical developments which have arisen only within some societies. To say that they inhere in individuals "naturally" is to speak metaphorically if not actually dangerously loosely. Within our historic constitutional scheme, the "liberty of conscience" involving the "conception of religious duty" (593) is limited by "the truth that no single principle can answer for all of life's complexities....to affirm that the freedom to follow conscience has itself no limits in the life of a society would deny that very plurality of principles which, as a matter of history, underlies protection of religious toleration" (594). Although

F.F. does not make the point, the word "toleration" was only introduced in the seventeenth century after more than a century of violence between Roman and Anglo-Catholics.[36]

In considering authority, "We are dealing with an interest inferior to none in the hierarchy of legal values" (595). This centrality is elaborated:

> ...the case before us is not concerned with an exertion of legislative power for the promotion of some specific need or interest of secular society—the protection of the family, the promotion of health, the common defense, the raising of public revenue to defray the cost of government. But all these specific activities of government presuppose the existence of an organized political society. The ultimate foundation of a free society is the binding tie of cohesive sentiment. Such a sentiment is fostered by all those agencies of the mind and spirit which may serve to gather up the traditions of a people, transmit them from generation to generation, and thereby create that continuity of a treasured common life which constitutes a civilization. "We live by symbols." The flag is the symbol of our national unity, transcending all internal differences, however large, within the framework of the Constitution. (596)[37]

On its face, the school rules requiring the flag salute and pledge of allegiance were "of general scope not directed against doctrinal loyalties of particular sects....[c]onscientious scruples have not, in the course of the long struggle for religious toleration, relieved the individual from obedience to a general law not aimed at the promotion or restriction of religious beliefs" (594). (Again, I draw on my own recollection in believing that the flag salute was not introduced with the purpose of entangling Witnesses.) Frankfurter makes three qualifying comments on the balance favoring permitting the salute and pledge to stand. In the first instance, he refers to the requirement as a "gesture of respect" (592). The case, moreover, involves school children who were twelve and ten when it arose; this is "the formative period in the development of citizenship" about which there is "[g]reat diversity of psychological and ethical opinion" about the best methods of training (598). (F.F. uses the word "train" rather than "educate.") "[F]reedom from conveying what may be deemed an implied but rejected affirmation" may be different in considering the "liberty of conscience" of adults. Finally, Frankfurter is personally "tempted to say that the deepest patriotism is best engendered by giving unfettered scope to the most crotchety beliefs" (598).

Frankfurter refers rather casually to the "First Amendment, and the Fourteenth through its absorption of the First" (593). (He was later to consider the character of "absorption" with much greater care.) He is also rather brief in circumscribing the judicial role. Since he sees the "development of citizenship" as a task of great importance as an objective but great uncertainty as to method, he considers it a matter for local experimentation among "competing considerations in the subtle process of securing effective loyalty to the traditional ideals of democracy" (598). He closes with reminders that the legislature "no less than" the courts has responsibility for the "guardianship of deeply-cherished liberties" and that "education in the abandonment of foolish legislation is itself training in liberty" (600). He thus employs the principles both of the federal system and of the "checks and balances" to dismiss any thought of the Supreme Court as the philosopher kings of the Constitution.

Justice Harlan Stone, in lonely dissent on a Court including both Black and Douglas, takes a quite different view of the case. Stone's argument counters Frankfurter's "gesture of respect" language. What the school has done is to "coerce the pupil to make affirmation contrary to his belief and in violation of his religious principles" (602). What F.F. sees as a competition of principles is for Stone a "prohibited infringement of personal liberty" unless the "state's power over public education" requires employing this particular method to "indoctrinate the minds of the young" in order "to survive" (601-602). The school is merely put to some "inconveniences" if it adjusts to the "religious convictions" of the Gobitis children (607), who are earlier (601) identified by Stone as "now fifteen and sixteen years of age" (thus subtly modifying the training versus education alternative).

Stone briefly repudiates Frankfurter's points. "The guarantees of civil liberty are but guarantees of freedom of the human mind and spirit" (604) which freedoms apparently exist independently of government. There is no proper balancing of the claims of freedom with the claims of authority. Nor should there be any deference to state experimentation or legislative responsibility: "This seems to me no less than the surrender of the constitutional protection of the liberty of small minorities to the popular will" (606). In this case, there is a "small and helpless minority" holding to "belief, which is such a departure from the usual course of human conduct, that most persons are disposed to regard it with little toleration or concern" (606). Concern for a "unifying sentiment without which there can be no liberties" must give way to a "command that freedom of the mind and spirit must be preserved" (606).

The future lay with Stone. Two kinds of public reaction were unfavorable to the maintenance of Frankfurter's Court majority. Many legal commentators were hostile to his arguments; and local popular majorities, feeling they had the blessing of the Supreme Court, became even more hostile to the Witnesses. After preliminary signals of a change of heart by some of its members, the Court reversed itself and F.F. in West Virginia Board of Education v. Barnette, 319 U.S. 624 (1943). The opinion of the Court was written by a new Justice, Robert Jackson. Frankfurter responded with an anguished and personal dissent. Two Justices briefly noted they would adhere to Gobitis. Justices Black and Douglas, in a short concurrence, explained their shift from Gobitis, relying in part on their recognition that what is involved is a "test oath."

Justice Hugo Black was, like Frankfurter, concerned about limiting judicial discretion in interpreting the Due Process Clause of the Fourteenth Amendment. His solution was to "define" the clause by asserting that it simply made the Bill of Rights applicable in toto to the States even though certain clauses, such as the Due Process Clause of the Fifth Amendment, did not seem to fit. In Barnette he tries to solve the problem by the use of "test oath," though that does not fit in its historic meaning. Frankfurter dismisses the "test oath" comparison as of "no kinship whatever" (663). Black tried to solve another case *United States v. Lovett*, 328 U.S. 303 (1946), by asserting it was an instance of a "bill of attainder." These efforts to explain due process by transforming terms which had historically well-defined meaning were especially irritating to Frankfurter since they blurred what he thought a useful distinction between terms well-defined by usage and terms of "convenient generality."

Jackson's opinion is a thorough-going and at times sarcastic rebuttal of Frankfurter's *Gobitis* opinion. The heart of Jackson's argument is that "such a compulsory rite" as the salute and pledge infringes the "constitutional liberty of the individual" (635). The First Amendment, applied to the States through the Fourteenth, insures that "no official, high or petty, can prescribe what shall be orthodox in politics, nationalism, religion, or other matters of opinion or force citizens to confess by word or act their faith therein" (642). In the course of establishing this, Jackson repeats but modifies Frankfurter's terminology to undercut its argumentative force.

For Jackson, the "sole conflict is between authority and rights of the individual" (630). No case is made for "authority" which is left to stand on its rather unfavorable connotations to many freedom-loving Americans. Symbolism is diminished as "primitive" and a "short-cut," invoking as a response "a salute, a bowed or bared head, a bended knee" (632). The school regulations involved in *Gobitis* and *Barnette* are dismissed as "local matters relatively trivial to the welfare of the nation" (638) which would offer only "slender grounds" for infringing "freedoms of speech and of press, of assembly, and of worship" (639). The fact that the school boards "are numerous and their territorial jurisdiction often small" is thought of not as an opportunity for local experimentation but as offering opportunities for "village tyrants" (637-638). No distinctions are made based on age. What is in question is not so much a training or educational effort aimed at school children as an "asserted power to force an American citizen publicly to profess [a] statement of belief" (635). Insofar as it is an educational effort to cultivate national unity, it is a misguided effort to "coerce uniformity" which is most likely to lead to "an ever-increasing severity" (640-641). Historical examples are cited and lead to the conclusion that "[c]ompulsory unification of opinion achieves only the unanimity of the graveyard" (641). "Persuasion and example" suffice as a basis for national unity, for there "is no mysticism in the American concept of the State." To think otherwise is to hold "an unflattering estimate of the appeal of our institutions to free minds" (640-641).

Jackson expresses a robust confidence in the power of reason and the attractiveness of American institutions. It is evident not just from his slighting reference to symbolism as "primitive" that he considers education to be concerned solely with the "rational" in the sense of that which can be articulated in a clear and direct fashion. He quotes from Justice Stone's *Gobitis* dissent that the State may "require teaching by instruction and study of all in our history and in the structure and organization of our government, including the guarantees of civil liberty, which tend to inspire patriotism and love of country" (631). Education, even at the elementary level, is apparently a matter of rational discourse and not, for example, habituation. Free speech is free speech for Justice Jackson, and no consideration need be given to implications for the education of the young. (The problem has not gone away. One may wonder what would have happened if the Barnette children had given "creationist" answers to classroom questions about biology and justified themselves on the grounds that to give "evolutionary" explanations without contradiction is a sin. If free speech is free speech, what is the principle which distinguishes the two situations?) The majority opinion, in its reliance on a simple and self-applying principle of free speech and its identification of elementary training with adult rational discourse, ignores the developmental problems of education.

Frankfurter's dissent takes up more space in the Reports than the opinion and two concurrences together. It begins with a highly personal reference. "One who belongs to the most vilified and persecuted minority in history is not likely to be insensible to the freedoms guaranteed by our Constitution. Were my purely personal attitude relevant I should wholeheartedly associate myself with the general libertarian views in the Court's opinion, representing as they do the thought and action of a lifetime" (646-647). This introduces an "admonition" in behalf of "judicial self-restraint" (648) and against "writing [one's] private notions of policy into the Constitution" (647). In his diaries, F.F. reports that from

> the time of the *Gobitis* case I was literally flooded with letters by people who said that I, as a Jew, ought to protect minorities....And when the Flag Salute issue again became prominent...I began to have a new trickle of letters telling me my duty, more particularly because I was a Jew and an immigrant. I therefore thought for once and for all I ought to put on record that in relation to our work on this Court, all considerations of race, religion, or antecedence of citizenship, are wholly irrelevant. (D: 254)

The dissent is one of F.F.'s most spectacular applications of his position on judicial restraint. The majority employed "freedom of speech" without elaborate explanation. Frankfurter finds himself obliged to explain judicial restraint at length and bolsters his argument with the authority not only of Holmes and Brandeis but also of the Framers, Jefferson, and Thayer.

At the end of the nineteenth century, the Supreme Court began using the

180   FELIX FRANKFURTER

Due Process Clause of the Fourteenth Amendment to protect "property rights" against State regulations. During the second decade of this century, the Court seemed to be more permissive of such State efforts; but in the 1920s and 1930s, the Court, returned to its earlier "activism." It was this use which led F.F. to argue that "due process" ought to be abandoned. A good deal of controversy surrounded the question of "interpreting" the Due Process Clause. One of the easiest because most explicit approaches was to argue or at least suggest that "Due Process" had simply applied the Bill of Rights to the States, but certain clauses seemed clearly irrelevant. Justices Holmes and Brandeis and then Cardozo began to suggest, or at least seemed to do so, that a distinction might be made between certain rights which were in some way fundamental and other rights which were in some sense secondary.

Frankfurter acknowledges this by quoting from what was for him the controlling (and basically troubling) statement by Cardozo: "When we are dealing with the Constitution of the United States, and more particularly with the great safeguards of the Bill of Rights, we are dealing with principles of liberty and justice 'so rooted in the traditions and conscience of our people as to be ranked as fundamental'—something without which 'a fair and enlightened system of justice would be impossible.' *Palko v. Connecticut*, 302 U.S. 319, 325; *Hurtado v. California*, 110 U.S. 516, 530, 531" (652). No clear agreement was achieved about the nature of the "fundamental," however—whether fundamental in the way they inhere in the individual or fundamental to the democratic political process. In either case, it was urged by some that these rights enjoyed a "preferred position" so the Supreme Court had a different and unique responsibility when they were in question. Frankfurter—loyal as he was to the positions of Holmes, Brandeis, and Cardozo—had intellectual difficulty with this distinction. While at times over the years he seemed to wish to make use of some such distinction, in *Barnette*, he vigorously repudiated it:

> Our power does not vary according to the particular provision of the Bill of Rights which is invoked. The right not to have property taken without just compensation has, so far as the scope of judicial power is concerned, the same constitutional dignity as the right to be protected against unreasonable searches and seizures, and the latter no less claim than freedom of the press or freedom of speech or religious freedom....each specific Amendment [of the Bill of Rights], in so far as embraced within the Fourteenth Amendment, must beequally respected, and the function of this Court does not differ in passing on the constitutionality of legislation challenged under different Amendments. (648-649)

The dissent closes with an extended quotation from Thayer's essay, discussed above, and takes Thayer at his most extreme: the only question is whether "legislators could in reason have enacted such a law" (647). It is "beyond [the

Court's] constitutional power to assert [its] view as to the wisdom of this law..."
(667). When the Court substitutes its "wisdom" for that of a legislature, it is "not
discharging the basic function of this Court as the mediator of powers within the
federal system. To strike down a law like this is to deny a power to all government" (667). The majority, and indeed most subsequent students of the Court,
disagreed with Frankfurter on precisely this point about the "basic function" of
the Supreme Court. For them, the basic function is to "deny a power to all government," that is, to protect individual rights. For Frankfurter, as for Thayer,
"[r]eliance for the most precious interests of civilization...must be found outside
of their vindication in courts of law" in the "convictions and habits and actions of
[the] community" (670-671).

> Our constant preoccupation with the constitutionality of legislation rather than
> its wisdom tends to preoccupation of the American mind with a false value.
> The tendency of focusing attention on constitutionality is to make
> constitutionality synonymous with wisdom, to regard a law as all right if it is
> constitutional. Such an attitude is a great enemy of liberalism. (671)

And of democracy, which Frankfurter sees as inherently linked with liberty.

Frankfurter's discussion, here as typically elsewhere, addresses "democracy"
more explicitly than "liberty"; but even democracy is not subjected to any inten-
sive exposition. After his initial discussion of the need for judicial restraint, he
asserts: "The reason why from the beginning even the narrow judicial authority
to nullify legislation has been viewed with a jealous eye is that it serves to prevent
the full play of the democratic process" (650). We should note that "from the
beginning" is very abbreviated. The authors of *The Federalist* did not speak of
"democratic process." Few of the Founders viewed "democracy" favorably. By
the time Chief Justice Marshall asserted the Court's power of judicial review in
Marbury v. Madison, however, the Jeffersonians had begun to think more favorably of a direct popular action which resembled the democracy of the ancients.
Perhaps the most extreme version of Jefferson's thought were his 1787 suggestions in letters that "a little rebellion, now and then, is a good thing, and as necessary in the political world as storms in the physical" and that the "tree of liberty
must be refreshed from time to time, with the blood of patriots and tyrants."[38] As
F.F. notes at 667, Jefferson certainly objected to judicial review although he found
little way at the time to do anything about it. The phrase "democratic process" is
employed again on 651 and is assumed without discussion. What F.F. thought in
detail about democracy must be examined below.

Frankfurter addresses religious freedom and the rights entailed in some detail. His position is summarized: "The constitutional protection of religious freedom terminated disabilities, it did not create new privileges" (653). While
"[r]eligion is outside the sphere of political government...this does not mean that

all matters on which religious organizations or beliefs may pronounce are outside
the sphere of government" (654). Justice Murphy, in his concurrence with the
majority, says: "Reflection has convinced me that as a judge I have no loftier duty
or responsibility than to uphold that spiritual freedom to its farthest reaches" (645).
F.F. gives no such status to "conscientious scruples" (652); they do not provide
"exceptional immunity from civic measures of general applicability" (653).

> An act compelling profession of allegiance to a religion, no matter how subtly
> or tenuously promoted, is bad. But an act promoting good citizenship and
> national allegiance is within the domain of governmental authority and is
> therefore to be judged by the same considerations of power and of
> constitutionality as those involved in many claims of immunity from civil
> obedience because of religious scruples." (654-655)

For F.F., "[l]aw is concerned with external behavior" (655); requiring the Pledge
of Allegiance to the Flag does not oblige a person to believe it. "Compelling
belief implies denial of opportunity to combat it and to assert dissident views"
(656). In requiring the flag salute, neither the schools nor the State had done
anything to oblige the students to believe anything. Since the "linguistic movement" in English philosophy identified especially with Wittgenstein and John
Austin, we are in a position to make considerably finer distinctions among pledges,
statements of belief, promises, assertions of fact, and so forth. To pursue that is
unnecessary here. Frankfurter is surely correct in denying that the pledge requires
a "compulsion of belief," but he has a Roman obliviousness to the Christian conscience—a sacrifice to the emperor to acknowledge the sovereignty of Rome should
not conflict with a commitment of conscience to a jealous God, but it does. F.F.'s
concern is with the "process of making and unmaking laws" (655). (We may add
that Frankfurter has little attachment to "sincerity" either. Had he lived to see its
elevation to be a major virtue in the late 1960s, he would have demurred.) Liberal
thought, even when agnostic, has tended to follow Murphy and has promoted
individual spiritual freedom to "reaches" which even Murphy's reflections are
unlikely to have encompassed. The Court has, for example, permitted hallucina-
tory drugs to Native Americans in the practice of their religion even though the
general illegality of the drugs was not questioned. We may wonder what would
have happened if the Mormon practice of polygamy had first been raised in such
a judicial environment.

In *Hamilton v. Regents*, 293 U.S. 245 (1934), cited at 656, Frankfurter has
on his side a strong precedent which Jackson attempts to distinguish from the
case at hand since it involved the conditions for attending a State-maintained
university. In Jackson's view, higher education is optional while elementary education is obligatory. Frankfurter rejoins that public education is not obligatory
and argues that in each case attendance at a public institution may be contingent

on compliance with certain requirements. His argument underplays the distinction between elementary and higher education and might have been stronger had he not done so. His treatment of symbolism is suggestive, though. Jackson quotes Stone in *Gobitis* that the "State may 'require teaching by instruction and study'" to imply that the school's business is narrowly rational (631). But necessary traits cannot be taught simply by discursive lessons. In teaching children not to resort to force in the resolution of disputes, the school uses the playground and punishment as well as, and probably more effectively than, booklearning. For elementary school children, the "teaching by instruction and study" is not adequate if the young are to develop a basic attachment to our society and forms of life. This involves no exotic or mysterious theory about education but is as old as Aristotle's discussion of the role of habituation in the development of moral virtue and as new as the work influenced by Jean Piaget.[39] Perhaps we do not now have enough book-learning in our elementary schools, but we cannot deny that children learn through several avenues. The significance of this for *Barnette* is that "freedom of speech" in the education of elementary pupils is a principle to be cultivated and developed rather than a standard to be applied. Empirical study at the time showed that many young people saying the Pledge did not really even know the words: for example, "'I pledge a legion...,' 'connation, invisible...,' 'with liberty and jesta straw,'" This does not prove that the Pledge did not serve the purpose of cultivating basic attachment to the community, however.[40]

Perhaps in some small part, elite opinion and Court doctrine have developed as they have because Frankfurter lost out to Jackson in their debate over "symbolism." Here too F.F. seems to have been of two minds. In both *Gobitis* and *Barnette*, he acknowledges that the Flag Salute may be of dubious value and that, if he were a legislator, he would make another choice of means. On the other hand, he responds vigorously to the assertion that "symbolism is a dramatic but primitive way of communicating ideas" by pointing out that "[s]ymbolism is inescapable" and "[e]ven the most sophisticated live by symbols" (662). (See the discussion of "compounded, abstract words" in Chapter 5 on Burke.) He charges Jackson with "flippancy" for associating the flag salute with a salute to a dictator. Jackson implies a slippery slope; F.F. responds with distinctions and choices (to be made by the legislative branch).

Frankfurter drew on Alfred North Whitehead's *Symbolism: Its Meaning and Effect* for his understanding of the role of symbolism in reason. Unfortunately for his argument, the book cannot readily be summarized both persuasively and briefly, for it is highly condensed. While Whitehead was not an academic skeptic, he shared the belief that attempting to erect philosophy on clear and distinct ideas is an error—what he called the "dogmatic fallacy." The best that can be hoped for is "a gradual approach to ideas of clarity and generality" by competent and sincere men.[41] The first two parts of his book examine the way symbolism permits the connection of sense perceptions ("presentational immediacy") with "causal efficacy"—the interactions of all things. The third section applies the insights of the first two to human societies. Symbolism both binds human communities together and permits their progressive modification. Critical reason accounts for only a small, though very important, portion of this. Understandably, says Whitehead, the brightest people over-estimate the place of critical reason and the need for change and underestimate the need for binding and continuity and the place of other forms of symbolic behavior. It would seem to be a case in point that neither the American Civil Liberties Union nor the Supreme Court have ever persuaded most Americans that requiring the Pledge of Allegiance of school children is a bad thing.[42]

Symbolism, like Whitehead himself, fell out of favor with most professional philosophers by the end of the 1950s. The major contributor to the discussion of symbolism was Ernst Cassirer whose work was popularized by Susanne K. Langer. Symbolism remains a subject of interest in some anthropological, sociological, and humanistic areas; but I am not aware that these have touched legal studies.[43]

7. Democracy

As a youth, Frankfurter was drawn to the populism of William Jennings Bryan and then to the progressivism of Theodore Roosevelt. Like the academic skeptics of Cicero's *Academica*, Frankfurter drew together positions others saw in conflict. For F.F., both Bryan and the first Roosevelt were champions of "democracy." The second Roosevelt promoted in practice what F.F. felt instinctively: the cause of the people—the "common man"—should be promoted by a vigorous government. There is some irony in identifying Frankfurter's reputation with judicial restraint because he was a persistent advocate of the cooperative enterprise he called democracy.

Democracy has been associated from the first with two other ideas, freedom and equality. The word is so commonly valued in our political discourse today that we seldom remember that it has not always enjoyed such status. Early in *The History of the Peloponnesian War*, Thucydides puts in the mouth of Pericles a funeral oration praising the Athenian democracy for its equal justice before the law, its political openness to the advancement of talent, and its personal freedom. These characteristics result in an open society where prosperity and culture flourish for both the community and the individual.[44] Plato, looking back after the loss of the war, gives a contrary assessment, one which dominated political thought until the nineteenth century. He writes in the *Republic* that democracy is the next worst form of government and society (in Greek thought, the "polis" stands for what we distinguish, both government and society). In such a democracy, "freedom" means doing whatever the individual wishes; and all persons, and even animals, are treated as equals. Immediate pleasures, disorderly souls, and lawlessness reign. Aristotle also associates democracy with freedom and equality.

While he too rates democracy as a perverse form of government, his treatment is quite different because he differentiates kinds of democracies. Some are not so bad. "Freedom" means ruling and being ruled in turn as well as doing as one pleases. "Equality" is equality of access to public office. What history remembered most about democracy, whether fairly or unfairly, was its instability. This lesson still stalks the pages of the writings of the Founding Fathers, including *The Federalist*.

Only as the nineteenth century progressed did democracy's status change. The party of Jefferson, we should remember, was called Republican; later Democratic-Republican; and only with Andrew Jackson did it become Democratic. The decade of Jackson also saw the writing of the first volume of Tocqueville's *Democracy in America*. Tocqueville equated democracy with equality of condition, worried that such democracy threatened liberty, and expounded the teachings of *The Federalist* as a new science of politics. John Stuart Mill promoted Tocqueville's work, and democracy came to be seen as a good as well as an inevitable thing. The "liberalism" of the second half of the century tended to treat democracy as a means to protect the primary end, liberty. What had been, for the authors of *The Federalist*, "popular" government was broadened in the United States and then Britain by the extension of the franchise to lower economic classes and, in this century, to women and Blacks. By the time of Frankfurter's youth, democracy had come, once again, to have a meaning approximating that held by Pericles.

Frankfurter associated Pericles with Thomas Jefferson in a short essay published in 1941, "The Paths Must Be Kept Open" (LM: 236-238). Like others of Frankfurter's occasional pieces, the ideas dart rapidly like a fight of hummingbirds—moving so quickly it is hard to distinguish them. Both Pericles, in the "Funeral Oration" referred to above, and Jefferson, in the "Declaration of Independence," associated freedom with the pursuit of happiness. While happiness is individual, its pursuit through freedom is a common enterprise. In the United States, the "Constitution is...an instrument of government under which the pursuit of happiness through freedom may be realized" (236). The Bill of Rights, praise of which occasioned the essay, is the product of "experience" guarding "against the recurrence of well-defined historic grievances" by making "explicit the conditions of freedom...." These "conditions" are procedures, developed over time, for responding to criminal charges, preventing unreasonable intrusions into privacy, and protecting "thought and conscience" (236-237). Even more important than these procedures, however, is "the conception of man's dignity and destiny which underlies" them. "Nature herself is democratic" in planting the capacity for excellence throughout society and not in a particular class (237). To reprise, the pursuit of happiness depends upon freedom which requires the proper kind of government which depends upon respect for and cultivation of the talents which are spread throughout society. This is the democratic attitude.

Jefferson, celebrated on his bicentenary in a 1943 F.F. essay "The Permanence of Jefferson" (LM: 228-235), is important as a symbol of that attitude rather than as providing "a book of precepts for the solution of specific problems" (234). "It is the permanence of his meaning—to establish sentiments of freedom as the enduring habits of a people" and to do so at the very time the nation was "founding its life upon ultimate principles of faith in human nature" (230). Jefferson put into words and thus reinforced "an expression of the American mind" (232)—the mind of a "people whose mission was the free unfolding of the human spirit" (233). He accomplished this because he was "sanguine" and "passionately and persistently followed his insight that the permanence of the American scheme could rest on nothing less than the whole American democracy" (235). Even Jefferson—occasional "antifederalist" though he seemed—realized, however, that democracy is not an "automatic device" but is "dependent on knowledge and wisdom beyond all other forms of government" and is the "reign of reason and justice on the most extensive scale" (235). Jefferson, according to F.F., "was no simple-minded believer in the popular will" (235). (F.F. does not go so far, however, as to argue that Jefferson was attached to the elaborate "checks and balances" which Madison had justified. Frankfurter combined Jeffersonian enthusiasm and Madisonian caution in his own unique blend.) At the beginning of his essay, F.F. refers to faith as "moral energy stored up in the past" (228). He closes on Jefferson's faith that, whatever the difficulties, democracy is the "exhilarating adventure of a free people determining its own destiny" (235). Thus, faith, habit, reason, freedom, and democracy are woven together through language, exemplars, and other "symbols."

Another short essay "The Bold Experiment of Freedom," given originally as an address in 1949, helps in distinguishing the strands. The opening sentence—"By its Founders this nation was committed to democracy"—seems to contradict the well-known contrary opinions of the Founders but in fact helps to clarify what Frankfurter means by "democracy." He goes on to say: "...democracy is the only form of social arrangement that fully respects the richness of human society and, by respecting it, helps to unfold it. Democracy is thus the only adequate response to the deepest human needs and justified as such by the long course of history. All the devices of political machinery—parties and platforms and votes—are merely instruments for enabling men to live together under conditions that bring forth the maximum gifts of each for the fullest enjoyment of all" (LM: 221). Several observations are in order.

Although they denigrated the governmental form they called democracy, the Founders were committed to freedom and, with few exceptions, to "popular government." In subscribing to the Declaration of Independence and the Constitution, they were acknowledging a common enterprise of persons created as equals. As the Tenth *Federalist* makes clear, individuals - though equal - are not identical in their opinions, passions, or faculties. The government established by the Founders had as its "first object" the "protection of these [diverse] faculties" (F:

130-131). In "respecting" this "richness of human society," the Founders recognized the truth about their American contemporaries; and because they did so, they established "political machinery" to—in the words of the Preamble—"promote the general welfare, and secure the blessings of liberty to ourselves and our posterity." In Frankfurter's view, the freedom promoted by the Constitution serves both historical progress and individual "enjoyment."

Properly understood, democracy is the "rule of the people" and not the particular "political machinery" of the ancient Greeks which the Founders repudiated because of its instability. Democracy "places ultimate faith for attaining the common good in the responsibility of the individual" (222). It includes economic as well as political institutions—institutions which "allow these mysterious natural bounties" of human diversity their "fullest outlet" (222). The institutions, created over time, continue to change and constitute a "bold experiment"—an "unremitting endeavor, never a final achievement" (222). F.F.'s praise of the United States matches in enthusiasm and attitude that of Cicero for Rome: both countries have met unique challenges by developing unique free institutions. But the scope of freedom has expanded. Frankfurter's America is more advanced in "the most difficult of all arts—the art of living together in a free society" because of "our belief in the worth of the individual" and our commitment to "common intrinsic human qualities" (222-223). The comprehensive "democracy" of Periclean Athens has been added to the "republicanism" of Rome. The American experiment has a "special destiny" because it involves "the most significant racial and religious admixture in history" (222-223). F.F. quotes FDR on what holds this admixture together: "'They [the immigrants passing the Statue of Liberty] came to us speaking many tongues—but a single language, the universal language of human aspiration'" (224). This language sounds so much like F.F. that one wonders whether he helped to draft it and is thus, once again, quoting himself.

In Frankfurter's thought, as in Dewey's, freedom and democracy are linked in the concept of self-development. Every individual has the capacity for self-development, and institutions should facilitate this self-development both individually and in common enterprises. As individuals develop, institutions must develop. Both lines of development depend upon the "continuous exercise of reason, and self-discipline of the highest order" (222). Thus, no office in the "political machinery" is "more important than that of being a citizen" (222).

With this as preface, we can consider a trio of Supreme Court cases which concerned "voting rights"—performing the primary responsibility of citizenship: *Colgrove v. Green*, 328 U.S. 549 (1946), *Gomillion v. Lightfoot*, 364 U.S. 339 (1960), and *Baker v. Carr* 369 U.S. 186 (1962). Frankfurter wrote for the Court in the first two and in dissent in *Baker*—an opinion written by one of F.F.'s former students, Justice William Brennan, who used Frankfurter's *Gomillion* opinion as precedent for overruling *Colgrove*.

At issue in *Colgrove* was the reapportionment of Congressional districts in

Illinois. Decision was rendered by a reduced and divided Court. Chief Justice
Stone had recently died, and Justice Jackson was absent while prosecuting the
Nurenburg Trials. Frankfurter announced the judgment and an opinion joined
only by Burton and Reed. Black dissented with Douglas and Murphy. Justice
Wiley Rutledge—who often allied himself with Black, Douglas, and Murphy—
in this case concurred in the judgment without joining the opinion.

Frankfurter settled the case on legal precedent which was based on the
grounds that the relevant Reapportionment Act contained no reference to com-
pactness or equality of Congressional districts. He went even further with the
precedent, however, to "agree with the four Justices (Brandeis, Stone, Roberts,
and Cardozo) who were of the opinion that [the ruling case] should have been
'dismissed from want of equity'" (551). The underpinning of *Colgrove* is thus
somewhat stronger than it at first seems. Brandeis and Cardozo provide strong
credentials from F.F.'s point of view; and presumably Stone, had he lived, would
have voted consistently with himself. Other things being equal, Jackson would
have been more likely to vote with Frankfurter than with Black out of personal
animus. Jackson blamed Black when Fred Vinson rather than Jackson himself
was chosen as Chief (D: 262-264). [45]

Frankfurter does not stop with simple citation of precedent, however, and
goes on to explain why the Court should not intervene in a case such as this—a
case presenting an "issue of a particularly political nature." Such an issue is "not
meet for judicial determination" for two related reasons. First, the "basis for [the]
suit is not a private wrong, but a wrong suffered by Illinois as a polity" (552).
Second, "this controversy concerns matters that bring courts into immediate and
active relations with party contests....It is hostile to a democratic system to involve the judiciary in the politics of the people" even if the contest "be dressed up
in the abstract phrases of the law" (553-554). A legal "case or controversy" has
two parties who disagree about specifiable particulars of what is at issue and what
would be appropriate remedy. In this situation, there are too many choices—too
many principles which can be claimed for justification. As he was to make much
clearer in dissent in *Baker v. Carr,* F.F. doubts that there is any remedy which a
court could provide without simply abandoning any semblance of judicial "neutrality." This is not basically a question of legalistic subtlety to be "met by verbal
fencing about 'jurisdiction'" (552). It is a very straightforward judgment that, in
fact, drawing the boundaries of legislative districts is a matter of partisan fencing
and compromise. Getting involved can only besmirch a court with politics in its
stickiest, dirtiest form: "the one stark fact that emerges from a study of the history
of Congressional apportionment is its embroilment in politics, in the sense of
party contests and party interests" (554).

In *Gomillion v. Lightfoot*, the situation was quite different in Frankfurter's
view. The Alabama state legislature had redrawn the boundaries of the city of
Tuskegee to exclude virtually all Blacks. The plaintiff sued for the right to vote in

Democracy

city elections. Frankfurter wrote for a unanimous Court. This was simply another instance of southern State efforts to undo the Fifteenth Amendment and deprive Blacks of voting rights. This gave the case specificity. Unlike *Baker* which was to follow, it involved none of the vagaries of "Equal Protection." Laws make all sorts of distinctions and classifications. The problem of what constitutes reasonable classification is addressed repeatedly. The State action attacked in *Gomillion* blatantly involved one distinct and clearly forbidden classification, race.

Frankfurter's concern that lawyers would see the issue in *Colgrove* as "verbal fencing about 'jurisdiction'" was validated with a vengeance in *Baker v. Carr*. The case involved the failure of the Tennessee legislature to redistrict the State for legislative elections as called for by the Tennessee Constitution. The central challenge to the State was made on alleged violation of the Equal Protection Clause of the Fourteenth Amendment. The opinion was written by Justice Brennan. He used *Gomillion* to overturn Frankfurter's *Colgrove* precedent and even stole the majority in *Colgrove* itself by claiming that the crucial point was that Rutledge joined Black and his colleagues in asserting jurisdiction. The *Baker* opinion, indeed, only dealt with jurisdiction. It did not resolve the basic problem but remanded it back to the lower court which had earlier dismissed the suit for want of jurisdiction. Both Brennan's opinion and F.F.'s dissent bristle with citations of precedent, usually referring to the same cases but drawing different lessons from them. In addressing the traditional "political question" ground for avoiding judicial intervention, Brennan makes a good deal of the fact that the co-equal branches (Congress and the President) are not involved in the case; but only Court supervision of the States.

Justice Tom Clark, concurring, was prepared to go all the way to decide the case on its merits, since "the controlling facts cannot be disputed" (253). Brennan and the two other concurring Justices Douglas and Stewart are not yet ready to address the question of principled distinctions and remedy, however, but assume something will come along. Justice Clark points out that "[n]o one—except the dissenters...- contends that mathematical equality among voters is required by the Equal Protection Clause" (258). What came along, however, has been judicial drawing of district boundaries at all levels on just such a mathematical equality— a "one person, one vote" basis.

Frankfurter was joined only by Justice J.M. Harlan who added his own dissenting opinion. F.F. marshals precedent to establish that the Court has previously avoided involving itself in redistricting cases "in the absence of an explicit and clear constitutional imperative" such as the fulfillment of the Fifteenth Amendment. Without saying so explicitly, he harkens back to his long-held view that "equal protection," like "due process," is all too dangerously vague and prompts the Court to decide matters it is not fit to decide. In this case, the appellants'

complaint is simply that [their] representatives are not sufficiently numerous

or powerful—in short, that Tennessee has adopted a basis of representation
with which they are dissatisfied....One cannot talk of "debasement" or
"dilution" of the value of a vote until there is first defined a standard of
reference as to what a vote should be worth. What is actually asked of the
Court in this case is to choose among competing bases of representation—
ultimately, really, among competing theories of political philosophy. (299-
300)

Much of the remainder of the dissent is given over to establishing the "stark
fact" that "if among the numerous widely varying principles and practices that
control state legislative apportionment today there is any generally prevailing
feature, that feature is geographic inequality in relation to the population standard" (321). F.F.'s solution to the complaint, ridiculed by Clark, is appeal "to an
informed, civically militant electorate" and an "aroused popular conscience" (270).
From Clark's point of view, this is impossible precisely because those who want
change find themselves in the legislative minority. Even appeal to Congress (which
has remedial authority) is "from a practical standpoint...without substance" because Congress is unlikely to act (259). The disagreement here is at the heart of
Frankfurter's "judicial restraint" and marks his separation from the "liberalism"
of Justices Black and Douglas and the Warren Court. In F.F.'s view, not every
problem has a satisfactory solution. In a democracy, a Supreme Court of philosopher kings does not provide a satisfactory solution to every case of mistreatment
of a minority. This is a practical matter, albeit a long-run one. The point, made by
Thayer and so-often reiterated by Frankfurter, is that a democracy will not survive without an "informed, civically militant electorate": such an electorate can
only be sustained by a "popular conscience" which is "aroused" by the need to
make important decisions.

Many who have espoused an "active" Court to protect minorities also emphasize the educational and leadership roles of the Supreme Court. They believe
the Court is at its finest when announcing high principle. Recent examples of this
attended speculation of the appointment of a successor to Justice Harry Blackmun.
David A. Kaplan said an "ideological cat fight is precisely what this soporific
court needs."[46] In Frankfurter's view, the leadership role of the Court is highly
circumscribed and basically limited to supervisory authority over lower courts
and the judiciary system. Political leadership in the broader sense properly lies
with the "political" branches. F.F. believed in an educational role for the Supreme
Court but also feared its potential for miseducation—most especially in training
people to expect a judicial quick-fix for complex and troubling social problems.

Even such monuments as *Brown v. Board of Education*, 347 U.S. 483 (1954)
and *Roe v. Wade*, 93 U.S. 705 (1973) are now being questioned by persons who
agree with the policies advanced but who doubt the efficacy or wisdom of having
promoted those policies through "great" Supreme Court cases.[47]

8. Legal Reasoning

In two essays published after joining the Supreme Court, Frankfurter addressed in some detail the characteristics of reasoning as it is applied to existing legislation and to the Constitution of the United States. Both deal with a particular kind of "practical reason"—the interpretation of "political" documents in the operation of government. The treatment is thus of a very specialized kind. It is of interest precisely because of this specialization. It reveals the importance of the environment of reasoning and the complex structures employed to respond to political problems.

In 1947, Frankfurter delivered the Sixth Annual Benjamin N. Cardozo Lecture before the Bar of the City of New York, published as "Some Reflections on the Reading of Statutes." The essay begins with a review of changes in the business coming before the Court—most specifically the dramatic increase in the quantity of legislation and the shift from common law litigation to cases resting on statutes. Thus, the "center of gravity of lawmaking" has shifted and "courts have ceased to be the primary makers of the law in the sense in which they 'legislated' the common law" (LM: 45). F.F. is both describing and approving: lawmaking is primarily the responsibility of the legislative branch which is immediately accountable to the people. He later quotes Bishop Hoadley: "Whoever hath an *absolute authority to interpret* any written or spoken laws, it is he who is truly the lawgiver to all intents and purposes, and not the person who first wrote or spoke them" (LM: 53). But F.F. admits only to a limited truth in this. Legislators make law wholesale; judges only retail—as he says, quoting Holmes. The Bishop's quote puts the emphasis in the wrong place. It is the responsibility of the courts to construe the meaning which the legislature has given to a law and not to make the law the judges might prefer. In common law reasoning, the judge is fashioning her or his own adjustment of the law to the resolution of the problem presented by the case. In statutory interpretation, the judge is attempting to determine what resolution the legislative branch has decided appropriate. To recognize the shift of business is to recognize a shift in responsibility. This is only the first of a series of dichotomies structuring the essay, each of which distinguishes a proper from an alternative but misguided approach. The truth is approximated by the selection of preferred choices.

The meaning of a statute is often straight-forward enough, elicits no controversy, and thus requires no "construing." The problem of construing arises where there is a "fair contest between two readings" (LM: 45). We are dealing with problems arising from what Madison called "inadequateness of the vehicle of ideas." F.F. first addresses difficulties inherent in the very nature of words. The task of determining meaning is not unique to judges. Judicial construction is merely one subset of meaning problems. F.F.'s discussion contains no reference to the later work of Wittgenstein or the "linguistic movement," although he knew A.J.

Ayer and knew of Wittgenstein. As mentioned above, his philosopher of reference was Alfred North Whitehead and especially his book on symbolism. Whitehead was not a skeptic, and F.F.'s reliance on him illustrates the skeptical tendency to borrow from whatever other traditions seem useful. Following Whitehead, Frankfurter does not think the usefulness of words depends upon their exactness. Words easily seem more exact than they are, or rather, words are more
exact than their referents and easily mislead us by the appearance of exactness.
F.F. refers to words which may be "inexact symbols, with shifting variables." He
is not concerned with the variations of common usage nor with the resolution of
philosophical problems typical of the linguistic movement.

From the point of view of legal analysis, the contrast F.F. finds most useful
is between univocal and multivocal words, mathematical symbols and inexact
symbols. He later expands this into a three-fold distinction: "mathematical" symbols, "other" symbols, and what he calls "not symbols at all, but labels." Some
terms in the law, as in other disciplines, are so defined by their history and by
legal, disciplinary usage that they can be considered univocal, almost the equiva-
lent of mathematical terms. Some of Frankfurter's most detailed lectures to his
colleagues concerned efforts by them to expand the meaning of terms which, in
his view, were explicitly defined by history. He found such terms useful as they
are—islands of stability in seas of verbal flux. As the century has advanced, however, various intellectual movements have resulted in calling almost all such stability of meaning into question.

"Other" terms, not peculiar to the law, share the vagueness of many words
in common usage. Some terms in the law have a "convenient vagueness," quoting
Judge C.M. Hough (MJH: 42). In his essay, F.F. treats "labels" only briefly, giving as an example "police power" which he say is not a symbol at all but a label
"for the results of the whole process of adjudication" (LM: 55). What he apparently means is that a judge when using the phrase is not referring to anything but
the results of her or his own, and similar, decisions. There is no preexisting and
coherent category of governmental power to which the judge is referring. The
"police power" is simply a miscellany of governmental actions which the courts
have decided are allowable. The more important distinction, however, is between
univocal symbols and other symbols—"a whole gamut of words with different
denotations as well as connotations. There are varying shades of compulsion for
judges behind different words, differences that are due to the words themselves,
their setting in a text, their setting in history" (LM: 55).

In some settings, ambiguity can be "productive."[48] The judge, however, faces
the task of eliminating or minimizing ambiguity in the specific case by identifying or choosing one meaning among those available. Frankfurter provides two
approaches to making that specification in the appositives "setting in a text" and
"setting in history." We shall return to these shortly. In addition to the uncertainty
introduced by words, however, are two further levels produced by the combina-

tion of words into statements and by the nature of the legislative process.

In considering statements, Frankfurter employs another dichotomy: a statement of the law is "not an equation or a formula" (LM: 45) and reading it is not "an exercise in logic....the aids of formal logic are not irrelevant: they may simply be inadequate" (LM: 47). This harkens back to Holmes' dismissal of the adequacy of formal logic. F.F. also contrasts both words and statements with "empty vessels" (into which the interpreter can put anything he or she wishes) and their interpretation with a "ritual." Humpty Dumpty, and apparently many others, act as though words are "'empty vessels into which he can pour anything he will'— his caprices, fixed notions, even statesmanlike beliefs in a particular policy." The judge is not free to do this and is not meeting her or his responsibilities in behaving this way. "Nor...is the process a ritual to be observed by unimaginative adherence to well-born professional phrases." Statutory interpretation is an active process which involves choices and not simply a ritualistic following out of established procedures (LM: 47).

The uncertainty which arises from the character of statutes exemplifies all the lesser problems of interpretation. Statutes, viewed in the light of the entire process which produces them, have many authors; and the authors may not have spoken with completely one voice. They are not "an expression of individual thought to which is imparted the definiteness which individual authorship can give" (LM: 45-46). Moreover, statutes have practical purposes and are groping efforts to achieve those purposes. They are experiments and carry with them two possibilities of error: the problem may have been misdefined or the proposed solution may not be an effective one. Sometimes, to complicate matters even further, the legislature "solves problems by shelving them temporarily" (LM: 46): it enacts something which is intentionally vague out of the felt need to appear to be doing something. Finally, because of the unforeseeability of the future, the statutes must be applied to situations unforeseen and unanticipated by their authors in the legislative process. Each situation has its own configuration of elements: individuals with particular characteristics and background, actions with particular structures.

The light which can be shed on difficulties of interpretation by examining the "setting in the text" is produced by the careful reading which any complex text requires. The "setting in history" is reformulated as "the determination of the extent to which extraneous documentation and external circumstance may be allowed to infiltrate the text on the theory that they were a part of it, written in ink discernable to the judicial eye" (LM: 48). This is later expanded and specified even more by the distinction of text and context. In his discussion, F.F. provides a list of places a judge may look when attempting to give specificity of meaning to the "other," non-mathematical symbols. In doing so, he rejects two alternatives which others have put forward. For once, he does not follow the British lead. The English rules of construction are "confined to" the words of the statute. F.F. says interpretation must only be "confined by" the words of the statute. The British rules "are too simple. If the purpose of construction is the ascertainment of meaning, nothing that is logically relevant should be excluded. The rigidity of English courts in interpreting language merely by reading it disregards the fact that enactments are, as it were, organisms which exist in their environment" (LM: 64). This is to think words, not things. It is tempting to see this as a rebuttal to Justice Black who attempted to confine the Constitution "to" its words.[49]

F.F. also rejects "the intent of the framers" as a locus or rubric of interpretation. "We are not concerned with anything subjective. We do not delve into the minds of legislators, or their draftsmen, or committee members" (LM: 61). What is of importance is that "[l]egislation has an aim; it seeks to obviate some mischief, to supply an inadequacy, to effect some change of policy, to formulate some plan of government. That aim, that policy is not drawn, like nitrogen, out of the air; it is evinced in the language of the statute, as read in the light of other external manifestations of purpose" (LM: 60). "Interpretation" in the law must focus on what is public and shared, not on what is private and idiosyncratic. Both the antecedents and the subsequent history of legislation and other legislation may shed light on the problem of concern to the legislature and its efforts to cope with that problem. Frankfurter would thus avoid the effects of one of the most peculiar efforts in American Constitutional interpretation: the effort to prove that the framers of the Fourteenth Amendment secretly intended to protect business enterprises rather than the emancipated former slaves. By F.F.'s approach, the drafters' secret intent is irrelevant.

We should look at the audience for which the legislation was intended: "If a statute is written for ordinary folk, it would be arbitrary not to assume that Congress intended its words to be read with the minds of ordinary men. If they are addressed to specialists, they must be read by judges with the minds of the specialists" (LM: 57). Some are "words of art" which have a special meaning appropriate within a specialized area.

Frankfurter enters potentially more controversial ground in suggesting that judges should also assume two environing considerations of all legislation: the Constitution and the federal system. It should begin with assumptions that Congress would not put forward legislation contrary to the Constitution or casually subversive of established State interests. To effectuate these assumptions sometimes produces interpretations which seem strained to the non-judicial or even the judicial reader. This option of straining does not mean, however, that the Court can properly "effectuate...that which Congress should have enacted" but did not (LM: 61).

Frankfurter claims to find the principles underlying his views of interpretation in a review of the work of three judicial masters—Holmes, Brandeis, and Cardozo. It would at first appear he prepared for the lecture by rereading some two thousand opinions by the three Justices (LM: 48-49); but we learn from his diaries that his law clerks "Phil Kurland and Lou Henkin....are helping me to analyze the opinions of these three Justices" (D: 289). F.F. found the three in basic agreement. Apparent differences are a matter of style, and in this each is distinctive. In F.F.'s reading, their opinions reveal "no private attitude for or against the extension of governmental authority by legislation" nor any private attitude "toward the policy of particular legislation" (LM: 49). That is to say, while these paragons each had private attitudes and opinions about the wisdom or probable efficacy of the general extension or restriction of governmental power and of particular policies, they did not let these private views intrude into their judicial opinions or, to use a word which F.F. liked a great deal, undermine their disinterested consideration of the issue before them. Judging the wisdom of the legislation was not a part of the determination of its meaning. One need not concur completely with F.F.'s assessment in this to approve such a distinction and to acknowledge that these three Justices made conscientious efforts to live by it.

All three Justices, according to F.F., accepted the fact that the determination of meaning involves an act of judgment: "The area of free judicial movement is considerable" (LM: 52). Judgment is not simply some sort of logical unfolding. There is a choice of possibilities, and the judge must accept responsibility for making the choice. Thus, "pretensions of certainty" should be distrusted. In matters of such controversy as to reach the Supreme Court there is no certainty: the Justices must ultimately make a choice among possible and competing interpretations. The skeptical philosophy which these three Justices shared leaves a judge undoctrinaire and able to exercise choice relatively free from over-attachment to her or his own beliefs and preferences. They were able to control their "private attitudes" and not let them affect their "judicial function in construing laws" (LM: 49).

All three of the exemplars also understood that a statute must be viewed in its entirety as an expression of policy arising out of a legislative grasp of a specific situation and a legislative choice of particular ends. Individual words, phrases, and clauses must be viewed in terms of the totality of the statute. Statutory interpretation is not statutory nitpicking. "Judges must retain the associations, hear the echoes, and capture the overtones" in grasping the whole piece of legislation (LM: 49-53).

The essay closes with a brief comment on the importance of careful legislative draftsmanship. The Court should not encourage hasty and careless draftsmanship of the part of Congress by its own generosity and looseness of interpretation.

> In a democracy the legislative impulse and its expression should come from those popularly chosen to legislate, and equipped to devise policy, as courts are not. The pressure on legislatures to discharge their responsibility with care, understanding, and imagination should be stiffened, not relaxed. Above

all, they must not be encouraged in irresponsible or undisciplined use of language....Perfection of draftsmanship is as unattainable as demonstrable correctness of judicial reading of legislation. Fit legislation and fair adjudication are attainable. (LM: 71-72)

Frankfurter addressed judicial reasoning even more explicitly as it pertains to the Supreme Court in a paper delivered before the American Philosophical Society in 1954, "The Judicial Process and the Supreme Court." While acknowledging that he is dealing with "complicated and subtle problems," he stresses the importance of them to all citizens because "an appreciation of the nature of the enterprise...in which [the] court is engaged" is "indispensable ...for the country's welfare....the chief reliance of law in a democracy is the habit of popular respect for law" and this in turn depends to a high degree "upon the confidence of the people in the Supreme Court" (LM: 31).

These few remarks imply much. They may seem obvious, but not everyone has adhered to them. A few contrasts help to illuminate. According to F.F., the stuff of politics is complicated. This is congruent with Madison in *The Federalist* 37. F.F. disagrees with a long tradition on this continent of advocates of democracy including such favorites as Thomas Paine, Henry David Thoreau, and the authors of the "Port Huron Statement" which initiated the Students for a Democratic Society in the 1960s. All of these considered the stuff of politics basically simple. Frankfurter and Madison, unlike Burke and earlier writers, do not draw from this complexity the conclusion that government must be restricted to the few. They too speak for popular government. Instead of expecting the many to understand all of the complexities of politics, F.F. believes the people need only understand the general character of the democratic enterprise—the institutions of government. They must also, however, possess a "habit" of "respect for law." This combination of understanding and habit is already evident in Aristotle.[50] The people must recognize that the Court makes judgments (and does not simply enunciate something which is logically inevitable) but must also have confidence that the members of the Court are making every effort to be, as F.F. quotes John Adams, "as free, impartial, and independent as the lot of humanity will admit..." (LM: 41). It would be hard to have respect for a Humpty-Dumpty Court which says the law is whatever it pleases.

F.F. begins his examination of what it is the Justices are doing—"the nature of their endeavor"—with a brief reflection on the books of Cardozo, especially *The Nature of the Judicial Process*.[51] Cardozo's writings, he says, are irrelevant because they are based upon a court with "very different business" than that of the Supreme Court. Once he had moved to the Supreme Court, Cardozo was "keenly alive" to the "resulting differences in the nature of the judicial process in which the two courts were engaged." The "raw materials of the adjudicatory process " were "very different" (LM: 32-33). Judicial reasoning is only one kind of practical reason, but even that is subdivided by the kind of court within which it operates. Frankfurter's language throughout the essay is the language of the title: it focuses on "process." Reasoning is not a "logic" but a "process," and the process differs with the institutional context and allocation of responsibilities. The formal character of thoughts takes second place to the character of the persons and the procedures they follow.

The essay then turns to the "two provisions" of the Constitution which have been invoked in the "most exacting problems that in recent years have come before the Court" (LM: 34) and have thus defined the distinctive business of the Supreme Court. The Commerce Clause and the Due Process Clauses are the "very different business" of the Supreme Court. The Commerce Clause concerns the "distribution of authority" between the Federal and State governments. The Due Process Clauses present "the most delicate and pervasive of all issues to come before the Court...the accommodation by a court of the interest of an individual over against the interest of society" (LM: 34-35). The two clauses evoke different kinds of reasoning, or rather, they require different kinds of reasons. They appeal to different sets of justifications. Here reasoning is clearly the offering of reasons.

In view of the diminished role of federalism and the Commerce Clause, mentioned above, we may plausibly reverse F.F.'s order and treat it first and only briefly. The central issue for Frankfurter is that of "striking the balance between the respective spheres of federal and state power." Again quoting himself, this time from *Polish National Alliance v. Labor Board*, 322 U.S. 643, 650-651 (1943), "The interpenetrations of modern society have not wiped out state lines." Federalism is of continuing validity, although much leeway is given to the federal government in controlling commerce. It is a "matter of practical judgment...[entrusted]...primarily and very largely to Congress, subject to the latter's control by the electorate." The Court "is concerned with the bounds of legal power and not with the bounds of wisdom in its exercise by Congress." In these cases, the Court's task is similar to that of chief courts of other federal states—"that of determining whether the Congress has exceeded limits allowable in reason for the judgment which it has exercised." What is "allowable in reason" is contrasted with "gossamer threads." Much leeway must be allowed for Congressional discretion. Federalism never lost its importance to Frankfurter: the States are the laboratories for democratic experiment.

The Due Process Clauses, especially that of the Fourteenth Amendment, have continued to provide a great source of business for the Supreme Court—though perhaps somewhat diminished since F.F.'s time by the alternative use by litigants of the Equal Protection Clause. Perhaps by the 1930s and certainly by the time he himself joined the Court, Frankfurter had come to accept that the due process clauses would not "go." They are a part of the American legal-political process. The issue is how to interpret and apply them.

Both "due process" and "equal protection" are, for F.F., phrases of tempting

generality—the apple attractive to Eve and leading to the Fall or that cast before
the three goddesses and leading to the Trojan War. In this essay, he puts his most
attractive light on "due process":

> Human society keeps changing. Needs emerge, first vaguely felt and
> unexpressed, imperceptively gathering strength, steadily becoming more and
> more exigent, generating a force which, if left unheeded and denied response
> so as to satisfy the impulse behind it at least in part, may burst forth with an
> intensity that exacts more than reasonable satisfaction. Law as the response
> to these needs is not merely a system of logical deduction, though
> considerations of logic are far from irrelevant. Law presupposes sociological
> wisdom as well as logical unfolding. (35)

After quoting Whitehead on the shocks which attend necessary change and the
role of symbols in mediating that change, F.F. goes on: "The Due Process Clauses
of our Constitution are the vehicles for giving response by law to this felt need by
allowing accommodations or modifications in the rules and standards that govern
the conduct of men" (35).

"[D]ue process as a concept is neither fixed nor finished" (35). Unlike terms
which are closely determined by legal tradition or legislative definition, due process, "is not a technical conception with a fixed content unrelated to time, place,
and circumstances." It expresses a "feeling of just treatment which has evolved
through centuries of Anglo-American constitutional history and civilization" and
thus "cannot be imprisoned within the treacherous limits of any formula" (36:
quoting himself from *Joint Anti-Fascist Refugee Committee v. McGrath*, 341 U.S.
123, 162-163). Due process is to be understood as freedom is understood by Burke:
the result of an on-going cummulation of institutions, practices, and standards
introduced over generations experimentally and without full understanding of
their implications.

Due process is "not a mechanical instrument. It is not a yardstick." It is "a
delicate process of adjustment inescapably involving the exercise of judgment by
those to whom the Constitution entrusts with the unfolding of the process." It
represents an "attitude of fairness between man and man, and more particularly
between the individual and government..." (36). It is thus something more than
the parts which make it up, but that something is not a comprehensive definition.
It is a "process" which draws upon the sentiments of the Anglo-American community and particularizes those sentiments and their implications in an instant
case. It depends upon the "judgment" of persons assigned a responsibility. This is
the heart of F.F.'s long disagreement with Justice Black. Black believed that due
process could and should be confined by definition as exactly as possible to the
provisions of the "Bill of Rights" and long argued for "incorporation" by proceeding on the conviction that the Fourteenth Amendment's reference to due process was best interpreted as applying the "Bill of Rights" to the States. The Jus-

tices should be left with a minimum of discretion. Frankfurter believed that "due process" has an independent, historically-developing meaning which the Court has the responsibility of redefining during the course of addressing changing circumstance. The Justices cannot escape their responsibility by any formula.

That judgment which these responsible persons makes draws on "history, reason, the past course of [judicial] decisions, and stout confidence in the strength of the democratic faith which we profess" (36). Such a judge

> should be compounded of the faculties that are demanded of the historian and the philosopher and the prophet. The last demand upon him—to make some forecast of the consequences of his action—is perhaps the heaviest. To pierce the curtain of the future, to give shape and visage to mysteries still in the womb of time, is the gift of imagination. It requires poetic sensibilities with which judges are rarely endowed and which their education does not normally develop. These judges...must have something of the creative artist in them; they must have antennas registering feeling and judgment beyond logical, let alone quantitative, proof. (39)

Frankfurter makes no attempt to extract the meaning of "due process" from the intentions of those who inserted the phrase into the Fifth and Fourteenth Amendments or to derive it from more primitive concepts by anything like a deductive procedure. The Justices—exercising a responsibility given by Anglo-American legal tradition, the Constitution, and the usages which have been developed since its adoption—make a judgment based on their grasp of the consensus of the community. It is a judgment of the best sense of fairness of the community as it pertains to the case at hand.

The required reading of consensus occurs at two levels. What is the consensus of the most insightful and unbiased observers as to the view of the community? And, what is the consensus of, as Madison put it in *The Federalist* 63, "the cool and deliberate sense of the community" about what is fair? It is important to keep these two levels distinct, since the "most insightful" persons in the community may—and indeed are likely to—have a different view of what is fair than does the community at large. The Court should not write into law what it perceives the most "advanced" portion of the community to think correct. That is a matter for legislation. On the other hand, assessment of the view of the community at large cannot be treated as a matter for an opinion poll—"quantitative" proof. The Court, even less than the Senate, should not be responsive to the temporary majority. What it seeks should be "the expression of the views and feelings that may fairly be deemed representative of the community as a continuing society" (40), free from the passions of the moment.[52]

Compare this with Cass Sunstein's recent and stimulating book, *The Partial Constitution*, in which he discusses "Text, Structure, History" as the "basic foundations of constitutional decisions." The section closes with: "Always there is (for good reasons) an overriding commitment of fidelity to text, structure, and history, and these will discipline the inquiry. But the discipline is not a straightjacket. Reasonable people will differ." He concludes the passage, however, "And in solving those differences that remain, interpretive principles must have some other source." He shortly explains: "My most general response is that such principles should be derived from the general commitment to deliberative democracy." His "interpretive principles" and their "source" in a "general commitment to deliberative democracy" seem to be developments consistent with the "stout faith" of Frankfurter, whom Sunstein simply groups with Holmes. Sunstein's "principles," however, have a shortcoming which does not pertain to the "stout faith."

Sunstein's main argument is against "status quo neutrality" which, apparently usually thoughtlessly, takes what exists as a "neutral" starting point. The advocates of the position attacked thus take departures from the status quo as violations of an appropriate judicial neutrality. Sunstein's concern with "status quo neutrality" has its analogue in Frankfurter's preoccupation with "alert self-scrutiny" and "exploring the influences which have shaped one's unanalyzed views." (See the discussion of *Haley v. Ohio* below.) "What is" is, we may agree, often "unfair." But "what is" is not so much a neutral starting point as a necessary starting point. Sunstein attempts to appeal to his set of "interpretive principles" derived from his "general commitment." This seems in danger of slipping back into the search for an Archimedean lever—a set of principles which will free us from the necessities of responsible choice and underlying faith.

Sunstein's argument has another short-coming, one that must be understood in the light of the teachings of Hume, Burke, and F.A. Hayek. The problem is summed up in Sunstein's assertion that "government has conferred on them a right." He confuses the use of governmental institutions and procedures to enforce or protect a right (for example, trespass) with "conferral." The "rights" in question have grown up over time and under many governments. While they are not "natural" in the sense of inhering in or arising from the biological nature of human beings and can continue to be "improved" over time, they now approach the status of "eternal verities." They have not been "conferred" by the "government" of here and now, to be withdrawn at that government's discretion.

Sunstein's interpretations of Frankfurter, Burke, and Hayek differ from mine. His is the sort of case I mention in the "Preface": I can only regret he has not made use of Frank Knight's understanding of—and recognition of the limitations of—the free market and has, apparently, limited his use of Hayek to *The Road to Serfdom* without benefit of *Law, Legislation and Liberty*.[53]

Of both the Commerce Clause and the Due Process Clauses, F.F. says: "Judicial judgment in these two classes of the most difficult cases must take deep account, if I may paraphrase Maitland, of the day before yesterday in order that yesterday may not paralyze today, and it must take account of what it decrees for today in order that today may not paralyze tomorrow" (39). Such judgment "derives from the totality of a man's nature and experience" (39-40). This broad charter requires restraints. For Frankfurter, these restraints lie not in a "meretricious authority" grounded in "the uncritical assumption that it is founded on compelling reason or the coercive power of a syllogism" (40). Rather, the restraint is grounded in the possibility that human beings may "avoid the cult of cynicism" which treats it as "at best a self-delusion for judges to profess to pursue disinterestedness" (40). A person does not change her or his character by becoming a judge, but "a judge worth his salt is in the grip of his function" (41). Frankfurter copes with Sunstein's concern with "status quo neutrality" by the demand that a judge must seek "true humility and its off-spring, disinterestedness" and have a "capacity for self-searching" (41-42).

Frankfurter's essay closes with a reformulation of skepticism drawing on the statements of others. "Inevitably there are bound to be fair differences of opinion" (42). He quotes Chief Justice Hughes: "How amazing it is that, in the midst of controversies on every conceivable subject, one should expect unanimity of opinion upon difficult legal questions! In the highest ranges of thought, in theology, philosophy and science, we find differences of view on the part of the most distinguished experts..." (42). The problem is that "there is hardly a question of any real difficulty before the court that does not entail more than one so-called principle" (43). F.F. then quotes Holmes: "All rights tend to declare themselves absolute to their logical extreme. Yet all in fact are limited by the neighborhood" of other, and competing, principles (43). Compare the epigraph to this book by Frank H. Knight. The final writer quoted is an anonymous reviewer: "But when, in the field of human observation, two truths appear in conflict it is wiser to assume that neither is exclusive, and that their contradiction, though it may be hard to bear, is part of the mystery of things." But judges cannot leave it at that. Like Cicero's man of practical affairs, the judge has to decide. "Judges cannot leave such a contradiction between two conflicting 'truths' as 'part of the mystery of things.' They have to adjudicate"—to decide the practical problem (42-43).

In these passages, Frankfurter turns us from the lessons of the past to the creation of the future. Cicero and Burke described the coral-like accretion of institutions, standards, and ideals but shed little light on how the process progresses. Frankfurter shows us that there is no magic formula—no template against which decisions can be compared to guarantee that the future is, indeed, an improvement. We must try to do the best we can to avoid pitfalls and to cultivate good judging.

9. Due Process

Due Process, and especially the Due Process clause of the Fourteenth Amendment with all its implications for action by the States, has been touched upon repeatedly. It deserves more focused attention. Its interpretation played an important role in the business of the Supreme Court during Frankfurter's career on the Court. More importantly for our purposes here, it illustrates the challenge facing the academic skeptic who, for better or worse, lacks any universal and certain criterion for distinguishing better from worse. For the past hundred years, "due process" has been—along with "freedom of speech"—a primary rubric for the "coral-like accretion of institutions, standards, and ideals" mentioned in the last paragraph. F.F.'s contribution to an understanding of "due process" has been greater than that to "freedom of speech" and best illustrates the problems and processes.

This use of "due process" is ironic since, as reported above, Frankfurter argued in the 1920s that the Due Process clauses should be eliminated because their meaning was so vague that their interpretation and application conferred more power than a court should properly have. They invited broad judicial innovation. At the time F.F. wrote his editorial on due process, the Court's attention was primarily focused on issues involving the "right of contract"; and the relevant "facts" were economic, social, and industrial. Presidential candidates Coolidge and Davis had given speeches asserting that the Court had a responsibility to protect the rights of a minority (in management and labor) from intrusions by a majority acting through legislatures and wishing to restrict these rights in the cause of social justice. By the time Frankfurter was well settled onto the Court, these restrictive powers were conceded to Congress and the State legislatures, and these rights were demoted, as it were, to the second-class status of "property rights." He had accepted that the clauses would not be repealed and that he would have to make the best of an unsatisfactory situation. The cases which have divided the Court on issues of restricting legislative power from the 1940s to the present have involved political, religious, personal, or human rights. The status, as well as the kinds, of facts which are thought relevant has changed also. From Frankfurter's point of view, however, the difficulties attendant upon the Justices filling the "vacuum" with their own "controlling notions" did not change.

One solution—that promoted by Justice Hugo Black—was to give specificity to the clause in the Fourteenth Amendment by postulating that it simply applies the particulars of the "Bill of Rights" to the States. (The First Amendment was drafted as a limitation on the Federal government. The others were interpreted by the Court in *Barron v. Mayor and City Council of Baltimore*, 7 Pet. 243, 8 L.Ed. 672 [1833] to apply only to the Federal government.) This approach was unsatisfactory to F.F. in part because the Court still had to pick and choose among the articles of the Bill of Rights. The Fifth Amendment, for example, includes "due process" itself; the Seventh requires a jury trial if more than twenty dollars is at stake in a suit at common law. Instead, F.F. preferred to follow the lead of Justice Cardozo in *Palko v. Connecticut,* 302 U.S. 319 (1937) in focusing on those aspects which are a necessary part of a "scheme of ordered liberty." This formulation still left the Justices great leeway in interpretation and choice. Frankfurter was often to be criticized during his years on the Court for the choices he made.

The discussion of "The Judicial Process and the Supreme Court" above quoted F.F. extensively on the meaning of "due process." It is a subject he felt forced to return to frequently in his years on the Court and inspired a number of concurrences as well as opinions and dissents.

The phrase "due process" seems at first to refer to procedure, the "process" by which a result is reached. The procedures are ones created during the slow growth of the Anglo-American system. Their articulation and application in individual cases have been the lesser source of controversy. The real issues are whether there are some results which are not to be reached by any procedure, what those "rights" are, and what is their source or origin. These are the issues of "substantive" rather than "procedural" due process. F.F. revealed his basic understanding of "due process" in *McNabb v. United States*, 318 U.S. 332 (1943), a case dealing with "[j]udicial supervision of the administration of criminal justice in the federal courts" which "implies the duty of establishing and maintaining civilized standards of procedure and evidence. Such standards are not satisfied merely by observance of those minimal safeguards for securing trial by reason which are summarized as 'due process of law' and below which we reach what is really trial by force" (340). By focusing on supervision of the federal courts, he found it "unnecessary to reach the constitutional issue [application of the Due Process Clause] pressed upon us" (340). He nonetheless took advantage of the occasion to preach on the subject of criminal procedure.

> A democratic society, in which respect for the dignity of all men is central, naturally guards against the misuse of the law enforcement process. Disinterestedness in law enforcement does not alone prevent disregard of cherished liberties. Experience has therefore counseled that safeguards must be provided against the dangers of the overzealous as well as the despotic. The awful instruments of the criminal law cannot be entrusted to a single functionary. (343)

Promptly bringing the accused before a judicial officer thus "constitutes an important safeguard—not only in assuring protection for the innocent but also in securing conviction of the guilty by methods that comment themselves to a progressive and self-confident society" (344). That the federal courts should set such an example, however, does not necessarily imply that the States, by application of the Fourteenth Amendment, must be required to follow suit: "review by this Court of state action expressing its notion of what will best further its own security in the administration of criminal justice demands appropriate respect for the deliberative judgment of a state in so basic an exercise of its jurisdiction" (340). Many people have a strong tendency to think of all "rights" as inhering in each individual's humanity. Frankfurter recognized that at least some "rights" are the product of a particular history and express a tentative and experimental reaching toward generality which must be balanced against other important needs and even other rights. The federal system can be used as a productive laboratory if every unit within it is not forced into conformity with the formulation perceived at any one time to be the "best."

In *Malinski v. New York*, 324 U.S. 401, 412 (1945), F.F. took the occasion in a case involving a confession of dubious worth to dispute the "incorporation" approach to interpreting the Due Process Clause. He concurred with Douglas in the result but not with the line of reasoning. "Due process" and "equal protection of the laws" are

> all phrases of large generalities. But they are not generalities of unillumined vagueness; they are generalities circumscribed by history and appropriate to the largeness of the problems of government with which they were concerned....The safeguards of "due process of law" and "the equal protection of the law" summarize the history of freedom of English-speaking peoples running back to Magna Charta and reflected in the constitutional development of our own people. The history of American freedom is, in no small measure, the history of procedure. (413-414)
>
> Experience has confirmed the wisdom of our predecessors in refusing to give rigid scope to [due process]. It expresses a demand for civilized standards of law. It is thus not a stagnant formulation of what has been achieved in the past but a standard for judgment in the progressive evolution in the institutions of a free society. (414)

Our understanding of the meanings of freedom and our views of the best institutions for promoting freedom are the products of our history; and our ways of formulating these understandings and views are limited by the characteristics of our language. We aspire toward universality for all times and all peoples in our formulations, but we should not assume we have achieved it. We use such guidance as we have from our history and study and reflection and what seem to be our current "best formulations" to chose the next step.

The Bill of Rights illustrates the problem rather than providing a conclusive solution to it.

> In the Bill of Rights, Eighteenth Century statesmen formulated safeguards against the recurrence of well-defined historic grievances. Some of these safeguards, such as the right to trial by a jury of twelve and the immunity for prosecution unless initiated by a grand jury, were built on experience of relative and limited validity....Others, like the freedom of the press or the free exercise of religion or freedom from condemnation without a fair trial, express rights the denial of which is repugnant to the conscience of a free people. They express those "fundamental principles of liberty and justice which lie at the

base of all our civil and political institutions," *Hebert v. Louisiana* 272 U.S.
312, 316, and are implied in the comprehensive concept of "due process of
law." (414)

That is, even though we may recognize in theory that no formulation is final and
impervious to improvement, some "rights" seem to be so nearly so as to excuse
the use of "fundamental." As Frankfurter, in another concurrence, approvingly
quoted Cardozo in *Louisiana ex rel Francis v. Resweber, Sheriff, et al.*, 329 U.S.
459, 466 (1947): "'some principles of justice [are] so rooted in the traditions and
conscience of our people as to be ranked as fundamental' *Snyder v. Massachusetts*," [291 U.S. 97, 105] (469). He later noted, in *Wolf v. Colorado*, 338 U.S. 25
(1949), that "basic rights do not become petrified as of any one time, even though,
as a matter of human experience, some may not too rhetorically be called eternal
verities" (27).

In still another concurrence in *Adamson v. California*, 332 U.S. 46, 59 (1947),
F.F. argued against expanding the Fifth Amendment right not to "be compelled in
any criminal case to be a witness against" oneself into a State-restricting "right to
remain silent" without negative interpretation.

> Only a technical rule of law would exclude from consideration that which is
> relevant, as a matter of fair reasoning, to the solution of a problem. Sensible
> and fair-minded men, in important affairs of life, deem it significant that a
> man remains silent when confronted with serious and responsible evidence
> against himself which it is within his power to contradict. The notion that to
> allow jurors to do that which sensible and right-minded men do every day
> violates the "immutable principles of justice" as conceived by a civilized
> society is to trivialize the importance of "due process." (60)

He also used *Adamson* to attack the idea that the "Due Process Clause" in
the Fourteenth Amendment should be interpreted as "incorporating" the Bill of
Rights so as to apply it to the States. As in *Hebert v. Louisiana*, he calls attention
to distinctions between those provisions of the Bill of Rights which are "enduring
reflections of experience with human nature" and those which "express the restricted views of Eighteenth Century England regarding the best methods for the
ascertainment of facts" (63). Incorporation would lump these together or necessi-
tate "subjective selection" among the provisions. Despite his own earlier preferences, F.F. thought the Court inescapably committed to make an "exercise of
judgment upon the whole course of the proceedings [at issue] in order to ascertain
whether they offend those canons of decency and fairness which express the notions of justice of English-speaking peoples..." (67). While the standards at issue
are "not authoritatively formulated anywhere," the "judges are not wholly at large"
with their own personal preferences: "The judicial judgment...must move within
the limits of accepted notions of justice" and not be simply "based upon the idio-

syncracies of a merely personal judgment. The fact that judges among themselves may differ whether in a particular case a trial offends accepted notions of justice is not disproof that general rather than idiosyncratic standards are applied" (68). The object is complex (the "notions of justice"); judgment is difficult (unanimity is not always achieved); but the responsibility for choice is assigned ultimately to the Court.

In *Haley v. Ohio*, 332 U.S. 596, 601 (1948), the Court opinion was written by Justice Douglas for himself, Black, Murphy, and Rutledge. Justice Burton dissented for himself, Chief Justice Vinson, Reed, and Jackson. Frankfurter concurred. Since the Court reversed a State court conviction on due process grounds, F.F. thought "it appropriate to state as explicitly as possible why...I cannot support affirmance of the conviction." The situation called for "an alert self-scrutiny so as to avoid infusing into the vagueness of a Constitutional command one's merely private notions"—a skeptical shower-bath preparatory to judging. "Like other mortals, judges, though unaware, may be in the grip of prepossessions. The only way to relax such a grip, the only way to avoid finding in the Constitution the personal bias one has placed in it, is to explore the influences that have shaped one's unanalyzed views in order to lay bare prepossessions" (602). He proceeded to do so.

At issue in *Haley* was whether the confession of a fifteen year old boy was "'voluntary' and as such admissible [as evidence], or 'coerced' and thus wanting in due process." This is "essentially" a "psychological judgment" (603). In F.F.'s view, however, it is what may be called a second order psychological judgment: not the judge's judgment of the boy's state of mind but the judge's judgment of what is the "pervasive feeling of society regarding such psychological factors" (605). "Judges must divine that feeling as best they can from all the relevant evidence and light which they can bring to bear...and with every endeavor to detach themselves from their merely private views" (603). There are no psychological or other experts available to guide such a second order judgment because: "Our Constitutional system makes it the Court's duty to interpret those feelings of society to which the Due Process Clause gives legal protection. Because of their inherent vagueness the tests by which we are to be guided are most unsatisfactory, but such as they are we must apply them" (605).

In this case, F.F. draws on "judicial experience with the conduct of criminal trials as they pass in review before" the Supreme Court (605). He characterizes what happened as "detention for purposes of eliciting confession through secret, persistent, long-continued interrogation" (606). "...conduct devoid of physical pressure but not leaving a free exercise of choice is the product of duress as much...as choice reflecting physical constraint" (606) and as such violates due process.

A series of cases over the next few years gave Frankfurter occasion to repeat and expand his views of due process as a developing concept. In dissent in *Irvine v. California*, 347 U.S. 128, 142 (1954), he commented on the process of inclusion and exclusion:

> The series of cases whereby...the scope of the Due Process Clause has been unfolded is the most striking, because the liveliest, manifestation of the wide and deep areas of law in which adjudication "depends upon differences of degree"....It is especially true of the concept of due process that between the differences of degree which that inherently undefinable concept entails, "and the simple universality of the rules in the Twelve Tables or the Leges Barbarorum, there lies the culture of two thousand years." (143; the quotations are from Holmes)

In one of these cases, *Rochin v. California*, 342 U.S. 165, 174 (1952), Justice Black made use of a concurrence to ask why only "English-speaking peoples" should be considered "to determine what are immutable and fundamental principles of justice" (176). He criticized Frankfurter for endowing the Court with "boundless power" under "natural law." But F.F. repeatedly disavowed "immutable" principles. He had already, in *Francis v. Resweber*—in the quotation from Cardozo cited above—noted that these are "principles...so rooted in the traditions...of our people" and in *Wolf*—also quoted above—that some rights are called "eternal verities" but only "not too rhetorically." That is, Frankfurter locates "due process" in an historic legal tradition rather than in the verbal formulas of a particular text or, at the other extreme, in a universal "natural law" rooted in human nature or in divine prescription. Other societies and language traditions have developed other institutions and other words in what we hope is a converging search for what we call justice and fairness.

In *Griffin et al. v. Illinois*, 351 U.S. 12, 20 (1956), F.F. repudiated any use of "natural law." "We should not indulge in the fiction that the law now announced has always been the law" (26). "'Due process' is, perhaps the least frozen concept of our law—the least confined to history and the most absorptive of powerful social standards of a progressive society" (20-21). By avoiding the "fiction," F.F. would avoid prejudging the cases of those held in jail under the previous legal situation.

10. Exemplars

In *The Public and Its Government*, Frankfurter remarked on "how slender a reed is reason...how deep the countervailing instincts and passions" and on the "dark recesses of man's nature, which pioneers like Freud and Jung are slowly" making accessible (128-129). He believed that a Justice of the Supreme Court must constantly reexamine her or his own presuppositions and urged the many benefits of judicial biography. His opinions are filled with efforts at self-exposure, but there is no reason to think he would have enjoyed the psychobiography by H.N. Hirsch.

That is not to say, however, that he would disapprove on general grounds. "A biography is to be judged by the insight it gives into the complexities of character, not by the satisfaction it affords the reader's presuppositions" (LM: 108). He attempted to set a number of his former students and clerks at work on searching biographies of various Justices. His own contribution to our view of humankind is of a sort different from that of Hirsch or even the series he proposed.

Above, Frankfurter's use of Holmes and Brandeis was explored; and later his regard for Cardozo was noted. It has been argued that F.F. played an important part in creating the legal persona of Holmes, just as he played a role in Brandeis's confirmation by the Senate. Especially in the cases of Holmes and Brandeis, F.F. repeated himself in several different papers and even in his Court writings and gave his thoughts the appearance of authority by their repetition. The treatment of these three Justices is connected to his broader preoccupation with biography but focuses on what may best be called "public character." It is represented in F.F.'s corpus by a large number of occasional speeches and memorials. None of these explore the "dark recesses of man's nature." The phrase "public character" is in quotes to call attention to a somewhat special usage, since "character" is a common enough English word.

Frankfurter's occasional contributions to biography are only fragmentary; his character sketches are remarkable. The biographies by his proteges were to portray some contemporary Justices; the character sketches are of acquaintances across a spectrum from fame to obscurity. The former were to show the impact of character and accident on judgment; the latter display the diverse citizens produced by and contributing to "the exhilarating adventure of a free people determining their own destiny" (LM: 235). The former were to have been done by former students and clerks; the latter were delivered or written by F.F. himself.

Two enterprises associated with the word "biography" must be distinguished in Frankfurter's thought: true biographies and the character sketches. F.F. envisioned a group of biographies covering at least Holmes, Brandeis, Cardozo, Jackson, and himself and selected persons he hoped would do the writing.[54] The project confirmed Mark DeWolfe Howe on a long path of Holmes scholarship which generated a number of books, though never the completed biography. The other projects have never ripened. F.F.'s interest in having detailed biographies of those who have served on the Supreme Court was career-long. The Justices he selected have at least received biographic attention from others but perhaps treatment which would not have satisfied F.F.

As mentioned, F.F. himself left a few biographical notes in addition to his small book on Holmes. To the essays on Holmes and Brandeis, there were added others on Hughes, Stone, Cardozo, and Jackson. An especial curiosity is an essay on Justice Owen Roberts who had chosen F.F. as the conduit for his own account of the famous "switch in time that saved nine"—the 1937 doctrinal shift which signaled the end of Supreme Court's blocking of the New Deal. For the most part, these essays are not actually biographical in the sense of giving detailed "insight into the complexities of character." They focus on the ways the subjects approached judging, the modes of reasoning they employed, and their visions of the law. In the cases of the Chief Justices, F.F. treated the way they managed the business of the Court. The same focus appears in the transcript of a talk he gave at the University of Virginia and printed as "Chief Justices I Have Known."[55] Throughout these and elsewhere, F.F. left thoughts on judicial biography.

Judicial biographies, and especially biographies of the Supreme Court Justices, were important to Frankfurter because he thought individuals make a difference and because he thought people can be educated to be better judges.

> ...the work of the Supreme Court is the history of relatively few personalities. However much they may have represented or resisted their *Zeitgeist*, symbolized forces outside their own individualities, they were also individuals. The fact that they were *"there"* and that others were not, surely made crucial differences. To understand what manner of men they were is crucial to an understanding of the Court. [We should seek to understand something of the] inner forces that directed their action and stamped the impress of their unique influence upon the Court. (FC: 247-248; footnote omitted)

The importance of the individual who was "there" is well-illustrated by John Marshall who did so much "to educate the country to a spacious view of the Constitution" (FC: 537). That he became Chief Justice was highly contingent.

> Surely the course of American history would have been markedly different if the Senate had not rejected the nomination of John Rutledge to succeed Jay as Chief Justice; if the benign Cushing, a Federalist of different composition from Marshall's had not withdrawn after a week and had continued as Chief Justice till his death in 1810; if Ellsworth's resignation had come later; if John Adams had persuaded Jay to return as Chief Justice; or if some other readily imaginable circumstance had delayed Ellsworth's replacement till John Adams was out of the White House so that the new Chief Justice would have been a Jeffersonian....John Marshall is a conspicuous instance of Cleopatra's nose. (FC: 237-238)

In view of the importance of choice in F.F.'s understanding of judging, it is not surprising that the biographies of those who have judged, both wisely and unwisely, should be of supreme interest. Those chosen to judge can learn to appreciate their responsibilities in the mirror of the great Justices. Neither judge nor statesman nor citizen can see the future, but we can partially see how past choices produced the present. The public cannot derive from biography any sure key to judicial selection, but it can better understand the importance of careful selection. F.F. was sure that judicial biography would have a common thread: the importance of getting persons

who bring to their task, first and foremost, humility and an understanding of
the range of problems and of their own inadequacy in dealing with them,
disinterestedness, and allegiance to nothing except the effort, amid tangled
words and limited insights, to find the path through precedent, through policy,
through history, to the best judgment that fallible creatures can reach in that
most difficult of all tasks: the achievement of justice between man and man,
between man and the state, through reason called law. (LM: 138)

Frankfurter's own contribution in the biographical vein was of a quite different sort than what he hoped others would produce, his displays of character.

The word "character" is of Greek origin and, according to the Oxford English dictionary initially referred to an "instrument for marking or engraving" or
the "impress, stamp, distinctive mark [or] distinctive nature" produced by such
an instrument. The contemplation of character is not simply the recounting of
biographical anecdote. Character both marks the person who possesses it and
impresses itself upon those with whom that person has contact.

Greek tragedy presented characters, in our sense of the word; but though
these usually had dominating characteristics, their "message" was carried mainly
by their actions and by what happened to them. In his early and middle dialogues,
Plato employed characterization of the participants to supplement his argumentation. This is sharply illustrated, for example, by *Euthyphro*. The dialogue about
impiety is inconclusive in arriving at a definition of the subject but clearly portrays an impious person in Euthyphro himself who has denounced his own father.
In the case of the more famous *Republic*, we are given portraits of two just men:
the host Cephalus who exemplifies the common picture of a just man and Socrates
who exemplifies the just man in a true understanding of justice. The dialogue
employs movement from a lower to a higher level: from the world of appearances
to the world of reality and from opinion to truth. In the common understandings
of justice, Cephalus is a just man. In a true understanding, however, he can be
seen not to possess that unity of soul (wisdom, courage, and temperance) which is
justice properly understood. And thus, in the myth of Er which concludes the
dialogue, a person such as Cephalus who had lived a sort of just life through habit
rather than understanding is consigned to a terrible fate in his next life. Socrates,
on the other hand, may seem to common opinion an eccentric but in truth he
embodies a balanced soul of justice and sanity. In each case, Plato is making use
of the complementarity of word, argument, and image discussed in the "Seventh
Letter."

Theophrastus, Aristotle's principal successor, created something new with
his "Charakteres"—a series of sketches of human types. Only a part of the original plan has come down to us showing the bad types: the dissembler, the flatterer,
the garrulous man, the boor, and so on. The portraits are not of real individuals
but give concrete examples of behavior to make a point about unacceptable and

acceptable behavior. In his dedication, Theophrastus explains his purposes:

I...having observed human nature a long time...have thought it incumbent upon me to write in a book the manners of each several kind of men both good and bad. And you shall have set down sort by sort the behavior proper to them and the fashion of their life; for I am persuaded...that our sons will prove the better men if there be left them such memorials as will, if they imitate them, make them choose the friendship and converse of the better sort, in the hope they may be as good as they.[56]

The work was apparently popular and influential.

Cicero claimed, as one attached to academic skepticism, to be an intellectual heir of Plato. As discussed in the chapter on him, Cicero employed real characters in his dialogues and made extensive use of character to reinforce his argument. Cicero borrowed liberally from others in his portraits—all a part of finding, or creating where he could not find, connections and common qualities amidst the variety of public leaders. The most famous and successful contribution to the genre, Plutarch's *The Lives of the Noble Grecians and Romans*,[57] overlaps with biography in our sense of the word.[58] Originally *The Lives* paired a Greek public figure, political or military, with a comparable Roman to illustrate a moral/political point. Much anecdotal, gossipy, and apocryphal material is included; and some of those featured are only legendary. The result nonetheless displays the place of character in public affairs.

In F.F.'s work, I have found no specific plan such as those of Theophrastus or Plutarch to illuminate character types, nor does he reveal any exhaustive system. His many essays in this genre are responses to his admirations and affections and to the many occasions he was called upon to express them, but they are also congruent with his views of law and government and are consistent with his academic skepticism. Like Cicero, he found many people worthy of memorialization; and, like Cicero, he borrowed as liberally as he praised.

Most of the published pieces concern the recently deceased, but a few were occasioned by *Festschriften*. Some praise famous persons, and others the near-famous. Most call attention to those at the edge of the public view. Some were his colleagues and students at Harvard. In many cases, F.F. had been called upon to say something. A surprising number of the essays, however, were at his own initiative, especially "letters to the editor." At times, he wished to correct the public record. At other times, it is as though he wished to insure that the falling of a tree had not passed unnoticed, with no lesson drawn from it.

Frankfurter described one of his Harvard classmates who carried on a personal campaign of letters and telegrams fighting "those who overtly or covertly resisted President Roosevelt's efforts" to aid the Allies before U.S. entry into World War II (LM: 302-307). His description of his friend aptly describes his own "indefatigable industry and legal imagination [and] felicitous command of language" in his efforts to "preserve in the amber" of the written word a multitude of characters. A long-time friend and Harvard professor of clinical psychology, in a tribute, captured the point essential to the worth of these essays: "...someplace in the soul of F.F.—not far from the center, I would guess—is a compass of sensitive vitality whose magnetic needle can be counted on to point with unexcelled precision to indubitable human worth in whatever man or woman this may happen to reside" (T: 11).

The general function of these pieces is summed up on one occasion after quoting "Let us now praise famous men." This "was not an exhortation for a gesture of pietistic generosity, the placing of verbal flowers on the graves of famous men. It is for our sake that we are to praise them, for, as Ecclesiasticus added, they have given us an 'inheritance.' We commune with them to enlighten our understanding of the significance of life, to refine our faculties as assayers of values, to fortify our will in pursuing worthy ends" (LL: 77). Our understanding is deepened by dwelling on exemplars, but something more is involved than just understanding. F.F. speaks of philosopher Morris Cohen, his former roommate at Harvard, as having "that magical ability to make life richer and deeper because he had that divine gift of making his students more important than they ever thought themselves to be" (LL: 111). F.F. might as well have been speaking of himself, for he uses the exemplars to call his auditors or readers to their better selves.

Two short pieces printed in *Of Law and Men* concern former students who died in World War II. Of one dead at thirty in the aftermath of fighting in the South Pacific, F.F. refers to his possessing "all the gentler qualities—loyalty, modesty, high courtesy, regard for the tender places in life...[combined with] sterner qualities...deep reserves, of a strong, even stubborn will, and a maturity far beyond his years" (315-316). Frankfurter gives these attributes their civic setting and makes the sacrifice of life more than thoughtless bravery: "The Greeks had such as Bill Sheldon in mind when they said the good die young. No one saw more clearly than he the moral issues of this war, and he felt his life belonged to his country not as a devouring state but to an organized way for leading civilized lives" (316). Participating in the dedication to another former student of a part of the Law School Library at Harvard, F.F. evokes shades of the "Gettysburg Address" to explain the occasion: "We are here not to memorialize Guido Pantaleoni, but to invigorate our weakness from his strength, to fortify our purposes from his vindication of them" (317). After quoting Holmes on the fullness of life, F.F. refers to Pantaleoni's "driving energy...[which was not] self aggrandizing...[but] tender and gay and energizing of others" (318). His virtues too are given their civic setting in his understanding "that freedom rests on those intricate arrangements for self-rule which is law" (319).

Frankfurter told a story on himself and Chief Justice Hughes concerning

F.F.'s early days on the Court. When they were in disagreement in conference, Hughes was prone to address his colleague "in a mischievous way" as "Professor Frankfurter" and then correct himself. Finally, F.F. responded "I hope with equal good humor, 'Chief Justice...I know of no title that I deem more honorable than that of Professor of the Harvard Law School'" (LL: 28).

Frankfurter held the professoriat in high standing, and a number of F.F.'s memorial essays concern academics. Many of these were law professors—especially teachers and colleagues at Harvard. The striking thing about his characterizations is their variety. In very few words, distinctive personalities emerge, each in his own peculiar style a contributor to the legal professoriat: writers and nonwriters, the disinterested and the doctrinaire, bullies and the convivial. Clearly, however, if the scholar "has one guiding function...one virtue about which there should be no question, it is disinterestedness" (LL: 173). F.F. in fact saw this as central to legal education and the profession: "...the training of the lawyer is to a great degree training for disinterested analysis not true to such a degree in any other profession" (LL: 154). That this should be so is curious since we call a lawyer an "advocate." The lawyer should be able to construct the best argument possible in the circumstances, and the judge to choose the better argument presented. Both construction and choice require the ability to view the situation and the range of possible arguments in a disinterested fashion. This may sound harsh because it does not seem to include "justice" in the calculations. Justice is a part of the calculation; only a part because, to the skeptical mind, it does not come with guarantee of authenticity attached. Disinterestedness does not imply blandness. These legal professors as well as other lawyers praised by F.F. are shown as colorful figures, well deserving recollection and contemplation.

As a famous man himself, Frankfurter was called upon to praise other famous men, including the two most widely-known philosophers of his age: John Dewey and Alfred North Whitehead. As mentioned earlier, Dewey and Holmes were intellectual cousins; and F.F. and Whitehead knew each other from Harvard. F.F. found Dewey's philosophy compatible and made frequent use of Whitehead's book on symbolism. The appreciation of Whitehead is in a letter to the New York *Times* occasioned by Whitehead's death. It addresses the integrative impact of Whitehead. His "benign and beautiful presence" was in the service of a "pervasive influence" which promoted "an understanding of interdependence among the various disciplines" (LM: 288-290). Whitehead exemplified the universality of the university and the adventure of the intellectual enterprise, institutional characteristics now too often lost in departments and bureaucracies.

None of Dewey's writings had the explicit impact on Frankfurter of Whitehead's oft-quoted *Symbolism*. It is, indeed, hard to capture Dewey in quotations. In praising Dewey's content, on the occasion of his ninetieth birthday, F.F. could not resist an extended quotation from Holmes which interlards gibes at Dewey's style: "There are moments that suggest that he could write well, but then

comes obscurity....So methought god would have spoken had He been inarticulate but keenly desirous to tell you how it was" (LM: 285 [quotation only partially reproduced here]). What F.F. found especially compatible in Dewey is his
view of the richness of experience which eludes any particular effort to encapsu-
late it. For the academic skeptic, no particular formulation of "truth" has a finality which forecloses further elaboration or modification. "[Dewey's] philosophical outlook has not been imprisoned within a fixed system established by inexo-
rable syllogisms....Dewey taught us to use all that is fruitful in experience to gain
new experience in dealing with problems that too often defy the abstractions offered for their solution" (LM: 286).

Frankfurter's Harvard roommate Morris Cohen, like Dewey and Whitehead
a philosophy professor, was also praised for, among other things, his skepticism:
"If he had a doctrine it was to be critical of doctrines" (LM: 292).

Frankfurter's love-affair with England and the British produced many friends
and eventually many memorial pieces. Some of the friendships began during his
first term of service in the Federal government; others during the Peace Conference or in his term as Pitt Professor at Oxford; and still others were picked up
along the way. Though he would never have used the analogy, F.F. viewed Britain's
relation to the United States a bit like that of John the Baptist to Jesus. The American covenant is the greater, but it is prefigured in English government and laws
and in slowly-maturing attitudes that eventually produced the Commonwealth.
The Romans opened up citizenship to all people. The English too built an empire
of very diverse people. Though many Englishmen never escape the constraints of
ethnic prejudice, their culture developed a kind of potential for universality: they
have so loved law that their civility has tended toward civilization. Burke's prosecution of Hastings exemplifies the tendency to apply English standards of fairness to "the other fellow" too. Recent fiction also illustrates this. Paul Scott in
The *Raj Quartet* plays out these tendencies with all their ambivalences—all the
"good guys" and "bad guys" within English character. Many of those portrayed
believe they have to try to be fair, even though they find the Indian cultures distasteful.[59]

Some of those memorialized represent the friendly concern of the older for
the younger brother—keeping the somewhat isolated Americans informed of the
larger world in which Britain had so long been involved (LL: 104-106; 253-255).
Others typified the search for civilization. Ambassador A.J.K.C. Kerr was sensitive to the "claims of human dignity everywhere and in all shifts of society" (LM:
341). Ambassador Philip Kerr was compared by F.F. to Lincoln in his "compas-
sionate faith...in the moral worth of every individual" and his belief that it "should
become the dominant faith of the world, a faith achieved through works." Typify-
ing British appreciation of America's "significance to a civilized organization of
the world," Kerr gave to the library of the Indian federal court a copy of "Farrand's
edition of the records of the Constitutional Convention of Philadelphia" (LM:

338-339).

Frankfurter focused on the convergences of humanity even while he delighted in the diversity of individuals. Lincoln was his archetype: the homely and unpretentious man of the people writ large for all peoples; the self-taught democrat. Quotations and, even more, representations appear frequently in F.F.'s writings; but his published essays never centered on Lincoln himself - the man Frankfurter called "the moral symbol of this nation" (LM: 242). Frankfurter ended his appreciation of Thomas Mann with reference to Lincoln:

> The essence of the democratic faith is the equal claim of every man to pursue his faculties to the humanly fullest—for his sake, but no less for the sake of society. Nature is the greatest of democrats. She endows men with the noblest gifts, heedless of genealogy. Greatness always remains a mystery - but what is more fitting than that Lincoln should gradually but securely have become the uncontested symbol of America.   (LL: 351)

This folksy Lincoln and the polished English are his polar exemplars.

In *The Public and Its Government,* Frankfurter had called for informed and disinterested public servants; and he stressed the importance of citizenship itself. Henry Stimson was the prime exemplar of citizenship and public service in F.F.'s experience. Stimson, like Lincoln and unlike Holmes and Brandeis, shown quite independently of anything F.F. had contributed to the building of his reputation. Like Lincoln, Stimson was not the subject of any of F.F.'s encomia. On a number of occasions, however, F.F. recorded the achievements and virtues of such public servants and citizens—providing just enough detail to whet the appetite. Only a few people out of the vastness of humankind are the subjects of biography. Lincoln and Stimson have had their due. All too many biographical subjects, however, are "celebrities" whose weaknesses of character lower rather than raise our sights. Many of the men and women about whom F.F. spoke and wrote may well have had feet of clay and no doubt had weaknesses. He often shows us their foibles. Mostly, however, he informs or remind us of their services and their admirable and charming characteristics.

Frankfurter's occasional writings (but not all of them) have been collected in three volumes, each edited by different persons. The first of these volumes appeared as the professor was translated from Harvard to the Supreme Court and contains none of the memorial pieces. Each of the latter two contains a brief piece on Franklin Roosevelt: the first written in the first days after his death and the other a decade later. There is, as usual when F.F. revisited a topic, repetition. Both express high optimism about FDR's place in the American vision as an exemplary democratic leader: one of the few who "represent some universal element in the long adventure of man"—with "qualities that kindle the heart and fortify the spirit" (LL: 25). Roosevelt was "a democrat in feeling and not through ab-

stract speculation about governments" (LM: 360). F.F. catalogs FDR's political
virtues (friendliness, self-sufficiency, resoluteness, energy, understanding of
people, a consistent course, a silver voice, and a "charismatic quality that stirs
comfortable awe, that keeps a distance between men and leader and yet draws
them to him"), but they all center in his trust of the people.

One repetition regarding FDR is: "It has been wisely said that if the judgment of the time must be corrected by that of posterity, it is no less true that the
judgment of posterity must be corrected by that of the time" (LM: 360; LL: 22).
F.F. judged that his friend was to become something more than just another historical figure: "Franklin Roosevelt cannot escape becoming a national saga, en-
shrined in myths, if you will. Myths endure only when rooted in essential truth; as
such they serve to guide and sustain the high endeavors of a people." FF compares FDR with Lincoln:

> They both had the common touch—a sense of kinship with their fellows, the
> sense of the deep things men have in common, not common in the sense of
> what is vulgar and unedifying. The Roosevelt saga will never swallow up
> Roosevelt the man, whose friendship gave hope to millions who never knew
> him and whose death brought a feeling of intimate, personal loss to millions
> who never saw him. (LL: 22)

In view of his closeness to FDR and the buoyant optimism they shared and the
newness in 1956 of television, it is not surprising that F.F. may have misjudged.
Roosevelt at present appears mythic mostly for those born during his administration. A new era of appearances was ushered in with the 1960's. Even Lincoln and
the civic virtues which he represented have faded. The mythic figures today, including the politicians among them, are entertainers.

11. Conclusion

The reader cannot be immersed in the writings of Felix Frankfurter without real-
izing that he sought to be an exemplar as well as to praise the exemplary in others.
He often attributes to others what he must have hoped others would see in him.
This is not to say that he sought the company and friendship only of those who
mirrored himself. The range of his friends and admirers and the diversity of those
for whom he had praise definitively precludes such an assessment. By various
accounts, he could appear aggressive or devious. His least favorite colleague on
the Court, William O. Douglas, wrote in his final days: "Frankfurter's skein of
life was woven with a design that was duplicitous, for no one poured his emotions
more completely into decisions while professing the opposite."[60]

It is important to note in Frankfurter's own case, however, that he claimed
to be leaving everything of his own which would serve potential biographers. He

is rather like Cicero in leaving so much behind, whether intentionally or not, that he easily invokes disrespect or even dislike. Melvin Urofsky comments in his preface to *Felix Frankfurter: Judicial Restraint and Individual Liberties* that: "biographer Michael Parrish relates that he started out liking and admiring Frankfurter and then came to dislike him intensely; only after a long time did he reach a middle point, a guarded affection. I, too, began my work thinking of Frankfurter as a great man; the more I learned, the less I cared for him."[61]

The earliest biographies, those by Helen Thomas and by Livia Baker, now seem to the reader exercises in uncritical praise, written before crucial sources were available. "A Brahmin of the Law: A Biographical Essay" by Joseph Lash is decidedly favorable to F.F., but his own closest successors, his students and clerks, seem not to have had the temerity to try to encompass him within any covers other than his own. His chosen biographer Max Freedman did not live long enough to fulfill the assignment. He is thus in the curious position of being memorialized in accounts most interesting for their portrayals of Frankfurter as the "disappointing" Justice who held back while others "forged a modern jurisprudence of constitutionally protected individual rights and liberties" and who "poisoned the well of [Court] collegiality," in the words of Urofsky; or as the neurotic "in desperate need of self-confidence," in the view of Hirsch; or as the conspirator/myth-maker of B.A. Murphy.

Unlike Parrish and Urofsky as portrayed above, I did not start out "liking" Felix Frankfurter. Indeed, partly out of diffidence, I resisted a suggestion to visit the Justice. I found Frankfurter's approach to things legal and political to be appealing, and my personal attraction to or dislike for the man was and is not relevant. Would I have liked him or disliked him had we met? I do not know. It might have depended on accidents of first impression. If over a period of time I found him to be a scoundrel, that would be another matter. But I expected to find a human being much like and much unlike others I have met. I neither sought nor needed another friend, one within whose complexity and ambiguity I lose my self in affection. What has interested me is the public doctrine and the public figure. In our fascination with what Frankfurter himself called the "dark recesses of man's nature" (PG: 129), compounded today by a prurient interest in the private lives of public figures, we lose sight of that realm of civic character in which we should expect to interact with one another with honesty and honor. Whether or not Frankfurter was himself always honest and honorable or whether he was sometimes devious and mischievous, he expounded a philosophy of moderation, toleration, participation, responsibility, democracy, and progress.

It is clear from his own and others' accounts that Frankfurter was very deeply moved by individual cases—especially when the death penalty was involved. The executions of Sacco and Vanzetti, Willie Francis, and the Rosenbergs drove him to distraction. In the first case, he was sure the prosecution was deeply flawed. In the second, the repeated effort to carry through the electrocution made worse an already dreadful act. In the third, he thought there remained serious doubts about the adequacy of the trial and appeals, an undue haste, and submission to public hysteria. As he made clear in the closing passages of his book on Sacco and Vanzetti, he realized that no system of justice will always operate perfectly. As he emphasized in the FELA cases, the Supreme Court cannot function to guarantee that every case within the jurisdiction of the United States will be decided the way the Supreme Court members would have decided them. Frankfurter thought that the most important function of the Supreme Court is to play its Constitutional roles of balancing the concerns of the States with those of the Federal government and of balancing the rights of the individual against the needs of the community. The Court has a narrow but crucial responsibility of choice.

Cicero recounted how nervous he became in presenting an argument because he was dealing with the most important issues of state. Frankfurter too thought he was dealing with the most important issues of state, the constitutional balances. Individual rights and general prosperity depend on the successful working and survival of the constitutional system. Under the pressure, he did not, like Cicero, respond by speaking so softly he could scarcely be heard. He may well, however, have responded by the seemingly endless restatement, the cajoling, and the maneuvering which his colleagues found so irritating and his biographers so unappealing. The issues as he saw them were not simply the doing of individual justice but the continuing of the whole system. And that depends on what the Court does not try to do as well as what it does do: its restraints as well as its choices.

To me after studying Felix Frankfurter for many years, Frankfurter stands, even if viewed with his alleged shortcomings, as an exemplar of responsible participation. We cannot depend upon any philosopher-king. No person or group is fit for such a role. Not even the Justices of the Supreme Court. Temperamentally and in manner, F.F. himself was far from kingly. Jovial yes; Jovian no. He was not a friend to every person but he was a friend to "everyman." A quite different kind of aristocrat than Franklin Roosevelt, he nonetheless shared his friend's natural attachment to freedom, to democracy, and to public service. Felix Frankfurter is well summed up by Alexander Meiklejohn's somewhat back-handed compliment: "As I have known and enjoyed F.F., however right or wrong he may have been in his theories of constitutional freedom, he has been clearly and persistently right about the way in which free men may hold different views as to what freedom really is" (T: 88).

12. Biographical and Critical Appendix

Biographical and critical treatment of Frankfurter is by no means at the definitive stage, since F.F. was a prolific writer, retained much himself, and sent "keepers" to many others. Interesting materials and new insights continue appearing in many places—not least the biographical material of his friends and acquaintances, former students, New Dealers, and colleagues and critics. I do not believe new material will damage my general thesis. By filling in details, it should further illustrate an academic skeptic making the hard choices of government.

For an easily readable selection from F.F.'s opinions, see Philip B. Kurland, *Mr. Justice Frankfurter and the Constitution* (Chicago: University of Chicago Press, 1971). An earlier collection covers only part of his Court career: Samuel J. Konefsky, *The Constitutional World of Mr. Justice Frankfurter: Some Representative Opinions* (New York: Macmillan, 1949).

The best biography of Frankfurter covers only his pre-Court years: Michael E. Parrish, *Felix Frankfurter and his Times: The Reform Years* (New York: Free Press, 1982); it was presumably to be followed by another volume. Helen Shirley Thomas wrote *Felix Frankfurter: Scholar on the Bench* (Baltimore: The Johns Hopkins Press, 1960) while F.F. was still on the Court. Like Thomas, Livia Baker, *Felix Frankfurter: A Biography* (New York: Cowart-McCann, 1969), provides a friendly work without the benefit of important material which became available only later. "A Brahmin of the Law: A Biographical Essay" by Joseph P. Lash, which introduces *From the Diaries of Felix Frankfurter* (New York: W.W. Norton & Company, Inc., 1975) is an excellent short view. Bruce Allen Murphy, *The Brandeis/Frankfurter Connection: The Secret Political Activities of Two Supreme Court Justices* (New York: Anchor Press/Doubleday & Company, 1983) writes in the spirit of a muck-raker, even when discussing what has been common knowledge all along, but adds much interesting detail to the common store. Leonard Baker, *Brandeis and Frankfurter: A Dual Biography* (New York: New York University Press, 1986) covers much the same ground without quite the same verve. The psychobiography by H.N. Hirsch, *The Enigma of Felix Frankfurter* (New York: Basic Books, 1981), is structured by a psycho-analytic interpretation and provides many colorful details.

The comparison of F.F. with Hugo Black is almost a book industry in itself, beginning with Wallace Mendelson, *Justices Black and Frankfurter: Conflict in the Court* (Chicago: University of Chicago Press, 1961), which is generally favorable to Frankfurter. More recent studies shed many additional details on Frankfurter: Mark Silverstein, *Constitutional Faiths: Felix Frankfurter, Hugo Black, and the Process of Judicial Decision Making* (Ithaca: Cornell University Press, 1984) and Melvin L. Urofsky, *Felix Frankfurter: Judicial Restraint and Individual Liberties* (Boston: Twayne, 1991). James F. Simon, *The Antagonists: Hugo Black, Felix Frankfurter, and Civil Liberties in America* (New York: Simon and Schuster, 1989), is "written... for the general reader." All three books tend to emphasize the role of Frankfurter in pushing Black to develop his ideas more fully.

This chapter was completed after many drafts before I looked at any of these more recent books. I wished to make my comments based primarily on the public works of Felix Frankfurter—what he had to say for himself. Silverstein and Urofsky both make stimulating reading, however. The former book explores the tension between liberalism and democracy. It structures a contrast between Frankfurter as an advocate of an educational elite with judges who are competent to be disinterested and Black as a advocate of limits on all power with judges who are restricted to literal interpretations. The former thus, despite his professions to the contrary, expanded the sphere of judicial judgment, while the latter sought to decrease it. This approach has the curious result of placing Frankfurter in the tradition of Jefferson in wishing to educate and promote an aristocracy of virtue and talent and Black in the tradition of John Adams who thought the aristocracy of wealth, beauty, and family name would always triumph over virtue and talent and thus all power should be greatly restrained. (See the Preface.)

Urofsky's book expands upon the thesis that Frankfurter, in an excess of consistency, applied to the protection of "personal liberties" the same standards of judicial restraint which had appropriately been used earlier to criticize the efforts of the Court to protect "economic liberties." He thus missed the opportunity to participate with Black and others in the forging of "a modern jurisprudence of constitutionally protected individual rights and liberties" (p. xi). The book concludes with a useful "Bibliographic Essay," although my views of Frankfurter were well fixed long before I had the benefit of Urofsky's work. It would seem worthy of note that Urofsky earlier edited the Douglas letters.

New studies and biographies of others shed additional information about Frankfurter, and many more are no doubt in the pipeline. James J. Magee, *Mr. Justice Black: Absolutist on the Court* (Charlottesville: University of Virginia Press, 1980), is a sympathetic yet critical study of Black's "search [for] an objectivity which does not exist." Roger K. Newman, *Hugo Black: A Biography* (New York: Pantheon, 1994) permitted some interesting last-minute additions to this chapter. Gerald Gunther, *Learned Hand: The Man and the Judge* (New York: Alfred A. Knopf, 1994) uses the Frankfurter-Hand correspondence extensively and gives perspective on their shared skepticism. It provides little new about F.F. but gives a splendid portrait of another great skeptic.

Seven

POSTSCRIPTS

In his later years, having contributed to the theory of economics and then to the nature of theory in economics, Frank Knight spent most of his time considering human nature—especially the aspects of human beings which lead them not to use the knowledge which is readily available to them. He acknowledged that "man is a rational animal": we know it, he said, because man tells us so himself. Knight reminds his reader of the whole catalogue of adjectives which pertain uniquely to the human animal. Human beings are game-players, liars, cheats, and—Knight's consummate summary—"romantic fools."[1]

We human beings like to dress up our lives with ornamentation in both garb and behavior. In the western world we are especially inclined to fashions and fads in these matters. This faddishness is nowhere stronger than in American society, though we are also most strongly inclined to praise our "individualism." In fact, custom and tradition, which are the deeper social forms of which fashion and fad are the surface veneer, are necessary to us. I have quoted above passages from Tocqueville in which he emphasizes the dependence of even the most independent minds upon opinions which must be assumed without proof. He also suggested that our love of individualism would be likely to have the ironic result of making us ever more completely the captive of mass opinion and fads.[2] We are given to romanticism and fad even in our views of rationality. The history of philosophy, for example, is a history of fashion, and at no time has fashion changed more rapidly than in the twentieth century.

Americans assume and often assert explicitly that "all problems are solvable." One business enterprise has recently asserted in its advertising that anything that can be imagined can be done since this is America. We expect to resolve everything wrong with what our parents and teachers thought and did. It is a long-standing joke at school and college graduation exercises that the speaker urges the students to solve the problems all previous generations have found intractable. Alternately, some of us prove to our own satisfaction that no efforts will accomplish anything (Pyrrhonian skepticism or cynicism). Our widespread, diluted higher education may have made us more aware of and thus even more subject to intellectual fads. All too often, it also seems to produce a debilitating cynicism rather than a healthy skepticism. We have forgot the lesson put into words by Cicero: there can be no "nobler motive for entering public life than the resolution not to be ruled by wicked men and not to allow the republic to be destroyed by them...(*On the Republic*: 25). The word here translated as "wicked" ["inprobis"] comes from the root which gives us "probity" (moral uprightness, integrity) and means just the opposite. "Lacking in integrity" might be an apt translation for our time.

The skepticism of Cicero and Frankfurter with its emphasis on procedure and the "long run" runs against our romantic grain. It is probably no accident that each of the writers discussed here was—in one or more ways—an "outsider" as well as an insider. All were white males comfortably situated within the ruling class. As previously noted, however, Cicero and Burke were "new men" admitted to the inner circles of power. Cicero's family came from a small town, and he was the first (and last) member of it to rise to high office. Burke was an Irishman and came into the government affiliated with a distinguished but small group, the Rockingham Whigs. Hume had no political ambitions, but he too was an outsider, a Scot in London. Frankfurter was the ultimate outsider for a Westerner, a Jew. Even Madison, though elected President of the United States and acknowledged as "Father of the Constitution," had something of a the outsider's mentality. He could observe, as well as participate in, the Constitutional Convention and thus keep what seems to be a remarkably objective account of the debates. Ketcham tells us that "Madison's health presents perplexing problems [for he] was described frequently as 'feeble,' 'pale,' or 'sickly,' and he wrote repeatedly of bouts of illness and fears that poor health would prevent him from doing something or other."[3] He married a widow when he was forty-three, and he sired no children. Cicero's family life was filled with disappointments. Hume never married. Burke's son was something of a worry and predeceased him. And Frankfurter's wife seems to have been psychologically fragile and bore no children. Each man stood somewhat apart from his contemporaries.

Their sort of moderate, intellectual skepticism has never been the overt majority position, even in the periods of its greatest influence. Academic skepticism is an approach for those who seek knowledge: a kind of epistemology which warns not to expect too much. Most people are not so self-reflective. As Madison makes clear in *The Federalist* 49, most individuals are timid and their opinions depend on perception of "the number which he supposes to have entertained the same opinion." Thus, our election campaigns now largely focus on public opinion polls, temporary cross-sections of samples, rather than substantive discourse.

Another kind of skepticism verging on cynicism is widespread in American society today. The platitudes pronounced by most politicians imply almost complete consensus (that is, the success of the "melting pot") and a highly cohesive set of fundamental symbols and economic and political institutions. This nearly complete consensus is not true and has never been true in the United States. Consensus has been achieved by a series of overlapping symbols, institutions, and elites. Reality is widely seen to be in conflict with the simple myth of unity. In some people, skepticism slips into corroding cynicism and withdrawal from public affairs. Other people are manipulated by politicians who thrive on tactics of division. Now as never before, it is important to make the actual principles upon which the Constitution is based widely understood.

People, including most politicians, are inarticulate about occupying that middle ground of moderation so dear to the Founders. Most political discourse is left to the extremes. The elites in the middle do not readily identify themselves as "skeptics" for fear of being taken for cynics. All too many of them are weak on the fundamentals of the American political system. While there is a long-standing tradition of popular skepticism about political extremes represented by Josh Billings, Mark Twain, Peter Finley Dunne ("Mr. Dooley"), Will Rogers, and now in some comic strips, the politicians themselves are almost entirely platitudinous. The general populace, for example, seems to hold some middle ground on abortion and to be in practice skeptical of both the "freedom of choice" and the "right to life" absolutist formulations; yet few politicians try to articulate the moderate consensus.

These popular currents and cross-currents have received a great deal of attention from academic commentators. Unfortunately, university work has put excessive emphasis on clarity (whether or not the subject matter lends itself to clarity) and to the setting out of a distinctive position. (There is much more room around the circumference of a circle than near the center.) There are two distinct trends. One has led to a bias in favor of mathematical formulations; the other to extreme specialization.

In the 1950s, academic exponents of political moderation such as historian Daniel Boorstin drew on Tocqueville and Burke—both of whom enjoyed a period of academic popularity. While many of these scholars remained quite productive in the following decades, the intellectual fashions of the 1960s and since have changed. Some among the bookish moved to a recreated, doctrinaire "conservatism." Many of the generation of the 1960s found renewed vitality in the writings of Karl Marx, albeit not in his masterwork *Das Kapital*. Oliver Wendell Holmes continued for some time to be generally admired among lawyers for his contribution to First Amendment law, but even his reputation began to suffer as the younger generation correctly associated his arguments with his skepticism rather than with his belief in the leftward march of humanity. Many law schools now seem far from skepticism and are veritable battlegrounds for enthusiasms or dogmatisms rather than the "reservoirs of disinterestedness" which Frankfurter hoped for.

Our inclinations toward enthusiasms and dogmatisms illustrate Knight's observations about our not using the knowledge available to us. History has never witnessed information made so widely available, and our century has been especially and unfortunately rich in relevant experience. Yet how much have we learned? Enthusiasm for dogmatic Marxism produced catastrophe after catastrophe. Stalin's "purges" are especially incredible since many of the believers were complicitous in their own "trials." Equally remarkable is the example set by the mass enthusiasm of the Germans for Adolf Hitler. How can anyone watch the films of the adulation bestowed on Hitler and the monstrous havoc he created and not develop some antibodies of healthy skepticism toward those who claim to have answers for everything? Yet even in the United States, where the most complete information is readily available and in fact regularly presented, James Joneses and David Koreshes and numerous others can draw together people who will die for the sake of romantic nonsense.

There has been in the dominant American culture a strong strain of optimism accompanying confidence in our reasoning powers. We not only assume that every problem is solvable, but we are also inclined to believe—despite our common strong attachment to the Constitution—that we can remake our institutions at will. This confidence in our ability to control human behavior is closely associated with our long-standing inclination to think we can solve every problem with a law of some sort. In *The Federalist* 1, Hamilton calls attention to the possibility that good government can only be established "from reflection and choice" under quite special circumstances. In the American case, the unusual circumstances were the leadership and character of the Revolution. Good government, where it has existed, has been mostly the product of a long historical winnowing and has been the exception rather than the rule. Its survival is something of a wonder. Gibbon's *Decline and Fall* begins with the question of how it was that people living under such untypically pleasant conditions should throw it all away. Government is absolutely necessary, but through most of history it has been an unpleasant necessity.

The fall of the Roman Republic was mentioned at the conclusion of the Introduction. In the first century, B.C., the Romans were unable to sustain republican institutions under changing social and economic circumstances because they were unable to make necessary improvements in their government. They had greatly enlarged and diversified their citizenry. They had acquired a vast client population, much of it very poor and virtually all of it poorly trained in the arts of self-government. They had become litigious and used the legal system as a tool of partisan warfare. They had created a class of "insiders" able to manipulate civic business for personal profit. Cicero tried to rise above short-term interests and party conflict and to find or create common ground between the "Optimates" and the "Populares." His philosophical dialogues were one part of this effort. His political imagination was inadequate to the task. Neither his statesmanship nor his philosophy found common acceptance by the short-sighted and venal general public, the rigidly virtuous Stoics such as Cato and Brutus, or the cultivated Epicureans who saw politics as a dirty and pointless business. The "public business" (the "res publica") which Cicero advocated was replaced by a regime which operated a system of imperial bureaucracy behind the appearances of popular government.

The fall of the Roman republic—put in very simplified terms—can be attributed to a failure of imagination in adapting their institutions and practices to deal with new circumstances, to preoccupation with the private at the expense of the public, and to a decline in temperance, moderation, and decorum (a sense of what is proper). What the Romans got, after a certain amount of turmoil, was the rather pleasant life, comparatively speaking, from which in Gibbon's terms they "fell." Only "comparatively speaking" because of the slaves and the many poor people who had mostly "bread and circuses" to brighten their lives. Even the rich suffered a degree of uncertainty created by an occasional emperor who, acting from whimsy or policy, might dispose of their lives as well as their wealth. The Roman world fell from this state of grace, according to Gibbon, when the emperor Septimius Severus and his army put aside the forms and appearances which both cloaked and guided and restrained authority. Henceforward, the Romans faced life realistically and directly—and saw only brute force.

We are not the ancient Romans and neither our institutions nor our problems are as theirs. Aside from all else, events move much more swiftly today. Historical analogies are almost always intellectual snares, especially as they lead one to predictions. They are tempting, though.

For about two hundred years after Augustus transferred the real operating system of the Roman state to the control of the imperial bureaucracy, political figures continued to talk about "restoring the republic" by transferring effective control of the state back to the Senate (which still enjoyed the forms of government) and the assemblies (which did not). Such talk was entirely unrealistic: the institutions had been supplanted because they had failed to function. By the time the state was reconstituted a century later by Diocletian, such talk had ceased; but the provinces of the empire were still controlled centrally. By the end of another century, the empire had fragmented.

Today, the government of this country is largely in the hands of a centralized bureaucracy; and legislators are trying to restore earlier and somewhat romanticized governmental forms. The Roman experience may warn us to be careful lest we manage to compress the fragmentation of the United States into a couple of decades. Our need for imagination, participation, moderation, and a sense of the subtleties of humane life is much more pressing than theirs was and should be much more obvious to us. When the imperfect Roman institutions of peace and freedom passed from the scene, it took some fifteen hundred years for the West to develop comparable ones.

Hume, Madison, and Burke developed the constitutional implications of academic skepticism during the great creative period of modern constitutionalism. In the 1760s, the young George III made a nearly-successful effort to reclaim royal dominance in the British constitution and lost America in the effort. By the end of his reign in the second decade of the next century, constitutional, and increasingly popular, government was firmly established on both sides of the Atlantic. Only Madison and Burke were active in the governmental arena, but both drew on Hume. They helped to create the stable and moderate tradition of popular government.

Frankfurter was acutely conscious of the dramatic social changes which accompanied the revolutions in economic organization and production, transportation, and communication which have roiled this century. He was skeptical of doctrinaire solutions to the many problems generated by these changes. He looked to a legal profession committed to both continuity and progress to help the people find new solutions to both old and new problems. He saw the legislative branch as both primary teacher and primary agent of the people themselves. He saw competing but complementary vital principles in individual and government and in State and Nation. He repeatedly warned against hiding behind or confusing ourselves by verbal formulas. He was deeply committed to democracy, but he saw clearly its problems and pitfalls. The titles of two essays say much: "The Bold Experiment of Democracy" and "The Paths Must Be Kept Open."

The failure of Cicero, the success of the eighteenth century trio, and the warnings of Frankfurter alike provide counsel for the current day. The principles central to the American tradition are ones of cautious adaptation. They are procedural principles which may approach the status of "absolutes" but are nonetheless themselves subject to reformulation and modification. "Federalism" is one such procedural principle. For sixty years it has been in decline and for much of that time has lain under the shadow of "States rights" as a cover for race prejudice. Now, the principle is being given a new vitality. The experiment with decentralization which dominates current popular political discourse cannot rely on formulas or on simply the old ways of thinking and doing. State and local governments are not what they were seventy years ago. Business corporations are not what they were. Local communities are not what they were. The legal and communications professions are not what they were. The world is not what it was.

Two illustrations must suffice. Seventy years ago, before the long Democratic predominance and the accompanying centralization, every city and most towns had multiple newspapers. Corrupt practices were common in local and State government, but the media competed in exposés. The long-run environmental effects of industrialization and urbanization were largely unrecognized. "Pollution" was only vaguely perceived, in such things as food processing, for example. Now our vision of both corruption and pollution has broadened greatly. Within the media and despite the "professionalization" of journalists, however, the "hype" and the "breaking story" of William Randolph Hearst have prevailed over the long view of the likes of Walter Lippmann and Edward R. Murrow. Even many of the larger cities lack significant media competition, and the journalists of both print and airwaves are all too likely to flock rather than to study. They display widespread ignorance of elementary economic principles. For example, much discussion of pollution recognizes the dangers but does not face the costs of obviating these changes. This weakens the effectiveness of arguments against local and often blind self-interest.

The legal system has grown more dense: laws are more complex and lawyers more specialized. The same adjectives apply to higher education. In neither education, journalism, nor law has disinterested public service or a concern for educating the public flourished to the extent required. Local politicians and businessmen are just as open to corrupting temptations as ever; the opportunities and benefits of polluting are much greater; and a lot more money is involved. How will the public interest be monitored in the new era of decentralization? We have seen the excesses of centralized bureaucracy, but we must not forget the excesses of tunnel-vision self-interest nor the corruptibility of unmonitored public officials.

The other illustration is closely related. The large cities are now densely surrounded by suburbs and exurbs, each operating independently and often in competition. Few metropolitan areas possess civic elites with a coherent political, economic, and cultural vision. Competing within themselves and competing among themselves, these metropolitan congeries must also contend with one or even more State legislatures partially controlled by "down-state" or "up-state" representatives who are uninterested in or hostile to urban-suburban life and problems. Petty municipal rivalries in the face of overwhelming problems are reminiscent of the Balkan cities and princelings in the face of the Ottoman advance in the fifteenth century. Many of them preferred the Turks to their rivals.[4] Federated metropolitan government, almost certainly premised on the division of the central cities into neighborhoods comparable in size to the suburban units, seems to me an absolute necessity but remains at the farthest margins of public thought.

The Founders of the United States shared a common language not just in English but in the vocabulary of politics. They shared a common agreement on both the necessities and dangers of government. They shared ideals of free, popular government—albeit with many disagreements on details. Today, we speak with many languages. The principal problem is not, however, the politically lively one of "English as the official language." It is our loss of a usable common vocabulary of politics. Much has been made of the preoccupation with "rights" in recent decades, and in this respect we share an important common term. By a curious twist, this has been a source of division rather than unity. Holmes remarked on the tendency of all rights to "declare themselves absolute to their logical extreme." The proliferation of vigorously defended rights seems to have encouraged the proliferation of extremists, often talking on completely different channels. I suggest, without arguing the matters here, that there are at least three other sources of our political Tower of Babel. The first is the development of a number of academic languages apparently relevant to the study of humankind and each with its own dictionary of technical terms and special definitions of common terms. Fragments of these academic languages have entered media discourse stripped of their defining disciplinary contexts. The second is the focus of practicing politicians as well as academics and the media on opinion polling and a statistical approach to "public relations" rather than a rhetorical (explanatory) approach to relations with the public. The third is the language of "values": values are almost infinite in number, are only commensurable in economic terms, and thus are no adequate substitute for "ideals."

While *The Federalist*—like the Constitution itself—papered over a great many divisions, the current fashion is to emphasize and even magnify divisions. The writing castes in the academy and the media (I write loosely here and include both the news and entertainment businesses in the term "media") achieve distinction by identifying and making distinctions. Two of the "flash points" of current political discourse are "multiculturalism" and "family values." Instead of being recognized and developed as long-standing principles of American society, they are widely cultivated as issues of division. Higher education and the media could seek to build the liberally-educated, culturally-open, civic-minded public which a democratic, free society requires. The distinction-making of higher education, however, operates to promote the esoteric in specialization and research. The distinction-making of the media operates to publicize, if not actually promote, conflict and to debase taste. These trends have generated reactions from those who perceive them to have gone too far. The challenge is to correct without destroying: criticism tends to go to its own extreme.

The audiences for Athenian drama were not limited to an intellectual and wealthy elite. The same citizens who appreciated the somber tragedies of Sophocles and Euripides watched the accompanying satyr plays and the bawdy works of Aristophanes. Athenian democracy had a narrow citizenship. The American democracy is far more expansive. The United States has had its literate and literary democrats who spoke both for and to the people. Jefferson and Lincoln were two such. It has even had democratic literary critics such as Walt Whitman. It is important that politicians and professionals help us reestablish a common political vocabulary, build community bridges, and rebuild connections between democracy and artistic excellence. We could reverse that strange perversion of the democratic spirit which insists on every distinction except those of character.

The tradition of Cicero and Hume and Burke and Madison and Frankfurter provides no absolutely certain criterion which permits us to distinguish better from worse in any field of judgment. That does not mean we cannot make distinction between better and worse, though. As Frank Knight often put it, there is no point in saying something is impossible if we have to do it and it makes a difference whether it is done better or worse. If distinctions in political thought cannot be based on certainty, neither can they be made by opinion polls. Polls probably more often confuse than illuminate common sense. Our political society will only be sustained if there is some shared sense of good-will and some common sense of what is fair—that "spirit of moderation" so often referred to in the preceding pages. As we jointly explore issues of better and worse, we must be especially aware of the dangers arising from the excesses of enthusiasm. Better judgments are made and tentative "truths" found when concerned and well-meaning persons speak to and listen to one another over a period of time. And no formula dictates how much time is appropriate. Vigorous pursuit of principle is not the same as blind or violent pursuit of principle. Distinctions of politics, like distinctions of taste, must be made by the highly fallible judgments of those who have "paid attention." We are dependent on a vast division of labor in government as in economics. We were warned by Tocqueville of our weakness in recognizing our interdependence: "The practice of Americans leads their minds...to fixing the standards of judgments in themselves alone...."[5] Every opinion is not equal, however, and those in government have been assigned responsibility for making judgments. They should be given a fair chance to do so. The great challenge of citizenship is deciding whom to trust, for we must trust many people. In view of our often fleeting attention, we exercise our responsibility as citizens by granting responsibility to office holders for a term. This arrangement may be highly unsatisfactory; it is just the best available.

NOTES

Epigraph

1. From Frank H. Knight "The Role of Principles in Economics and Politics," published originally in the *American Economic Review* and reprinted in *On the History and Method of Economics* (Chicago: University of Chicago Press, 1956).

Preface

1. For example, see the beginning of Felix Frankfurter, *The Public and Its Government* (Boston: Beacon Press, 1964), p. 2, where Frankfurter quotes from Holmes's *"Collected Legal Papers* (1920), p. 202." He quotes again, without citation, in a lecture reprinted as "The Supreme Court in the Mirror of Justices" in *Of Law and Life and Other Things that Matter* (Cambridge, Mass.: Harvard University Press, 1965), p. 78. He even quotes it in a private letter to Franklin Roosevelt in *Roosevelt and Frankfurter: Their Correspondence 1928 -1945*, annotated by Max Freedman (Boston: Little, Brown and Company, 1967), p. 462.

2. See, for example, Alexander Hamilton, James Madison, and John Jay, *The Federalist* (Cambridge, Mass.: Harvard University Press, 1961), Numbers 1, p. 90 (by Hamilton), and 37, pp. 266 and 271-272 (by Madison).

3. Daniel J. Boorstin, *The Genius of American Politics* (Chicago: University of Chicago Press, 1953). Edward Shils, *Collected Essays* (Chicago: University of Chicago Press, 1972, 1975, and 1980) and *Tradition* (Chicago: University of Chicago Press, 1981). Leo Tolstoy, *War and Peace*, trans. Louise and Aylmer Maude (New York: The Heritage Press, n.d.). Stendahl, *The Charterhouse of Parma*, trans. Lady Mary Lloyd, revised Robert Cantwell (New York: The Heritage Press, 1955). Henry James, *Portrait of a Lady* (New York: Modern Library, 1951). Cao Xuequin, *The Story of the Stone* (also called *The Dream of the Red Chamber*), vols. 1, 2, 3 trans. David Hawkes, vols. 4, 5 trans. John Minford (Great Britain and New York: Penguin Books, 1973-1986). Lady Murisaki, *The Tale of Genji*, trans. Arthur Waley (New York: Modern Library, 1960).

4. Edmund Burke, *Reflections on the Revolution in France* (Indianapolis: Library of Liberal Arts, 1955), p. 181.

5. Alexis de Tocqueville, *The European Revolution & Correspondence with*

Gobineau, ed. and trans. John Lukacs, (Garden City, N.Y.: Anchor, 1959), pp. 33-34.

6. *Cf.*, Peter Laslett, "The Face to Face Society" reprinted in *Philosophy, Politics, and Society* (Oxford: Basil Blackwell, 1956) and Edward Shils, "Center and Periphery," reprinted in *Center and Periphery: Essays in Macrosociology* (Chicago: University of Chicago Press, 1975). The Adams-Jefferson correspondence, in edited form, appears in *The People Shall Judge*, Vol. 1 (Chicago: University of Chicago Press, 1965), pp. 228-235.

7. *Cf.*, Richard Rorty, "Philosophy in America Today," in *Consequences of Pragmatism* (Minneapolis: University of Minnesota Press, 1982), pp. 211-230.

Chapter One

1. G.E.M. Anscombe's translation of Ludwig Wittgenstein, *Philosophical Investigations* (Oxford: Basil Blackwell) was published in 1953; and her translation of Wittgenstein's *Remarks on the Foundations of Mathematics* (New York: Macmillan), in 1956.

2. Aristotle, *Nicomachean Ethics* in *Introduction to Aristotle*, ed. and intro. Richard P. McKeon (Chicago: University of Chicago Press, 1973), Bk. 1, ch. 3. All subsequent references in this volume to Aristotle's *Ethics* will be to the *Nicomachean Ethics*.

3. See, for example, Richard P. McKeon, *Freedom and History and Other Essays*, ed. Zahava K. McKeon (Chicago: University of Chicago Press, 1990); Walter Watson, *The Architectonics of Meaning: Foundations of the New Pluralism* (Albany: State University of New York Press, 1985); and David A. Dilworth, *Philosophy in World Perspective: A Comparative Hermeneutic of Major Theories* (New Haven: Yale University Press, 1989).

4. Richard Rorty, *Essays on Heidegger and Others* (New York: Cambridge University Press, 1991).

5. *Genesis: A New Translation with Introduction and Commentary*, by E.A. Speiser (New York: Doubleday & Company, Inc., 1981).

6. Michael Polanyi, *Science, Faith, and Society* (Chicago: University of Chicago Press reprint, 1966), *The Logic of Liberty* (Chicago: University of Chicago Press, 1951), and *Personal Knowledge* (Chicago: University of Chicago Press, 1958). Gilbert Ryle, *The Concept of Mind* (London: Hutchinson, 1949). Stephen Toulmin,

Human Understanding (Princeton: Princeton University Press, 1972). Thomas Kuhn, *The Structure of Scientific Revolutions* (Chicago: University of Chicago Press, 1970).

7. John Dewey, *Logic: The Theory of Inquiry* (New York: Henry Holt and Company, 1938).

8. Richard Rorty, *Objectivism, Relativism, and Truth* (New York: Cambridge University Press, 1991).

9. My reworking of John Dewey comes mainly from *Reconstruction in Philosophy* (Boston: Beacon Press, 1957); *The Quest for Certainty* (New York: Minton, Balch & company, 1929); *Experience and Nature* (New York: Dover Publications, 1958); and *Art as Experience* (New York: Minton, Balch, & Company, 1934). Though the book came to my attention only after this book was completed, see Joseph J. Schwab, *Science, Curriculum, and Liberal Education* (Chicago: University of Chicago Press, 1978).

10. Frank H. Knight, "Fact and Value in Social Science" in *Freedom and Reform* (New York: Harper & Brothers, 1947). Cf., Michael Polanyi, "Life's Irreducible Structure," reprinted in Michael Polanyi, *Knowing and Being: Essays*, ed. Marjorie Grene (Chicago: University of Chicago Press, 1969).

11. *Cf.*, Talcott Parsons, *The Structure of Social Action* (Glencoe, Ill.: The Free Press, 1949).

12. See Note 4 above.

13. *Cf.*, McKeon in Note 3 above and also Mortimer J. Adler, *The Idea of Freedom* (New York: Doubleday, 1958-1961).

14. This was written before I read Michael Crawford, *The Roman Republic* (Cambridge, Mass.: Harvard University Press, 1993) which emphasizes the failure to adjust institutions to changing conditions.

Chapter Two

1. Unless otherwise explained, all page references are to *The Federalist*, by Alexander Hamilton, James Madison, and John Jay; ed. Benjamin Fletcher Wright, (Cambridge, Mass.: Harvard University Press, 1961).

2. James Madison, *The Papers of James Madison*, vols. 1-10, ed. William T.

234   NOTES

Hutchinson, W.M.E. Rachel, *et al.* and Robert A. Rutland, *et al.* (Chicago: University of Chicago Press, 1962-1977).

3. Ralph Ketcham, *James Madison: A Biography* (New York: Macmillan, 1971), pp. 46, 244. Neal Riemer, *James Madison: Creating the American Constitution* (Washington: Congressional Quarterly, 1986), pp 29-30, 41. See Michael G. Ketcham, *Transparent Designs: Reading, Performance, and Form in the Spectator Papers* (Athens, Ga.: University of Georgia Press, 1985), pp. 20, 168, who mentions complaint that *The Spectator* too often quoted or drew upon Cicero, especially *De Officiis.*

4. Alexander Hamilton, James Madison, and John Jay, *The Federalist Papers* (New York: Mentor, 1961), p.vii.

5. Leo Strauss and Joseph Cropsey (eds.), *History of Political Theory* (Chicago: Rand McNally, 1963). The quotations come from, in order, pp. 574, 579, and 580.

6. David Epstein, *The Political Theory of the Federalist* (Chicago: University of Chicago Press, 1984). See pp. 117, 10, and 2 for the quotations.

7. George W. Carey, *The Federalist: Design for a Constitutional Republic* (Urbana, Ill.: University of Illinois Press, 1989), p. 161.

8. Gottfried Dietze, *The Federalist: A Classic on Federalism and Freedom* (Baltimore: Johns Hopkins University Press, 1960).

9. David Hume, "Idea of a Perfect Commonwealth," in *Essays Moral, Political, and Literary* (Indianapolis: Liberty Fund, 1985), pp. 512-513.

10. Edmund Burke, *Reflections on the Revolution in France* (Indianapolis: Bobbs-Merrill, 1955), p. 106.

11. Alexis de Tocqueville, *Democracy in America*, Vol. 1 (New York: Vintage, 1945), p. 7. For Comte and Marx, see F.A. Hayek, *The Counter-Revolution of Science* (Glencoe, Ill.: The Free Press, 1952).

Chapter Three

1. My approach to Cicero is deeply indebted to Richard P. McKeon's "Introduction" to Marcus Tullius Cicero, *Brutus; On the Nature of the Gods; On Divination; On Duties*, trans. by Hubert M. Poteat (Chicago: University of Chicago Press, 1950).

2. Richard H. Popkin, *The History of Scepticism: from Erasmus to Spinoza* (Berkeley: University of California Press, 1979).

3. David Hume, A *Treatise of Human Nature* ed. by L.A. Selby-Bigge (Oxford: Oxford University Press, 1951), Book 1, Part 4. For a survey of ideas of epistemology, logic, and metaphysics in this century, see John Passmore, *A Hundred Years of Philosophy* (Baltimore: Penguin Books, 1966).

4. Diogenes Laertius, *Lives of the Eminent Philosophers*, Vo. 2, trans. R.D. Hicks (Cambridge, Mass: Harvard University Press, Loeb Classical Library, 1970), p. 487.

5. For Hume, see Peter Jones, *Hume's Sentiments: Their Ciceronian and French Context* (Edinburgh: University of Edinburgh Press, 1982). For Burke, see his early, and only philosophical, work Edmund Burke, *A Philosophical Enquiry into the Origin of our Ideas of the Sublime and the Beautiful* (New York: Columbia University Press, 1958), pp. 4-5. *Cf.*, Thomas Jefferson, *The Life and Selected Writings of Thomas Jefferson*, edited by Adrienne Koch and William Peden (New York: Modern Library, 1944), p. 568.

6. There are many biographies of Cicero. *Cf.*, D.R. Shakleton Bailey, *Cicero* (New York: Scribner, 1972). H.J. Haskell's *This Was Cicero: Modern Politics in a Roman Toga* (New York: A.A. Knopf, 1942). For political thought, *cf.*, Neal Wood, *Cicero's Social and Political Thought* (Berkeley: University of California Press, 1988).

Cicero's writings are most readily available in their entirety from the Loeb Library (Cambridge, Mass., Harvard University Press), in Latin with English translation. These editions will be used, and translations will follow as in the editions unless otherwise noted. Citations will be made in parentheses in the text, employing the following abbreviations.

I   *De Inventione, et al.*, trans. by H.M. Hubbell, 1960.
ND   *De Natura Deorum* and
A   *Academica*, trans. by H. Rackham, 1961.
Of   *De Officiis*, trans. by Walter Miller, 1961.
Or   *De Oratore*, trans. by E.W. Sutton and H. Rackham, 1967.
R   *De Re Publica* and
L   *De Legibus*, trans. by C.W. Keyes, 1961.

Where a series of quotations from the same text follows in order, the source abbreviation will not precede the page number.

In a number of cases, I have included the Latin when it has an arresting English cognate.

7. For Cicero's difficulties with Clodius, see D.R. Shackleton-Bailey, *Cicero's Letters to Atticus* (London: Penguin Books, 1979), pp. 78-9 and 58. Plutarch, in his "Cicero" in *The Lives of the Noble Greeks and Romans*, trans. John Dryden and revised by Arthur Hugh Clough (New York: Modern Library, n.d.), p. 1043, recounts many examples of Cicero's biting wit and misplaced humor.

8. George H. Sabine, *A History of Political Theory* (London: Harrap, third edition reprinted, 1959). Neal Wood, *Cicero's Social and Political Thought*, see esp. pp. 70-72 for the assumption of Stoicism. For the assumption that the characters are simply mouthpieces, see esp. p. 145 (where Scipio's history is treated as spoken directly by Cicero) and note 4 on p. 229 (where words spoken by Laelius are given the same treatment).

9. James E. Holton, "Marcus Tullius Cicero," *History of Political Philosophy,* ed. Leo Strauss and Joseph Cropsey (Chicago: Rand McNally, 1963). Page references to this essay are shown in the text simply by numbers in parentheses.

10. Cicero, *De Natura Deorum*, p. xii.

11. Cicero, *Cicero's Letters to Atticus*, trans. Shackleton Bailey, p. 45.

12. Shackleton Bailey, *Cicero*, p. 20.

13. Aristotle, *Introduction to Aristotle*, ed. and intro. R.P. McKeon (Chicago: University of Chicago Press, 1973), p. xlv.

14. Erich S. Gruen, *The Last Generation of the Roman Republic* (Berkeley: University of California Press, 1974).

15. Cf., Aristotle, *Nicomachean Ethics*, Bk. 7, ch. 1 and Bk. 8, chs. 9-10.

16. See the Loeb Edition of Cicero, *Tusculan Disputations* (Cambridge, Mass.: Harvard University Press, 1966), p. 495, note 2. See also Emile Brehier, *The Hellenistic and Roman Age*, trans. Wade Baskin (Chicago: University of Chicago Press, 1965), p. 37.

17. *Cicero's Letters to Atticus*, p. 533.

18. See Aristotle's *Politics*, Bk. 4, ch. 11.

19. Frank H. Knight, "Human Nature and World Democracy," reprinted in *Freedom and Reform* (New York: Harper & Brothers, 1947), pp. 302-303.

20. See Passmore, *A Hundred Years of Philosophy*.

21. See Plato, *The Republic*, Bks. 5 and esp. 6.

22. Cf., Aristotle, *Topics*, Aristotle, *Nicomachean Ethics*, Bk. 6, chs. 6 and 8-13, and Aristotle, *Rhetoric*.

23. Plato, *Collected Works*, ed. Edith Hamilton and Huntington Cairns with the "Letters" trans. L.A. Post (New York: Pantheon Books, 1961), p. 1589.

24. For a good general history of the transition, see Ronald Syme, *The Roman Revolution* (Oxford: Oxford University Press, 1963).

25. Plutarch, *The Lives of the Noble Greeks and Romans*, trans. John Dryden, revised Arthur Hugh Clough (New York: Modern Library, n.d.).

26. Cf., David Grene, *Man in His Pride* (Chicago: University of Chicago Press, 1950).

27. Isaiah Berlin, *Personal Impressions* (New York: Penguin Books, 1982), p. xxx.

28. Leo Strauss, *Natural Right and History* (Chicago: University of Chicago Press, 1953), p. 156.

29. George Sabine, *A History of Political Theory*, pp. 148, 217.

30. Leo Strauss, *Natural Right*, p. 154.

31. F.A. Hayek, *Law, Legislation, and Liberty* (Chicago: University of Chicago Press, 1973-79).

32. Edmund Burke, *Reflections on the Revolution in France* (Indianapolis: Bobbs-Merrill, 1955), p. 87.

33. For a general discussion of the idea of liberty among the Romans, see Ch. Wirszubski, *Libertas: As a Political Idea at Rome during the Late Republic and Early Principate* (Cambridge, UK.: Cambridge University Press, 1960).

34. Aristotle, *Politics*, Bk. 3, Ch. 11.

35. *Ibid.*, Bk. 6, Ch. 2.

238   NOTES

36. M. Cary, *A History of Rome down to the Reign of Constantine* (London: Macmillan, 1962), p. 252.

37. Plutarch, *The Lives*, p. 428.

38. Polybius, trans. Ian Scott-Kilvert and selected and with an introduction by F.W. Walbank as *The Rise of the Roman Empire* (London: Penguin Books, 1979), p. 311.

39. Cf., Michael Polanyi, *Personal Knowledge* (London: Routledge & Kegan Paul, 1958), esp. ch. 5, "Articulation."

40. *Federalist*, Number 51.

41. J.J. Rousseau. *The Social Contract* (New York: Hafner, 1960), Bk. 2, ch. 7, "Of the Legislator."

42. For Aristotle, see *Politics*, Bk. 4, on the sort of constitution fitting a particular people. For Rousseau, *The Social Contract*, Bk. 2, chs. 8-10, "Of the People."

43. Aristotle, *Nicomachean Ethics*, Bk. 6, ch. 3.

44. *Ibid.*, Bk. 10, ch. 9.

45. Madison, *Federalist*, Number 47, p. 336. Tocqueville, *Democracy in America*, trans. George Lawrence (New York: Harper and Rowe, 1966), p. 231.

46. Plato, *Republic*, Bk. 4, 424-5.

47. See H. M. Hubbell's "Introduction" to his translation for the Loeb Classical Library edition (Cambridge, Mass.: Harvard University Press, 1960). Quotations in what follows are from this translation unless otherwise noted.

48. M. Gelzer's *The Roman Nobility*, trans. Robin Seager (New York: Barnes & Noble, 1969), p. 66. The page references to *De Officiis* are from the translation by Walter Miller for the Loeb Library Edition (Cambridge, Mass.: Harvard University Press), 1961.

49. Cf., McKeon "Introduction" to Cicero, *Brutus, et al.*

Chapter Four

1. For biographical purposes, see Ernest Campbell Mossner, *The Life of David Hume* (Austin: University of Texas Press, 1954). On Hume's philosophy, see *The Philosophy of David Hume*, ed. V.C. Chappell (New York: Modern Library, 1963) and *Hume: A Collection of Critical Essays*, ed. V.C. Chappell (Garden City, N.Y.: Doubleday Anchor, 1966). Hume's own cited works will be referred to as follows in notes within the text:

E   David Hume, *Essays Moral, Political, and Literary* (Indianapolis: Liberty Fund, 1987), ed. and with a Foreword by Eugene F. Miller.

HU   David Hume, *An Enquiry Concerning Human Understanding* (Indianapolis: Hackett Publishing Company, 1977), edited and with an Introduction by Eric Steinberg.

The two principal commentators and their works will be referred to as follows:

H   F.A. Hayek, "The Legal and Political Philosophy of David Hume (1711-1776)" in *The Collected Works of F.A. Hayek:* Volume 3*: The Trend of Economic Thinking* (Chicago: University of Chicago Press, 1991).

LLLi   F.A. Hayek, *Law, Legislation, and Liberty:* Volume 1, *Rules and Order* (Chicago: University of Chicago Press, 1973).

CL   Donald W. Livingston, *Hume's Philosophy of Common Life* (Chicago: University of Chicago Press, 1984).

2. Douglass Adair, "'That Politics May Be Reduced to a Science': David Hume, James Madison and the Tenth Federalist," *Huntington Library Quarterly*, 20:4 (1957), pp. 343-360.

3. Chappell, *The Philosophy of David Hume* and Chappell, *Hume: A Collection of Critical Essays*, pp. 35, 11, 106.

4. Richard H. Popkin, *The History of Scepticism: From Erasmus to Spinoza* (Berkeley: University of California Press, 1979), p. 132. Peter Jones, *Hume's Sentiments: Their Ciceronian and French Context* (Edinburgh: University of Edinburgh, 1982).

5. F.A. Hayek, *The Road to Serfdom* (Chicago: University of Chicago Press, 1944).

6. F.A. Hayek, *The Constitution of Liberty* (Chicago: University of Chicago Press, 1960)

7. F.A. Hayek, *Law, Legislation, and Liberty* (Chicago: University of Chicago Press, 1973-79).

8. F.A. Hayek, *Hayek on Hayek: An Autobiographical Dialogue*, ed. Stephen Kresge and Leif Wenar (Chicago: University of Chicago Press, 1994), p. 23.

9. "Iuris consensu" in Cicero, *On the Republic*, 1, 25. See Chapter Three on Cicero.

10. Hayek, *The Constitution of Liberty*, pp. 57, 166-173, and Notes.

11. See R.P. McKeon, "Introduction," *Introduction to Aristotle* (Chicago: University of Chicago Press, 1973).

12. These views were popularized in the United States by A.J. Ayer, *Language, Truth, and Logic* (New York: Dover, 1952) and by T.D. Weldon, *The Vocabulary of Politics* (Baltimore: Penguin, 1953). For a survey, see Jorgen Jorgensen, *The Development of Logical Empiricism* (Chicago: University of Chicago Press, 1951).

13. F.A. Hayek, *The Counter-Revolution of Science* (Glencoe, Ill.: Free Press, 1952) and Hayek, *The Fatal Conceit*.

14. Alexis de Tocqueville, *Democracy in America*, Vol. 2 (New York: Random House, Vintage Book, 1961), pp. 3-7.

15. *Ibid.*

16. *Ibid.*, p. 10.

17. See John U. Nef, *Cultural Foundations of Industrial Civilization* (New York: Harper & Brothers, 1960), p. 79, and the *Oxford English Dictionary*.

Chapter Five

1. For a biography of Burke, see Conor Cruse O'Brien, *The Great Melody: A Thematic Biography of Edmund Burke* (Chicago: University of Chicago Press, 1992). My text was largely completed before I read O'Brien. His discussion of the Hastings impeachment was helpful, however. Page references to Burke will

be to the following editions and employ the following volume abbreviations.

A   Edmund Burke, *An Appeal from the New to the Old Whigs*, edited and
      with an Introduction by John M. Robson (Indianapolis: Bobbs-Merrill,
      1962).

C   Edmund Burke, *Conciliation with the Colonies*, edited by Archibald Free-
      man and Arthur W. Leonard (Cambridge, Mass.: Riverside, 1943).

R   Edmund Burke, *Reflections on the Revolution in France*, edited and with
      an Introduction by Thomas H.D. Mahoney (Indianapolis: Bobbs-Merrill,
      1955).

S   Edmund Burke, *A Philosophical Enquiry into the Origin of our Ideas of
      the Sublime and Beautiful*, edited and with an Introduction and notes by
      J.T. Boulton (New York: Columbia University Press, 1958).

W   Edmund Burke, *Selected Writings and Speeches*, edited by Peter J. Stanlis
      (Garden City, N.Y.: Anchor Books, 1963).

2. Leo Strauss and Joseph Cropsey, eds., *History of Political Theory* (Chicago:
Rand McNally, 1963), p. 601.

3. Burke, *Reflections*, pp. 56-57.

4. Richard Weaver, *The Ethics of Rhetoric* (Chicago: H. Regnery Co., 1965), pp.
74-75.

5. See Kirk's "Forward" to Peter J. Stanlis, *Edmund Burke and the Natural Law*
(Ann Arbor: University of Michigan Press, 1965). The reference to Thomism is
on p. 249. Page numbers in the discussion of Stanlis refer to this volume.

6. Leo Strauss, *Natural Right and History* (Chicago: University of Chicago Press,
1953), pp. 156, 314-315.

7. John Morley, *Edmund Burke: A Historical Study* (London: Macmillan, 1867;
reprinted New York: Arno Press, 1979), p. 243.

8. *Ibid.*, pp. 144-145.

9. *Ibid.*, pp. 253, 255-256.

10. See Frank H. Knight's essay "Freedom as Fact and Criterion" reprinted in Frank H. Knight, *Freedom and Reform* (New York: Harper & Brothers, 1947).

11. *Ibid.*, p. 14.

12. Ludwig Wittgenstein, *Philosophical Investigations*, trans. G.E.M. Anscombe (Oxford: Basil Blackwell, 1953), p. 32e.

13. *Ibid.*, p. 11e.

14. *Ibid.*, 81e-82e.

15. *Ibid.*, p. 47e-48e; italics in the original.

16. *Ibid.*, 103e.

17. Cf., Carl L. Becker, *The Declaration of Independence: A Study in the History of Political Ideas* (New York: Vintage, 1958) and Garry Wills, *Inventing America: Jefferson's Declaration of Independence* (Garden City, N.Y.: Doubleday, 1978).

18. J-J Rousseau, *The Social Contract* (New York: Hafner, 1960), Bk. 1, ch. 8. For the "innovator," see Bk. 2, ch. 7, on "The Legislator."

19. See O'Brien, *Thematic Biography*, for details.

20. Wittgenstein, *Philosophical Investigations*, p. 8e.

21. Cf., Alexander Hamilton, James Madison, and John Jay, *The Federalist*, ed. Benjamin Fletcher Wright (Cambridge, Mass.: Harvard University Press, 1961), Number 10.

22. John Stuart Mill, *Principles of Political Economy* (Reprint New York: Augustus M. Kelly, 1961), p. 968. See F.A. Hayek, *Capitalism and the Historians* (Chicago: University of Chicago Press, 1954).

23. Felix Frankfurter, *The Public and Its Government* (Boston: Beacon Press, 1964), p. 127.

Chapter Six

1. References to Felix Frankfurter's many essays will be to pages in the several collections which have been published in book form. The collections are readily

available, while the journals and magazines in which they were first published are not. These collections and other books by Frankfurter will be abbreviated as follows in page citations within the text:

BSC *The Business of the Supreme Court*, with James M. Landis (New York: Macmillan, 1927).

CC   *The Commerce Clause: Under Marshall, Taney, and Waite*, with Introduction and Epilogue by Wallace Mendelson (Chicago: Quadrangle Books, 1964).

D   *From the Diaries of Felix Frankfurter*, with a Biographical Essay and Notes by Joseph P. Lash (New York: W.W. Norton & Company, 1975).

FC   *Felix Frankfurter on the Supreme Court: Extrajudicial Essays on the Court and the Constitution*, edited by Philip B. Kurland (Cambridge, Mass: Harvard University Press, 1970).

LI   *The Labor Injunction* (New York: Macmillan, 1930).

LL   *Of Law and Life & Other Things that Matter: Papers and Addresses of Felix Frankfurter, 1956-1963*, edited by Philip B. Kurland (Cambridge, MA: Harvard University Press, 1965).

LM   *Of Law and Men: Papers and Addresses of Felix Frankfurter*, edited by Philip Elman (reprinted Hamden, Conn.: Archon Books, 1965).

LP   *Law and Politics*, edited by E.F. Prichard, Jr., and Archibald MacLeish (New York: Capricorn Books, 1962).

MJH *Mr. Justice Holmes and the Supreme Court* (Cambridge, Mass.: Harvard University Press, 1961).

PG   *The Public and Its Government* (Boston: Beacon Press, 1964).

RF   *Roosevelt and Frankfurter: Their Correspondence, 1928-1945*, annotated by Max Friedman (Boston: Little, Brown and Company, 1967).

SV   *The Case of Sacco and Vanzetti* (New York: Grosset & Dunlap, 1961).

Three volumes published following FF's retirement from the court will be cited enough to merit abbreviation. Two contain essays about Frankfurter and the

NOTES

other is oral history.

J   *Felix Frankfurter: The Judge*, edited by Wallace Mendelson (New York: Reynal & Company, 1964).

R   *Felix Frankfurter Reminisces: Recorded in Talks with Harlan B. Phillips* (New York: Reynal & Company, 1962).

T   *Felix Frankfurter: A Tribute*, edited by Wallace Mendelson (New York: Reynal & Company, 1964).

When citations in sequence are to pages in the same volume, the volume abbreviation will not be repeated.

Two spellings—"skepticism" and "scepticism"—occur in both Frankfurter and Holmes and will be quoted as in the original. The "c" spelling was in vogue for some decades.

2. Oliver Wendell Holmes, Jr., "The Path of the Law," reprinted in *Landmarks of Law*, ed. Ray D. Henson, (Boston: Beacon Press, 1960), p. 43.

3. On the richness of institutions involved in a "legal system," see: Aristotle's *Politics*, Book IV, ch. 15, and Book VI, ch. 8; H.F. Jolowicz, *Historical Introduction to the Study of Roman Law* (Cambridge, UK: The University Press, 1967); and Bruce W. Frier, *The Rise of the Roman Jurists: Studies in Cicero's 'pro Caecina'* (Princeton: Princeton University Press, 1985); A.K.R. Kiralfy, *Potter's Historical Introduction to English Law and Its Institutions* (London: Sweet & Maxwell, 1958) and F.W. Maitland, *A Constitutional History of England* (Cambridge, UK: The University Press, 1955); *Oxford History of England*, 17 vols. (Oxford, UK: Oxford University Press, 1936-1962); Lawrence Friedman, *A History of American Law* (New York: Simon and Schuster, 1973); Lewis Mayers, *The Machinery of Justice: An Introduction to Legal Structure and Process* (Englewood Cliffs, N.J.: Prentice Hall, 1963); Julius Stone, *Legal System and Lawyer's Reasonings* (Stanford: Stanford University Press, 1964) and the companion volumes *Human Law and Human Justice* (1965) and *Social Dimensions of Law and Justice* (1966). On "recognizing" the law by articulating the rules of fairness, see F.A. Hayek, *Law, Legislation, and Liberty;* Vol 1: *Rules and Order* (Chicago: University of Chicago Press, 1973), pp. 94 ff.

4. *Cf.*, Jolowicz, *Historical Introduction*, and Bruce Frier, *The Rise of the Roman Jurists*.

5. See John Dewey, *Logic: The Theory of Inquiry* (New York: Henry Holt &

Company, 1938), pp. 101 and 120. See also Dewey's essay, "Logical Method and Law," reprinted in *Landmarks of Law*.

6. Stephen Toulmin, *The Uses of Argument* (Cambridge, UK: The University Press, 1958). Edward H. Levi, *An Introduction to Legal Reasoning* (Chicago: University of Chicago Press, 1948), pp. 3-4. Cf., John Dewey, *The Quest for Certainty* (New York: Minton, Balch & Company, 1929).

7. See the Biographical and Critical Appendix which concludes this chapter.

8. Robert H. Bork, *The Tempting of America: The Political Seduction of the Law* (New York: Free Press, 1990).

9. Richard A. Posner, *Cardozo: A Study in Reputation* (Chicago: University of Chicago Press, 1990), pp. 76-78.

10. For "the renunciation of civil collaboration," see Edward Shils, "Intellectuals and the Center of Society in the U.S." in *The Constitution of Society* (Chicago: University of Chicago Press, 1982), pp. 224-272.

11. The other books were the *Federalist* and John Morley's *On Compromise* discussed below (RF: 721).

12. The classic work on this transformation is A. V. Dicey, *Lectures on the Relation between Law and Opinion in England in the Nineteenth Century* (London: Macmilian, 1914).

13. *Felix Frankfurter: A Tribute* includes contributions by statesman Jean Monnet, philosopher Isaiah Berlin, playwright Garson Kanin, cabinet member Francis Biddle, columnist James Reston, educator Alexander Meiklejohn, and poet Archibald MacLeish, as well as lawyers and legal scholars.

14. For F.F.'s account of his protégés in the government, see "The Young Men Go to Washington" (LP: 238-49).

15. Bruce Allen Murphy, *The Brandeis/Frankfurter Connection: The Secret Political Activities of Two Supreme Court Justices* (New York: Anchor Press/Doubleday & Company, 1983).

16. Cf., Arthur Schlesinger, Jr., *The Coming of the New Deal* and *The Politics of Upheaval* (New York: Houghton Miflin, 1958; 1960) for numerous references to Brandeis suggestions; and also F.F.'s diary (D: 134-135).

17. Roger K. Newman, *Hugo Black: A Biography* (New York: Pantheon, 1994), pp. 306-309, 328-329, 312-313.

18. *Ibid.*, pp. 258, 682, 482-487, 508-509, 518-520, 621-622.

19. *Ibid*, p. 453.

20. Alexander M. Bickel, *The Supreme Court and the Idea of Progress* (New York: Harper & Row, 1970), p. 31.

21. John Morley, *On Compromise* (London: Macmillan, 1886), pp. 229, 242.

22. *Ibid.*, p. 283.

23. James Bradley Thayer, "The Origin and Scope of the American Doctrine of Constitutional Law" in *Harvard Law Review*, 8:3 (October 1893).

24. *Ibid.*, Footnote 2, p. 156.

25. See G. Edward White, *Justice Oliver Wendell Holmes: Law and the Inner Self* (Oxford: Oxford University Press, 1993), ch. 10. Much of my chapter was drafted years before White's book was available, but White's information and insights have been invaluable in its final formulation.

26. White, *Oliver Wendell Holmes*, pp. 192, 323.

27. Quoted from an article by Holmes in *MJH*, p. 57.

28. White, *Oliver Wendell Holmes*, pp. 162-163, 380-381, 162.

29. Alexis de Tocqueville, *Democracy in America* (New York: Random House, Vintage Books, 1954).

30. See Levi, *An Introduction to Legal Reasoning*, pp. 24 ff.

31. Wallace Mendelson, *Justices Black and Frankfurter: Conflict on the Court* (Chicago: University of Chicago Press, 1961), pp. 16 ff.

32. Gilbert Ryle in *The Concept of Mind* (New York: Barnes & Noble, n.d.), pp. 27 ff. Michael Polanyi, *Personal Knowledge* (Chicago: University of Chicago Press, 1958).

33. Michael E. Parrish, *Felix Frankfurter and His Times: The Reform Years* (New York: Free Press, 1982), pp. 195-196.

34. For a detailed account of these cases, see David Manwaring, *Render unto Caesar: The Flag-Salute Controversy* (Chicago: University of Chicago Press, 1962).

35. *Ibid.*

36. See the entry in the *Oxford English Dictionary.*

37. *Cf.*, Alfred North Whitehead, *Symbolism: Its Meaning and Effect* (New York: Capricorn, 1959) and *The Function of Reason* (Boston: Beacon Press, 1958).

38. Both quotations are from *The Life and Selected Writings of Thomas Jefferson*, ed. Adrienne Koch and William Peden (New York: Modern Library, 1944), pp. 413, 436.

39. For Aristotle, see the *Nicomachean Ethics*, Book 2 and generally, and the *Politics*, Book 7. For Jean Piaget, see *The Moral Judgment of the Child* (Glencoe, Ill.: The Free Press, 1948).

40. Manwarring, *Render unto Caesar,* p. 9.

41. The quotation is from Whitehead, *The Function of Reason*, pp. 87-88.

42. See Burke's treatment of "prejudice" in Chapter Five above.

43. Ernst Cassirer, *The Philosophy of Symbolic Forms*, trans. Ralph Manheim, (New Haven: Yale University Press, 1953-57). Susanne K. Langer, *Philosophy in a New Key: A Study in the Symbolism of Reason, Rite, and Art* (New York: New American Library, Mentor Book, 1951).

44. Thucydides, *The History of the Peloponnesian War*, trans. Thomas Hobbes, ed. David Grene (Ann Arbor: University of Michigan Press, 1959), Book 2, sections 38-40.

45. Eugene C. Gerhart, *America's Advocate: Robert H. Jackson* (Indianapolis, Bobbs-Merrill, 1958); Newman, *Hugo Black: A Biography.*

46. *Newsweek* (18 April 1994), p. 25.

248 NOTES

47. See Gerald N. Rosenberg, *The Hollow Hope* (Chicago: University of Chicago Press, 1991).

48. See, for example, the works of Richard McKeon, and Daniel Boorstin, *The Genius of American Politics* (Chicago: University of Chicago Press, 1953).

49. See James J. Magee, *Mr. Justice Black: Absolutist on the Court* (Charlottesville: University of Virginia Press, 1980).

50. Aristotle, *Politics*, Book 7, ch. 13.

51. Benjamin Cardozo, *The Nature of the Judicial Process*, reprinted in *Selected Writings: Benjamin Nathan Cardozo*, ed. Margaret E. Hall (New York: Fallon, 1947).

52. *Cf.*, David Hume, "Essay on Taste" discussed in Chapter Four above on Hume and also Alexis de Tocqueville, *Democracy in America* (New York: Vintage, 1961), p. 269, on "appeal from the sovereignty of the people to the sovereignty of mankind."

53. Cass Sunstein, *The Partial Constitution* (Cambridge, Mass.: Harvard University Press, 1993), pp. 119-122, 123, 124, 130, 208.

54. H.N. Hirsch, *The Enigma of Felix Frankfurter* (New York: Basic Books, 1981), pp. 198-199.

55. See Felix Frankfurter, *Of Law and Men* and *Felix Frankfurter on the Supreme Court,* for these essays.

56. *The Characters of Theophrastus*, newly ed. and trans. J.M. Edmonds (Cambridge, Mass.: Harvard University Press, 1967), pp. 37-38. For the influence of the work, see the Introduction by Edmonds.

57. Plutarch, *The Lives of the Noble Greeks and Romans*, trans. John Dryden, revised Arthur Hugh Clough (New York: Modern Library, n.d.).

58. *Ibid.*

59. Paul Scott, *The Raj Quartet* (New York: William Morrow and Company, 1976).

60. William O. Douglas, *The Court Years, 1938-1975: The Autobiography of William O. Douglas* (New York: Random House, 1980), p. 34.

61. Melvin L. Urofsky, *Felix Frankfurter: Judicial Restraint and Individual Liberties* (Boston: Twayne, 1991), pp. xii-xiii.

Chapter Seven

1. F.H. Knight, *Intelligence and Democratic Action* (Cambridge, Mass.: Harvard University Press, 1960). *Cf.*, Alexis de Tocqueville, *Democracy in America* (New York: Random House, Vintage Books, 1945); Daniel Boorstin, *The Genius of American Politics* (Chicago: University of Chicago Press, 1953); and Edward Shils, *The Intellectuals and the Powers and Other Essays* (Chicago: University of Chicago Press, 1972).

2. See Tocqueville, *Democracy in America*, Vol. 2, Bk. 1, ch. 2 and Bk. 3, ch. 21.

3. Ralph Ketcham, *James Madison: A Biography* (New York: Macmillan, 1971), p. 51.

4. John V.A. Fine, *The Late Medieval Balkans: A Critical Survey from the Late Twelfth Century to the Ottoman Conquest* (Ann Arbor: University of Michigan Press, 1987).

5. Tocqueville, *Democracy in America*, Second Part, Bk 1, ch. 1.

BIBLIOGRAPHY

Adair, Douglass, "That Politics May Be Reduced to a Science: David Hume, James Madison, and the Tenth Federalist," *Huntington Library Quarterly,* 20:4 (1957).

Adler, Mortimer J., *The Idea of Freedom* (New York: Doubleday, 1958, 1961).

Aristotle, *The Complete Works of Aristotle: The Revised Oxford Translation,* ed. Jonathan Barnes, 2 vols. (Princeton: Princeton University Press, Bollingen Series, 1985).

————, *Introduction to Aristotle,* ed. and intro. Richard McKeon (Chicago: University of Chicago Press, 1973).

Ayer, A.J., *Language, Truth, and Logic* (New York: Dover, 1952).

Baker, Leonard, *Brandeis and Frankfurter: A Dual Biography* (New York: New York University Press, 1986).

Baker, Livia, *Felix Frankfurter: A Biography* (New York: Cowart-McCann, 1969).

Bailey, D.R. Shakleton, *Cicero* (New York: Scribner, 1972).

————, *Cicero's Letters to Atticus* (London: Penguin Books, 1979).

Bay, Christian, *The Structure of Freedom* (Palo Alto: Stanford University Press, 1958).

Becker, Carl L., *The Declaration of Independence: A Study in the History of Political Ideas* (New York: Vintage, 1958).

Berlin, Isaiah, *Personal Impressions* (New York: Penguin Books, 1982).

Bickel, Alexander M., *The Supreme Court and the Idea of Progress* (New York: Harper & Row, 1970).

Boorstin, Daniel J., *The Genius of American Politics* (Chicago: University of Chicago Press, 1953).

Bork, Robert H., *The Tempting of America: The Political Seduction of the Law* (New York: Free Press, 1990).

Brehier, Emile, *The Hellenistic and Roman Age*, trans. Wade Baskin (Chicago: University of Chicago Press, 1965).

Burke, Edmund, *An Appeal from the New to the Old Whigs*, ed. John M. Robson (Indianapolis: Bobbs-Merrill, 1962).

————, *Conciliation with the Colonies*, ed. Archibald Freeman and Arthur W. Leonard (Cambridge, Mass.: Riverside, 1943).

————, *A Philosophical Enquiry into the Origin of our Ideas of the Sublime and the Beautiful* (New York: Columbia University Press, 1958).

————, *Reflections on the Revolution in France* (Indianapolis: Library of Liberal Arts, 1955).

————, *Selected Writings and Speeches*, ed. Peter J. Stanlis (Garden City, N.J.: Anchor Books, 1963).

Cao Xueguin, *The Story of the Stone*, vols. 1, 2, and 3, trans. David Hawkes (Great Britain: Penguin, 1973, 1977, 1980).

Cao Xuegin and Gao E., *The Story of the Stone*, vols. 4 and 5, trans. John Minford (New York: Penguin Books, 1982, 1986).

Cardozo, Benjamin, *Selected Writings: Benjamin Nathan Cardozo,* ed. Margaret E. Hall (New York: Fallon, 1947).

Carey, George W., *The Federalist: Design for a Constitutional Republic* (Urbana, Ill.: University of Illinois Press, 1989).

Cary, M., *A History of Rome down to the Reign of Constantine* (London: Macmillan, 1962).

Cassirer, Ernst, *The Philosophy of Symbolic Forms*, trans. Ralph Manheim (New Haven: Yale University Press, 1953-1957).

Cervantes, Miguel de, *Don Quixote: The Ingenious Gentleman of La Mancha*, trans. John Ormsby (New York: The Heritage Press, n.d.).

Cicero, Marcus Tullius, *Brutus; On the Nature of the Gods; On Divination; On Duties*, trans. Hubert M. Poteat, intro. Richard P. McKeon (Chicago: University of Chicago Press, 1950).

————, *De Inventione, et al*, trans. H.M. Hubbell (Cambridge, Mass.: Harvard University Press, Loeb Library, 1960).

————, *De Natura Deorum and Academica*, trans. H. Rackham (Cambridge, Mass.: Harvard University Press, Loeb Library, 1961).

————, *De Officiis*, trans. Walter Miller (Cambridge, Mass.: Harvard University Press, 1961).

————, *De Oratore*, trans. E.W. Sutton and H. Rackham (Cambridge, Mass.: Harvard University Press, Loeb Library, 1967).

————, *De Re Publica and De Legibus*, trans. C.W. Keyes (Cambridge, Mass.: Harvard University Press, Loeb Library, 1961).

————, *Tusculan Disputations*, trans. J.E. King (Cambridge, Mass.: Harvard University Press, Loeb Library, 1966).

Crawford, Michael, *The Roman Republic* (Cambridge Mass.: Harvard University Press, 1993).

Croly, Herbert D., *The Promise of American Life* (Hamden, Conn.: Archon Books, 1963).

Descartes, René, *The Discourse on Method and Meditations* (New York: Liberal Arts Press, 1960).

Dewey, John, *Art as Experience* (New York: Minton, Balch & Company, 1934).

————, *Experience and Nature* (New York: Dover Publications, 1958).

————, *Logic: The Theory of Inquiry* (New York: Henry Holt and Company, 1938).

————, *The Quest for Certainty* (New York: Minton, Balch & Company, 1929).

————, *Reconstruction in Philosophy* (Boston: Beacon Press, 1957).

Dicey, A.V., *Lectures on the Relation between Law and Opinion in England in the Nineteenth Century* (London: Macmillan, 1914).

Dietze, Gottfried, *The Federalist: A Classic on Federalism and Freedom* (Baltimore: Johns Hopkins University Press, 1960).

Dilworth, David A., *Philosophy in World Perspective: A Comparative Hermeneutic of Major Theories* (New Haven: Yale University Press, 1989).

Diogenes Laertius, *Lives of the Eminent Philosophers*, trans. R.D. Hicks (Cambridge, Mass.: Harvard University Press, Loeb Library, 1970).

Douglas, William O., *The Court Years, 1938-1975: The Autobiography of William O. Douglas* (New York: Random House, 1980).

Epstein, David, *The Political Theory of the Federalist* (Chicago: University of Chicago Press, 1984).

Fine, John V.A., *The Late Medieval Balkans: A Critical Survey from the Late Twelfth Century to the Ottoman Conquest* (Ann Arbor: University of Michigan Press, 1987).

Forster, E.M., *A Passage to India* (New York: Harcourt, Brace & World, 1952).

Frankfurter, Felix, with James Landis, *The Business of the Supreme Court* (New York: Macmillan, 1927).

———, *The Case of Sacco and Vanzetti* (New York: Grosset & Dunlap, 1961).

———, *The Commerce Clause: Under Marshall, Taney, and Waite*, intro. and epilogue Wallace Mendelson (Chicago: Quadrangle Books, 1964).

———, *Felix Frankfurter Reminisces: Recorded in Talks with Harlan B. Phillips* (New York: Raynal & Company, 1962).

———, *Felix Frankfurter on the Supreme Court: Extrajudicial Essays on the Court and the Constitution*, ed. Philip B. Kurland (Cambridge, Mass.: Harvard University Press, 1970).

———, *From the Diaries of Felix Frankfurter*, intro. Joseph P. Lash (New York: W.W. Norton & Company, Inc., 1975).

————, *Mr. Justice Holmes and the Supreme Court*, (Cambridge, Mass.: Harvard University Press, 1961).

————, *The Labor Injunction* (New York: Macmillan, 1930).

————, *Of Law and Life & Other Things That Matter: Papers and Addresses of Felix Frankfurter 1956-1963*, ed. Philip B. Kurland (Cambridge, Mass.: Harvard University Press, 1965).

————, *Of Law and Men: Papers and Addresses of Felix Frankfurter*, ed. Philip Elman (Reprinted Hamden, Conn.: Archon Books, 1965).

————, *Law and Politics*, ed. E.F. Prichard, Jr., and Archibald MacLeish (New York: Capricorn Books, 1962).

————, *The Public and Its Government* (Boston: Beacon Press, 1964).

Felix Frankfurter: A Tribute, ed. Wallace Mendelson (New York: Reynal & Company, 1964).

Felix Frankfurter: The Judge, ed. Wallace Mendelson (New York: Reynal & Company, 1964).

Frankfurter, Felix and F.D. Roosevelt, *Roosevelt and Frankfurter: Their Correspondence, 1928-1945*, annot. Max Friedman (Boston: Little, Brown and Company, 1967).

Friedman, Lawrence, *A History of American Law* (New York: Simon and Schuster, 1973).

Frier, Bruce W., *The Rise of the Roman Jurists: Studies in Cicero's 'pro Caecina'* (Princeton: Princeton University Press, 1985).

Gelzner, M., *The Roman Nobility*, trans. and intro. Robin Seager (New York: Barnes & Noble, 1969).

Genesis: A New Translation with Introduction and Commentary, trans. E.A. Speiser (New York: Doubleday & Company, Inc., 1981).

Gerhart, Eugene, *America's Advocate: Robert H. Jackson* (Indianapolis: Bobbs-Merrill, 1958).

Gibbon, Edward, *The Decline and Fall of the Roman Empire*, ed. J.B. Bury (New York: Heritage Press, 1946).

Grene, David, *Man in his Pride* (Chicago: University of Chicago Press, 1950).

Gruen, Erich S., *The Last Generation of the Roman Republic* (Berkeley: University of California Press, 1974).

Gunther, Gerald, *Learned Hand: The Man and the Judge* (New York: Alfred A. Knopf, 1994).

Hamilton, Alexander, James Madison, and John Jay, *The Federalist,* ed. Benjamin Fletcher Wright (Cambridge, Mass.: Harvard University Press).

————, *The Federalist Papers*, intro. Clinton Rossiter (New York: Mentor, 1961).

Haskell, H.J., *This Was Cicero: Modern Politics in a Roman Toga* (New York: A.A. Knopf, 1942).

Hayek, F.A., *Capitalism and the Historians* (Chicago: University of Chicago Press, 1954).

————, *The Collected Works of F.A. Hayek:* Vol. 3, *The Trend of Economic Thinking* (Chicago: University of Chicago Press, 1991).

————, *The Constitution of Liberty* (Chicago: University of Chicago Press, 1960).

————, *The Counter-Revolution of Science* (Glencoe, Ill.: The Free Press, 1952).

————, *The Fatal Conceit: The Errors of Socialism* (Chicago: University of Chicago Press, 1988).

————, *Hayek on Hayek: An Autobiographical Dialogue*, ed. Stephen Kresge and Leif Wenar (Chicago: University of Chicago Press, 1994).

————, *Law, Legislation, and Liberty* (Chicago: University of Chicago Press, 1973-1979).

————, *The Road to Serfdom* (Chicago: University of Chicago Press, 1944).

Hirsch, H.N., *The Enigma of Felix Frankfurter* (New York: Basic Books, 1981).

Homer, *The Iliad*, trans. Richard Lattimore (Chicago: University of Chicago Press, 1962).

Hume, David, *An Enquiry Concerning Human Understanding* (Indianapolis: Hackett Publishing Company, 1977).

———, *An Enquiry Concerning the Principles of Morals* (Indianapolis: Hackett Publishing Company, 1983).

———, *Essays Moral, Political, and Literary* (Indianapolis: Liberty Fund, 1987).

———, *A History of England* (Indianapolis: LibertyClassics, 1983).

———, *The Philosophy of David Hume*, ed. V.C. Chappell (New York: Modern Library, 1963).

———, *A Treatise of Human Nature*, ed. L.A. Selby-Bigge (Oxford: Oxford University Press, 1951).

Hume: A Collection of Critical Essays, ed. V.C. Chappell (Garden City, N.J.: Doubleday Anchor, 1966).

James, Henry, *Portrait of a Lady* (New York: Modern Library, 1951).

Jefferson, Thomas, *The Life and Selected Writings of Thomas Jefferson*, ed. Adrienne Koch and William Peden (New York: Modern Library, 1944).

Jolowicz, H.F., *Historical Introduction to the Study of Roman Law* (Cambridge, UK: The University Press, 1967).

Jones, Peter, *Hume's Sentiments: Their Ciceronian and French Context* (Edinburgh: University of Edinburgh Press, 1982).

Jorgensen, Jorgen, *The Development of Logical Empiricism* (Chicago: University of Chicago Press, 1951).

Ketcham, Michael G., *Transparent Designs: Reading, Performance, and Form in the Spectator Papers* (Athens, Ga.: University of Georgia Press).

Ketcham, Ralph, *James Madison: A Biography* (New York: Macmillan, 1971).

Kiralfy, A.K.R., *Potter's Historical Introduction to English Law and Its Institutions* (London: Sweet & Maxwell, 1958).

Knight, Frank H., *Freedom and Reform* (New York: Harper & Brothers, 1947).

————, *On the History and Method of Economics* (Chicago: University of Chicago Press, 1956).

————, *Intelligence and Democratic Action* (Cambridge, MA.: Harvard University Press, 1960).

Konefsky, Samuel J., *The Constitutional World of Mr. Justice Frankfurter: Some Representative Opinion* (New York: Macmillan, 1949).

Kuhn, Thomas, *The Structure of Scientific Revolutions* (Chicago: University of Chicago Press, 1970).

Kurland, Philip B., *Mr. Justice Frankfurter and the Constitution* (Chicago: University of Chicago Press, 1971).

Landmarks of Law, ed. Ray D. Henson (Boston, Beacon Press, 1960).

Langer, Susanne K., *Philosophy in a New Key: A Study in the Symbolism of Reason, Rite, and Art* (New York: Mentor, New American Library, 1951).

Laslett, Peter, ed., *Philosophy, Politics and Society* (Oxford: Basil Blackwell, 1956).

Levi, Edward H., *An Introduction to Legal Reasoning* (Chicago: University of Chicago Press, 1948).

Livingston, David, *Hume's Philosophy of the Common Life* (Chicago: University of Chicago Press, 1984).

Madison, James, *The Papers of James Madison*, Vols. 1-10, ed. William T. Hutchinson, W.M.E. Rachel, *et al.* and Robert A. Rutland *et al.* (Chicago: University of Chicago Press, 1962-1977).

Magee, James J., *Mr. Justice Black: Absolutist on the Court* (Charlottesville: University of Virginia Press, 1980).

Maitland, F.W., *A Constitutional History of England* (Cambridge, UK: The University Press, 1955).

Manwaring, David, *Render unto Caesar: The Flag-Salute Controversy* (Chicago: University of Chicago Press, 1962).

Mayers, Lewis, *The Machinery of Justice: An Introduction to Legal Structure and Process* (Englewood Cliffs, NJ: Prentice Hall, 1963).

McKeon, Richard P., *Freedom and History and Other Essays*, ed. Zahava K. McKeon (Chicago: University of Chicago Press, 1990).

Mendelson, Wallace, *Justices Black and Frankfurter: Conflict in the Court* (Chicago: University of Chicago Press, 1961).

Mill, John Stuart, *Principles of Political Economy* (Reprint New York: Augustus M. Kelley, 1961).

Morley, John, *On Compromise* (London: Macmillan, 1886).

————, *Edmund Burke: A Historical Study* (London: Macmillan, 1867).

Mossner, Ernest Campbell, *The Life of David Hume* (Austin: University of Texas Press, 1954).

Lady Murasaki, *The Tale of Genji*, trans. Arthur Waley (New York: Modern Library, 1960).

Murphy, Bruce Allen, *The Brandeis-Frankfurter Connection: The Secret Political Activities of Two Supreme Court Justices* (New York: Anchor Press/Doubleday & Company, 1983).

Nef, John U., *Cultural Foundations of Industrial Civilization* (New York: Harper & Brothers, 1960).

Newman, Roger K., *Hugo Black: A Biography* (New York: Pantheon, 1994).

O'Brien, Conor Cruse, *The Great Melody: A Thematic Biography of Edmund Burke* (Chicago: University of Chicago Press, 1992).

Oxford History of England, 17 vols. (Oxford: Oxford University Press, 1936-1962).

Parrish, Michael E., *Felix Frankfurter and His Times: The Reform Years* (New York: Free Press, 1982).

Parsons, Talcott, *The Structure of Social Action* (Glencoe, Ill.: The Free Press, 1949).

Passmore, John, *A Hundred Years of Philosophy* (Baltimore: Penguin Books, 1966).

The People Shall Judge, Vol. 1 (Chicago: University of Chicago Press, 1965).

Piaget, Jean, *The Moral Judgment of the Child* (Glencoe, IL: The Free Press, 1948).

Plato, *Collected Works*, ed. Edith Hamilton and Huntington Cairns (New York: Pantheon Books, 1961).

Plutarch, *The Lives of the Noble Greeks and Romans*, trans. John Dryden, revised Arthur Hugh Clough (New York: Modern Library, n.d.).

Polanyi, Michael, *Knowing and Being*, ed. Marjorie Grene (Chicago: University of Chicago Press, 1969).

————, *The Logic of Liberty* (Chicago: University of Chicago Press, 1951).

————, *Personal Knowledge* (Chicago: University of Chicago Press, 1958).

————, *Science, Faith and Society* (Chicago: University of Chicago Press reprint, 1966).

Polybius, *The Rise of the Roman Empire*, trans. Ian Scott-Kilvert and selected with an introduction by F. W. Walbank (London: Penguin Books, 1979).

Popkin, Richard H., *The History of Scepticism: From Erasmus to Spinoza* (Berkeley: University of California Press, 1979).

Posner, Richard A., *Cardozo: A Study in Reputation* (Chicago: University of Chicago Press, 1990).

Riemer, Neal, *James Madison: Creating the American Constitution* (Washington: Congressional Quarterly, 1986).

Rorty, Richard, *Consequences of Pragmatism* (Minneapolis: University of Minnesota Press, 1982).

————, *Essays on Heidegger and Others* (New York: Cambridge University Press, 1991).

————, *Objectivism, Relativism, and Truth* (New York: Cambridge University Press, 1991).

Rosenberg, Gerald N., *The Hollow Hope* (Chicago: University of Chicago Press, 1991).

Rousseau, J.J., *The Social Contract* (New York: Hafner, 1960).

Ryle, Gilbert, *The Concept of Mind* (New York: Barnes & Noble, n.d.).

Sabine, George, *A History of Political Theory* (London: George G. Harrap & Co. Ltd., 1959).

Schlesinger, Jr., Arthur, *The Coming of the New Deal* (New York: Houghton Miflin, 1958).

————, *The Politics of Upheaval* (New York: Houghton Miflin, 1960).

Schwab, Joseph J., *Science, Curriculum, and Liberal Education* (Chicago: University of Chicago Press, 1978).

Scott, Paul, *The Raj Quartet* (New York: William Morrow and Company, 1976).

Seth, Vikram, *A Suitable Boy* (New York: HarperCollins, 1993).

Shils, Edward, *Collected Essays* (Chicago: University of Chicago Press, 1972, 1975, 1980).

————, *Tradition* (Chicago: University of Chicago Press, 1981).

Silverstein, Mark, *Constitutional Faiths: Felix Frankfurter, Hugo Black, and the Process of Judicial Decision Making* (Ithaca, N.Y.: Cornell University Press, 1984).

Simon, James F., *The Antagonists: Hugo Black, Felix Frankfurter and Civil Liberties in America* (New York: Simon and Schuster, 1989).

Stanlis, Peter J., *Edmund Burke and the Natural Law* (Ann Arbor: University of Michigan Press, 1965).

262 BIBLIOGRAPHY

Stendahl, *The Charterhouse of Parma*, trans. Lady Mary Lloyd, revised Robert Cantwell (New York: Heritage Press, 1955).

Stone, Julius, *Human Law and Human Justice* (Stanford: Stanford University Press, 1965).

———, *Legal System and Lawyer's Reasonings* (Stanford: Stanford University Press, 1964).

———, *Social Dimensions of Law and Justice* (Stanford: Stanford University Press, 1966).

Strauss, Leo, *Natural Right and History* (Chicago: University of Chicago Press, 1953).

Strauss, Leo and Joseph Cropsey (eds.), *History of Political Theory* (Chicago: Rand McNally, 1963).

Sunstein, Cass, *The Partial Constitution* (Cambridge, Mass.: Harvard University Press, 1993).

Supreme Court Decisions:

Adams, Warden v. United States ex rel McCann, 317 U.S. 269 (1942).

Adamson v. California, 332 U.S. 46 (1947).

Bunting v. Oregon, 243 U.S. 426 (1917).

Baker v. Carr, 369 U.S. 186 (19620.

Barron v. Mayor and City Council of Baltimore, 7 Pet. 243 (1833).

Brown v. Board of Education, 347 U.S. 483 (1954).

Colgrove v. Green, 328 U.S. 549 (1946).

Dennis J. Driscoll v. Edison Light and Power Co., 307 U.S. 104 (1939).

F.C.C. v. Pottsville Broadcasting Co., 309 U.S. 134 (1940).

Ferguson v. Moore-McCormack Lines, Inc., 352 U.S. 521 (1957).

Gomillion v. Lightfoot, 364 U.S. 339 (1960).

Griffin et al. v. Illinois, 351 U.S. 12 (1956)

Haley v. Ohio, 332 U.S. 596 (1948).

Hamilton v. Regents, 293 U.S. 245 (1934).

Harris v. United States, 331 U.S. 145 (1947).

Irvine v. California, 347 U.S. 128 (1954).

Joint Anti-Fascist Refugee Committee v. McGrath, Attorney General, et al., 341 U.S. 123 (1951).

Lochner v. New York, 198 U.S. 45 (1905)

Louisiana ex rel Francis v. Resweber, Sheriff, et al., 329 U.S. 459 (1947).

Malinski v. New York, 324 U.S. 401 (1945).

Marbury v. Madison, 1 Cranch 137 (1803).

McNabb v. United States, 318 U.S. 332 (1943).

M'Culloch v. Maryland, 1 Wheat. 316 (1819).

Minersville School District v. Gobitis, 310 U.S. 586 (1939).

National Broadcasting Company, Inc. v. United States, 319 U.S. 190 (1943).

National Labor Relations Board v. Mexia Textile Mills, Inc., 339 U.S. 563 (1950).

Palko v. Connecticut, 302 U.S. 319 (1937).

Polish National Alliance v. Labor Board, 322 U.S. 643 (1943).

Radio Corporation of America et al. v. United States et al., 341 U.S. 412 (1951).

Rochin v. California, 342 U.S. 165 (1952).

Roe v. Wade, 93 U.S. 705 (1973).

Securities and Exchange Commission v. Chenery Corporation, 318 U.S. 80 (1943).

Sherman v. United States, 356 U.S. 369 (1958).

Stark v. Wickard, Secretary of Agriculture, 321 U.S. 288 (1944).

West Virginia Board of Education v. Barnette, 319 U.S. 624 (1943).

Wolf v. Colorado, 338 U.S. 25 (1949).

Syme, Ronald, *The Roman Revolution* (Oxford: Oxford University Press, 1963).

Thayer, James Bradley, "The Origin and Scope of the American Doctrine of Constitutional Law," *Harvard Law Review*, 8:3 (October 1893).

Theophrastus, *The Characters of Theophrastus*, newly ed. and trans. J.M. Edmonds (Cambridge, Mass.: Harvard University Press, Loeb Library, 1967).

Thomas, Helen Shirley, *Felix Frankfurter: Scholar on the Bench* (Baltimore: The Johns Hopkins Press, 1960).

Thucydides, *The History of the Peloponnesian War*, trans. Thomas Hobbes, ed. David Grene (Ann Arbor: University of Michigan Press, 1959).

Tocqueville, Alexis de, *Democracy in America* (New York, Vintage, 1945).

————, *Democracy in America*, trans. George Lawrence (New York: Harper and Rowe, 1966).

————, *The European Revolution and Correspondence with Gobineau*, ed. and trans. John Lukacs (Garden City, N.Y.: Doubleday Anchor, 1959).

Tolstoy, Leo, *War and Peace*, trans. Louise and Aylmer Maude (New York: The Heritage Club, n.d.).

Toulmin, Stephen, *Human Understanding* (Princeton: Princeton University Press, 1972).

————, *The Uses of Argument* (Cambridge, UK: The University Press, 1958).

Urofsky, Melvin L., *Felix Frankfurter: Judicial Restraint and Individual Liberties* (Boston: Twayne, 1991).

Watson, Walker, *The Architectonics of Meaning: Foundations of the New Pluralism* (Albany: State University of New York Press, 1985).

Weldon, T.D., *The Vocabulary of Politics* (Baltimore: Penguin, 1953).

White, G. Edward, *Justice Oliver Wendell Holmes: Law and the Inner Self* (Oxford: Oxford University Press, 1993).

Whitehead, Alfred North, *The Function of Reason* (Boston: Beacon Press, 1958).

————, *Symbolism: Its Meaning and Effect* (New York: Capricorn, 1959).

Wills, Garry, *Inventing America: Jefferson's Declaration of Independence* (Garden City, N.Y.: Doubleday, 1978).

Wirszubski, Ch., *Libertas: As a Political Idea at Rome during the Late Republic and Early Principate* (Cambridge, UK: Cambridge University Press, 1960).

Wittgenstein, Ludwig, *Philosophical Investigations*, trans. G.E.M. Anscombe (Oxford: Basil Blackwell, 1953).

————, *Remarks on the Foundations of Mathematics*, trans. G.E.M. Anscombe (New York: Macmillan, 1956).

Wood, Neal, *Cicero's Social and Political Thought* (Berkeley: University of California Press, 1988).

ABOUT THE AUTHOR

James W. Vice was born on a farm in Wabash County, Indiana. His family moved into the city of Wabash while he was still a small child, and he was graduated from Wabash High School in 1951. He attended the University of Chicago, where he dropped the "Jr." from his name in all but official documents, and from which he received an A.M. in American history and literature in 1954. He continued his studies in the Committee on Social Thought and began a career in university administration and teaching. After twenty-four years in different positions at Chicago and an unsuccessful effort to succeed his father as mayor of Wabash, he moved to the Illinois Institute of Technology as Dean of Student Life. At IIT, he also taught in political science. In 1991, he became Ombudsperson for Loyola University Chicago. He has published essays on student affairs, university administration, and ombudsing.

INDEX

VIBS

The **Value Inquiry Book Series** is co-sponsored by:

American Maritain Association
American Society for Value Inquiry
Association for Personalist Studies
Association for Process Philosophy of Education
Center for East European Dialogue and Development, Rochester Institute of
Technology
Centre for Cultural Research, Aarhus University
College of Education and Allied Professions, Bowling Green State University
Concerned Philosophers for Peace
Conference of Philosophical Societies
Instituto de Filosofía del Consejo Superior de Investigaciones Científicas
International Academy of Philosophy of the Principality of Liechtenstein
International Society for Universalism
Natural Law Society
Philosophical Society of Finland
Philosophy Born of Struggle Association
Philosophy Seminar, University of Mainz
R.S. Hartman Institute for Formal and Applied Axiology
Society for Iberian and Latin-American Thought
Society for the Philosophic Study of Genocide and the Holocaust
Society for the Philosophy of Sex and Love
Yves R. Simon Institute.

Titles Published

1. Noel Balzer, *The Human Being as a Logical Thinker.*

2. Archie J. Bahm, *Axiology: The Science of Values.*

3. H. P. P. (Hennie) Lötter, *Justice for an Unjust Society.*

4. H. G. Callaway, *Context for Meaning and Analysis: A Critical Study in the Philosophy of Language.*

5. Benjamin S. Llamzon, *A Humane Case for Moral Intuition.*

6. James R. Watson, *Between Auschwitz and Tradition: Postmodern Reflections on the Task of Thinking.* A volume in **Holocaust and Genocide Studies.**

7. Robert S. Hartman, *Freedom to Live: The Robert Hartman Story,* edited by Arthur R. Ellis. A volume in **Hartman Institute Axiology Studies.**

8. Archie J. Bahm, *Ethics: The Science of Oughtness.*

9. George David Miller, *An Idiosyncratic Ethics; Or, the Lauramachean Ethics.*

10. Joseph P. DeMarco, *A Coherence Theory in Ethics.*

11. Frank G. Forrest, *Valuemetrics: The Science of Personal and Professional Ethics.* A volume in **Hartman Institute Axiology Studies.**

12. William Gerber, *The Meaning of Life: Insights of the World's Great Thinkers.*

13. Richard T. Hull, Editor, *A Quarter Century of Value Inquiry: Presidential Addresses of the American Society for Value Inquiry.* A volume in **Histories and Addresses of Philosophical Societies.**

14. William Gerber, *Nuggets of Wisdom from Great Jewish Thinkers: From Biblical Times to the Present.*

30. Robin Attfield, *Value, Obligation, and Meta-Ethics.*

31. William Gerber, *The Deepest Questions You Can Ask About God: As Answered by the World's Great Thinkers.*

32. Daniel Statman, *Moral Dilemmas.*

33. Rem B. Edwards, Editor, *Formal Axiology and Its Critics.* A volume in **Hartman Institute Axiology Studies.**

34. George David Miller and Conrad P. Pritscher, *On Education and Values: In Praise of Pariahs and Nomads.* A volume in **Philosophy of Education.**

35. Paul S. Penner, *Altruistic Behavior: An Inquiry into Motivation.*

36. Corbin Fowler, *Morality for Moderns.*

37. Giambattista Vico, *The Art of Rhetoric (Institutiones Oratoriae,* 1711-1741), from the definitive Latin text and notes, Italian commentary and introduction by Giuliano Crifò, translated and edited by Giorgio A. Pinton and Arthur W. Shippee. A volume in **Values in Italian Philosophy.**

38. W. H. Werkmeister, *Martin Heidegger on the Way,* edited by Richard T. Hull. A volume in **Werkmeister Studies.**

39. Phillip Stambovsky, *Myth and the Limits of Reason.*

40. Samantha Brennan, Tracy Isaacs, and Michael Milde, Editors, *A Question of Values: New Canadian Perspectives in Ethics and Political Philosophy.*

41. Peter A. Redpath, *Cartesian Nightmare: An Introduction to Transcendental Sophistry.* A volume in **Studies in the History of Western Philosophy.**

42. Clark Butler, *History as the Story of Freedom: Philosophy in Intercultural Context,* with Responses by sixteen scholars.

43. Dennis Rohatyn, *Philosophy History Sophistry.*

44. Leon Shaskolsky Sheleff, *Social Cohesion and Legal Coercion: A Critique of Weber, Durkheim, and Marx.* Afterword by Virginia Black.

45. Alan Soble, Editor, *Sex, Love, and Friendship: Studies of the Society for the Philosophy of Sex and Love, 1977-1992.* A volume in **Histories and Addresses of Philosophical Societies.**

46. Peter A. Redpath, *Wisdom's Odyssey: From Philosophy to Transcendental Sophistry.* A volume in **Studies in the History of Western Philosophy.**

47. Albert A. Anderson, *Universal Justice: A Dialectical Approach.* A volume in **Universal Justice.**

48. Pio Colonnello, *The Philosophy of José Gaos.* Translated from Italian by Peter Cocozzella. Edited by Myra Moss. Introduction by Giovanni Gullace. A volume in **Values in Italian Philosophy.**

49. Laura Duhan Kaplan and Laurence F. Bove, Editors, *Philosophical Perspectives on Power and Domination: Theories and Practices.* A volume in **Philosophy of Peace.**

50. Gregory F. Mellema, *Collective Responsibility.*

51. Josef Seifert, *What Is Life? The Originality, Irreducibility, and Value of Life.* A volume in **Central-European Value Studies.**

52. William Gerber, *Anatomy of What We Value Most.*

53. Armando Molina, *Our Ways: Values and Character,* edited by Rem B. Edwards. A volume in **Hartman Institute Axiology Studies.**

54. Kathleen J. Wininger, *Nietzsche's Reclamation of Philosophy.* A volume in **Central-European Value Studies.**

55. Thomas Magnell, Editor, *Explorations of Value.*

56. HPP (Hennie) Lötter, *Injustice, Violence, and Peace: The Case of South Africa.* A volume in **Philosophy of Peace.**

57. Lennart Nordenfelt, *Talking About Health: A Philosophical Dialogue.* A volume in **Nordic Value Studies.**

58. Jon Mills and Janusz A. Polanowski, *The Ontology of Prejudice.* A volume in **Philosophy and Psychology.**

59. Leena Vilkka, *The Intrinsic Value of Nature*.

60. Palmer Talbutt, Jr., *Rough Dialectics: Sorokin's Philosophy of Value*, with Contributions by Lawrence T. Nichols and Pitirim A. Sorokin.

61. C. L. Sheng, *A Utilitarian General Theory of Value*.

62. George David Miller, *Negotiating Toward Truth: The Extinction of Teachers and Students*. Epilogue by Mark Roelof Eleveld. A volume in **Philosophy of Education.**

63. William Gerber, *Love, Poetry, and Immortality: Luminous Insights of the World's Great Thinkers*.

64. Dane R. Gordon, Editor, *Philosophy in Post-Communist Europe*. A volume in **Post-Communist European Thought.**

65. Dane R. Gordon and Józef Niznik, Editors, *Criticism and Defense of Rationality in Contemporary Philosophy*. A volume in **Post-Communist European Thought.**

66. John R. Shook, *Pragmatism: An Annotated Bibliography, 1898-1940*. With Contributions by E. Paul Colella, Lesley Friedman, Frank X. Ryan, and Ignas K. Skrupskelis.

67. Lansana Keita, *The Human Project and the Temptations of Science*.

68. Michael M. Kazanjian, *Phenomenology and Education: Cosmology, Co-Being, and Core Curriculum*. A volume in **Philosophy of Education.**

69. James W. Vice, *The Reopening of the American Mind: On Skepticism and Constitutionalism*.